The Art & Science o[...]

MW01698073

# THE WING-T FROM A TO Z

## VOLUME 2: INSTALLING THE SYSTEM

Dennis Creehan

COACHES CHOICE™

ISBN: 1-58518-250-8

Cover Design: Jennifer Bokelmann
Front Cover Photo: Ed Mailliard
Diagrams: James Hunt
Developmental Editor: Dan Robinson
Editor: David Hamburg
Production Manager: Michelle A. Summers

Coaches Choice Books is an imprint of:

Coaches Choice
P.O. Box 1828
Monterey, CA 93942
Web Site: http://www.coacheschoiceweb.com

# DEDICATION

I would like to dedicate this book to everyone in my family. They have all been so patient and understanding over the years as we have moved all around the country so that I could pursue my dream of coaching football.

To my loving wife, Linda, who is the best dance teacher in the country and has given up four different successful dance studios as we have moved. To my sons, Kevin and Casey, who attended four different schools while I chased my coaching dream. To Kevin, the older of my two sons, who is so intelligent that he has decided to use his brain power in the world of industrial engineering rather than in the arena of coaching–even though he could be a great coach, as evidenced by the American Legion state baseball championship his team won in his first and only coaching opportunity. To the younger Casey, who actually wants to go into the field of coaching and is just hardheaded enough to be a great coach.

Finally, I would also like to dedicate this book to my mother and father, Peggy and Jerry Creehan, who have been big fans of mine, no matter where I have coached. And to my brothers and sisters, Jerry Jr., Rick, Karen, Kathy, and Kenny. Rick and Kenny have already been quite successful as baseball coaches.

# ACKNOWLEDGMENTS

Many great coaches have touched my life, and I would like to thank all of them for their leadership and guidance. My high school coaches, Dan Galbraith and Joe Nicoletti, who instilled in me the desire to play the game and taught me the fundamentals at Bethel Park (PA) High School. My college head coach, Bill McDonald, who turned Edinboro University of Pennsylvania from a 40-year loser into a champion. My college position coaches, Sam Ruvolo, Jack Hyland, and Bill Straub, who helped me to achieve more personal success than I ever thought possible for myself.

Upon graduation from college, I had no idea that I would ever coach, but Jerry Mancini brought me into the profession at Keystone Oaks (PA) High School. Johnny Majors and Jackie Sherrill gave me my first taste of college football as a graduate assistant at the University of Pittsburgh. Joe Gasparella and Chuck Klausing gave me my first real college coaching position at Carnegie Mellon University. My first full-time position in college football came from Bill McDonald, my college coach at Edinboro. Three years later, I got a lucky break and succeeded Bill when he retired. During my 12 years as a head coach, I was very fortunate to have many great assistant coaches who have gone on to become college or pro head coaches themselves: John D'Ottavio, Utah Pioneers of the PSFL; Gerry Gallagher, St. Francis (PA) and William Patterson (NJ); Budgie Hamilton, San Francisco State; Tom Herman, Gannon University (PA); Mike Kelly, Valdosta State University; Malen Luke, Defiance (OH) and Clarion University (PA); Tom Menage, Westmar University (IA); Dave Lyon, Thiel College (PA); Ron Rankin, University of South Dakota; and Blair Hrovat, who is the new head coach at Allegheny College in Pennsylvania.

Finally, I would like to thank the coaches who taught me the wing-T offense: Ted Kempski of the University of Delaware and, most of all, John D'Ottavio, who is out of coaching, but who is, in my opinion, the most knowledgable wing-T coach I have ever met.

# CONTENTS

Page

# PREFACE

This two-volume set of books on *The Wing-T from A to Z* was written in order to provide coaches and players at all competitive levels with a useful tool that can enable them to better understand the intricacies of the wing-T offense. In this comprehensive overview of one of the game's most popular offensive schemes, the fundamentals and the nuances of the wing-T offense are presented in great detail.

The first volume in the set provides an excellent guide to understanding and developing a sound *base plan* for the wing-T offense. This volume features chapters on pholosophy and organization, goal line attack, and movements (20 series, 30 series, 60 series, and 80 series).

The second volume in the set explains how to install and implement this innovative offensive package. The responsibilities and techniques essential to each offensive player position are identified and reviewed in a step-by-step manner. This volume also includes deatailed chapters on establishing an efficient and effective plan for practicing the wing-T and developing a successful offensive game-day plan.

It is hoped that the insights and the information presented in these books will also enhance the reader's sense of appreciation for the wing-T. In my opinion, the more that an individual knows about this offensive scheme, the greater the level of appreciation. I can only hope that every coach and player who reads these books will enjoy them as much as I enjoyed writing them.

Dennis Creehan

# CHAPTER 1

## The Wing-T Practice Plan

In this chapter, I would like to illustrate the practice plan we use to teach and drill the offense. We think the plan is unique to the wing-T. It certainly has proven to be successful. We actually named the plan for the way we run our practices and operate our practice plans. We call it the "racehorse philosophy." We use the concept of "racehorse" even in our pre-practice meetings. In pre-practice meetings, we expect our players to pay attention and stay with us. We want them to sit upright with their feet on the floor-not lounging all over their chairs-and we tell them to take their hats off in meetings. This is because we want to make eye contact with them. During those meetings, we go quickly. We start on time and the coaches talk loud. They talk fast, and they repeat. The coaches must get their message across in pre-practice meetings. We go over anything new or different that we will do in practice that day, and we always review videotape of practice with the players.

### RACEHORSE PHILOSOPHY

What exactly does racehorse philosophy mean? Racehorse philosophy involves working at a pace that will allow for maximum repetitions and maximum learning to take place. For us, this means seven things:

1. Maximum repetitions
2. Mass teach when possible
3. All drills on sound
4. Shifting in team takeoff only
5. Shotgun two huddles
6. Coaches stay in centralized locations
7. Coaches make quick corrections

These are the concepts we refer to when we talk about racehorse philosophy. "Racehorse" would indicate that we are going to go fast. And that is exactly what we want to do.

What we want to accomplish with this philosophy is "maximum reps." Many coaches make that claim. Coaches are always trying to structure their practices for maximum repetitions. If you study many other practice plans and watch others practice, then watch the practice structure we use to teach wing-T. You will find that we really do get maximum reps! Everything we do in the structure of the practice is based on getting maximum reps. Everything within this philosophy is designed to facilitate getting maximum reps for teaching. We accomplish it with the very style with which we coach.

We mass teach whenever possible. This means that anytime we have drills being run on the practice field, we like to have every player in each group taking part in that drill at the same time. We do all drills on sound cadence. When we are doing drill work, we save time by not using long cadences during drills. By the time practice ends, you may have wasted a lot of time by calling cadences throughout practice. "On sound" means that the quarterback or the coach running the drill will say, "Set." On the '"s" in "set," the ball will be snapped and the players will take off. We will use "sound" cadence in as many drills as possible. If you have a 10-minute period and you want to get a lot of reps during that drill, start each rep with one command rather than a long cadence. We go on the first sound and do all our drills to get maximum reps.

Another way to guarantee maximum reps is to practice shifting in "team takeoff" only. In the wing-T offense, we run many shifts throughout the course of a game. We want to be good at shifting. However, we rarely work on shifting in team periods when we practice 11-on-11. We do not want to take those extra minutes out of team period, when we could be getting more reps. We will mix up the cadences in team period and shift if we think we need to see the timing of a shift along with the 11 players running a play. For the most part, 99 percent of the time, our shifting will be done during team takeoff period.

We shotgun two huddles. This means that during our team periods, there will be one huddle going and another huddle huddled up, ready to go. As soon as the players finish the first play, the second group should be saying, "Ready, break," and then sprint up to the line of scrimmage, ready to run the next play. Most of the time, the first group, which has just run the play, will have to hustle out of the way of the second group by running off toward the sideline and then coming back around to the huddle. As they get in tune with the practice tempo, the players will understand that they must get back to the huddle quickly in order to get out of the way of the next group. It is also vital for the scout team to hustle back. This is tough on the scout team. I would recommend having two scout teams, or having three players for every two positions so they can rotate in and out. They will become tired at times during team periods when we practice at this pace, and they will need a rest.

We tell our coaches to stay in a centralized location and make the players run past them for correction. In many programs, you will see a coach chase a player into the huddle to make a correction while the player is still in the huddle. What happens is that the next play gets run with another group, and the coach does not see anything in that next play because he is still correcting the player from the previous group. If you tell coaches to stay in a centralized location and have the players run past them for corrections, they cannot only make the corrections, but they can watch the next play. When coaches make corrections in our program, we do not want them to earn their doctorate by giving a dissertation on the field. We like to have the coaches make a quick, meaningful correction to the players on their way by. The players can thus hear the correction and know what they did wrong; the rest of the help comes from the film analysis. We videotape every practice. We do so with two cameras-one for offense and one for defense. Every day, there is plenty of film for players to watch . Our coaches can make longer explanations or demonstrations once they see the film. On the field, in order to get maximum reps, we have the players run past the coach, who then gives a short correction on the way into the huddle. If necessary, we will stop a play to explain something and make them repeat. That does not happen very often. It does happen at times, and we understand that. At times, it may be better to get a play stopped, make the corrections for everybody to hear, and get it cleared up, thus enabling the players to continue with the rest of the practice free of errors.

When our staff gets together for practice planning, the first thing we consider is how we can get maximum reps, how we can stay within the "racehorse philosophy." It starts with pre-practice and continues all the way through the practice. Our coaches meet to find ways to get more repetitions during practice. It is very important for coaches to make sure they are getting maximum reps and to make sure that each is taking time to think about how he can get more reps in the practice plan.

## TEAM TAKEOFF PERIOD

Team takeoff period will follow loosening and kicking, which are our first two periods in practice, according to our practice plan. We begin practice each day in this manner. We put 11 people on the line of scrimmage and we run a play. The offensive line's assignment is to get off the ball as fast as they can. This is a "get-off" drill for them. We want to see them come out low and hard for 10 yards and finish across the goal line to get reps on firing out. The backs, on the other hand, will run their play assignments in order to execute footwork. They will also sprint 10 yards across the goal line. We do this drill from the 10-yard line on in to the goal line. That way, the backs run across the goal line all the time. We will make the backs run across the goal line as many times as possible in practice. It sends a psychological message: "Across the goal line, across the goal line, across the goal line!" We want them to do that every time they run the football.

Diagram 1.1 illustrates our team takeoff period.

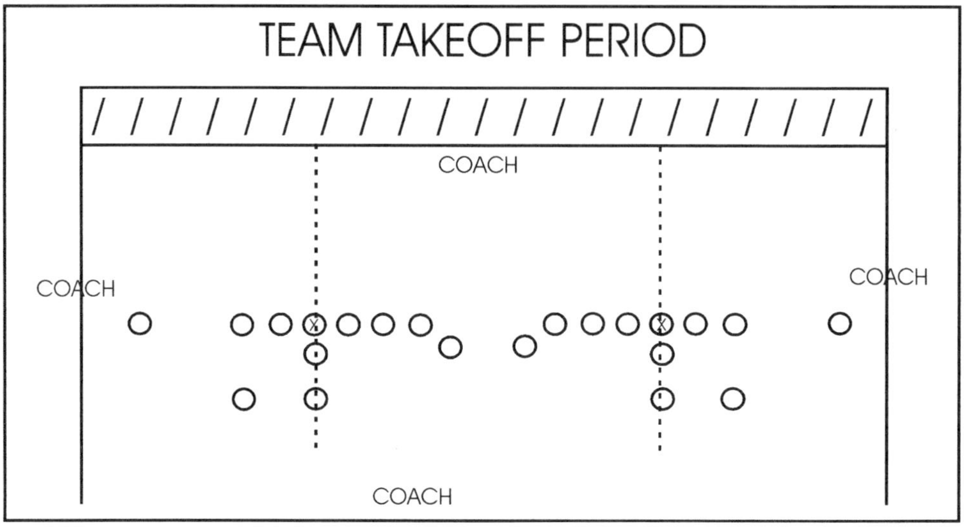


**Diagram 1.1**

One can see that we try to have two groups going at the same time. We will put one offensive group on the left hash mark and another offensive group on the right hash mark. Coaches will stand in centralized locations. We will have one coach down at the goal line to make sure they are firing out and crossing the goal line. We have other coaches on the sides, on the line of scrimmage, to see the team's takeoff and to note whether they are coming off the ball low. The coach running the drill will be behind the teams. He will tell the quarterback the play to be run and which quarterback will have the cadence. Both groups will go on one cadence. We can run the same plays with both groups or the mirrored play with both groups. If we are going to run "121 sweep" with the group on the right hash and "929 sweep" with the group on the left hash, then both units will go on the same cadence. If the coach designates that the left-side quarterback has the cadence, then the right side also listens for that cadence. Both groups fire off the line at the same time on one cadence. This is the period when we will work on shifting. The coach will say, "shift to 121," or "shift to 929." The backs and ends will execute their shift, and then the teams run the play. One day during each week, we will have the teams just fire off the ball and do team takeoff without any shifting. The next day we will execute all the shifts that we are going to prepare for that particular week. If you are going two groups at one time, it is amazing how many reps your entire team will get. If you have a third group and, possibly, even a fourth group, then they will wait in line behind the first two groups. As soon as those two groups are done, the next two groups sprint up to the line and run the same play. Even though each team only goes every other play, they still get plenty of reps.

Because we have done all our shifting during team takeoff, when we go to mixed group work or to team period, we do not have to work on our shifts. There may be times when we will need to include one shift during some other part of practice, but for the most part, shifting gets practiced in team takeoff period. Over the course of an entire practice, this saves time and allows for maximum reps during the other phases of our practice plan.

## SHOULDER SKILLS PERIOD

The next drill we do in practice is a shoulder skill period. Diagram 1.2 illustrates how our entire team is spaced during the shoulder skill period. This is an example of mass teaching. Every player on the offensive unit is involved in this drill and working at the same time. We take the big blocking bags and align them so that the bottom of the bag is intersected by one of the yard lines. One player will hold the bag while another player is down in a six- or two-point stance, ready to block the bag. The blockers are on the inside of the yard line and the bag is directly on the line. The bags are five yards apart.

If you feel you need more space, you can move them back so that they are 10 yards apart. In this drill, the coach is able to see all his players and coach them all at the same time. There is one bag for every two players. The blockers execute the drill and trade around to become the bag holders. The players who were holding the bags then become the blockers and execute the drill themselves.

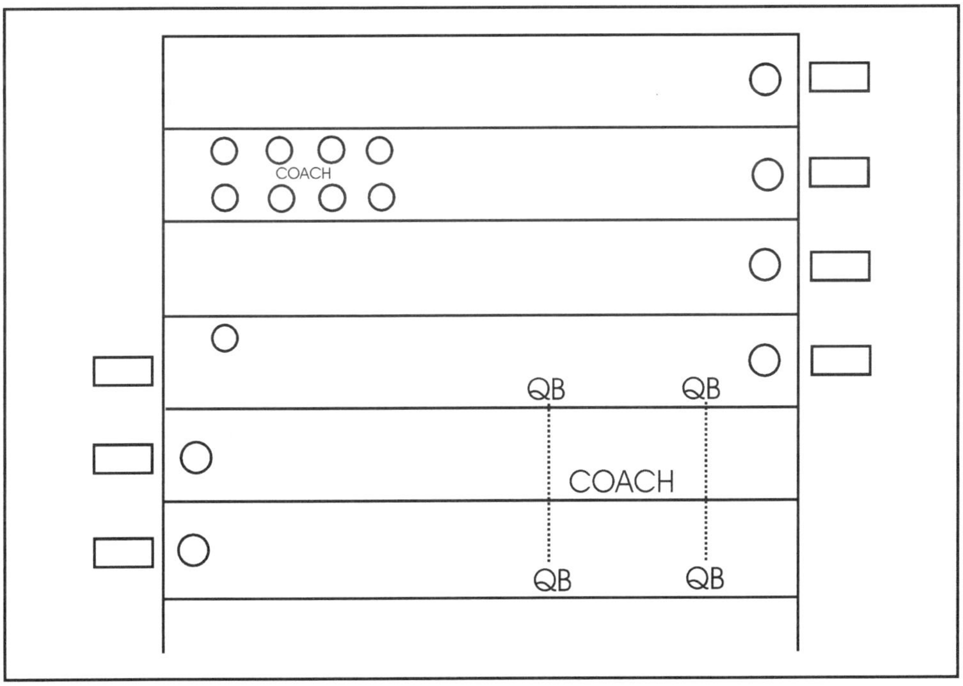


**Diagram 1.2**

In our shoulder skill period we start with "surface," which is nothing more than a form fit drill. The second drill we do is "strike a blow." Both of these drills start in a six-point stance. In the "surface" drill, we are working on how we fit into the bag. In the "strike a blow" drill, we strike the bag and roll our hips, keeping the bag between our legs. The third drill we do every day is "step and hit." When we "step and hit," we are working on making sure that the first step is exact. The second step is when we want contact to occur, and on the third step we want the body to follow through naturally. We practice this drill in progression, but we can also practice it by saying, "set," and the entire sequence is executed. The last drill we work on is either "run and hit" or "hit and run." "Run and hit" means that we will run four yards at the bag, strike the bag, drive it, and then turn it to finish the block. "Hit and run" is the opposite, with contact first and running after contact to emphasize leg drive. The blocker comes off, strikes the bag, which is directly on him, and then drives the bag off the line.

Everyone on the football team is doing shoulder skills at the same time. It is a very well-organized practice time period, but, more important, the players will get maximum reps in each of the drills. If a coach misses a correction, he will be able to catch it in time. We firmly believe that a player will learn more by doing than he will by watching. Our shoulder skills period is another example of what we call "mass teaching." The drill is also done "on sound." We do not waste time with cadence. Again, this drill facilitates getting maximum reps in a short amount of time. We use the entire field for this drill. While the offensive line coach is working in one area, the running backs coach is working in another area. In another area of the field, the receivers coach is also doing the same drill. We have quarterbacks throwing the ball to each other with the quarterbacks coach, in order to loosen up and do their daily drills. While all the other players are doing shoulder skills, the quarterbacks will be doing arm loosening or working on the center-quarterback exchange.

We teach everybody on the team how to execute a block. If you are the most gifted wide receiver or most talented running back, you will also get down in the dirt and get physical, just like our linemen. This is an unselfish offense. All skill players will get the ball, but they must also be willing to block when their teammate gets the ball. Therefore, everyone on the team (other than quarterbacks) learns how to execute shoulder skills, and he does it from day one, all the way through to the end of the season.

## ROUTINE PERIOD

The next period after shoulder skills drill is "routine" period. In routine, the offensive line will be lined up five yards apart. Each backup is five yards behind and five yards apart from left to right. We align them in their positions (Diagram 1.3) so that the left guard is on the coach's right, but on the offense's left as they face the coach. All players in the drill are facing the coach. While the line coach is doing his

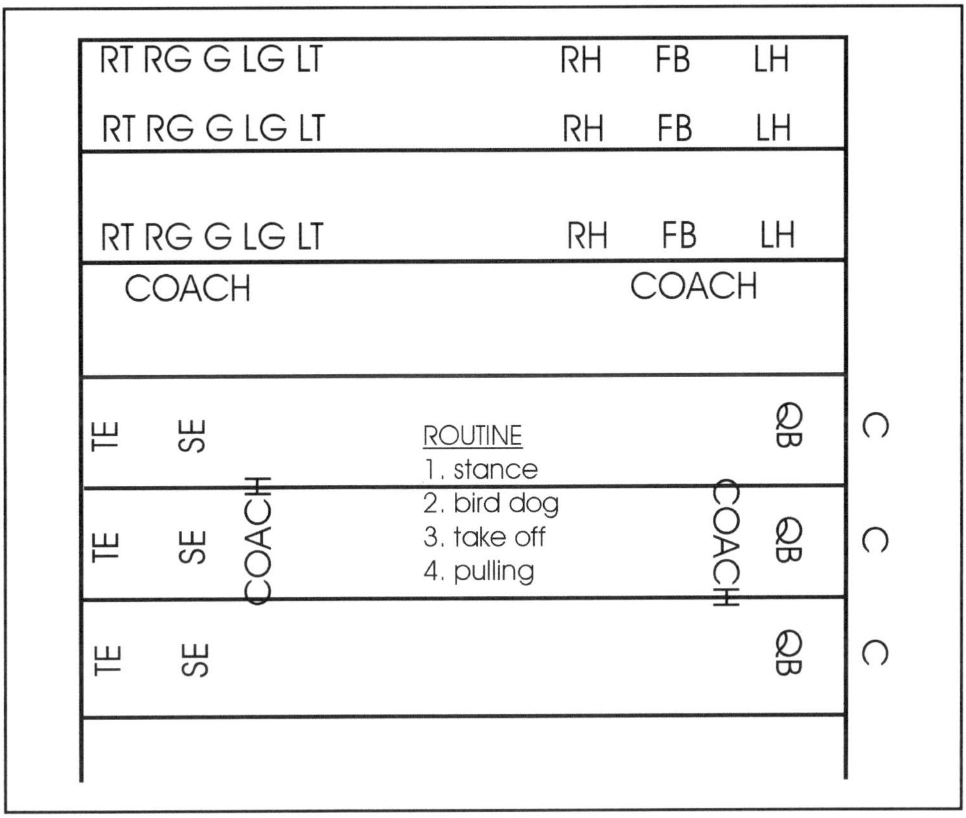


**Diagram 1.3**

drill, the running backs coach is doing his drills in another area of the field. The running backs align on lines five yards apart, and they are working on routine period as well. The receivers coach has his split ends and his tight ends five yards behind each other, doing the same drill as everyone else. The centers and quarterbacks are working on center-quarterback exchange. If you look over the entire field, you will observe everyone engaged in the same drill. This is another drill period where the entire team is active. Again, this is mass teaching! There is not one player standing around watching. Everybody on the team is learning the same skills.

There are four steps in progression during routine period. The first step is "teaching the stance." After the stance is taught, we check it every day. The ends and halfbacks have different types of stances because the ends put their inside hand down and the halfbacks also have to be comfortable with a wingback stance. The first fundamental we review at each position is proper stance. We have the coach stand in front of each group so he can see all of his players-this is coaching from a centralized location. He can make a quick check of all of his players and make necessary corrections or proceed to the next drill if everybody is performing satisfactorily.

The second phase, we call "bird-dog." We take one step and hold it to check the first step of whatever type of footwork we are emphasizing each day. We make sure the players have good opposite arm and leg action. We make sure that each player's chest is down on his thigh. We make sure his butt is over his heels and that he is not overextended. These are the points we emphasize during "bird-dog" period. It is a great drill for working on the first step, which is the most important step.

The third step in the progression is "takeoff." In takeoff period, the focus is on sprinting off the ball. This is not a long sprint; it is only a five-yard sprint, followed by five yards of jogging to slow down. Each player will have a five-yard "get-off" to see if

1. He is firing out low, and

2. He is coming off the ball with the proper footwork.

When players first start taking off with a certain foot, they begin to think too much. Eventually, you want your players not to have to think about their feet. They must automatically know, for example, that if they block with their right shoulder, then they must step with their left foot first. It has to become second nature to them. They should not have to think about it.

The last step in the progression is only for the line and the tight ends. It is an "11-step pulling drill," where they work on pulling techniques, log block techniques, and gut techniques. In these drills, we will pull to log and pull to gut. The first time we do this drill, we tell the players to walk through the drill step-by-step through all 11 steps. We do the drill by the numbers once or twice, then sprint all 11 steps. In this drill, we pull and log, or pull to wall off, or pull to gut. The purpose of this drill is to work on the footwork of both pulling and log blocking. If an offensive guard is going to pull to the right to log the defensive end, then on the fourth step (which is the point at which contact will occur), he will be on his inside foot, blocking with his inside shoulder. The fifth step must work directly up the field, while the sixth step starts back to the starting point.

The actual wing-T part of practice is made up of team takeoff, followed by shoulder skills, and finally routine. At the beginning of the year, these drills are longer. The shoulder skill period might be 15 minutes long so that we have plenty of time to explain it and teach it. The second and third days, we may cut it down to 10 minutes, and once the season begins, the shoulder skill period will be a five-minute period. Routine starts out being a 10-minute period, and by the end of the year, it will dwindle to two or three minutes long. By that time, the players will know what to do, they will be able to do it well, and they will know how to do it quickly.

## PRACTICE ORGANIZATION

The next phase of practice is the individual part of practice. It is necessary to divide the practice plan into three discrete practice plans in order for each group to work on the individual skills that relate to each position. Diagram 1.4 illustrates how the practice plan is typically divided up. The amount of time that's used for individual periods is up to the coaches, depending on how much time each coach needs for each of these drills.

| BACKS 40' | ENDS 40' | OFFENSIVE LINE 40' |
|---|---|---|
| 5' HAND OFFS | 15' BLOCKING TECH. | 15' BLOCKING TECHNIQUE |
| 5' PITCH DRILLS | 5' RELEASES | 5' SWEEPING DRILL |
| 20' FULL BACKFIELD TECH. | 5' PATTERNS | 5' WAGGLE DRILL W/QB |
| 10' PASSING WITH ENDS | 5' BALL DRILLS | 10' ASSIGNMENT PERIOD |
| | 10' PASSING WITH BACKS | 5' PASS PRO DRILLS |

**Diagram 1.4**

**Running Backs**

The backs do these drills during the individual portion of their practice plan. The first thing the backs do is "handoff drill" (Diagram 1.5). Handoff drill is set up with four stations, with a quarterback and a fullback in one station and a quarterback and a fullback in another station. The fullbacks are working on certain plays, including the corresponding footwork. If there are not enough quarterbacks and fullbacks to have two fullback stations, then we combine them into one. While the fullback stations are working on handoffs, the left halfbacks and a quarterback are

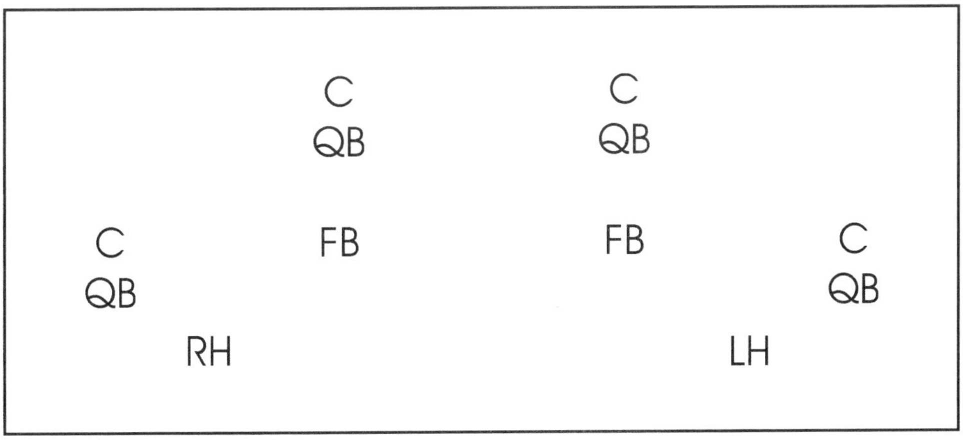


**Diagram 1.5**

working together on one side of the field, and a quarterback and the right halfback are working on the other side of the field. There are three different running back stations. This drill structure enables you to get maximum reps on handoffs and on plays where the quarterback hands the ball to a back. This is a five-minute period, and it is amazing how many repetitions you can get. Five minutes does not sound like much time, but if each station works independently of the other, each player will get enough reps to execute each play flawlessly.

The next drill for the running backs is called "pitch drill" (Diagram 1.6). During pitch drills, there are two groups going at the same time. There is a quarterback, a fullback, and a left halfback working on option plays to the right. There is also a quarterback, a fullback, and a right halfback working on option plays to the left. Both groups work independently. The left-side quarterback runs option to the right and emphasizes pitching the ball. The same thing occurs with the other group of quarterbacks, fullbacks, and right halfbacks. In order to make sure that they don't run into each other, the drill is offset 10 yards upfield. By conducting one drill 10 yards up the field from the other, each drill can be run at the same time without players having to wait for the other group. You can also do this drill with both groups going at the same time, running option into the boundary. Even though you don't want to run a lot of option into the boundaries, the backs learn to take good footwork, stay in bounds, and maximize their use of the field.

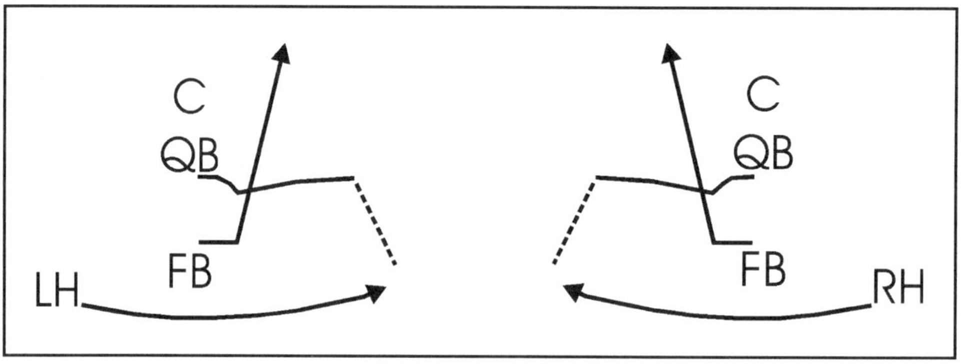


**Diagram 1.6**

"Full backfield technique" is the next drill. In this drill (Diagram 1.7), there is a full backfield, a quarterback, a fullback , a right half, and a left half. If we have enough backs, we put another group back-to-back with this group that goes in the opposite direction and runs the same play. If you have a quarterback coach and a running back coach, you have enough coaches to work two different drill groups and get a lot of reps.

"Passing with ends" is the last drill we work on during individual period with the running backs (Diagram 1.8). We also involve the ends, a quarterback, a fullback, a tight end, a split end, a left half, and a right half. We have all the backs, all the ends together to work on pass patterns. They can either work on pass patterns as a total group or practice different individual cuts. We also practice getting into our blocking techniques with the backs for pass protection.

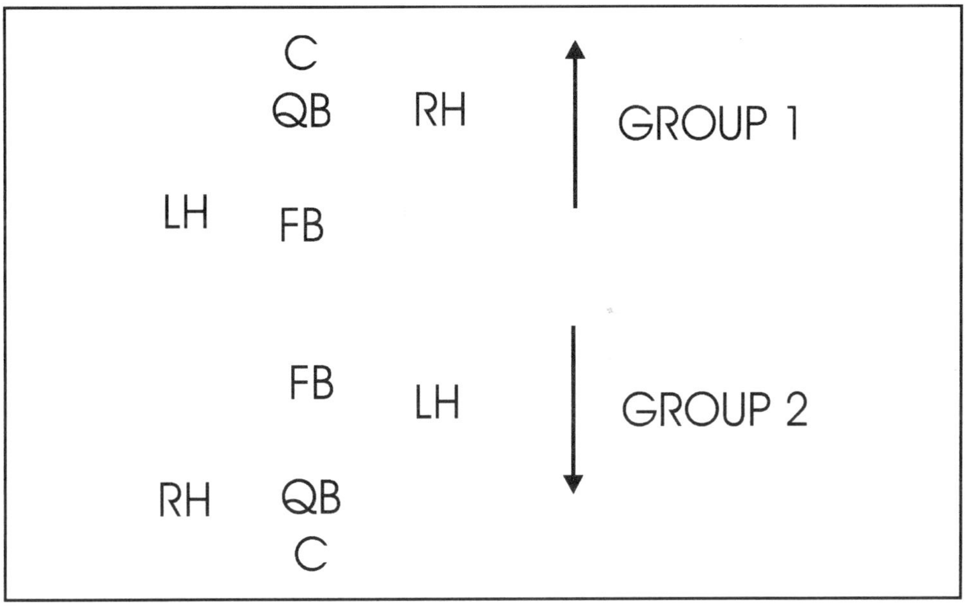


**Diagram 1.7**

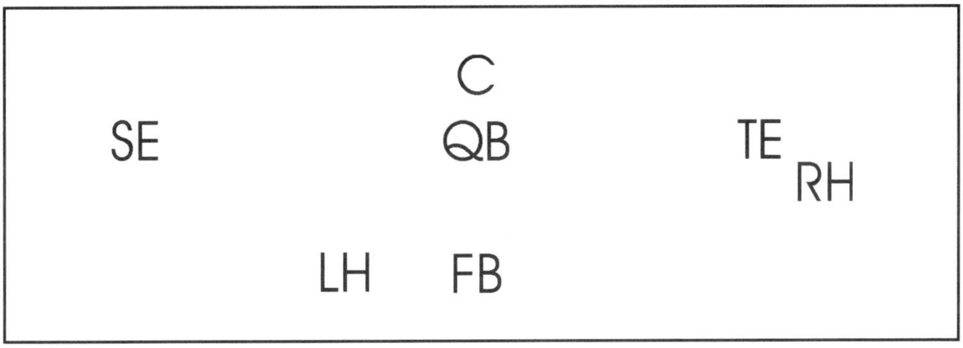


**Diagram 1.8**

"Handoff period" is no more than five minutes long. At the beginning of the year, it will be 10 minutes, but later in the year, it will be cut down to five minutes and will stay five minutes most of the year. In the last few weeks of the season, it might be cut down to two minutes. If a coach is maximizing reps, he can still get a lot of handoffs done in just two minutes. If the coach has the drill set up quickly, gets his players there quickly, and if they know what they are doing, then he can get plenty of reps in just two or three minutes.

"Pitch drill" will generally last about five minutes. Usually, our coaches would like to do "passing with ends" for a minimum of 10 minutes. That will account for 20 minutes of the individual time to do those three drills. If you have planned 40 minutes for individual practice period, then use 5 minutes for handoffs, 5 minutes for pitches, 20 minutes for full backfield, and 10 minutes for passing with ends. Full backfield technique takes up the most crucial period. It is the period that requires the most time and attention to detail. That is the period where we correct any mistakes that are being made. This is the time period in which to perfect any plays that need perfecting. It provides you within an excellent opportunity to work the flank plays that require the backs to block , or the flank passing plays.

**RECEIVERS**

The ends have five important drills to do in individual period. They will work on these five drills every day. The position coach decides what he needs to accomplish during each drill and how much time he needs to spend with each particular drill. At the beginning of the season, he has 40 minutes of individual period. As the season wears on, it will be closer to 20 minutes or half an hour. Early in the season, a coach must use these reps as quality teaching reps.

"Blocking technique period" is a period where the ends-both spread ends and tight ends-work on the different types of blocks they will use. In the receiver section, every block is explained in detail. During blocking-technique period, the coach might choose to have the tight ends work "gap" blocks and "down" blocks, while he has the split ends work on "stalk" blocks or "crack" blocks. Since each group has different blocks to work on, the coach may want to shotgun the groups. If there is only one receiver coach, then you may want to have the tight ends work a block and then the spread ends work a block, continuing to alternate in order for the coach to work with both groups at once. Another possibility is that both groups could go at the same time. If there are two coaches or somebody to help the receiver coach, then you can have two groups going at the same time, independent of each other, and get more quality reps and coaching.

During "release" period, the receivers work their releases from the line of scrimmage against a defender who is trying to stop them from releasing. The defender trying to jam their release may be on the line of scrimmage, or he might be five yards off. Our receivers work against all types of jams. The tight ends use different releases, while the spread ends work on the different types of releases needed on the perimeter. They can work at the same time if there are two coaches, so that each group has a coach available.

"Pattern" drill works on the actual pass patterns the receivers run. Anything new in the week's game plan or for that day of practice is taught and reinforced during this drill. The receivers will also work on correcting patterns that they need to perfect, or routes that have consistently posed problems for the players. One example might be the "trap option pass," because the spread ends are having a problem with the slant route. If that is the case, then the coaches make sure that the slant gets emphasis during this period. This period is usually filled by two different groups. For example, the tight ends may need work on the waggle route or their crossing route, while at the same time, the split ends are working on the slant route or the out route. Each group can work different types of pass patterns during the same drill.

"Ball" drills are a part of the individual practice plan that all the receivers do together. We use many ball drills, and most wing-T teams probably use drills similar to those used in other offenses. Some examples are distraction drills, one-hand-catch drills, drills in which the receiver must catch the ball and keep his feet in bounds, catching bad balls, jugs gun drills, and comeback drills. This drill period will usually last five minutes. If there are six to eight receivers in the group, they will be able to complete two or three different drills every day during this five-minute period.

"Passing with the backs" is the same drill as "passing with ends." The quarterbacks, fullbacks, right halfbacks, left halfbacks, tight ends, and spread ends work on patterns as a group at the same time, or sometimes we divide up in order to work on individual cuts. For example, the one set of quarterbacks might be throwing out routes to the split ends, while another set of quarterback is throwing waggle routes to all the tight ends.

Releases, patterns, and ball drills are each done for five minutes during every practice. At the end of the season, each might be cut down to three minutes, which forces everyone to really hustle. Our staff usually takes 10 minutes for blocking technique every day early in the season, but by late in the year, this drill gets cut down to five minutes. Passing with backs is usually done in a 10-minute period. That accounts for 35 minutes, with an extra five minutes for anything else the coaches feel they need more work on. Blocking-technique period usually gets the most emphasis. This added emphasis helps the players understand that blocking is the most important skill they need to learn. Some of the receivers may not want to hear that, but no matter what position you play in the wing-T, players will have to block. If players are willing to block with great effort, and are unselfish players, then they will be the kind of players who fit into the wing-T offense the best.

**OFFENSIVE LINE**

"Blocking technique" is the No. 1 drill that any offensive line has to work on. The linemen must be good blockers. Players must excel at combination blocks as well as single blocks. Each must understand every block, understand the techniques required, and understand how each type of block makes a contribution to winning. Offensive linemen are the ultimate team warriors in football. Football is the ultimate team game. Therefore, coaches look at offensive linemen as the ultimate team warriors in the ultimate team game. These players get very little recognition and stats. Playing offensive line is not like playing defense, where players get a certain number of tackles, sacks, pass breakups, interceptions, or other stats. An offensive lineman has no statistics, certainly none one reads in the next day's paper. We give an offensive lineman a grade every week, and we ask him to take pride in his grades. We also foster in them a feeling of pride in our total offense. Without them, there is no offense. The team can have great backs, but great backs can do only so much without good blocking for them. Without strong blocking, they will not be productive. The offensive line puts most of its individual time in blocking-technique period.

The "pulling" drills that the line does include "sweep" drill, with all the linemen playing guards, and "waggle" drill , with all the linemen also practicing as guards. Linemen also practice "gut" drill, "guard trap" drill , or several other combinations of pulling drills. These are each done in five-minute periods. The linemen also work together with the quarterbacks during "waggle" drill. This is very helpful for both the quarterbacks and the offensive linemen because they work together on the various pulling techniques, as well as on when to attack the flank or when to pull up, and the timing and spacing needed to react to the different defensive reactions we face. It is a drill we have some of our quarterbacks working on just about every day.

Following their pulling drills, the linemen have "assignment" period (Diagram 1.9). The assignment period is constructed similarly to an inside drill with a full offensive line. There is a center, a left guard, a left tackle, a right guard, and a right tackle, all of whom practice all plays against the interior of a defense. The defense will use the front four and the inside linebackers. The offensive linemen will be reviewing and practicing their blocking assignments. The defensive line will send a scout team or possibly defensive starters, if our opponent use a wing-T scheme. The No. 1 defensive line and linebackers can then work on reacting against the blocking schemes they will see that week. An injured player, a kicker, or one of the backups will be in the backfield, indicating the direction the ball will go. This is important so

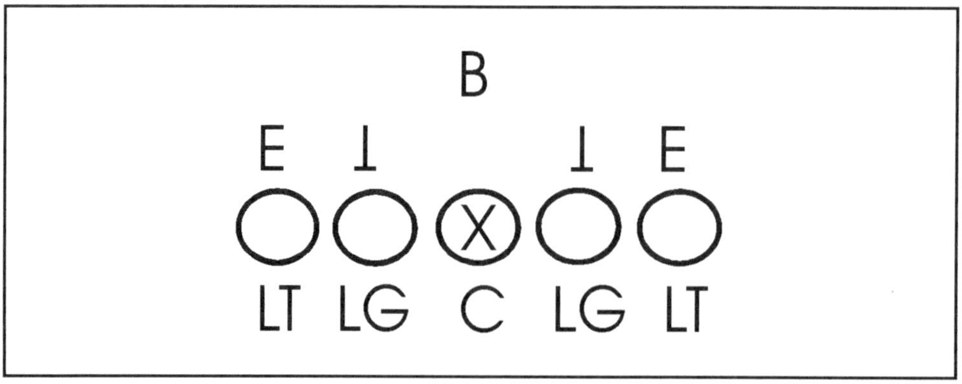


**Diagram 1.9**

that the defenders have a key to react to if they are keying flow. They also react to the blocking scheme that they see in front of them.

The last drills for the linemen during individual period are "pass protection" (pass pro) drills. In the beginning of the season, while learning their skills, the linemen do pass protection drills against themselves, and as the linemen become more proficient, they progress to blocking more active defensive players.

Each of the pulling drills takes five minutes. Pass pro drills should take no more than 10 minutes, and as the season progresses, we will be able to finish those in five minutes. Assignment period usually takes 10 minutes, which leaves 15 minutes for blocking technique.

What has been discussed thus far is what constitutes a normal practice plan for the offensive line, the ends, and the backs during individual period. With all of these drills to do, coaches must be very thoughtful in deciding how much time is necessary for each period and exactly which drills to use each day. Each coach must have a feel for his group and know exactly which drills need working on. In blocking-technique period, there are individual blocks and combination blocks in every practice plan. "Sweep" drill and "waggle" drill are the primary pulling drills. Either can be replaced by "guard trap" drill or "gut" drill. "Waggle" drill will be done as often as possible because the quarterbacks must get a feel for the waggle action and also because the play-action pass is key to our offensive success. Assignment period will be done every day. It will either be done with the offensive coach having his extra offensive linemen hold bags, or against the defense in a live setting. Pass pro drills can be done with offensive linemen blocking against other offensive linemen , working the techniques of pass protection. They will block one-on-one pass protection live against defensive players during mixed-group work period. That is a broad summary of the individual period for the practice plan.

There are two parts of daily practice following individual, shoulder skills, routine, and team takeoff periods. These last two parts of practice are "mixed group work" and "11-on-11."

## MIXED GROUP PERIOD

Three different types of drills are done during "mixed group" period. The first drill is called "four-corner drill" (Diagram 1.10). During this drill, the receivers, running backs, and quarterbacks are throwing one-on-one routes against defensive backs and linebackers in four separate sections of the field. During this drill, the defense is working on man coverage. The defensive coaches want to see how well the defensive players can cover a receiver in man coverage. The same idea holds true for the receivers and the backs. The offensive coaches want to emphasize running patterns against man coverage. Receiver technique versus man coverage plays a big

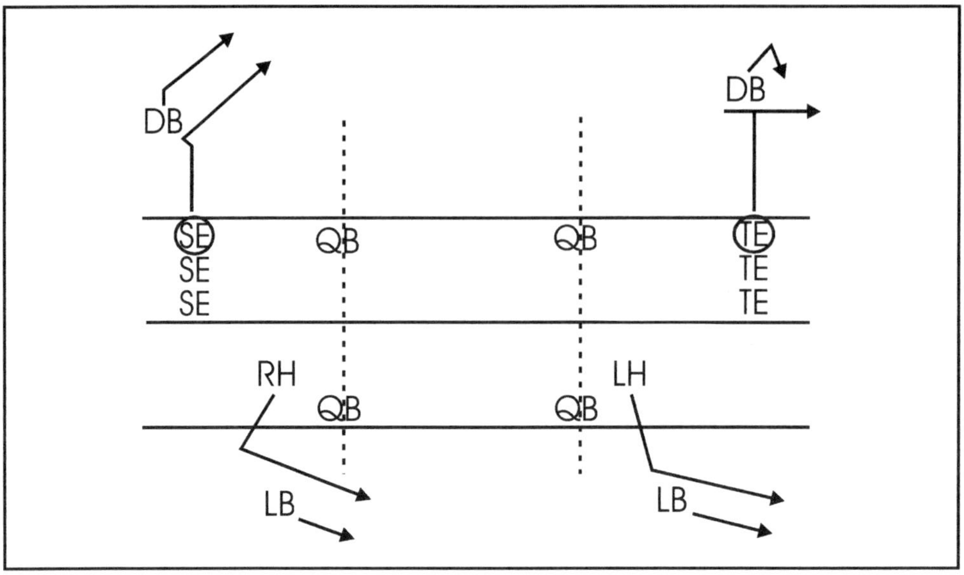


**Diagram 1.10**

part in our passing game. A key question we face is, "Can our receivers beat a coverage defender who is lined up across from them, one-on-one, in a man-to-man setting?" Our coaches tell the receivers that if they cannot get open against man coverage, then they cannot play in this league. Our receivers have to possess either (1) great speed or (2) great moves. Each receiver must have one of those two qualities, in addition to great hands. In order to get open, a receiver must have some good "shake and bake" moves and must be able to push the defense off. Certainly, it is much better if the receiver has good speed, because he can really back the defender off and sit down inside or outside, using any kind of break. If a receiver does not have great speed, then he really has to have shiftiness. He must be able to push a defender, work the defender in and out, get the defender to turn his shoulders, and then break.

## FOUR-CORNERS DRILL

During "four-corner drill," we set up near the 50-yard line. There will be a quarterback on the left hash throwing to the spread ends. On the right hash, there is another quarterback throwing to tight ends. The players decide what pass pattern they need to work on. It must be one that is used in our offense. The coaches make sure the players are running their patterns with the proper technique. The quarterback works on his drop-back mechanics and his throwing mechanics. The receiver is working on his patterns, and the defensive back is working on man coverage. Each quarterback will run his group independent of the other group.

Going in the other direction on one hash mark, we set up a quarterback throwing to the left halfbacks. Another quarterback is set up with the right halfbacks on the opposite hash. The linebackers will work against the running backs in order to work on man-to-man coverage. The quarterbacks, meanwhile, are working on throwing techniques, ball placement, and footwork. The receivers are working on specific patterns and pattern running techniques. The defensive backs and linebackers are working on coverage technique.

At the far end of the field, there is another drill set up in which our fullbacks will pass protect against a set of linebackers rushing the passer (Diagram 1.11). There are two outside linebackers and two inside linebackers. The fullbacks will step right or left and pass protect against either the outside rusher or the inside rusher. One of those two pass rushers will be the live rusher. The fullback steps to one side and pass protect against either linebacker on a blitz. Sometimes there will be halfbacks included in the drill to work on pass protection. At times, our fullbacks will be working in four-corners drill, running pass patterns against the linebackers.

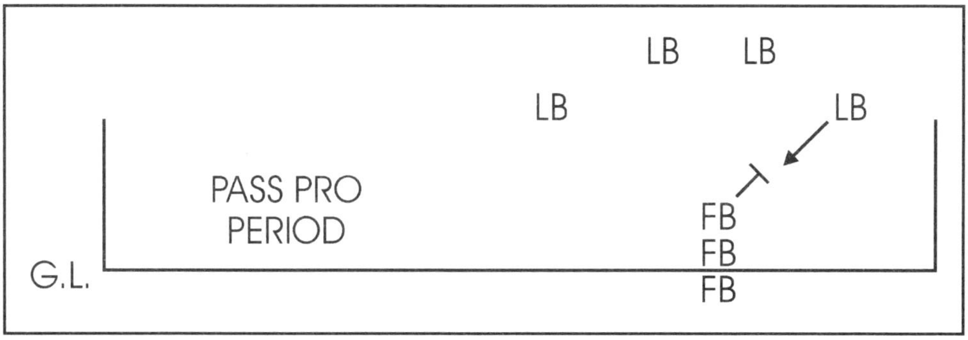


**Diagram 1.11**

At the other end of the field, while all this is going on, the defensive line and the offensive line will be working on pass protection or assignments versus various types of pass rushes Diagram 1.12).

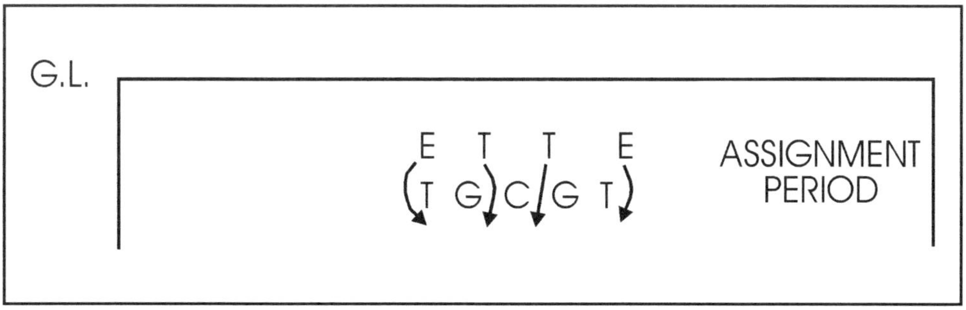


**Diagram 1.12**

Four corners and pass pro is one period where everybody on the field is active. Looking at this period from end to end, everybody on the field is active, there is mass teaching going on. In the middle of the field is the four corners. On one end of the field, there is an assignment period, and on the other end is the backfield pass protection period. All of this is going on at the same time. All the drills go on sound. All the coaches stay in centralized locations, and each group gets a ton of reps in just a five-minute period. Constructing this drill period in this fashion is another prime example of our "racehorse" philosophy. There are two other mixed-group periods-one period concentrating on runs, the other on passing.

## INTERNAL PERIOD

During "run play mixed group work," two different drills are going on at the same time. At one end of the field (Diagram 1.13), there is an "internal" drill working on inside runs. This drill includes the offensive line and the backs. The defensive players in the drill include the nose, the defensive ends, the outside linebackers,

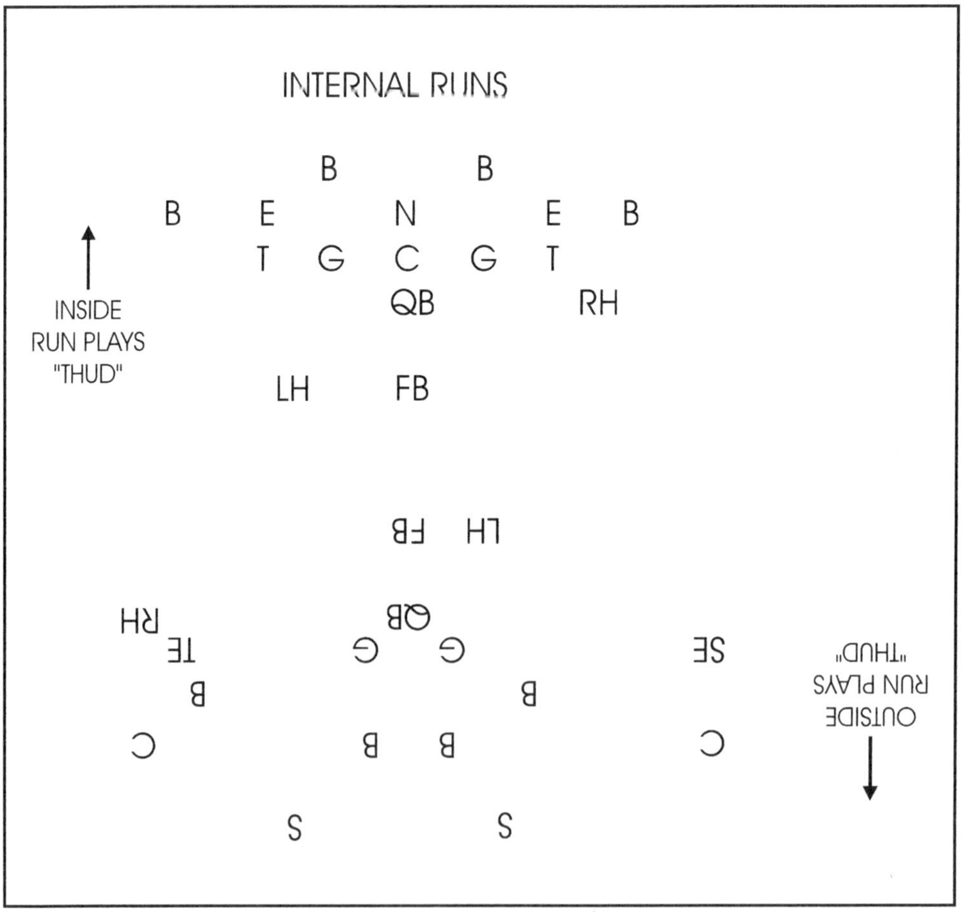


**Diagram 1.13**

and the inside linebackers. In this drill, the offense will run internal or inside run plays against the defense. These are the plays that hit between the tackles or off tackle. The tempo for the drill is live blocking. The backs will run the ball full speed. The defense tries to defeat the blocks and then tackle full go live to the ground, or to "thud" the backs. In this drill, coaches prefer "thud," or wrapping the backs up and not taking them to the ground. "Thud" keeps the backs healthier over the course of a season.

## PERIMETER PERIOD

While "internal" is going on, at the other end of the field there is a drill called "perimeter drill." Perimeter drill includes the guards, all the backs, and the receivers. The defense will include the defensive backs and the linebackers. In this drill, the offense will run all the outside plays, including all the sweeps, all options, and all of the passes where the quarterback is attacking the flank with a run-pass option.

Early in the season, the offensive coaches may see all of the offensive people getting their butt whipped in these drills. It may look bad the first day, and worse the second day. By the third day, the coach will feel as though it cannot possibly get any worse-then, it will start to get better.

Ten minutes is usually the amount of time given to mixed-group runs, both internal and perimeter drills. Within those 10 minutes, coaches can have the guards and backs switch drills after five minutes. We sometimes wait until the next day and then switch them. It is extremely important that the guards and the running backs get time at both drills. The ends and the quarterbacks need to be at "perimeter drill." Other than the guards, the offensive linemen are usually in "internal drill." Guards must work both drills. Other than one group of backs, all of the backs and receivers are at perimeter.

## MIXED-GROUP PASS

The final period in mixed-group work is called "mixed-group work pass period." In this period, everybody on the field will be active. Again, there will be two groups going at the same time. One group will be working on pass protection, and the other group will be working on pass routes (Diagram 1.14).

## PASS SKELETON

In "pass skeleton," the offense will have the quarterback, backs, and ends working passing plays against all four defensive backs and all of the linebackers. They will work pass plays against all pass defenses. The offensive coaches will ask the defense to mix in blitzes. We want them to blitz. We need to make sure the backs learn to pick up the blitz and execute their blocking assignments versus any kind of blitz. The quarterbacks also need a great deal of work on reading coverage and throwing the ball to the correct receiver.

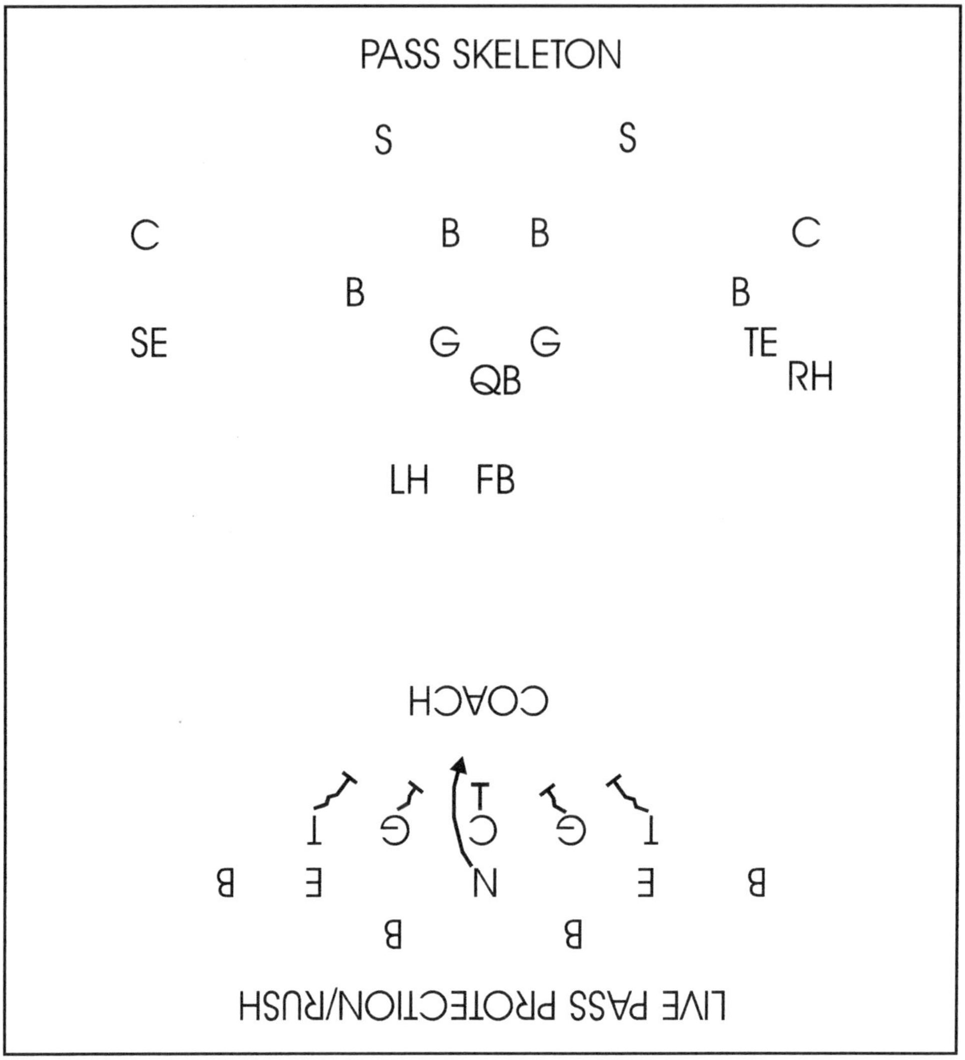


**Diagram 1.14**

## PASS-PROTECTION DRILL

While this "pass skeleton" drill is going on, there is another drill at the other end of the field called "live pass protection." In this drill, there will be a center, two guards, and two tackles. They will work against the defensive line and a set of linebackers so that the linebackers can get work on pass rush with the defensive line. Only one pass rusher at a time goes. All five linemen are lined up, and a coach stands behind the drill and points to one of those defensive rushers, who knows that he will be the live pass rusher. The entire defense gets in their stance. All the offense gets in their stance. When the coach gives the command, all five offensive linemen pass set at the same time. They are all getting reps on learning how to explode out of their stance and get set for pass pro. Only one of the defensive players is live when the ball is actually snapped, yet every lineman gets into a pass set . By having all linemen in their positions, there will not be a pass rush occurring with unrealistic rush lanes. The offensive line coach will want a realistic rush and will want all defenders to work in the gaps or in the confined areas they normally do during games.

### 11-ON-11

There is only one more part of daily practice to discuss and that is called "11-on-11." It is the whole offensive team going against the whole defensive team, and we do it three different ways:

### TEAM VS. BAGS

The first method is called "team vs. bags" (Diagram 1.5), which means 11 players going against bags. When coaches use "team vs. bags," it is a drill that can be done in T-shirts and shorts, and not necessarily with all pads on. The offense can still get a lot of work done. On defense, there is either a scout team or the No. 2 defense holding bags in the proper front spacing that the opponent will use in the upcoming game. The big linemen will hold big bags, and the linebackers will hold hand shields. The defensive backs do not hold anything, so that they will be able to cover full speed. The offense gets to block the front without having to get beat up and without having to hit live on each play. The offense will get a lot of good mental work done in this drill. The only problem is that a big bag doesn't move a whole lot. Team periods will look really sharp when blocking bags. It is a great drill

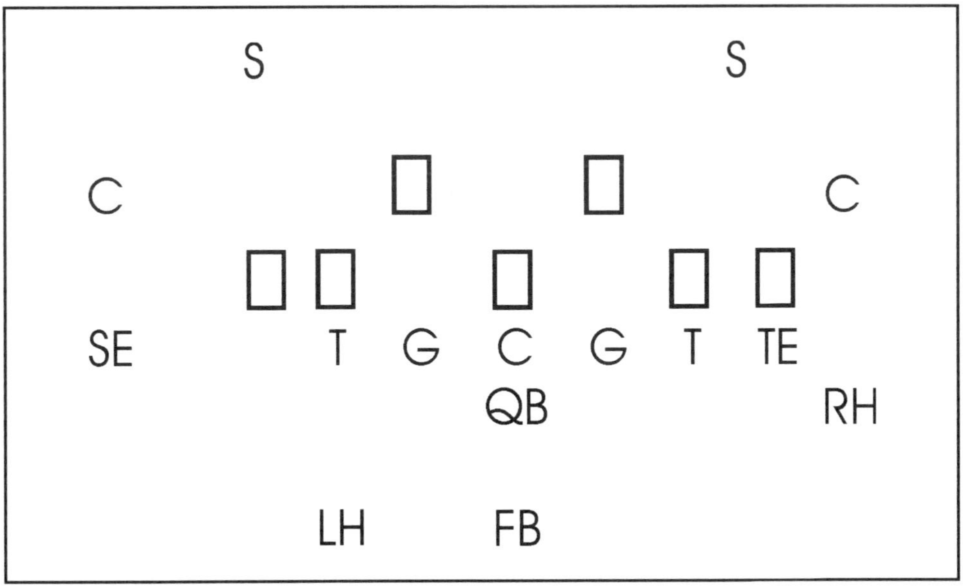


**Diagram 1.15**

to do on Thursday and Friday before a game to help promote confidence. It is not the greatest drill for blocking line stunts and movement. It does not get the players ready to play a live game at full speed. But it is a great review drill, and it is a good drill for practices before the players are allowed to wear full pads. It is also a good drill to run when players are banged up and coaches need to keep them healthy, yet still working on executing assignments.

**TEAM VS. SCOUTS**

Coaches can also do team versus live players. This is an 11-on-11 drill called "team vs. scouts." Here, the offense will work against the scout team. All 11 offensive players will work against a scout team defense (Diagram 1.16). When the offense does "team vs. scouts," the blocking is live.

The defense will run the kind of stunts and movements that our opponent will use against us when we play them on Saturday. If the opponent is a slant team, then we want the defensive line to execute slant 75 percent of the time. Everybody on the offense will block live and full speed. One thing we will never do against each other is cut block a teammate. Instead, we do cut drills on bags, or if the defense needs to work against cuts, then we do a cut drill live against them and warn them beforehand, "This is a cut drill." No coach wants to injure his own players by allowing cutting during his practice plan. Sometimes working on cutting during team period is necessary. If so, tell the defense so that your players always know it is coming, and from where, so that they are prepared to protect themselves.

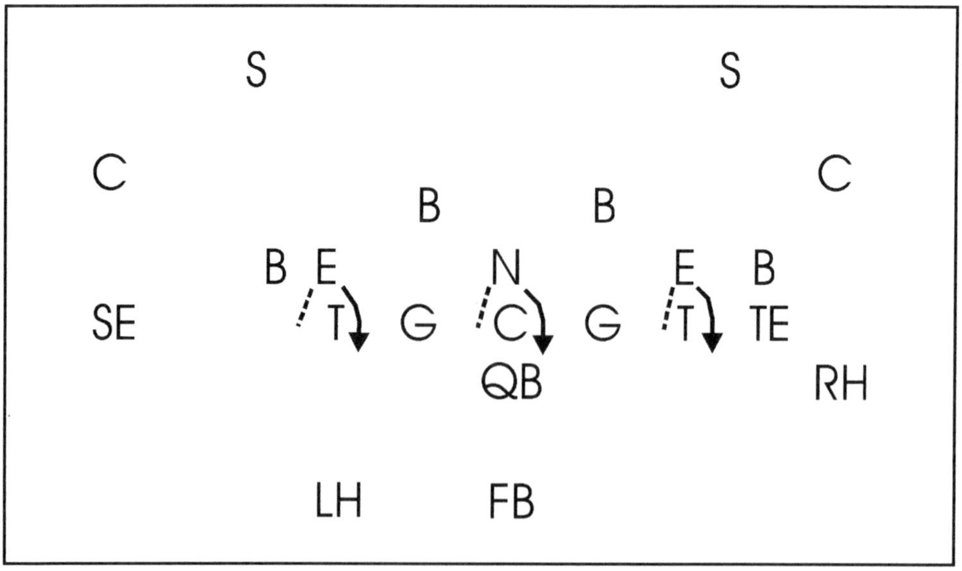


**Diagram 1.16**

In "team vs. scouts," the players are blocking live. The defenders are told that when they get to the ball carrier, they should wrap him up, but without taking him to the ground (thud). Late in the season, they are even told not to touch the backs, but just to let them run by. We coach our defense to sprint to the football, tag off on the back, and not hit them at all. This format takes away a lot of the hits on the running backs, yet coaches can still see which defenders are constantly getting to the ball. They can still evaluate each blocking scheme and solve any problems. Whichever defensive player gets to the ball, even if he just tags off, will show the coaches which offensive player is having problems in that blocking scheme. If the scheme is wrong, assignments are missed, or improper technique is used, the coaches should correct it or find a way to make it work better.

## SCRIMMAGE

The last drill is 11-on-11, full speed, live "scrimmage." We move the chains, make first downs, keep score, and conduct the period like a game. Coaches win no ball games or points for beating themselves up. However, during preseason and training camps, the players do need to scrimmage. They need to know what game speed feels like. Our coaches hold few scrimmages, but we make a big deal about them, as if it is game day. We keep score, draft teams in the spring, and do anything to help make the players have fun; but we also recognize that it is game day, and that they must compete. Our players must get accustomed to the full-speed aspect of what a game actually feels like, and to block and tackle where they have to take somebody to the ground.

Each spring, we have 15 practices and three scrimmages. The first scrimmage is a controlled, intrasquad scrimmage. The second is an intrasquad game, with teams drafted by the players. The third is an alumni game.

During preseason training camp, there is one controlled scrimmage after the first week of practice. The second scrimmage is as much like a game as possible. The coaches will divide the teams up equally or play the first unit against the second unit in order for the starters to gain confidence as they finish training camp.

We have about five scrimmages a year that are live, full-speed, in which we tackle the backs to the ground. There are few, if any, scrimmages in the normal daily practice. Occasionally, there will be a special-situation scrimmage that's 3rd-and-long , or possibly goal line, which becomes necessary. The varsity players who play every weekend are too important to beat up all week, especially when it does not count.

The one other type of scrimmage takes place with the freshmen who are redshirting and some of the sophomores who are not playing full time, yet who need the work. They scrimmage on Friday, at the end of practice. The redshirts love it, since it is their game day. All of the varsity coaches are there coaching their players. Our film man will also be there to film it. The coaches write up grades for the players, and they keep grades for each scrimmage, plus a composite of how each player grades over the course of the season. It is amazing how many times players who are not well thought of will perform over their heads in the scrimmages.

To review our wing-T practice plan, we progress from team takeoff at the beginning to shoulder skills, to routine period, to individual periods. There are three categories of individual drills, some for the backs, some for the ends, and some for the linemen. Next are mixed-group work drills and then 11-on-11 drills. That is how the practice breaks down. At any school in the country, practice will include working individually, working in groups, and then working as a team. Wing-T coaches are very proud of their practice plan because their players get so many repetitions-so much so that practice itself becomes a conditioner. Players hardly need to do extra conditioning after practice. The players get a lot of reps and a lot of practice on the techniques that they will use in a game. Such practice builds mental toughness; it also results in character and promotes proper execution. Players must be able to think and execute when they are tired. That is our "racehorse" philosophy and our wing-T practice plan.

# CHAPTER 2

## The Wing-T Quarterback

In this chapter, I will discuss the qualities of a wing-T quarterback, the traits that we look for in the man who will be our leader. I will also illustrate technique, including the exact stance we teach the quarterback, and show you the hand-up technique, which is the center-quarterback exchange, or "the snap." In addition, I will illustrate the arm-loosening drills that we teach our quarterbacks as we instruct them on how to throw with the proper technique. Finally, we will discuss our handoff drills, our pitch drills, our technique period, and that period in our practices that we call "passing with ends."

### QUALITIES OF THE WING-T QUARTERBACK

What are the qualities of a successful wing-T quarterback, and exactly what do we look for? To run the wing-T, or any offense in college football, you need a fierce competitor at the quarterback position. You need the kind of person who, if he were playing checkers with his roommate, playing video games, or playing a pickup basketball game, would be irate if he lost. You want a guy who does not want to lose at anything. That is what I mean by a fierce competitor. It follows, then, that this fellow will not want to lose a football game when he is out there in front of all those people as the starting quarterback.

One of the things we teach each of our quarterbacks is that he must show people that he is in control and that he should take control of the huddle. When our team steps into that huddle, the players in the huddle should be listening attentively. They should know that there is absolutely no question that this quarterback is

1. In charge

2. Confident

3. Knows what he is doing

4. Has the potential to lead the team into the end zone every time he is out there

We want the players in the huddle to have the utmost confidence in him. He must take control of the huddle! When he talks, nobody else should be talking. We tell our quarterbacks that, when they step in the huddle, they should call the play and the cadence only once. That way, his teammates will know that they are responsible for listening closely to the quarterback. As they run from the huddle to the line of scrimmage, we tell the rest of the players, "If any of you have forgotten anything, do not ask your buddy or the guy that plays next to you. You run to the quarterback, and he will tell you exactly the information that you missed in the huddle."

Another quality I like to see in the quarterback is his taking the blame when things go wrong, especially in front of his teammates. Say there is a fumbled snap in which the center rolled the snap back and never got it off the ground. Say it was the most horrible snap in the world. Our quarterback should turn around to the coach and say, "Coach, that's my fault. I messed up." He can grab the coach after practice and tell him exactly what went wrong. Or he can grab the center and practice with the center on the snap technique. If the quarterback is willing to take the blame in front of his teammates, he is thus showing them that he is their leader, that he is willing to take responsibility for anything.

Another issue that's very important for a quarterback concerns the people he associates with when he is not on the field. I believe the best quarterbacks are the ones who really befriend their offensive linemen. The offensive linemen are the ultimate team warriors, and football is the ultimate team game. Offensive linemen need to know that their quarterback is one of them. If he is, then they will work harder to protect him. If you have a quarterback who only hangs around with the captain of the cheerleading squad, the great tailback, or a certain wide receiver, then you have a quarterback who is distancing himself from the blue-collar guys on the team. This type of quarterback will not be accepted as a leader as much as the quarterback who gets down in there with the guys in the trenches. This is a vitally important trait for the quarterback.

It is also very important that the quarterback is unselfish. He is the guy who must put the team ahead of himself. He has to believe in "team first." When there is an option called, he must be the guy who makes the correct read, and he has to be willing to give the ball to the people as the read dictates. The same thing holds true on a passing play. In the wing-T, where you do so much bootleg and action pass with a run-pass option built into the plays, the quarterback must unselfishly distribute the ball. If he decided to, the quarterback could keep the ball and run every time. That is not what is always best for the team. It is the same idea on the option. The quarterback keeping the ball is not always the best option. He has to believe in the team first, and he has to be willing to distribute the ball to the other players on the team when the defense dictates as much. We tell our quarterback he must be a ball distributor.

The wing-T offense is basically built around unselfishness. The greatest team concept is that in which all skilled players take part in running the ball and pass receiving. Another selling point for the wing-T is that it is not built around only one player. You can have great running backs, great receivers, great quarterbacks, great tight ends, great offensive linemen, and they all can be featured in the wing-T. It is a team-oriented offense, and the quarterback must be the No. 1 team player. He must be willing to distribute the football to the players who are going to win the game. In some games, he will be the focus when he keeps the ball on the option or runs the ball on the flank pass. Often, he must deliver the ball to the correct back or receiver. He has to be a great distributor of the ball.

In any offense, and at any level, you must have a quarterback who is a great decision maker. That must be one of his outstanding qualities. You want a guy who can run. You want a guy who can throw. You would like to have a guy who can do both. However, a great decision maker will win for you before a guy with great talent who cannot make the correct choices. The quarterback must make the correct decisions, and he must make them on time. It does not matter what offense you use, the most important quality for a quarterback is decision making. He must get the ball to the correct player. It is the same thing if you are in the wishbone. Your quarterback is going to hand the ball off , or keep it, or pitch it. He must make the correct decision. A passing quarterback must certainly make correct decisions.

What gives the quarterback the ability to make the correct decision all the time? The quarterback has to have an understanding of what stops the offense. We teach our quarterbacks the four things that will stop an offense faster than anything else:

1. *Turnovers*—We look handoffs in, make accurate pitches, and throw to the correct receiver.

2. *15-yard penalties*—We preach to our players not to commit 15-yard penalties that disrupt or stall a drive. The wing-T is a ball-control offense and, therefore, a 15-yard penalty can be destructive to a drive. It is very difficult to overcome a 15-yard penalty.

3. *Poor execution*—Poor execution is the fastest way to stop an offense. A player misses a block or someone makes a mental error or someone turns the wrong way, and you have a disaster. How can this problem be cleared up? In practice, you must be sure to repeat. You must get flawless execution out of your team. When you put in your offense, you should start at step 1. You do not go to step 2 until step 1 has been done correctly. That is the best way to avoid poor execution.

4. *Poor play calling*—We give the quarterbacks a lot of latitude to call plays. Most of the passing and running game is called from the line of scrimmage. We usually give the quarterback two options, and he must pick the correct one. His job is not to call a perfect play, but to stay out of a bad play.

The next concept we need the quarterback to have an understanding of is what allows those first four things to happen. What allows turnovers to happen? What allows 15-yard penalties to happen? They are caused because you have not improved. If you do not improve every day in practice, eventually you will have turnovers, 15-yard penalties, and poor execution. You will have all those problems. You must improve as a football player every single day. When you do the same drill that you did yesterday, do the drill better the second day. Do it better the third day. Whatever it is, be better the next time, take it to the next level.

Another reason that mistakes continue to happen is that someone did not correct them. We grade the players on film, assigning any one of five different grades, from a -2 to a +2, each week, for every play, once they step on the field. When they make a mistake, the grade is either a -1 or a -2. A -1 is a physical error: the player knew what to do, but he did not get it done. A -2 is a mental error: the player did not know what to do or he gave a poor effort. When those things happen on film, I tell our coaches that if it is on the film, you are responsible for it. You either coached it that way, or you allowed it to happen. We do not want those mistakes to go uncorrected. We need to watch all of our film, whether it is practice film or game film, and make sure the players get those mistakes corrected.

Another problem is not being mentally ready to play. If you are not mentally ready to play a football game each weekend, then you will have the kind of poor execution that stops drives.

These are many of the personality traits we look for in a quarterback. We really like the intense competitor aspect of his personality. We know he has to be unselfish, but, most of all, he has to be a great decision maker.

## PHYSICAL QUALITIES

A wing-T offense can feature a great passing quarterback , even one who may not be fleet of foot. The offense, in that case, will be handoff oriented rather than option oriented. It will be pass oriented, and you the coach must be willing to accept that. If you have a great runner who does not throw the ball well, then the offense will probably tend to be more option oriented. Either type of quarterback can be effective in your offense, but the catalyst to the wing-T is the play-action passing. The waggle off the sweep, the keep pass off the belly, and the counter bootleg off the counter play-these are the plays that really spark the offense. Your quarterback must be able to complete those passes, or you will have trouble moving the ball with the wing-T. Therefore, the quarterback must be enough of a thrower to complete those plays. If he can do that-and run the option-he will be just fine at quarterback. Obviously, we would love to have a guy who can both run and pass.

In terms of your quarterback's height requirements, at the college level , 6'1" is fine.

However, many shorter and taller quarterbacks can also make the offense go. My personal opinion is that the "athletic-type" quarterback is going to do much more for your team in the long run than a slow-footed passer. Someone who has quick feet, not necessarily the greatest 40 time, but certainly quick feet and escapability, is the type of young man who will help your program more than somebody who is 6'6" and can really throw, but can't get out of his own way. Those kinds of quarterbacks have trouble, even in a passing offense, because their lack of mobility makes them a standing target. We want a quarterback who has good feet, who can handle the offense in all phases, and who can get out of trouble with quickness and agility once in awhile.

I think most offenses would ask for the same qualities we have discussed. Of all the characteristics of a successful quarterback I have mentioned, decision making is the most vital.

## QUARTERBACK DRILLS

### Stance

Both the quarterback's stance and the quarterback-center exchange, which we call "hand-up," are areas that are often overlooked. We consider them both to be extremely important.

The things we want to emphasize when we teach the quarterback's stance are

1. A narrow base

2. A slight knee bend

3. Only wrist deep under the center

We do not want the quarterback with his feet real wide apart, underneath the center, and squatted down low. I have seen that over and over when watching high school film. I can only tell you that we do not want to have our quarterback look like that. We would like to have our quarterback stand taller and not quite so far under the center. This action enables the quarterback to get away from the center quickly, but also does not impede the linemen in their pulling technique.

The first thing we emphasize is the width of the feet We want four to six inches between the insides of his two ankles. We want a parallel stance, with his toes straight ahead. If you look between the ankles, you will see four to six inches of space. That is all the farther apart we want the feet spread. We coach this way because the quarterback with the real wide stance has trouble gaining much ground on his first step. His foot will not strike as big an arc when he takes his first step away from center. We would like the first step to strike a big arc and gain distance away from the center. We want to be able to get away from the center quickly, to allow for the pulling which happens in the wing-T. We want to be able to get the ball to the backs as deep in the backfield as possible.

Second, we want our quarterback to stand tall. There should not be a lot of bend in the waist. We coach a slight arch in the back, with just a slight knee bend. Sometimes it appears that our quarterbacks look too upright or lock-kneed. We do not want that either, but we do want the knee bend to be as slight as possible so that he can stand up tall. We want quarterbacks as tall in the saddle as we can get them.

Finally, we do not want the quarterback too low under the center. He should only be wrist deep. As the quarterback takes the ball from the center, he will only be under the center as far as his wrist, and the ball will be snapped up to him. He is then in perfect position, after he takes the snap, to bring the ball to his belt, take a step, and gain ground away from the center. We constantly work on a good first step that gets distance away from the center.

We have all the quarterbacks practice with all the centers every day. They practice every five yards on the white sideline stripe. As we line up on the white stripe, the quarterbacks straddle the white stripe so that the white stripe goes right through the middle of their feet. When we bring the centers in, they put the ball down on the sideline. We have the center over the ball, and the quarterback behind the center. Remember, even with a short quarterback, we want him as tall in the saddle as we can get him. We do not want him to have a lot of waist bend. We do not want his feet too wide, and we do not want him crouched down low under the center.

## HAND UP

In the "hand-up" technique, which is the center snap, there are some important coaching points to emphasize. The snap is taught in a three-step progression. The first step is called "the fit." The second step is called "a six-inch snap." The third step is the "full snap."

The center is our best line athlete. We do a lot of different tests to find out who is the quickest, biggest, strongest lineman on the team, and then we combine those test results to find out who is the best big man. He is the player we play at center. We want to be strong down the middle in this offense. The center is as important to us as the quarterback and the fullback.

A necessary feature of the snap technique is that we should be able to teach this technique to anybody. When I speak at clinics, I take somebody out of the audience who has never snapped a ball in their life, and teach him quickly how to snap. It is amazing how a guy who has never snapped before can adapt to this snap technique, learning it quickly, and do it well. The best coach to coach the center is the quarterback himself. He will tell the center exactly where the snap needs to be and also help the center adjust the snap.

One of the most demoralizing occurrences for an offense is the fumbling of the snap. Nothing can happen in any offense without the ball being exchanged smoothly from the center to the quarterback. We do not want to demoralize our team by having fumbled snaps. Therefore, in the practice plan, we devote five minutes every day to what we call "hand-up period." The offensive line coach will send the centers to the quarterback coach, and the centers and the quarterbacks will work together on their snap technique. At the beginning of the season , this drill is as basic and elementary as it can be. As time goes on, we begin to have the center fire out after he snaps the ball, and we also have the quarterback practice any footwork he needs to work on. Sometimes the quarterback will explode off the snap, take one step, and hold it to see if that first step is correct. Other times, the quarterback takes two steps. On other occasions, he might step through a complete play. The center/quarterback exchange period in practice can accomplish many objectives. The most important of them is the exchange between the center and the quarterback.

The first part of the three-step process we use to teach the snap is called "the fit." We start with the center down in his stance. He should not have too wide of a base. He has to be comfortable, but the center does not want to have his feet too wide, because the wider his feet are, the more he creates gaps between his shoulders and the shoulders of the next adjacent blocker. His feet should be fairly narrow. He should reach the ball out in front of him as far as he can so that the defenders are farther away from the line. This maneuver will allow the offensive linemen extra space to get off the ball and execute their blocks.

When the quarterback receives the ball, he wants to receive the back end of the ball, and he would like to have the fat of the ball in the V of his fingers. The quarterback's right hand under the center is turned one-quarter of a turn to his right. In order to learn this technique, the quarterback will point his fingers directly up to the sky. As his hand is vertical, he will make a quarter turn to the right so that that V between his thumb and forefinger is now facing directly up to the sky. From there, he brings his hand down so that it is parallel to the ground, which will cause his wrist to bend. That is the position he wants his hand to assume just before he receives the snap from the center. He will be only wrist deep under the center.

'The fit" is when the quarterback holds the ball under the center where he wants to receive it, with his fingers near the passing grip, and the fat of the ball in the V of his hand on the back end of the ball. The quarterback places the football under the center in the position he wants to receive it. The center then takes the ball from the quarterback and places it on the ground in reverse motion from the snap. The center is thus getting a feel from the quarterback as to where the ball should be snapped. As the quarterback puts the ball under the center, the center is getting the feel for exactly where the quarterback wants that ball snapped.

The snapping motion by the center is the same motion he would use if he pulled a cord to turn on a light bulb. That pulling motion is the same motion he will use on the snap technique. The center should bring the ball straight up, without turning his wrist. He should not turn the ball sideways. The center should simply bring the ball straight up to the quarterback. These are the body mechanics that are involved in the "fit" drill. The center takes the ball from the quarterback and brings the ball back to the ground, using the reverse of his snap motion. The quarterback hands the ball to the center, who takes it and brings it back to the ground. From there, the center passes the ball around behind him. The quarterback refits the ball in his hand, gives it back to the center, and they continue to do this until both the quarterback and the center feel comfortable having the ball in the right place and knowing the kind of motion to use.

The second part of teaching the snap progression is what we call the "six-inch snap." In this drill, the center snaps the ball to the quarterback, but he starts with the ball about six inches off the ground, snaps it, and holds onto it. He does not actually give the ball to the quarterback. The center snaps the ball back and keeps control of it with the quarterback. The center takes the ball back from the quarterback to that six-inch position off the ground, and then snaps it again to the quarterback. In this phase, we want the quarterback to give directions to the center. The quarterback has to know how he wants to receive the ball from the center. As the center snaps the ball, the quarterback coaches him. He is going to tell him whether the ball is too far back, too far forward, turned to the right, or turned to the left.

The final step in the progression is to snap the ball full speed. The center will drive the ball back into the quarterback's hands. The quarterback should be able to have control of the ball with his right hand. He should not have to use his left hand at all. In fact, for all these drills, if he chooses to use just one hand to take the ball from the center, he will be building great confidence, because he will then find it much easier to eventually use both hands.

It is important to discuss what happens when the quarterback takes the ball in the wing-T. He will get the ball from the center in the same position in which he placed it under the center. When the quarterback takes the snap, the long axis of the ball will be parallel to the ground. He will be holding the ball on the back half of the ball, and he should have the fat of the ball in the V between his thumb and his forefinger. As he takes the ball from the center, he should rotate the ball one-quarter of a turn to the right, if he's right-handed; to the left, if he's left-handed. As the ball is rotated into his second hand, it should be quickly snapped to the belt buckle. The long axis of the football will be parallel to the ground, with the quarterback's elbows in, and with the back point of the ball in the belt buckle.

## ARM LOOSENING

The next drills I will discuss are the quarterback arm-loosening drills, or throwing drills. The first drill that the quarterbacks will work on is called "quick grips." The quarterbacks have the ball on the ground, and they do this drill with both their right and left knees down. With the ball resting on the ground, the quarterback takes the football from the ground, without his hands starting on the ball, gets it into the passing grip as quickly as possible, and then delivers the ball to another quarterback, who will be lined up in front of him. Coaches should instruct their quarterback to take the ball from the ground and up to the passing position as quickly as possible, while using the proper passing grip, and then deliver the ball.

One of the mechanics we look for in this drill is for the quarterback to keep the nose of the football turned outward as he brings it up to the ready position. If the quarterback is holding the ball with the nose down, then his elbow will be tight to his body. Consequently, as he throws the ball, he will short-arm it. If you take the nose of the ball and turn it out, the elbow comes out. The quarterback should release the ball as if there is somebody standing in front of him and forcing him to release the ball up and over. This technique will extend his arm, elevate his elbow, and give him better distance on his throw. The quarterback should do this drill with both his right knee and his left knee down. One good extension to this drill is to put two quarterbacks on opposite sides of the crossbar on a goalpost and then practice throwing over the crossbar. This will teach the quarterbacks to get the ball up as they release it.

The second extension we do is to have two quarterbacks throw the ball to each other as they practice throwing on the run. In this drill, one quarterback will run straight at the other quarterback he is playing catch with. That quarterback will be backing up to keep the spacing between them the same. What we try to accomplish in this drill is to teach the quarterback to throw on the run. We coach the quarterback to throw the ball, then follow the ball, so that his throwing and his running are both going in the same direction. You do not want to have your quarterbacks run in one direction and try to throw the ball in another direction. We coach the quarterbacks to throw the ball and follow it, to chase the ball as they deliver it. As the second quarterback backs up, the first quarterback throws him the ball. Next, the second quarterback runs forward, and the first quarterback runs backward. They throw the ball as they run forward, and chase the ball and follow the ball as they deliver it.

When quarterbacks throw on the run, they should have the throwing elbow wrench to the middle of the back. You will see their shoulders turn perpendicular as they deliver the ball. We want to emphasize wrenching the elbow, so it rotates into the middle of the quarterback's back before he releases the ball. Two quarterbacks can participate in this drill at the same time. As one quarterback runs forward, his partner runs backward. They get a feel for throwing the ball at a moving target and chasing the ball. Their running motion and their passing motion is all in the same direction.

The next arm-loosening drill for quarterbacks has them running in place and throwing the ball. This action gives them a feel for throwing with their feet moving. We coach the quarterback to chop his feet, run in place, and then throw the ball. The reason we do this drill is for accuracy. Sometimes when quarterbacks start to run, they become less accurate. We want to simulate running action and then have them throw the ball to the strike point. The quarterback has a strike point on every pass play. In order to practice this, we tell him to throw the ball for the front number, the back number, the nose, or the waist. This is the "run-in-place" drill: the quarterback can run in place and throw the ball to his partner, who is a minimum of 10 yards away. He should hit a different strike point with each throw.

The next drill is the "wave" drill. Start the quarterback in a throwing position, as if he has already dropped back, ready to throw the football. To simulate pressure coming through the line, the coach will point in a number of directions. The quarterback is set up to throw the ball, but now he feels pressure. He has to shuffle his feet, avoid the pressure, then be able to reset his feet to throw the football. He might have to shuffle his feet in another direction and again reset his feet to throw tho football. He must slide his feet back and forth, like a wave. As he slides his feet, he throws the ball as soon as he can get set up.

The next drill is called "roll-out drill." In this drill, the coach will line the quarterbacks up about 10 yards away from each other, on a yard line, as they run across the field to the other sideline. As they run across the field, they get a little bit of depth off the line, as if they are moving outside on a sprint play. Each quarterback's partner will also run down the line and get a little bit of depth. Both quarterbacks should then practice waggle and throwing to each other. As they practice this drill, they should start on one sideline and run across the field to the far sideline. They should do this all the way across the field: One quarterback throws the ball first, then the other quarterback gets the ball and throws it next. One quarterback will be moving to his right, the other quarterback will be moving to his left. As they run, they throw the ball, get it in the ready position, wrench their elbow into their back, turn their shoulders to their target, and follow the ball in the direction they are throwing.

## WAGGLE DRILL

The last throwing drill for the quarterbacks during practice is called the "waggle" drill. When quarterbacks do the waggle drill, all of the offensive linemen will be in the drill. Regardless of whether they play center, guard, or tackle, all linemen are taught the guard techniques for the waggle. This type of learning is called "cross-training," and in this case, all linemen learn to pull on the waggle. As a result, our best backup lineman can play any position on the line. All he has to do is brush up on his mental assignments to be able to step right in to play. This strategy keeps the five best linemen on the field.

The first play practiced in the drill is called 29 waggle, which means the quarterback fakes 29 sweep to the left and bootleg to the right. The right guard takes a flat pull step as he eyes the defensive end. As the guard log blocks the defensive end, he will work to strike with his inside shoulder while inside his foot. His next step will work up the field. He will finish the log block using the outside hand and driving it through the defensive end's outside number, bench pressing him, and finishing him back inside. This play has been set up by having the tight end release inside to see if the defensive player over him will seal inside or penetrate. If he penetrates across the line of scrimmage, run plays inside of him. If the tight end is releasing inside and the defender is jamming the tight end, he makes himself a perfect target for the log block. This log block should have contact on the fourth step. The first step should be a pull step, the second and third steps should continue in the same direction, flat down the line of scrimmage. On his fourth step, the contact should occur. On the fifth step, the guard will turn up the field and bench press the defender to the inside.

The backside guard will take a flat pull step on the first step, cross over for depth on the second step, then flatten out down the line of scrimmage. He is looking to kick out any penetration off the corner. If the defensive end decides to penetrate into the backfield, the first guard lets him go, the backside guard kicks him out, and the quarterback must learn to step inside the kick-out and then continue to attack the flank. If the end does not penetrate, the first guard will log him, and the second guard will now lead the quarterback to the flank, looking for the next defender. Against a corner blitz, if the defensive end crashes inside, the log block takes care of him, and as the corner comes off the edge, the second guard kicks him out. In this case, as the guard kicks him out, the quarterback will duck up inside.

The next possibility we practice involves the defensive end sealing and being logged by the first guard, with the corner dropping into coverage. The second guard will now block any defender who scrapes from the inside to the outside. The quarterback gives a "go" call if he runs the ball, and the backside guard will lead him down the field and block any defender he finds.

Quarterbacks and linemen repeat this drill to both sides. They do the drill in a rapid-fire fashion, getting as many reps as possible in a five-minute period, practicing the different reactions by the defense. The first group of players will fake sweep to the left and run waggle to the right. As they start, the next group is waiting in line behind them. Two more offensive linemen run up to become the next two guards to go.

Having completed 29 waggle, the quarterbacks will now fake the sweep to the right, while the guards pull to the left. The quarterback is led by the two guards around the left end on 21 waggle. The purpose of waggle drill is to learn to react to defenders coming off the edge. The quarterback should learn to anticipate whether penetration is going to happen or whether the guards will get the flank sealed down. The quarterbacks are in waggle drill every day.

## HANDOFF DRILL

There are four other drills we do with quarterbacks during practice: handoff, pitch, full backfield technique period, and passing with ends. Diagram 2.1 illustrates the "handoff drill," which includes four stations. We have a center, a quarterback, and a fullback in a middle station; a center, a quarterback, and a fullback in another middle station; a center, a quarterback, and a right halfback in a third station to the left; and a center, a quarterback, and a left halfback in a fourth station to the right. Now, in these four stations, they will work solely on the quarterback-running back exchange on selected running plays. They will get as many reps as they can in a five-minute period. It is amazing how many reps the backs will get in just a five-minute period. At the end of the season, we cut this drill down to two minutes and still get a lot of reps.

The centers in this drill are kickers, or anybody on the team who might be injured and cannot play, or somebody who is sitting out the season on a medical redshirt. The kickers make great snappers; during some parts of practice, they get bored being down at the other end of the field just kicking footballs all the time. One of the first things we do is to teach all kickers how to be snappers. This means the quarterback will always take the ball in exchange. As mentioned earlier, anybody can learn how to be a snapper in a very short period of time and execute at a very high percentage.

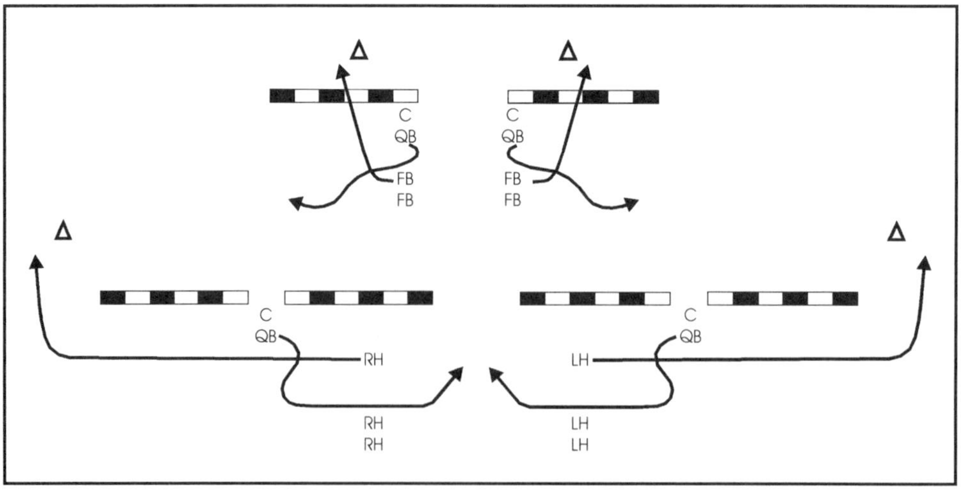


**Diagram 2.1**

The diagram shows that the four stations will be operating independent of each other. As soon as the quarterback and the running back are ready, the quarterback will snap the ball, and they will execute the play we are working on. If the fullbacks are working on the belly play, they take their footwork for the belly as the quarterback executes his handoff technique and then executes the fake he needs to perform. The ball is handed off to the running back, who bursts through the line of scrimmage full speed down the field past cones. It should be a habit for the backs to accept the handoff and burst through the line of scrimmage.

While the center, quarterback, and fullback work on belly to the right, another center, quarterback, and fullback work the same play to the left. While that is going on, the halfbacks are working on the handoff they have planned for the day. The right halfback might work on sweep to the left. The quarterback takes the center exchange, executes his footwork, hands the ball off to the halfback, and fakes waggle. The halfback executes his sweep technique with a good cut and must burst past the cones. At the same time the right halfback is working on sweep left, the left halfback is working on sweep right. The backup players are lined up behind the starters. The halfbacks and fullbacks are going to be getting maximum reps. They will go rapid-fire and get rep after rep. The coach should tell the fullbacks to keep switching sides. As soon as they have gone on one side, they should switch back to the other side. The halfbacks stay in the same place.

The quarterbacks will rotate in this drill. They will rotate on their own after one-quarter of the time through each drill. You will be amazed at how many reps on a handoff the players will get. If you have five minutes, work on two different types of handoffs in the period.

## PITCH DRILLS

The next drill is called "pitch drill." As seen in Diagram 2.2, pitch drills will involve two groups that are running option plays. On one hash mark is a center, a quarterback, a fullback, and a left halfback. They will be running option plays to the right. In another group is a center, a quarterback, a fullback, and a right halfback, who will be running option plays to the left. The groups are offset by 10 yards to avoid collisions. For example, if we work on trap option, the fullback will take his footwork and execute his blocking assignment for the play. We use big blocking bags on the field so that the fullback has to do a great job faking and also execute his block technique. The center will snap the ball to the quarterback, who will take his footwork. The left halfback is the pitchback. Another quarterback is in a read position to challenge the first quarterback. The quarterbacks should try to make it harder in practice than the defense will make it during a game. They should challenge each other during this drill. The halfback who is the pitchback should get good pitch relationship with the quarterback. Pitch relationship is 5 x 3, meaning 3 yards deep and 5 yards in front of the quarterback so the back can catch the ball

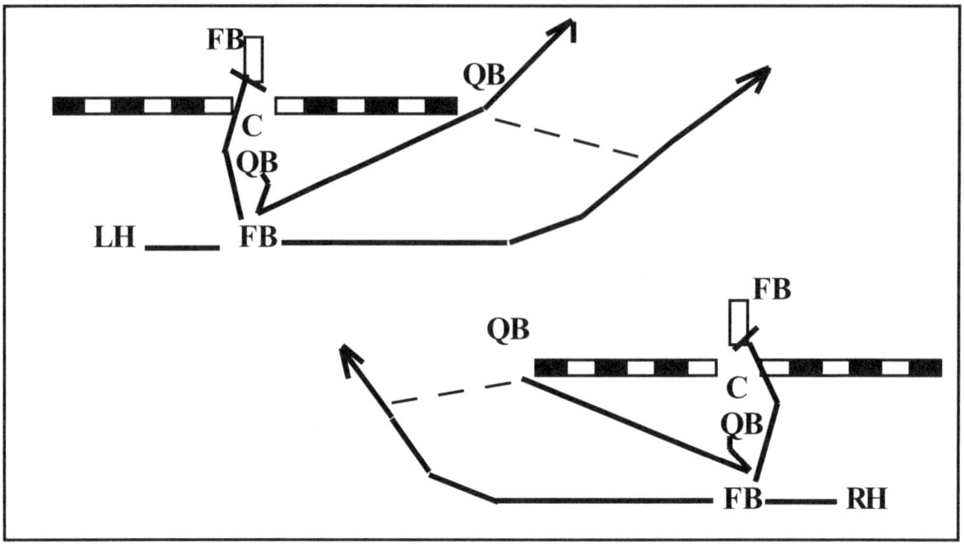


**Diagram 2.2**

running downhill, gaining maximum yardage. Coaches should make sure that, as they catch the pitch, the backs should not turn back into the free safety and the pursuit. Our backs work a technique where they bounce from the hash mark to the numbers to the sideline. They keep trying to stay outside, away from the free safety running through the alley. While this group is working on option to the right, another group will be working on option to the left. The right halfback is the pitchback, and the quarterback executes his option technique. Another quarterback is the pitch key.

### Full Backfield Technique

"Full backfield technique" (Diagram 2.3) is exactly what it sounds like-all backs working together to perfect plays and techniques. We work a lot on flank runs and on flank passing in this drill. Anything that needs to be perfected is in this drill. If we were working on 21 sweep, the right halfback would have to execute a blocking assignment so that another right halfback is holding a bag while the halfbacks work on sweep blocks. There will be another fullback holding a bag where the fullback is assigned to block. The quarterback will take the snap, and the ball carrier will take the ball from the quarterback as he works on his sweep cut. While this group is going in one direction, the young players will be working on the same play, going in the opposite direction. Sometimes it will be better for the younger players to watch the older players and only have one group; but, normally, it is better to learn by doing than by watching.

### Passing with Ends

The last drill we do is "passing with ends." When we do passing with ends (Diagram 2.4), we will have all the ends, receivers, backs, and quarterbacks in one group.

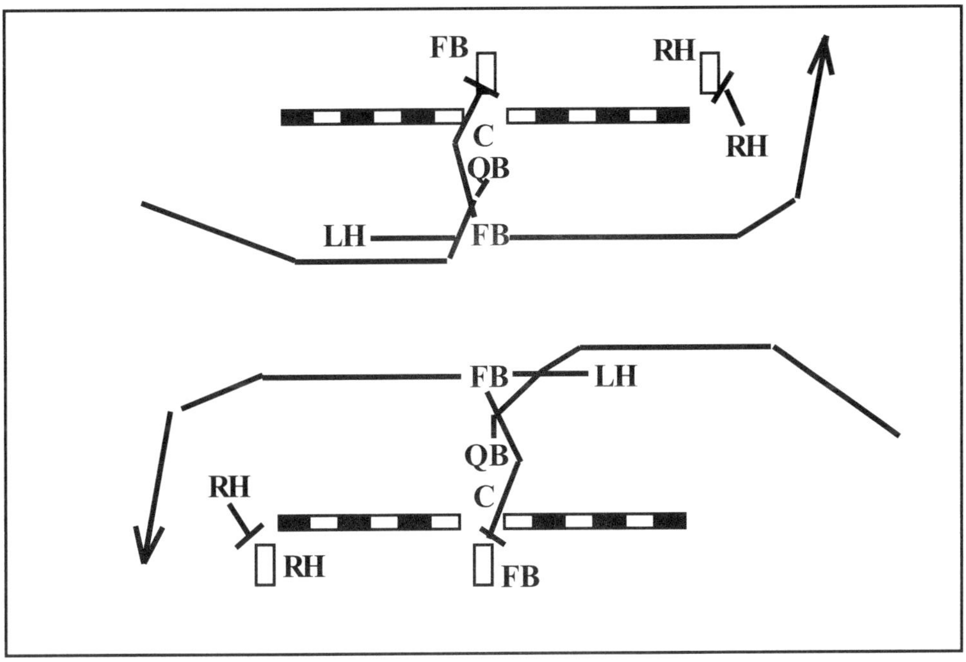


**Diagram 2.3**

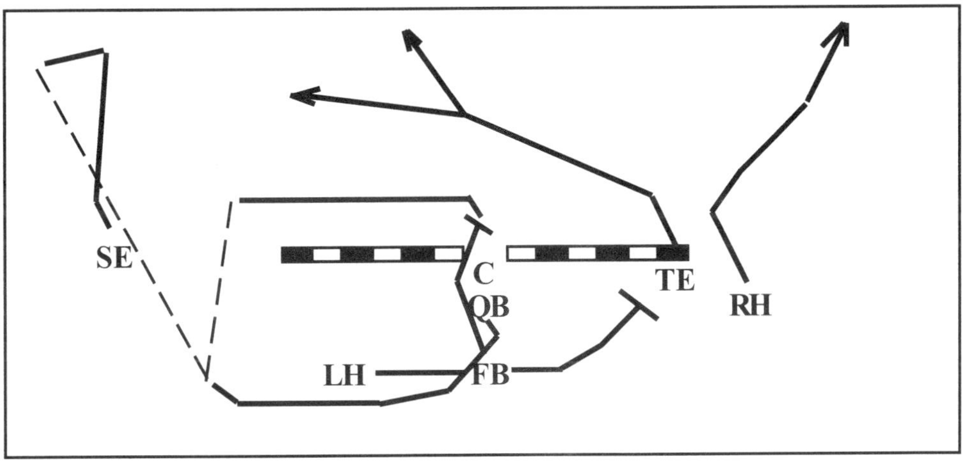


**Diargram 2.4**

If we are working on "waggle out," the spread end will practice his out cut, and the backfield will work on waggle. The fullback will be a blocker first and a receiver second. The tight end will run the crossing route or split the middle versus two-deep coverage. The right half runs the throw back, and the left half fakes the sweep and becomes a blocker to the back side. The quarterback makes the correct decision and throws to the proper receiver. We can drill as a full group, or we can work on individual cuts, with one quarterback and one receiver repeating routes over and over again.

To summarize the practice plan for the quarterbacks, the first thing they do is review their stance. They do that as they are working on hand-up technique with the center. They work on hand-ups every day in practice. They do their arm loosening and throwing drills early in the practice to get loosened up and to review the fundamentals of throwing. Next, our quarterbacks go to handoff drills. They work individual handoffs with the halfbacks and the fullbacks. The next drill is pitch drill, where they work on option plays and especially on pitch technique. Full backfield technique follows. The quarterbacks always finish by working "passing-with-ends" with all backs and all ends.

## PLAY SERIES TECHNIQUES

The most important coaching points I will cover in this chapter are the quarterback's footwork on the plays he will use in the wing-T offense. There are four series of plays, and each set of plays is fully discussed in other chapters of this book. In those chapters, each series will be diagrammed, detailing exactly who blocks whom and how to attack different defenses. Throughout the technique chapters, the footwork for each of these plays will be discussed for every position. The backfield technique chapter will demonstrate each play series for the running backs and the exact techniques used. Techniques we use for our linemen and receivers will be presented in those specific sections. In this chapter, our primary focus will be on the quarterback's techniques in each series.

### The 20 Series

The 20 series contains the basic plays in the wing-T offense. The first play will be the sweep play, which is the play too many coaches use to identify the wing-T offense. Too many coaches think the "wing-T" represents only the wing formation and the sweep play. But that is merely one play in a total system of offense. Because of its popularity, the sweep should be discussed first.

### The Sweep

Our first discussion about quarterback technique will be the technique we teach on 21 or sweep right. The quarterback should be in a good quarterback stance and receive the hand-up. He should use the proper stance, with his wrist deep under the center, a good arch in his back, and a slight knee bend, yet he should be upright. The quarterback's first step is to reverse pivot to the midline. On this play, it is important that the quarterback pivots his back foot. His right foot, the foot he will pivot on, pivots all the way around. A cardinal sin, and a common error that can be detected on film, is when the quarterback does not pivot his back foot and does not get his shoulders completely around, thus allowing the defense to see the ball. When looking at this from the back, the ball is exposed to the defense, and a defensive player in a linebacker position will have a clear look at the football. If the quarterback reverse pivots all the way around with his back to the defense, the defense will not know where the football is. The fullback will be stepping with his right foot for the left foot of the center.

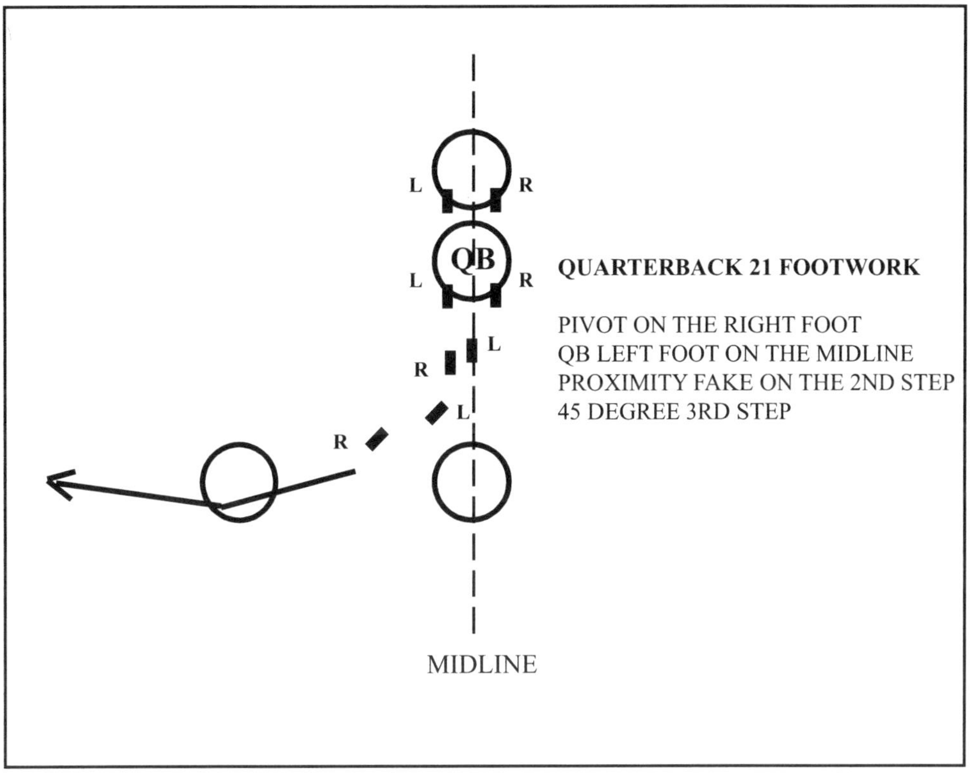
L
R
QB
L
R
QUARTERBACK 21 FOOTWORK
PIVOT ON THE RIGHT FOOT
QB LEFT FOOT ON THE MIDLINE
PROXIMITY FAKE ON THE 2ND STEP
45 DEGREE 3RD STEP
L
R
L
R
MIDLINE

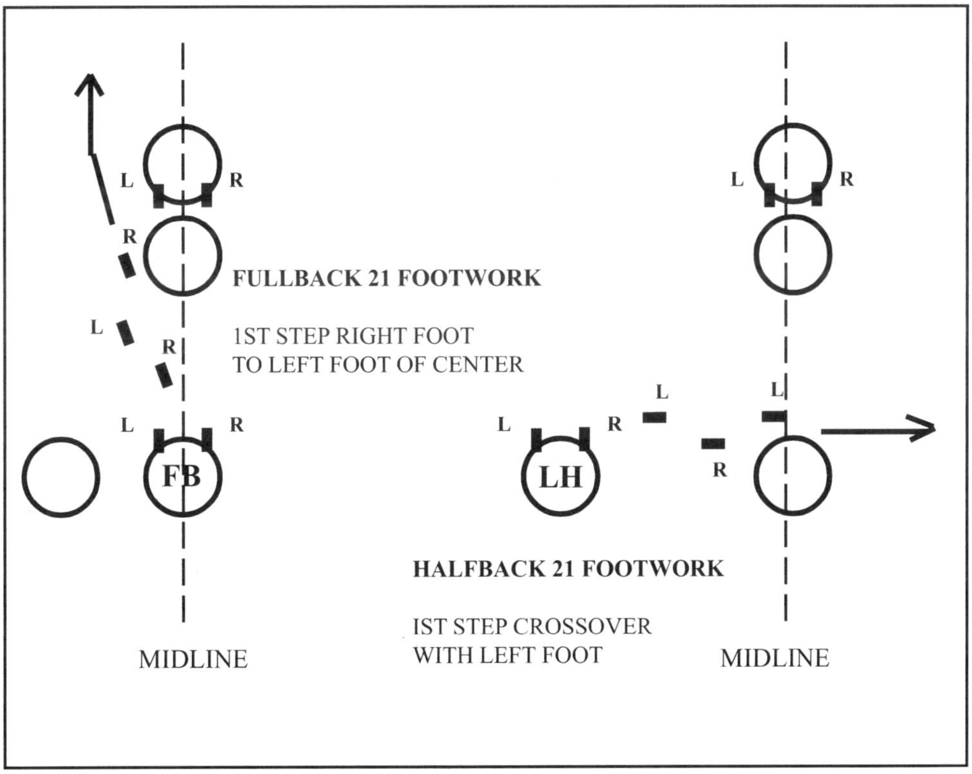
L
R
R
FULLBACK 21 FOOTWORK
L
R
1ST STEP RIGHT FOOT
TO LEFT FOOT OF CENTER
L
R
FB
L
R
L
R
LH
L
R
L
R
HALFBACK 21 FOOTWORK
IST STEP CROSSOVER
WITH LEFT FOOT
MIDLINE
MIDLINE

**Diagram 2.5**

On his second step, the quarterback continues to stay on the midline. The fullback fakes over an imaginary ball. The fake occurs between the first and second steps. The quarterback will not fake with the ball to the fullback. The fullback takes his first step for the backside foot of the center and, on the second step, will fake over an imaginary ball. The close proximity of the shoulders of the quarterback and the fullback lead us to call this a "proximity" fake. The nearness and the closeness of the shoulders and the fact that the fullback faked over an imaginary ball are enough for a good trap fake.

The quarterback will take his first two steps on the midline. His third step begins to cross over as the handoff to the halfback takes place. Our handoffs look like we're dealing cards. They are all at forearm's length only. The quarterback will not reach the ball. If the quarterback is reaching the ball, the defense will see the ball. If he keeps his elbows tight to the side of his body, then the defense will not be able to see the ball. The halfbacks will be coached to take the ball with the inside thumb down. Their footwork is to crossover step, run through the fullback's position on the second step, and receive the ball on the third step. After that, the quarterback will continue to threaten the flank, faking waggle. The halfback will run the sweep.

When the quarterback hands the ball off on sweep, he will need to read the free safety as he continues to fake waggle. As a result, he will know exactly what the free safety's reaction will be when we call waggle. As the quarterback fakes waggle, his inside arm should pump hard, and his outside hand, his backside hand, should be in the crotch, where the ball would be placed if he were running the waggle.

**The Fullback Trap**

The next play is 24 and 26, "guard trap" up the middle (Diagram 2.6). In this play, the footwork for the quarterback and the footwork for the fullback are determined by the spacing of the defense. If it is an even spacing, with the guards covered and the center uncovered, the fullback's footwork will be exactly the same as in the sweep. He will step with his right foot on "24 guard trap." His first step is right foot for left foot of the center. If the guards are uncovered and the center is covered, the defense is an odd spacing-the first step by the fullback is now on the midline. In an even defense, the center's block will be back to the man covering the left guard, and that is the block the fullback will be cutting off of. If it is an odd defense, the center will block the man directly on him. The fullback now steps right down the midline, where the center's block will occur. The fullback will cut off this block in either direction.

Against even defenses, the fullback steps for the backside foot of the center, so the quarterback can stay on the midline. His first two steps will be on the midline, and his footwork is exactly the same as it was on the sweep. The quarterback's second step continues on the midline, and the ball is handed off on the second step. His elbows are in tight, and the ball is handed off from no farther than forearm's

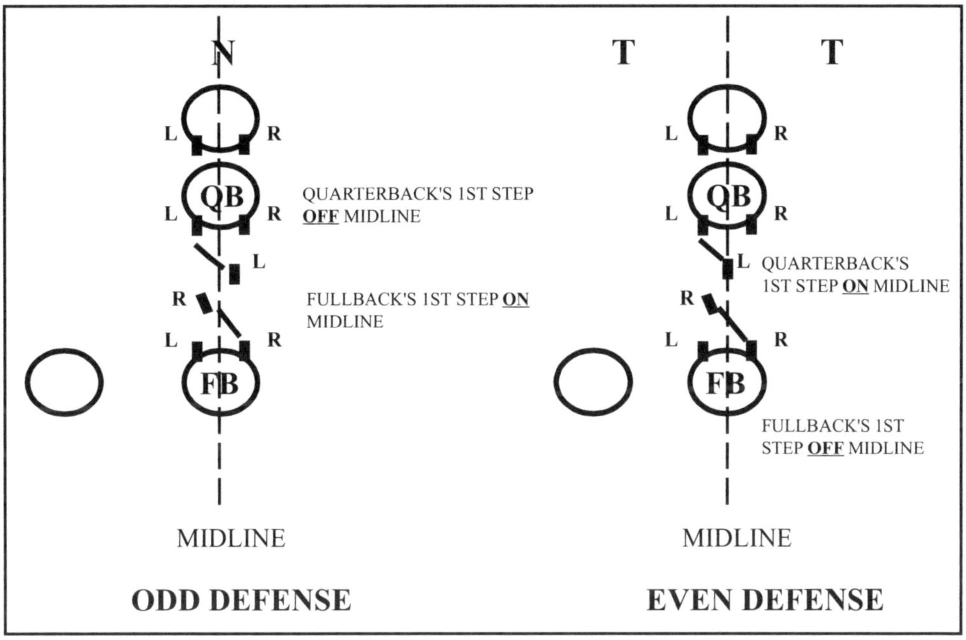


**Diagram 2.6**

distance away. When the quarterback has to reach the ball to the fullback, one of them has bad footwork or bad aiming points.

Techniques against the odd defense require the fullback's first step to be on the midline; therefore, the quarterback's first step must be beyond the midline to give the fullback the midline unimpeded. On the quarterback's second step, he will hand off to the fullback. On his third step, he will begin to cross over and make an effective fake to the left halfback. He will then continue to attack the flank and fake the waggle.

It does not matter if the line is blocking the play with "guard trap blocking," "on blocking," or "gut blocking." The line uses all those different blocking schemes, but the quarterback's footwork remains consistent. He and the fullback depend on the spacing of the defensive front. This will give the fullback the optimum chance to option run the most important block, which is the center's block, regardless of which defense we are facing.

### The Off Tackle

Our off-tackle play is 22 and 28. This play looks like the sweep (Diagram 2.7). We run this play if the third defender in the defense is a penetrating defensive end and is running up the field, making it hard to run the sweep. We try to make the play look just like the sweep, but turn up one hole short. The basic concept is to kick the penetrator out and run the ball off tackle.

Many coaches run 22 and 28 (the off-tackle play) like they run the sweep, and hand the ball to the halfback over the top. The halfback fakes the sweep and cuts it up inside.

Our coaches have found over the years that this is a tough cut. They have modified both the quarterback's footwork and the halfback's footwork. For the quarterback, the first two steps will reverse pivot to the midline like 21. The halfback will cross over just like 21 and take his second step just like the sweep. The left halfback, who is running 22 to the right, plants his right foot on his second step and then cuts off that right foot and turns up into the off-tackle hole. The quarterback will hand the ball off on the inside. His footwork is almost identical to that in the sweep. He will make the inside handoff on his third step. The halfback continues to the off-tackle hole, and the quarterback continues to the flank and fakes waggle.

For the first two steps, everything here is exactly the same as it is on the sweep. If the backs have taken poor footwork, the defense will recognize the play. This happens when the quarterback reverse pivots too far across the midline or the halfback takes the crossover step, forgets to take the second step, and then starts running for the off-tackle hole. This results in a play where the quarterback has to reach to give the ball and the defense can see the play. Coaches should make sure this play looks just like the sweep for as long as possible. If the backs execute good footwork, meaning the quarterback stays on the midline for two steps and the halfback takes two good steps, as in the sweep, then the play will look like sweep.

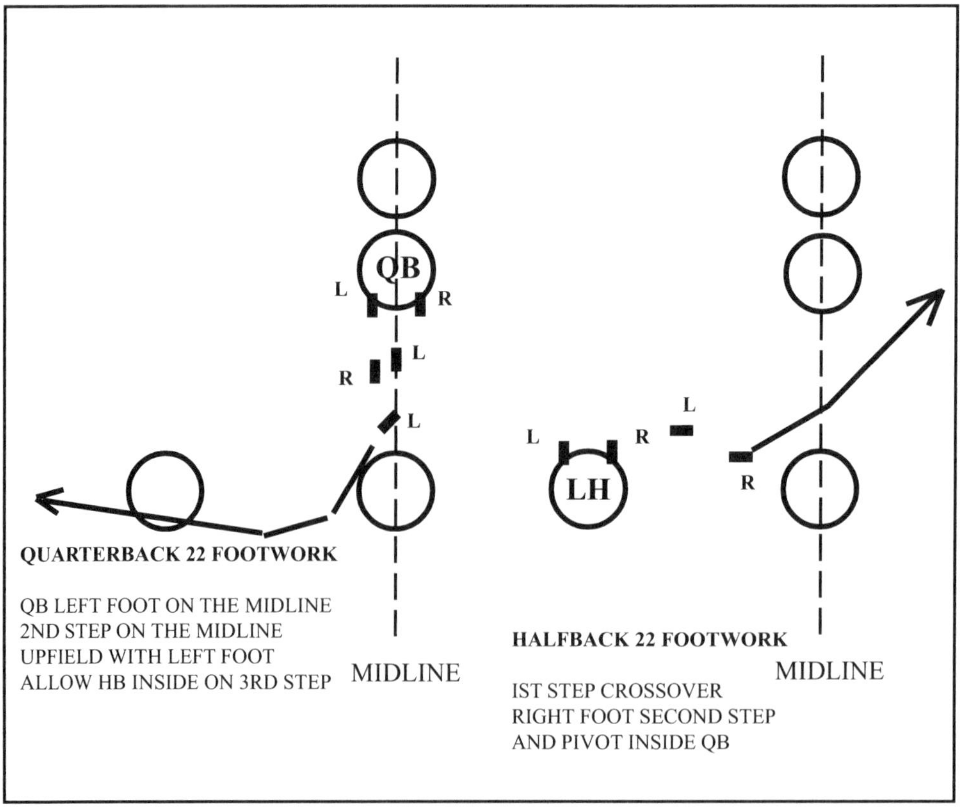


**Diagram 2.7**

## The Waggle

On this play, the quarterback will operate on the midline. The quarterback has the ball, so the fullback will step for the backside foot of the center. The quarterback owns the midline for the first two steps. The quarterback snaps the ball to his belt as he pivots-the long axis of the ball is parallel to the ground, the back point of the ball is at his belt buckle, and his elbows are in tight. With his elbows in tight, no one on the defense can see where the ball is. On the third step, the quarterback will fake the sweep with two hands. He will fake with two hands to the halfback to make the defense believe that the halfback has the ball. From there, he will tuck the ball into the crease of his pants and attack the flank on the waggle. The faking halfback has a blocking assignment on the backside of the quarterback.

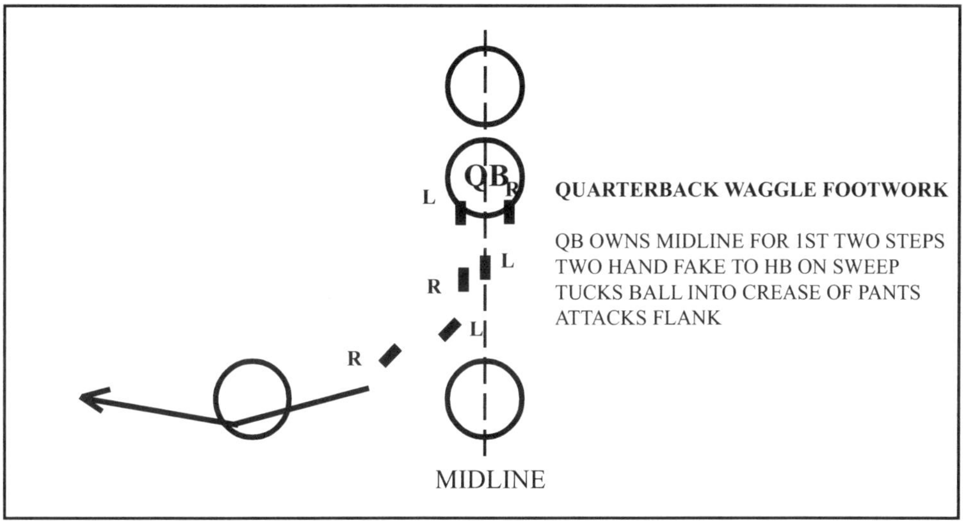


**Diagram 2.8**

As the quarterback runs to the flank on the waggle, different defensive adjustments may occur that will force blocking adjustments (Diagram 2.9). The quarterback must be keyed into this. It is a must to bring the quarterbacks to waggle drill every day, and it is important for them to know how to react when the defense is penetrating.

As the quarterback attacks the flank on the waggle, if the defensive end comes upfield, he gets trapped or kicked out. If the quarterback tries to outrun the defensive end, the play will result in a big loss. He will give up an 8-10-yard loss, a sack, and a big play for the defense.

The problem on the waggle play comes with the penetration. As the defensive end penetrates, the first guard will let him go and turn inside looking to help on any inside-out pursuit. The backside guard should kick out the penetrating defensive end. The quarterback will step underneath the kick-out block and then continue to the flank, where he can either drop the ball off quickly to an open receiver or run the ball.

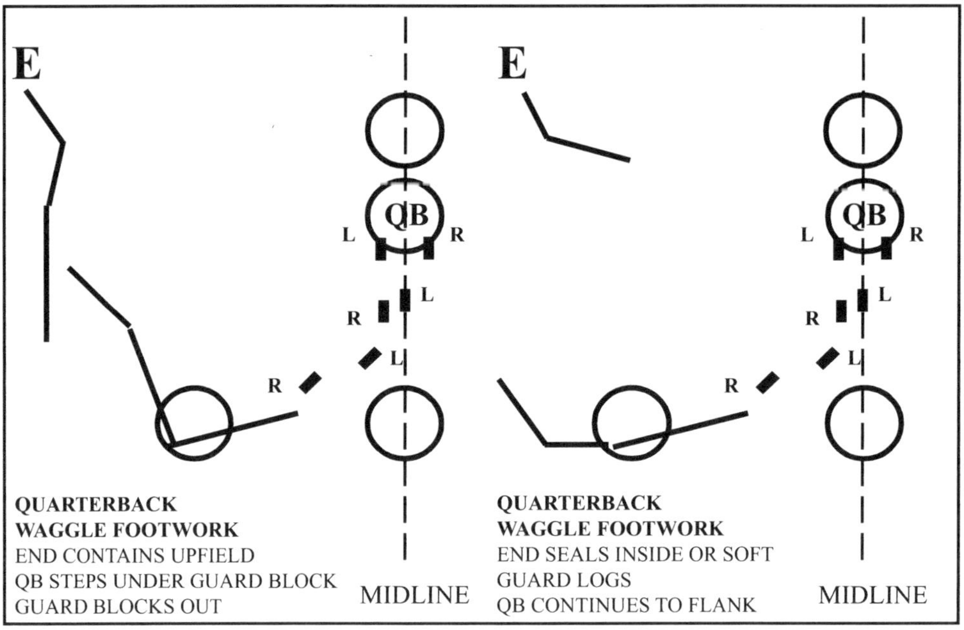


**Diagram 2.9**

If the defensive end seals down inside or plays soft, then the guard should be able to get a good "log block" on him, and there will be no problems for the quarterback. As he attacks the flank, nobody will be in his face. He should thus he able to continue outside and really threaten the flank with a run or pass option.

**Waggle Solid**

An alternative to waggle is "waggle solid" (Diagram 2.10). The quarterback is now a pure passer. The route combinations change to "waggle out," "waggle curl," and waggle with the wing breaking over the center position, which we call "wing at five." The split end can also run the same route, which is called "waggle at five." Another adjustment is waggle "switch," which means the fullback goes deep and the end is in the flat. There are many different ways to change these patterns. There is also a waggle keep play called "waggle run," where the flank is blocked like a sweep play. There are numerous variations to the waggle.

Against aggressive corners, an effective technique to use is "waggle solid." This means the quarterback will have a drop-back style of passing attack, but with 20 action. He uses the buck action, the misdirection in the backfield, and the deception of the play, but it is similar to drop-back passing. On this play, the fullback and the halfback who fake the sweep are blockers, and it is a three-man route. The fullback takes his footwork and the quarterback still owns the midline. On the third step, the quarterback will fake sweep, take one more step to the flank, and then start to drop back. It is now a drop-back pass, as the quarterback gets his shoulders turned and sets up to throw the pass. It is very similar to pocket protection. The fullback is a blocker. He will block his area inside. The halfback who fakes the sweep will gear down and become a blocker on the backside. Only one guard pulls; everybody else is cup protecting. The line blocks the defense from inside out. The quarterback will start to the flank for one step, but then he will drop back to pass. As such, he turns his shoulders, and now he can throw the ball from right to left and use the whole field.

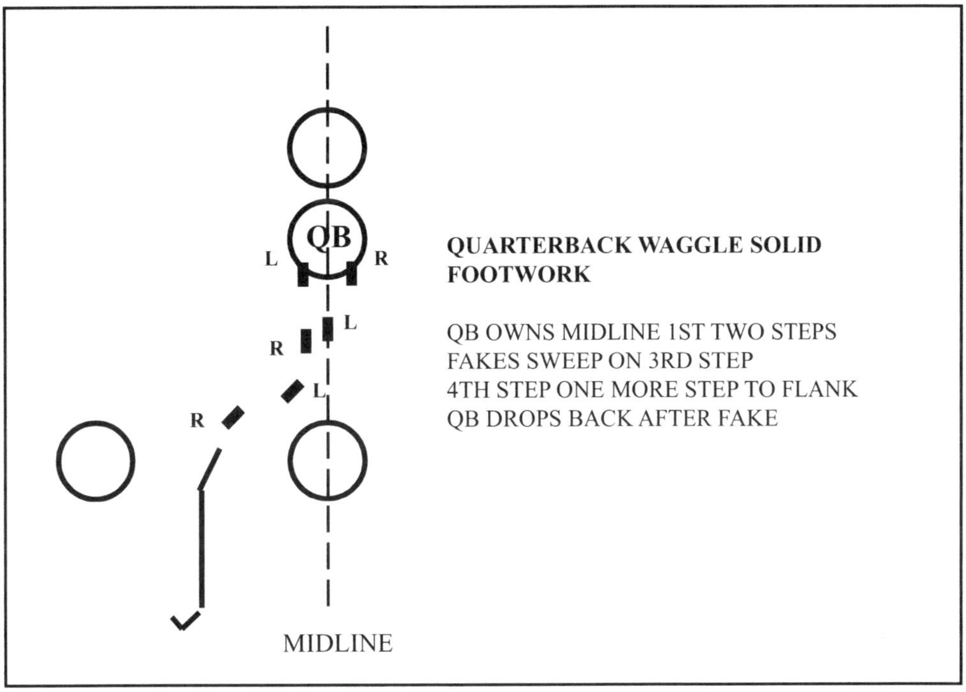


**Diagram 2.10**

## THE 60 SERIES

The next part of the offense is the "trap option" package, which is called 60s. The series number is changed to 60s instead of 20s because there are times when plays must be called at the line of scrimmage and it is difficult to tell the difference between 21 sweep, 21 waggle, 21 trap option, 21 trap-option pass, and other plays which can be run using buck action.

### The Wide Guard Trap

"Guard trap" is at the 3 or 7 hole. The quarterback can execute 20s technique, or the quarterback can use 60s technique. If the play is "23 guard trap," the ball will go to the fullback and the trap is at the 3 hole, which is one hole wider than a normal guard trap (Diagram 2.11). Against even defenses, instead of trapping the defensive tackle over the guard, we double-team him, take the play one hole wider, and trap the defensive end. If it is an odd, or 50, defense, the play reverts back to

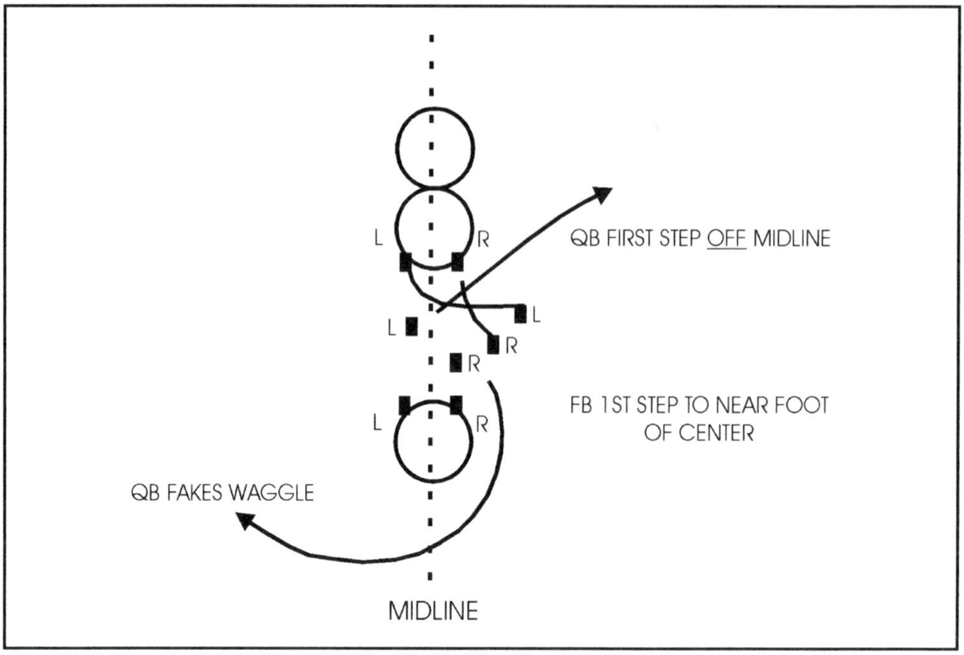


**Diagram 2.11**

24 guard trap. On 24 guard trap, the fullback will step with his right foot for the left foot of the center showing buck action. On 23 guard trap, he will step with his right foot, but since the trap is one hole wider, his right foot will step for the right foot of the center. The quarterback reverse pivots beyond the midline enough to allow the fullback his course. On the second step, the ball is handed off. On the third step, the fullback will veer to the 3 hole but stay tight to the tackle's down block. The quarterback's handoff fake is the same as his fake on the sweep to the left halfback. For "23 guard trap," he will fake the sweep and continue to show waggle action.

We can also run "63 guard trap" or "67 guard trap," with the quarterback faking trap option (Diagram 2.12). It will not change the fullback's footwork in any way. If the call is "63 guard trap," the fullback will step with his right foot for the right foot of the center. The difference is that the quarterback is beyond the midline on the first step, giving the fullback the midline. On the second step, the ball is handed off. The quarterback will then snap his chin to his frontside shoulder, pivot off his second step, and come downhill to fake the trap option to the right. When running the trap-option series, the defense might read trap option, overpursue, and allow the fullback to run inside of them on the trap. The alternative is to run the 20 action with the quarterback faking waggle, which is "23 guard trap."

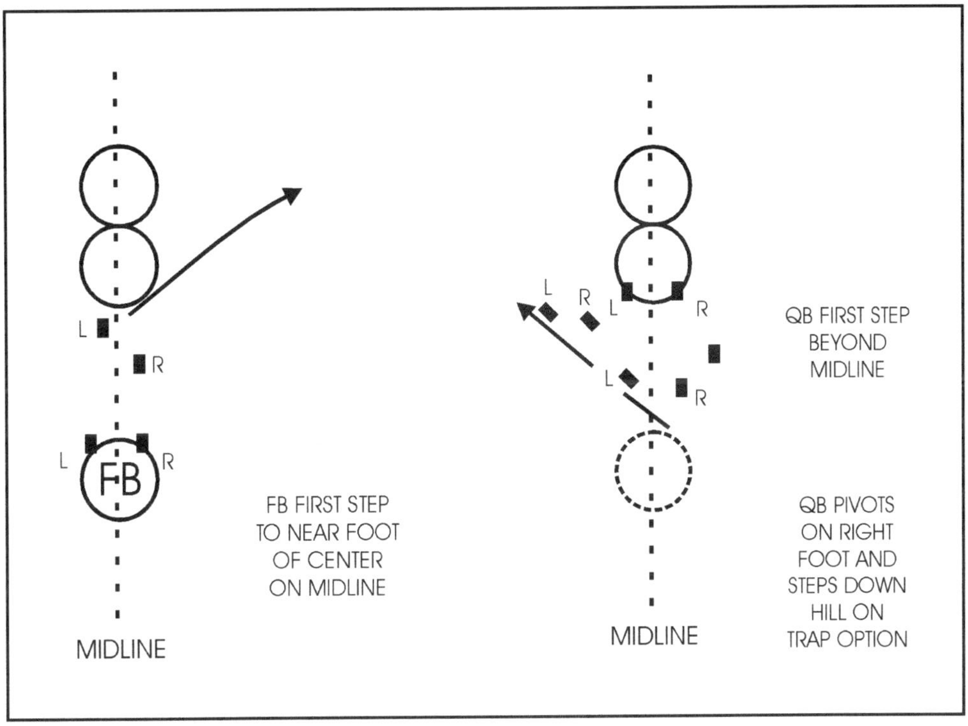


**Diagram 2.12**

### The Trap Option

On the "trap option" play, the quarterback owns the midline (Diagram 2.13). If the play is "trap option to the right," it is called "61 trap option," or "69 trap option," to the left. We will option the third defender. The quarterback will keep the ball or pitch it, depending on the reaction of the third defender, and the other defenders are blocked at the point of attack.

The first step for the quarterback on the "trap option" is on the midline. The backside foot must pivot. The second step is also on the midline, but from there, the quarterback begins to change from the 20 series. At this time, his right foot should begin to pivot and his chin should snap to his shoulder. This gives him a clear read on the defense. At the same time, he begins to pivot his foot, and his third step starts downhill, enabling him to attack the inside shoulder of the third defender playside. He will run downhill and keep the ball or else pitch the ball, depending on the third defender's reaction.

The third defender, usually the defensive end, can give him a number of different reactions (Diagram 2.14). He could come right at the quarterback. That is why the chin has to snap to the shoulder on the second step. As the quarterback starts downhill, if the defensive end is attacking quickly, he will not have a chance to run very far before he must get the ball pitched. This reaction is the reason why the

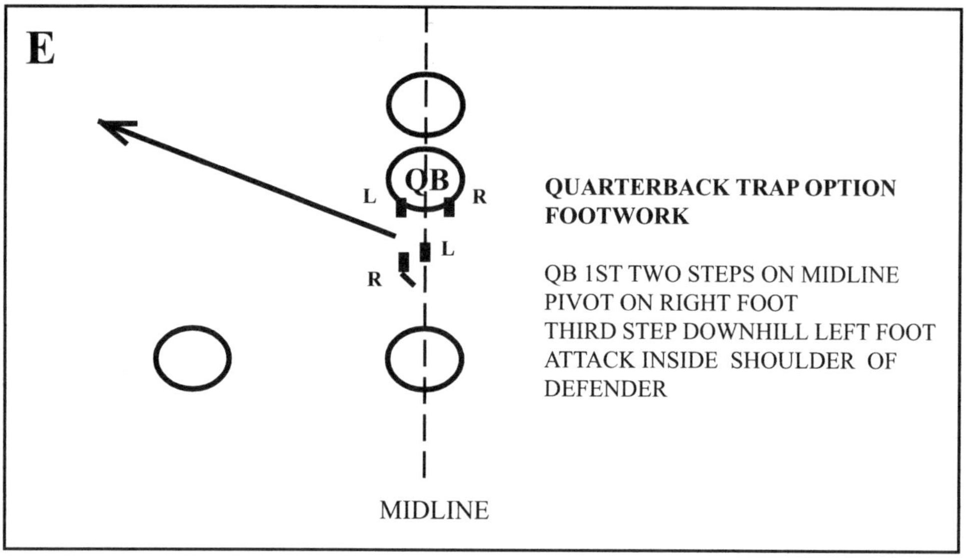


**Diagram 2.13**

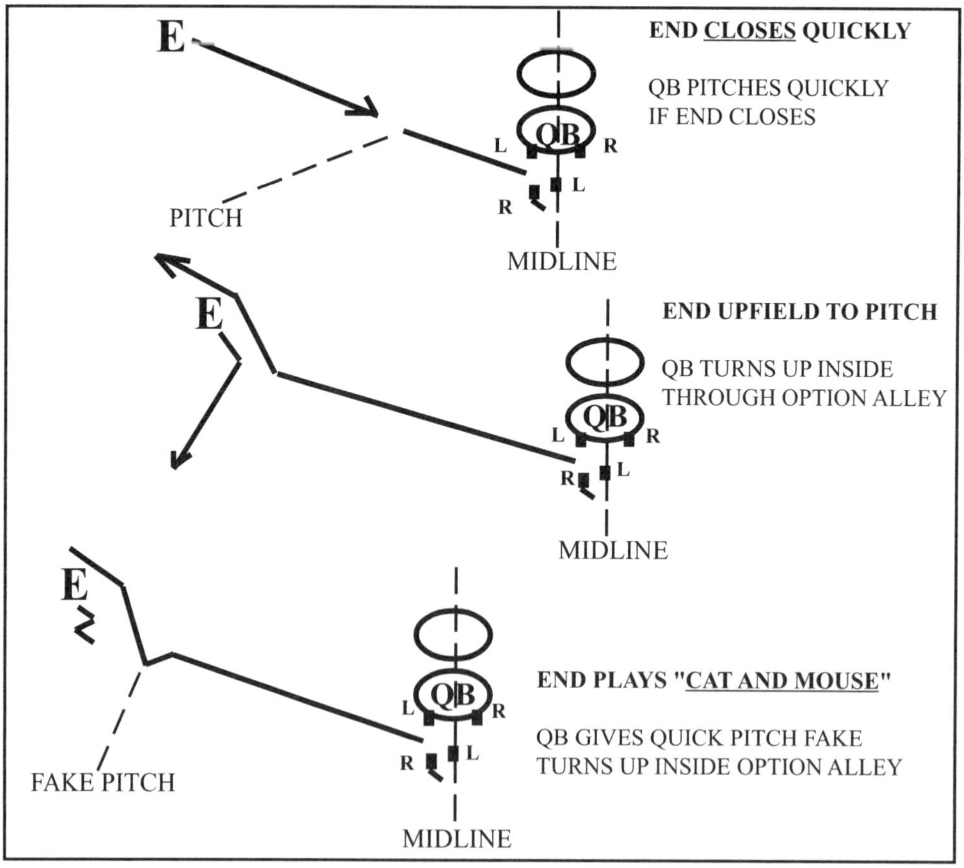


**Diagram 2.14**

chin has to be snapped to the shoulder and the foot will start to pivot on the second step. The defensive end could also run straight across the line and take the pitch, which will make him an easy read. This is a clearcut read for the quarterback to keep the ball and burst through the option alley. The quarterback will also get defenders who try to play in between the quarterback and the pitch back. The next reaction he might see is when defenders play cat-and-mouse or slow play. The defensive end will be shuffling his feet, trying to keep position on both threats. If this defender gives ground, the quarterback should make a little pitch fake to get the defender to bite and then turn up inside of him. If the defender is keeping good position on the quarterback shuffling, but not letting the quarterback outleverage him, then he should pitch the ball. The quarterback must get in his face and then pitch the ball to the halfback. We also get the defender who wants to play cat-and-mouse on the quarterback, but is responsible for the pitch. The quarterback should give him a quick pitch fake and then run up through the option alley.

**Trap Option Pass**

A natural complement to trap option, is "trap-option pass" (Diagram 2.15). To stop the trap-option crack, the fourth defender will read trap option, come flying up to beat the crack, and be in good position to stop the trap option. With "trap-option pass," there is a conflict for the fourth defender. If he comes hard on the option, the pass play is open. If he is soft on the option, the end should be able to block him with "crack blocking" or "stalk blocking." The strong safety, #4, when too aggressive, has come hard into the backfield and opened up the slant area for the quarterback to throw the ball quickly behind him.

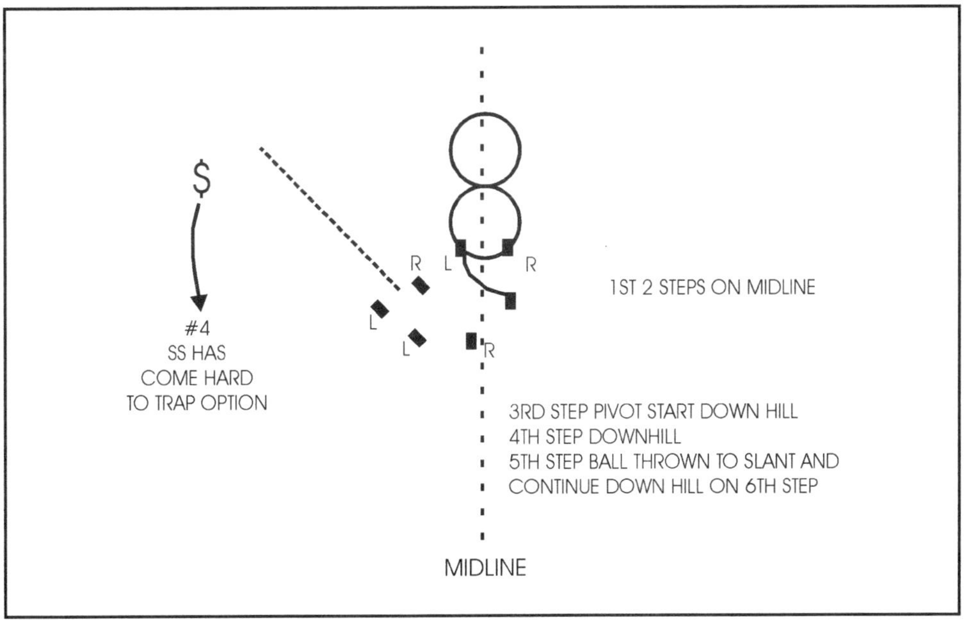


**Diagram 2.15**

The quarterback's first two steps will be on the midline and should resemble his action on the sweep. By this time, the halfback has crossed the backfield and has established pitch relationship. For the first two steps, the defense cannot recognize if the play is sweep or waggle. On the third step, the quarterback's chin has been snapped to his shoulder, and his toes begin to pivot into the third step in order to start downhill on the trap-option course. On the third step, he will have identified the strong safety's (#4's) reaction. As soon as the quarterback snaps his chin to his shoulder, his eyes need to go to the fourth defender. The fourth step continues downhill, and on the fifth step, the ball should be thrown off his left foot, followed by his right foot. The ball is released between the fifth and sixth steps. The quarterback follows through on the same course as the ball. The ball must be placed quickly in the passing position. The quarterback has to release the ball on the sixth step. Right-handed quarterbacks are more comfortable throwing off their right foot, and on their sixth step. The ball should go to the slanting receiver-or to the flaring halfback, if the corner chases the slant.

**Trap-Option Reverse**

"Trap-option reverse" is a great momentum-changing play (Diagram 2.16). You can establish flow with the trap option series, get the defense running, and then run a reverse. We pitch the ball to the spread end coming back through the backfield from a spread position. On this play, we coach everybody to show the picture of "trap option." The backside of the offense is going to look a lot like waggle, with a blocker for everybody on the defense making this play sound, regardless of what defense you face. The footwork for the quarterback should be exactly the same as on the "trap option": take two steps on the midline, snap the chin, pivot the toes, and start downhill playside on the third step.

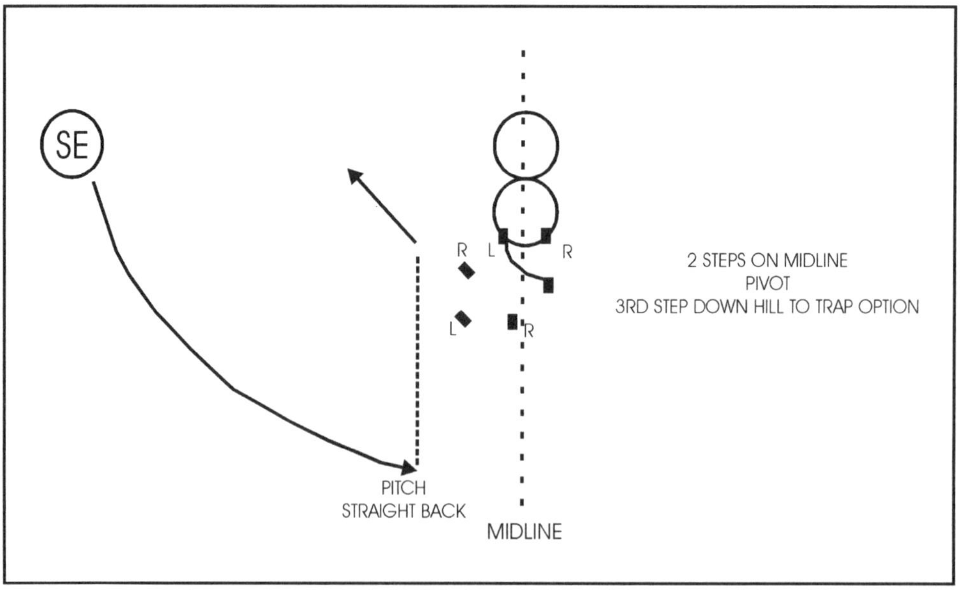


**Diagram 2.16**

The difference on this play is that the normal pitch relationship with the halfback is five yards out in front and three yards deep. The quarterback pitches the ball out in front for the halfback to catch the ball on the run. When running the trap option, the halfback should be receiving the pitch with his momentum going in the same direction as the quarterback. The ball needs to be pitched in front of the halfback so he can catch the pitch and make yards. When running "trap-option reverse," the spread end will come back through the right halfback's diveback position. The left halfback, who was the pitchback, will get a little more depth and fake catching the pitch, but the spread end will catch the pitch with his momentum going in the opposite direction. The pitch is straight back, as opposed to being pitched out in front of the halfback. The spread end can catch the ball without slowing his momentum and run to the flank in the opposite direction, as the quarterback continues to fake "trap option."

**67 Counter**

Within the 20 series, there is a counter package which uses 60s footwork for the quarterback. The first play is called "27 counter" or "67 counter." Since the quarterback will fake the trap option, these plays are called 67 instead of 27.

The quarterback will take two steps on the midline and start downhill on his third step, as in trap option. The wingback will run back to the diveback position and receive an inside handoff. The wingback does not go in motion! Instead, he runs the same course, as if he were going in motion, but he leaves on the snap. On the third step, the wingback starts downhill, and the quarterback, who is running trap-option footwork, will hand him the ball with an inside handoff. The wingback runs the 7-hole counter play, as the rest of the offense fakes the 60 trap-option package.

The "63 counter" is the same play to the right side (Diagram 2.17). The quarterback will fake "69 trap option" to the left, and as he comes downhill, he hands the ball to the left halfback coming inside on the same course attacking the 3 hole rightside. The quarterback continues to fake trap option.

**60 Counter Sweep**

Off of 60 counter action, we can run "counter bootleg," or we can run "counter sweep." The first of these is "61 or 69 counter sweep" (Diagram 2.18). The quarterback is doing nothing more than taking 61 to the right, or 69 to the left-trap-option footwork. The quarterback's first two steps are on the midline. On the second step, he snaps his chin, and his toes start to pivot. He will run downhill from there. This will also be an inside handoff. The wingback will take the same path he runs on "67 counter." He takes three steps, starts downhill, and receives the handoff from the quarterback. As the handoff is exchanged, the quarterback fakes counter bootleg, and the halfback gets extra depth around the opposite end. The quarterback will continue to fake the trap option. The line blocks the same as it does for 21 waggle.

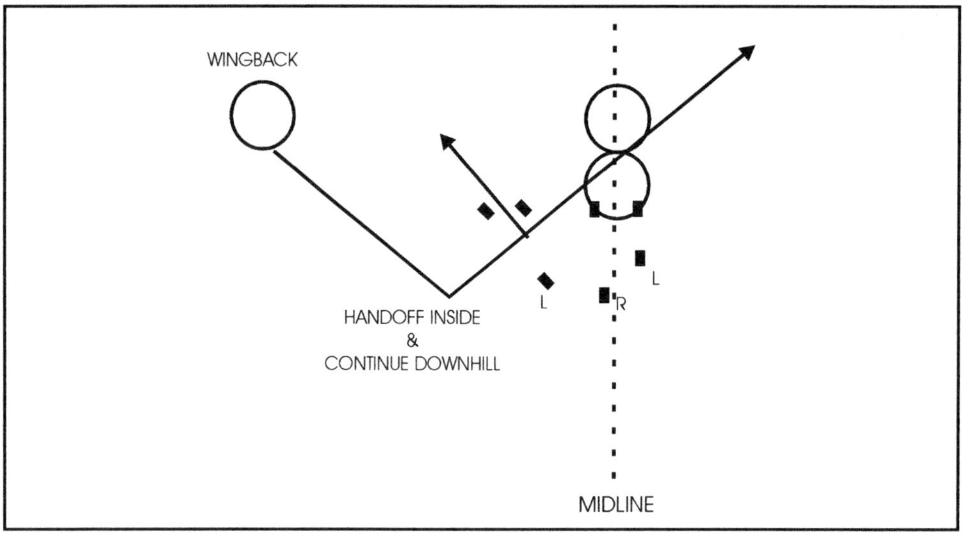


**Diagram 2.17**

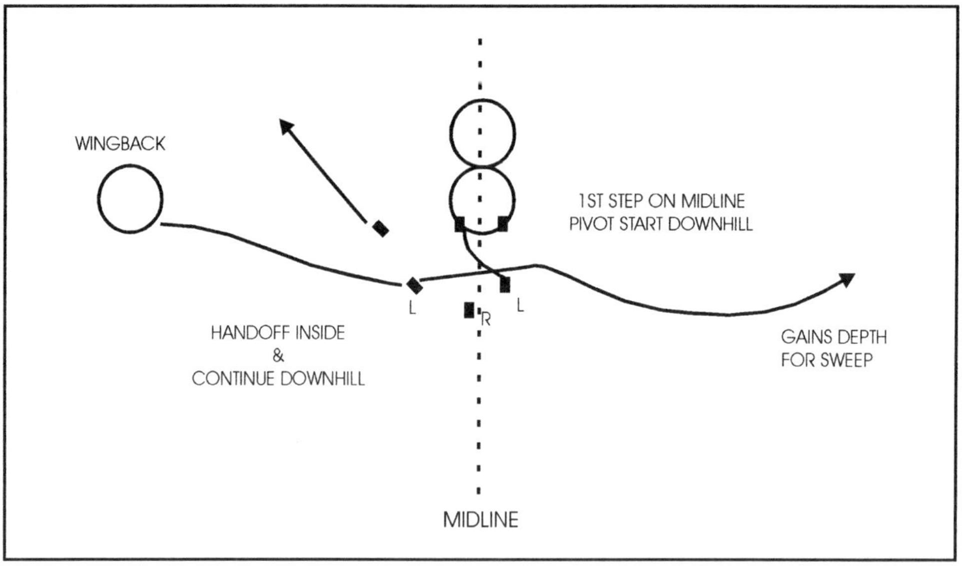


**Diagram 2.18**

## 60 Counter Bootleg

The next play in the package is "63 or 67 counter bootleg" (Diagram 2.19). On this play, the backs will fake 63 and 67 counter. The quarterback takes his two steps on the midline, snaps his chin, pivots his toe, and starts downhill. He will fake the handoff to the halfback coming back inside. The quarterback will fake the handoff, then get depth and run counter bootleg. The halfback who is normally the pitchback on trap option is the log blocker at the flank. The quarterback gets extra depth and will have a run-pass option at the flank.

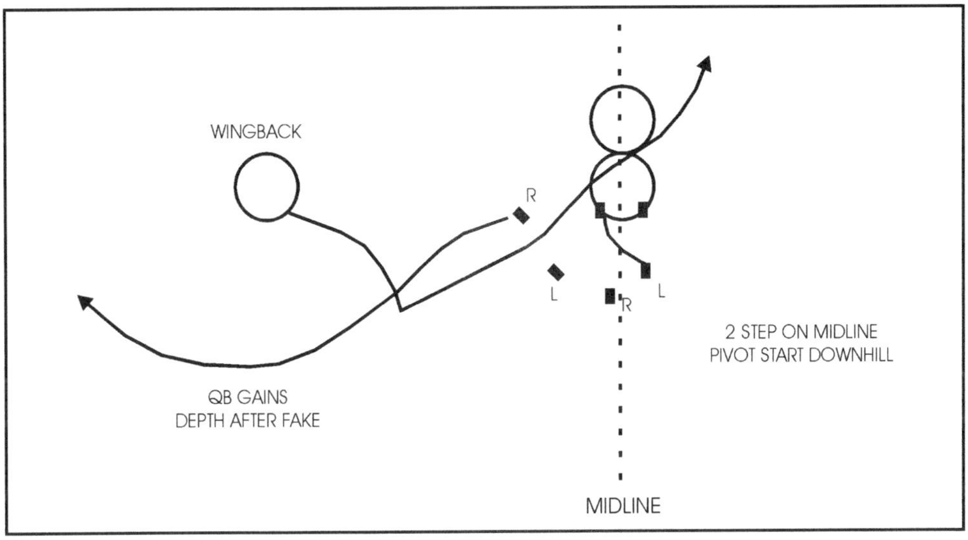


**Diagram 2.19**

## THE 30 SERIES

### The Power Sweep

The 30 series is closely related to the 20 series. The first play in the series is the "power sweep." On this play, the quarterback will execute the same footwork he uses on 20s, as will the ball carrier. If we run "31 power sweep right" (Diagram 2.20), the quarterback takes two steps on the midline, and his technique is exactly as it was on 21. He will make the handoff exchange on his third step. The ball is handed off, at forearm's distance, to the left halfback, who will run "31 sweep." The quarterback continues to fake the waggle and attack the flank. One key question: "Why run the 30 sweep instead of 20s?" We run the play when facing a blitzing eight-man-front defense. The defense is not reading, just trying to blitz, cause confusion, and wreak havoc in the backfield. Sometimes the 20 blocking scheme allows penetration because of the pulling, but in 30s, the line is blocking with fire technique and the back has a solid wall in front of him. The full flow is not a problem now, because the defense, if stunting, is not reading guards or backfield flow. The front will be well blocked, and the fullback will be the kick-out blocker instead of the frontside guard, who provides the kick-out on 21 and 29 sweep. This is a power sweep, but the footwork for the quarterback and the footwork for the ball carrier is exactly the same as in the buck sweep (20s): take two steps on the midline, cross over on the third step, make the handoff, and fake waggle.

### The Power Off Tackle

As in the 20 series, if the defensive end is a penetrator, not allowing the wing to block down on him, then there is a companion play to the sweep, which puts the end in a conflict. The 30 series play is called 32 and 38 (Diagram 2.21). On 32 and

38, the play is a direct shot off tackle. The halfback needs to run directly to the off-tackle hole. He will take his first step using a crossover step as the quarterback takes his first step directly at the halfback to hand the ball off. On the second step, the handoff will occur as the quarterback and the halfback have their hips open to each other. The halfback runs off tackle, and the quarterback will do the best job he can trying to make the play look like waggle. This play is nothing more than an off-tackle, double-team-down, fullback kick-out, power play.

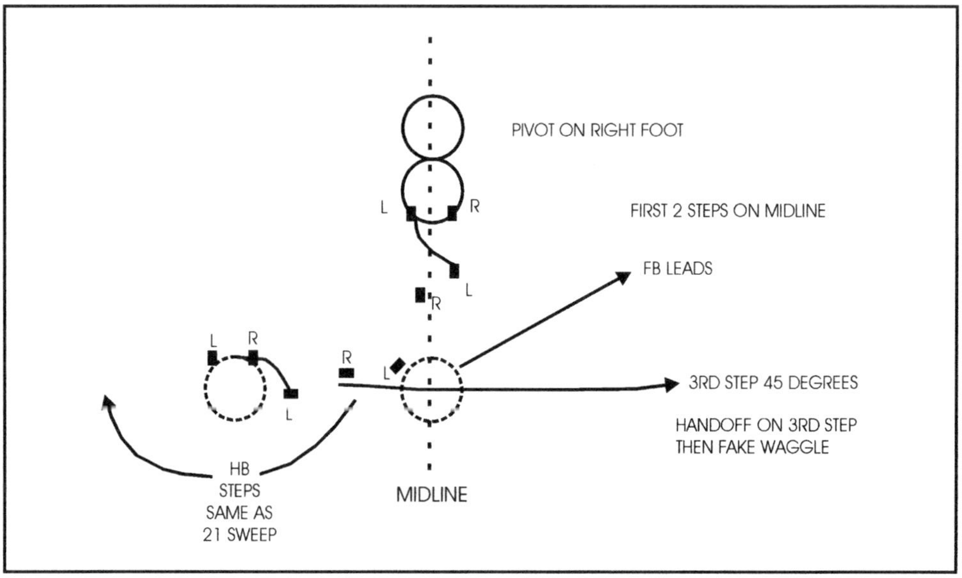


**Diagram 2.20**

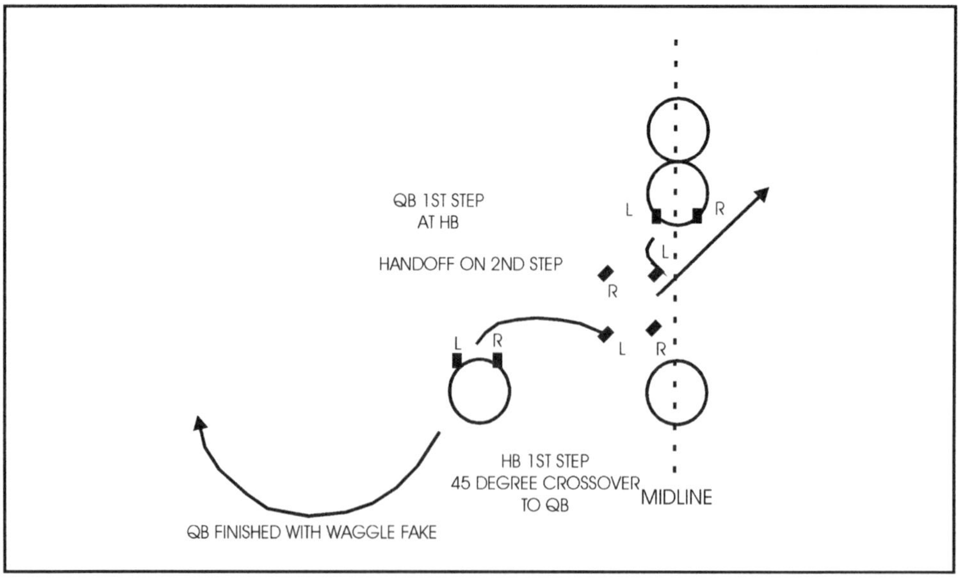


**Diagram 2.21**

## The Blast Play

The complete 30 series is power oriented. The series employs double-team and kick-out blocking, with a direct path for the running back at the point of attack. Within the same series, we have a play called "34 blast," which is similar to 32, except that the double-team is more inside. Against an odd defense with a man covering the center, the guard is uncovered and the tackle is covered and there will be a double-team on the noseguard. The tackle will turn out on the man covering him, and the fullback will run through to isolate on the frontside inside linebacker. The backside guard is responsible for the backside backer, and will fire straight ahead or pull around the center to block him (Diagram 2.22).

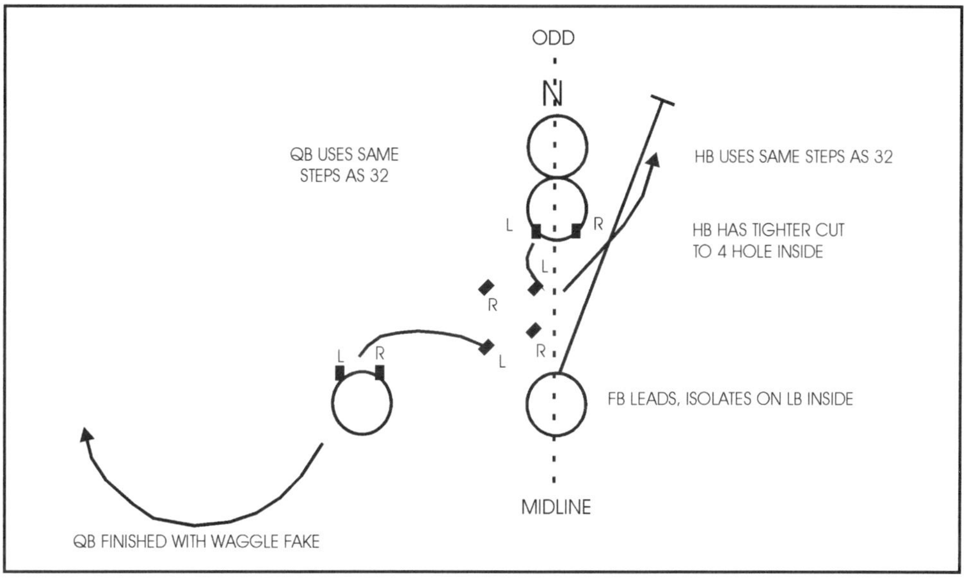


**Diagram 2.22**

On this play, the techniques for the quarterback and the left halfback are the same as on the off-tackle play. The quarterback will bring the ball directly to the halfback. The halfback will take a crossover step. On the second step, he receives the ball and makes a quicker cut to stay tight to the double-team He must make sure not to overrun the hole. As the quarterback gives the ball to the halfback, he will step right to him, make the handoff, and do the best he can with the waggle fake.

## The Counter Crisscross

The next play, which also looks like 32, is called "37 counter crisscross" (Diagram 2.23). The quarterback's footwork resembles that in 32 and 38. He will bring the ball directly to the halfback, but he will step a little bit deeper because the halfback will run a course similar to that on the power sweep. The halfback crosses over as he runs across the backfield, receives the handoff, and, as he approaches the opposite halfback, he hands the ball off to him. The play is a handoff-to-handoff reverse, with the quarterback faking waggle. The quarterback becomes an added feature to this play. As he attacks the flank, he should draw defenders with him. If the right halfback breaks through the line of scrimmage down the field , and then the defense collapses on him, he can option pitch back to the quarterback. The players have a lot of fun with this in practice. They are cautioned that they can pitch to the quarterback-anytime they are up by 40 points! Otherwise, they are to keep the ball and run it upfield.

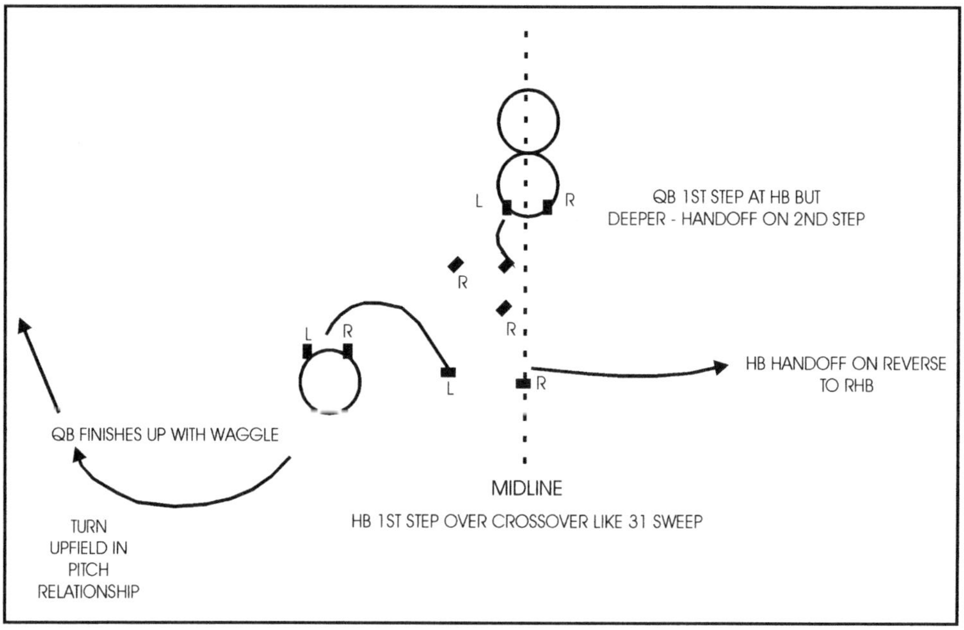


**Diagram 2.23**

The quarterback should be instructed to bring the ball to the halfback as quickly as possible and allow the defense to see it so that they will react with the sweep fake. The line can block the counter crisscross at 3 and at 7 with three different blocking schemes. We can also run another counter crisscross back to the tight end, which we call "32 and 38 counter crisscross." On that play, the techniques for the backs will not change at all.

## The Tackle Trap

The most classic counter play in the wing-T offense is the tackle trap counter, called "34 and 36 counter." This play is one of the outstanding plays in the offense, along with the bootleg that comes off of the counter. The backfield technique will be different on this play. The call "34 counter" indicates that the 4-hole is the point of attack , and the word "counter" tells all the backs who are not receiving the handoff to run in the opposite direction, away from the point of attack. The fullback on this play will run for the outside leg of the guard and then fake over an imaginary ball, thus giving the picture of a belly. The halfback is the ball carrier. If the halfback is in a diveback position, the fullback and the halfback show the picture of belly.

When running the belly play, the fullback runs the ball off tackle, and the halfback leads through the hole. The halfback will not jab step, but he will try to give that impression. The halfback rocks his weight, takes a lead step, a crossover step, and squares up into the hole to receive the handoff from the quarterback. The quarterback's first step is either on the midline, or a little beyond the midline, depending on the defensive front spacing. If the defense is odd (Diagram 2.24), with a man covering the center, the halfback takes his footwork, receives the handoff, and runs for the near foot of the offensive center. The center will post, the right guard will lead, and the two of them will drive the nose down the line of scrimmage as flat as possible. By having the halfback run for that landmark, he can stay tight to the double-team. If the nose fights across the double-team, the halfback could cut off the backside of the double-team.

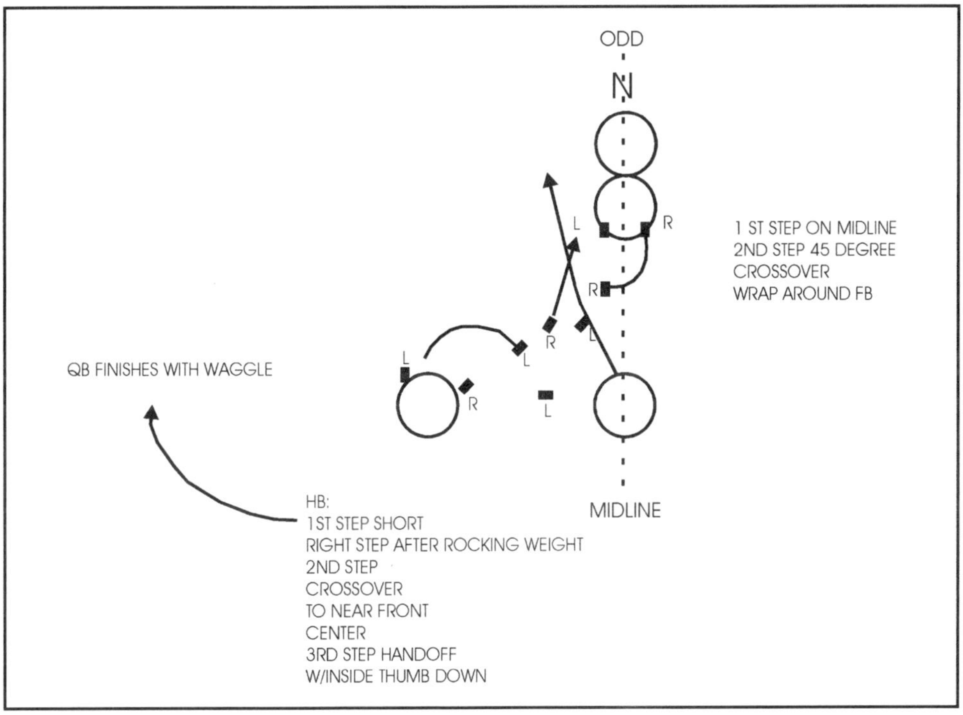


**Diagram 2.24**

The quarterback's first step will be on the midline. On his second step, he will wrap tight around the fullback's tail to make the handoff to the halfback. The quarterback then snaps his hands in. He will drag the hand to make it look like the counter bootleg. His left hand is in tight and his right arm is pumping as he attacks the flank. He shows good deception by not letting the defense see where the ball is.

The halfbacks take the handoff with their inside thumb down. This play, along with the counter crisscross, are the two main reasons we coach the inside thumb down. On the counter crisscross, the halfback receives the handoff, and as he crosses the backfield, he merely pushes the ball straight ahead to hand the ball off to the other halfback. This is opposed to receiving the handoff traditionally, and then having to turn the ball over in order to hand it to the other halfback. We merely push the ball to him. The second reason is the tackle trap counter play. If the halfback accepts the ball from the quarterback with his elbow up, what happens to his shoulders? His shoulders raise up. If he takes his footwork, and takes the ball from the quarterback with his inside thumb down his shoulders, he will maintain a good body lean. As a result, he will have a much better chance at deception because he has great body lean and he is tight to the quarterback.

We can hand the ball off to a halfback who is in a diveback position or run the same play to a halfback in three-step motion. The footwork for the quarterback is no different. It is up to the motion halfback to get the play timed up correctly and get the proper aiming point.

When running the "34 counter" against an even defense (Diaghram 2.25), the double team will occur over the backside guard. The center and the left guard execute the double-team. The left guard is the post blocker and the center is the lead blocker. On contact, they will work their butts together and drive the defender laterally down the line. The hole for the halfback is shorter or closer to the halfback. As the halfback takes his footwork, he will bend his path for the inside foot of the guard. The quarterback's first step will be six inches beyond the midline. On the second step, he wraps tight around the fullback, and on his third step, he will be in position to make the handoff without having to reach to the halfback. The ball can also be handed off to a halfback coming in motion. The halfback bursts through the line and the quarterback attacks the flank, faking counter bootleg.

**The Counter Bootleg**

The "counter bootleg" (Diagram 2.26) is the companion play to the "tackle trap." The fullback and halfback techniques are explained in the running back chapter. The quarterback keeps the football, and he will attack the flank with a run-pass option. The fullback's footwork is different and depends on what kind of defense he sees and whether the tackle pulls. The halfback and the quarterback will always use short-hole technique. Whether it is an odd or even defense makes no difference to the quarterback and the halfback. The halfback will bend his path to the inside foot of the guard, and the quarterback will reverse pivot beyond the midline. When pulling, the tackle must pull to the opposite guard and then break down. If the tackle pulls with speed, and the halfback fakes at a short hole, there will not be a collision between the halfback and the pulling tackle. Collisions occur because one player, or both, use poor technique. By using short-hole technique, the quarterback has also started his momentum moving faster to the flank. He will be attacking the flank with quickness. On his fourth step, the quarterback will drag his hand as he did when he handed off. The ball is hidden from the defense as he attacks the flank.

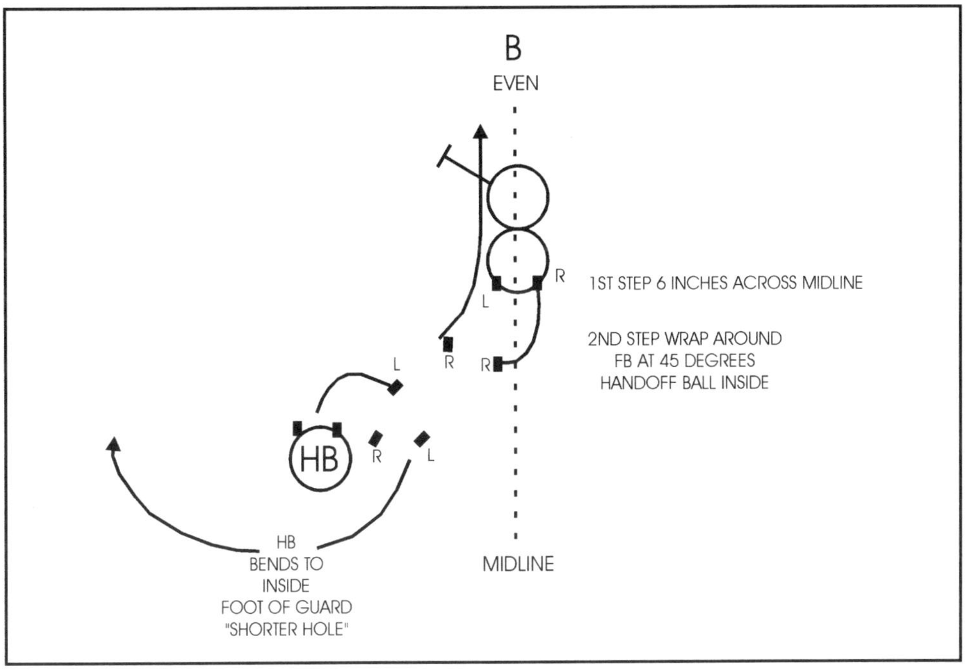


**Diagram 2.25**

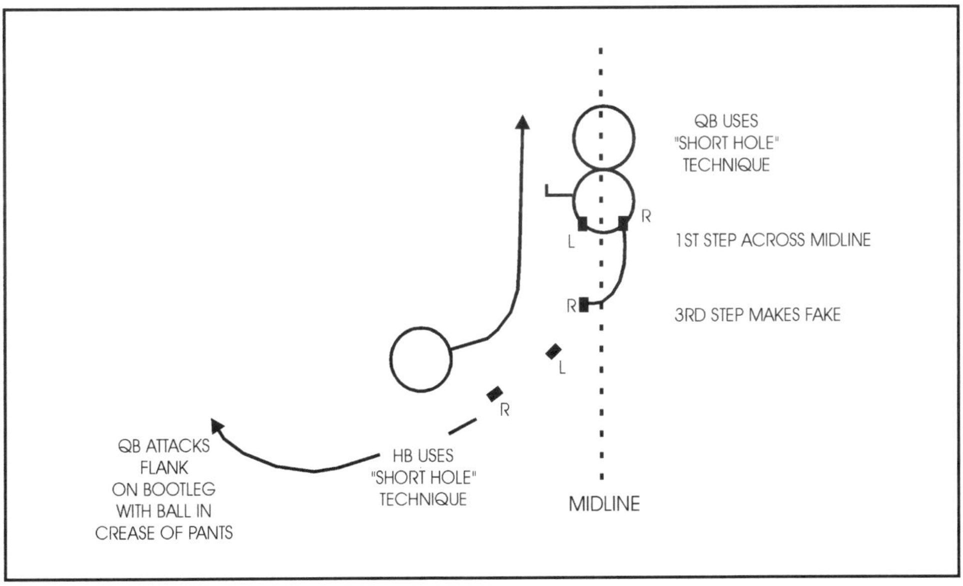


**Diagram 2.26**

## THE 80 SERIES

The final play series is the 80 series, and it contains important coaching points for the quarterback's footwork. The first play in the series is the fullback belly play, which is one of the big plays in the offense. The play can be blocked with a variety of different blocking schemes. We use "cross block" as the No. 1 scheme, but we also block the play with "on blocking," "blast blocking," "isolation blocking," or "fire blocking."

### The Fullback Belly

The belly play has always been a great play (Diagram 2.27). The fullback will take a lead step, crossover step, and square-up step. The fullback will take the handoff in the traditional manner, with his inside elbow up and his inside thumb down. The quarterback's technique on the belly is to reverse pivot beyond the midline on the first step. The fullback has taken a lead step, and on the second step, he crosses over. The quarterback's next step is toward the heels of the fullback. He will reach

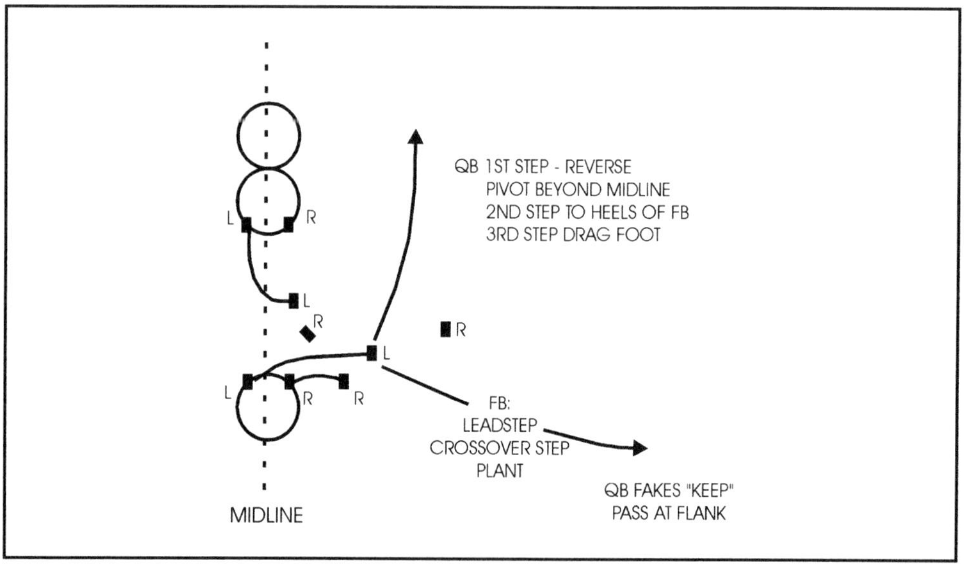


**Diagram 2.27**

the ball to the fullback's far hip. On the fullback's third step, he will square up, and the quarterback will give him the ball as he fakes keep pass. After the handoff is secure, the quarterback will drag his back foot out of the way to give the fullback a cutback lane and not trip him. The belly is the "sprint draw" play of the wing-T. The fullback will gain many yards in a variety of ways. He should be able to bend this play anywhere along the line of scrimmage where he sees daylight. Those coaches who have coached wing-T for a long time have probably run into the main problem with this play, which is that the quarterback has to keep his backside foot out of the way of the fullback so the fullback can cut anywhere.

Let's focus on the quarterback. His first step is on the midline. On his second step, he will wrap tight around the fullback and start to reach the ball. On his third step, the exchange is completed. Finally, on his fourth step, the quarterback begins to fake keep pass at the flank. It is important to make the defense believe that the quarterback has the ball. He must get his hands up quickly and into a ready position to throw the ball.

**The Keep Pass**

On the belly keep pass, the fullback takes the same footwork as usual, except that his path is a little wider because of his blocking assignment (Diagram 2.28). The quarterback will have the ball instead of the fullback, since he only fakes to the fullback. The fullback's first step is still a lead step; the second step is still a crossover. The quarterback will make a short arm's-length ride and snap the ball

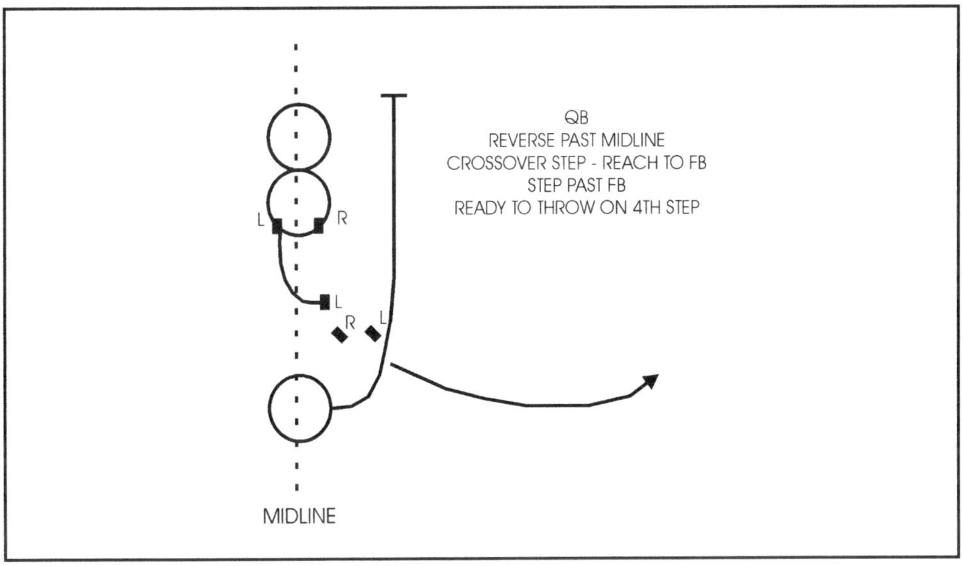


**Diagram 2.28**

into the ready position to throw the ball. As the quarterback comes off the fake, he brings the ball up quickly in the passing grip and in the passing position. On his fourth step, the quarterback will begin to attack the flank, ready to throw the football quickly. The quarterback should be ready to throw to the halfback in the flat as he comes off the mesh with the fullback. It is helpful to tighten the split of their playside end in order to outleverage the defense in the flat with the playside halfback.

As the quarterback reverse pivots and makes the fake, he will get the ball up into the ready position. As he attacks the flank, the ball may go back and forth or side to side. The ball is in the "carriage," and it is normal for this type of shoulder action to occur.

As the quarterback reverse pivots on the keep pass, his first step is slightly across the midline. On his second step, he will poke the ball quickly into the fullback's pocket. He gives a quick arm's-length ride to the fullback and snaps the ball up to the ready position as he comes off the fake. It remains in the carriage, and he must be able to throw the ball quickly to the back in the flat. If the play is run to a spread end-wingback flank, the spread end runs a fly and the halfback is in the flat. The quarterback can throw quickly to the halfback, allowing him to catch the ball and get turned up the field. If the corner in deep third coverage runs off with the split end, the halfback gets the ball. If the back breaks one tackle, he can run down the sideline for a big play. The quarterback will make his throw on his sixth step. We teach our quarterback to think "mesh, throw, mesh throw," and to get rid of the ball on his sixth step.

When running 89 keep pass to the left, the ball will be thrown on the fifth step. The quarterback should think, "mesh, throw." That way, he will get the ball up on his third step, ready to throw. He should then look to dump the ball off to the halfback in the flat quickly.

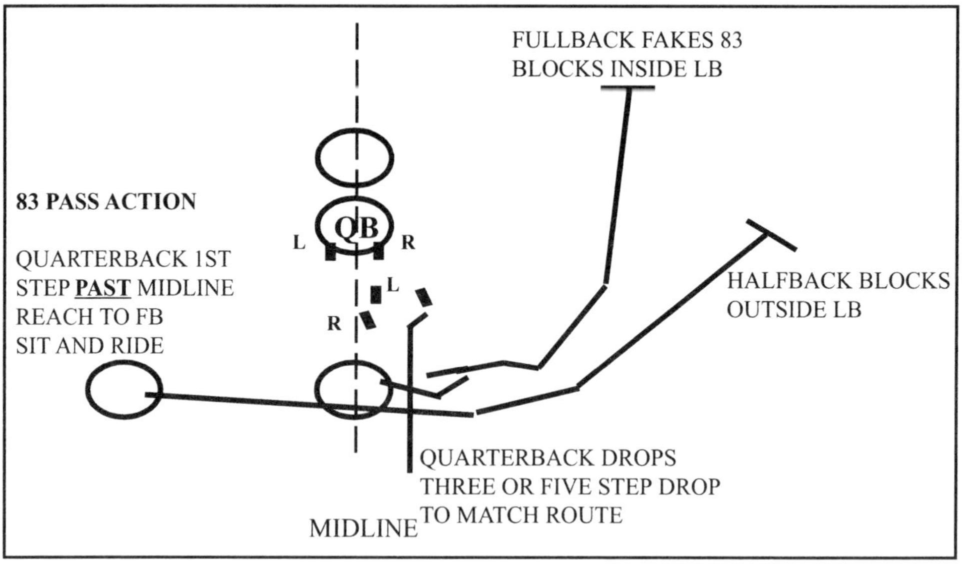


**Diagram 2.29**

It is common to call individual pass routes for the spread end in an attempt to get him the ball or to take advantage of the weakness of a certain coverage. Some examples include "keep pass out," "keep pass curl," "keep pass post wheel," and "keep pass with drag routes."

**Belly Drop-Back**

Very closely related to the keep pass is a play called 83 and 87 pass (Diagram 2.29).

The fullback will fake 83 or 87 with lead, crossover, and square-up footwork. As he fakes through the hole, he has a blocking assignment on the inside linebacker. The halfback is in motion on "83 pass," and he sets up after passing the quarterback-fullback mesh to pass-block the first defender outside the right tackle's block.

There are differences between this play and the keep pass for the quarterback. First of all, keep pass is called at the 1 hole (81), which tells the quarterback, fake 83 or 87 to the fullback, but then attack the flank with a run-pass option at the 1 or 9 hole. On 83 pass, the quarterback will make a more deliberate fake to the fullback, then drop back. The coaching point here is to "sit" on the ride. After that, the quarterback snaps the ball back quickly with his hands and drops back as the fullback fakes through the line.

The quarterback should drop back three to five steps, pushing off his front foot. This is a good time to use crossing patterns, since the backfield action the defense is seeing is full flow. Our "87 pass" is the same play to the left.

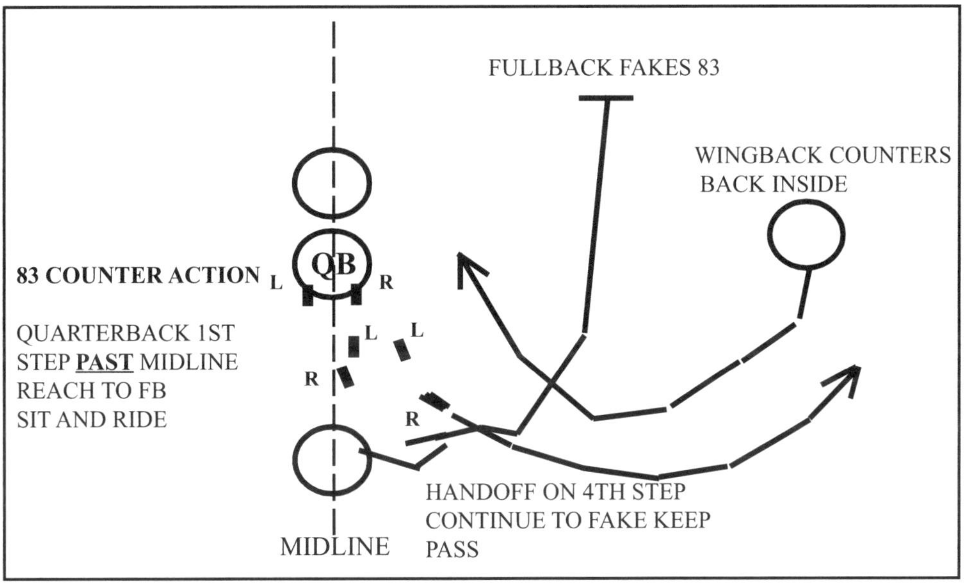


**Diagram 2.30**

**80 Counter**

Closely related to 83 pass is 83 and 87 counter (Diagram 2.30). On 83 and 87 counter, the footwork for the quarterback and the fullback remains the same. The term "counter" means that the backs who are not getting the ball run away from the play. The fullback will fake 83 to the right. He uses the same footwork as belly, but he then becomes a blocker. The quarterback will hand the ball to the wingback coming back inside. The quarterback's footwork consists of his reversing pivot just beyond the midline; reaching the ball to the fullback; pulling the ball out, as in keep pass; and then handing the ball to the halfback on the inside. The halfback runs the counter off tackle, and the quarterback continues to fake keep pass. The "87 counter" occurs when they fake 83 and counter back to the left. The opposite would be "83 counter."

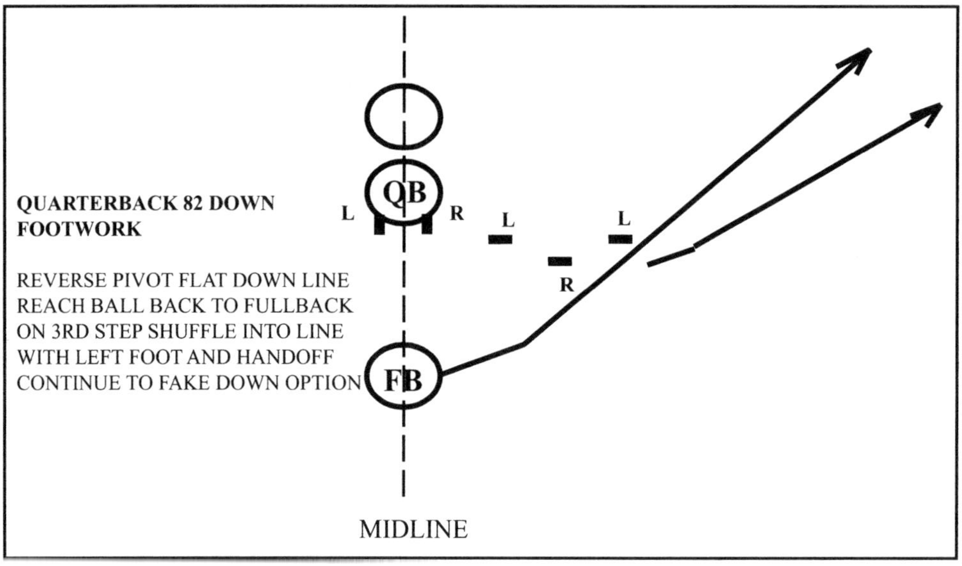


**Diagram 2.31**

## The Down Play

On 82 and 88 down, the fullback runs a direct path for the off-tackle hole (Diagram 2.31). The quarterback will reverse pivot flat down the line of scrimmage. The play could be blocked (82 and 88) "gut." Although there are different blocking schemes, the quarterback will use the same technique on each. The quarterback will reverse pivot down the line. On his second step, he will reach the ball out. On his third step, he will ride the fullback into the line, hand him the ball, and shuffle with him into the line. The quarterback will then fake down option at the flank. Instead of handing the ball to the fullback and faking the belly keep pass, the companion play to 82 down is "82 down option." This is why the quarterback will fake the option, setting up "82 down option" for future use. The quarterback may need to step around penetration when he rides the fullback. The ride helps to establish the fullback off tackle and also helps set up the option.

## Down Option

The "82 down option" contains alternate blocking schemes, including "82 load," "82 down load," and "82 down option." An important coaching point for the quarterback is to make sure the ball is in the ready position after he comes off the mesh with the fullback. He must be ready to pitch the ball. He will use a passing grip.

On "down option" (Diagram 2.32), the fullback should block the free safety. Depending on the reaction he gets from the defense, the fullback might be able to go through the line and cut the safety off. But this does not happen very often. Remember that this play is called because the third defender is sealing. If #3 were

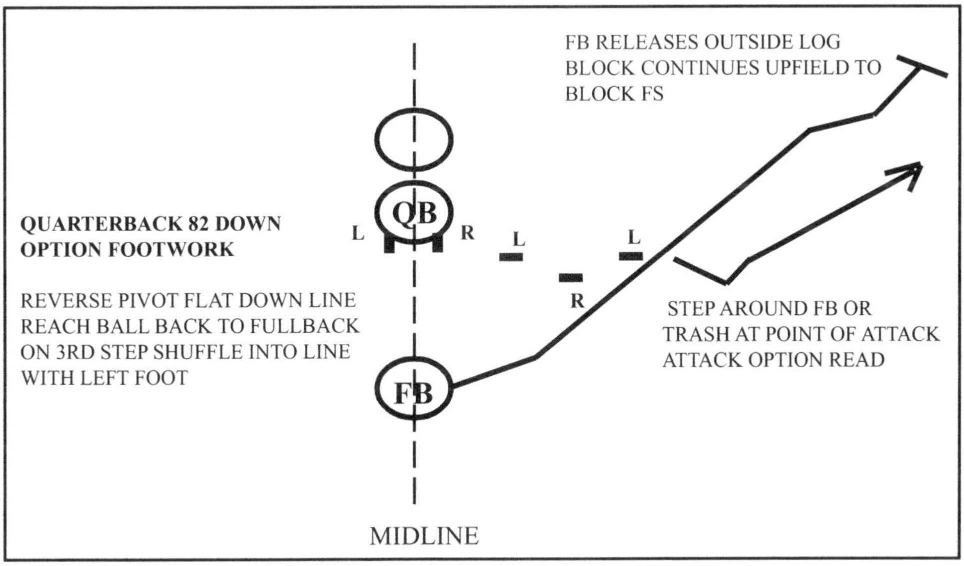


**Diagram 2.32**

penetrating, we would call "82 down" and run the ball off tackle. If #3 is sealing down inside, then the fullback should block him inside, take the ball outside, and run the option. If the fullback can make it through the line of scrimmage to block the free safety, that is optimal. What normally happens is the fullback has to bounce outside the log block on the defensive end in order to block the free safety. The quarterback's footwork does not change, and he should try to make the play look like 82 down, as if the fullback is carrying the ball through the line of scrimmage. After the shuffle, the quarterback may have to step around penetration, because that is where the log block will occur. We coach our quarterback to step around this "trash," so he can get to the fourth defender in order to option him.

### The Quick Belly

There is one more belly footwork you can use, and it is called '"quick belly" footwork (Diagram 2.33). The quick belly series includes a quick short belly to the fullback, an option off the quick belly, a "scissors" or "Sally" type of play, and "81 waggle," where the backs fake 80 action and the quarterback attacks the backside flank.

In this series, the quarterback does not need as much width. The fullback takes a quick jab step, as he does on cross block, except on his second step, he will dive for the butt of the guard. Since the quarterback does not need much width, his first step will be a jab step forward, which gets him into the line. He will then reverse pivot off the toes of his playside foot. After the quarterback reverse pivots flat, he will mesh with the fullback. On his third step, the quarterback reaches the ball back to the fullback; on his fourth step, he rides him into the line. From there, the quarterback will fake option.

The play will be blocked with "fire-on-backer" blocking, and it is a quick hitter to the fullback. To the split end-wingback flank, the play is a quick belly to the fullback with zone blocking, and it is a north-south play.

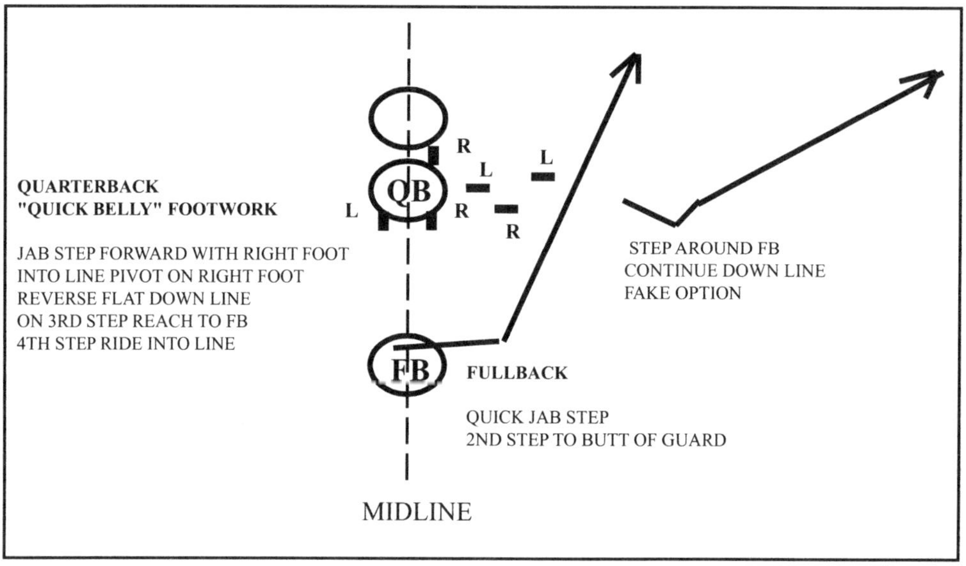


**Diagram 2.33**

## QUICK BELLY OPTION

The quick belly will set up 81 and 89 option (Daigram 2.34). The footwork for the fullback and quarterback will be the same. The fullback will not get the ball. He will become a blocker, and the quarterback will take the ball down the line of scrimmage to option the third defender.

The quarterback's technique is to jab step forward on his first step, reverse pivot on his second step, reach the ball back to the fullback on his third step, and ride the fullback to the front foot on his fourth step. The quarterback will then snap his hands in and continue down the line to option the defensive end. If we run the same play to the left, it will be called "89 option." The quarterback will jab step with his left foot, reverse pivot off that foot, reach back, ride the fullback, snap his hands back in, come downhill, attack the flank, and execute the read on the third defender. The backside halfback is in motion. He is the pitch back.

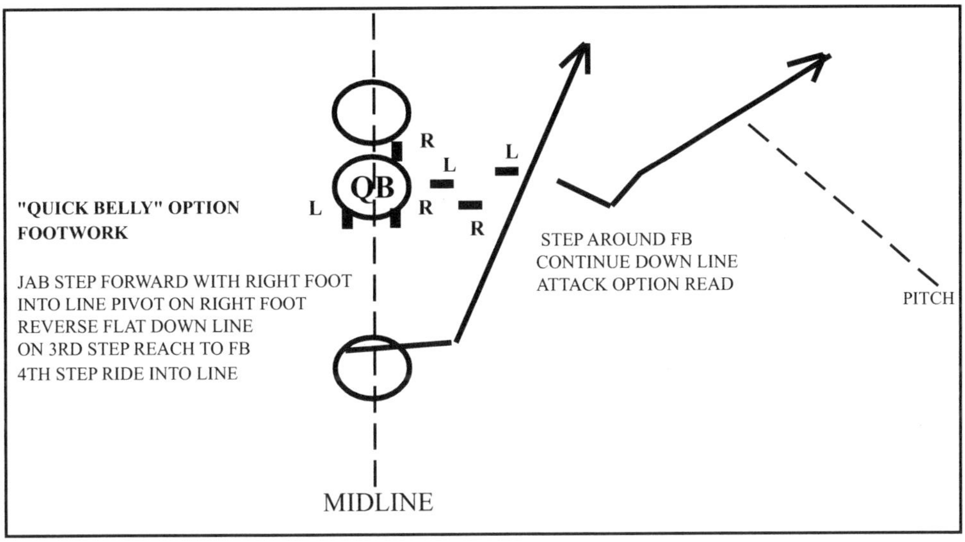


**Diagram 2.34**

### The Scissors

The next play in the series is a "scissors" play, which some coaches call "Sally." We block the scissors a bit differently from the coaches who run "Sally," but it is basically the same principle. The quarterback will use his normal footwork, except here he will fake to the fullback and hand the ball to the wingback coming back inside on an inside counter. After his fake to the fullback, the quarterback's footwork will change slightly. On his fifth step, the quarterback will step back and hand the ball inside to the wingback. From there, the quarterback will fake the option play. The wingback, who is running the football, does not go in motion! His first step will be back, for depth, which will open his shoulders to the quarterback. As the quarterback reverse pivots, the wingback will start to run for the tail of the center, which is his aiming point. The quarterback will step back and give the ball to the wingback. The wingback will then turn up the field north and south. We teach the wingback to option run the center's block. This scissors play is called "84 scissors at 6" (Diagram 2.35), which means we will fake 84, and the right halfback will "scissors" back toward the 6 hole. The opposite is "86 scissors at 4."

### The 80 Waggle

The last play I want to discuss is "81 and 89 waggle" (Diagram 2.36). The best time to run this is when the linebackers are keying the fullback. When they see the fullback start, the linebackers will fly in his direction. It is tougher to run this play if linebackers are blitzing, because the fullback in the waggle play is also responsible for blitz pickup. If the defense is blitzing inside linebackers, "81 or 89 waggle" is not a good call. When playing a team that does not blitz the inside backers, but will flow with the fullback, this play can be devastating. If the play is 81 waggle, the quarterback will simply run "21 waggle."

On this play, the fullback uses different footwork. He takes a jab step, which resembles his footwork on "84," then starts to attack the butt of the guard. The fullback will fake over an imaginary ball, and on his third step, he will start back to the side of the waggle. The fullback will then work to the front side and be a receiver. The quarterback will attack the flank. For the quarterback, there is no difference between this play and "21 waggle." Our "81 waggle" is a great key breaker for the defense, especially if they are keying the fullback. If the call is "89 waggle," the play will go to the right, away from the 9 hole, and the fullback will fake "86." The quarterback's technique is exactly the same as on "29 waggle."

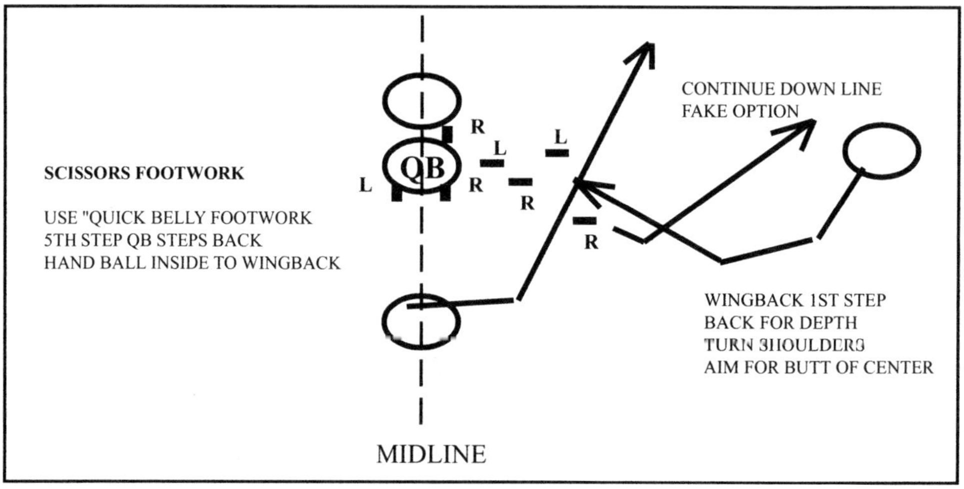


**Diagram 2.35**

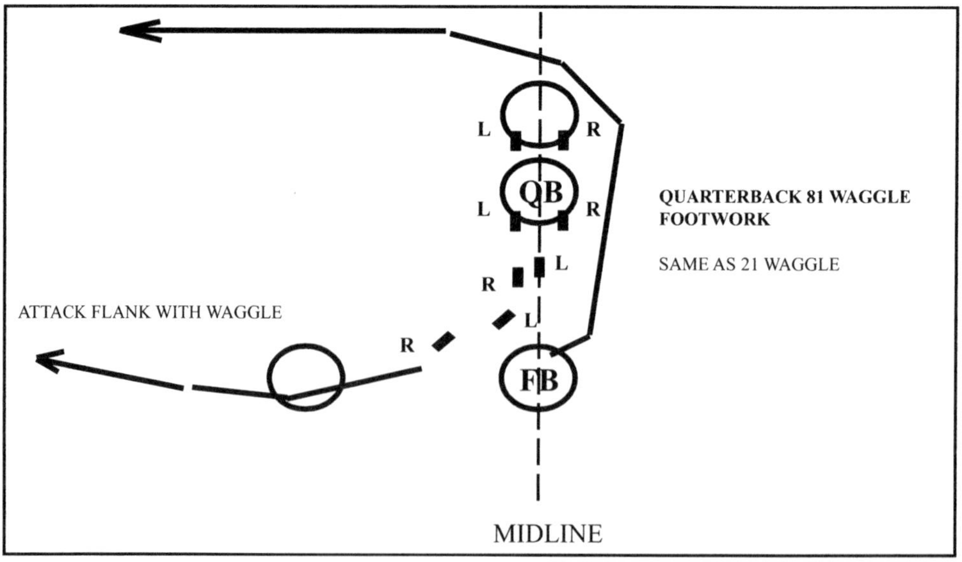


**Diagram 2.36**

# CHAPTER 3

# The Wing-T Running Back

## QUALITIES OF WING-T RUNNING BACKS

Before we discuss the techniques of wing-T running backs, we should address the qualities that are required to play those positions, along with the physical skills coaches look for. As with all positions in the wing-T, the running backs must be unselfish. They have to understand what their role is, and they have to understand that the ball will be spread to all of the skilled positions. This offense will get the ball to the spread end, the tight end, both halfbacks, and certainly the fullback. Everybody will share in the skill responsibilities. Coaches want players who are comfortable in this offense, but they also want the best talent possible at every position. They want players in these positions to be talented enough that the defense cannot key on just one back. If the halfbacks are having a big day, it might be because the defense is keying on the fullback, or vice versa.

The second vital quality is that the backs must be willing to block. They will not block all the time, but when their turn comes to block, they have to be willing to do it. No back will be allowed to have the attitude that he is going to get the ball all the time, while everyone else's job is to block. We will not think that way. Backs must be willing to block. There are many ways to get halfbacks and fullbacks to block in this offense without having to take the physical abuse that comes from blocking all the time. Often, people on the opposing team will out-size us. As long as our talented backs are willing to make an attempt, they will find that great running backs can also become great blockers.

The next qualities we look for are the physical tools we need at each position. At the college level, the fullback needs to weigh somewhere between 205 pounds and 225 pounds. He can be bigger, as long as he is also fast enough. Occasionally, he might be smaller, but smaller fullbacks are the exception, rather than the rule. We would like to have a fullback with powerful legs who can run through arm tackles, but is also capable in the open field. The fullback in this offense is somewhat like the tailback in the I. He will average the most carries in a game, because he gets to run plays to both sides of the formation. By the time the season is over, the fullback will have carried the ball a full third of the time more than the halfbacks. Which backs carry the ball in the wing-T depends on how the games go and who the defense is keying on.

The halfback in this offense is a player who needs to be a minimum of 185-200 pounds. Those are the sizes we try to recruit. Sometimes smaller backs can get the job done, but many times, the smaller players do not stay healthy for the whole season in our league. If you have smaller running backs, it is very important to also have backups.

The halfback needs to understand that his role in the offense is to rush for 500-1,000 yards in a season and catch from 300 to 700 yards' worth of passes. We look for halfbacks who have great hands, as well as great running skills. They will catch the ball a lot. In college football, it is critical to throw the ball efficiently. We do not throw the ball all the time, but we do throw it efficiently. You need to be able to complete passes when you decide to throw them.

The catalyst in this offense is the play-action passing game. A wing-T offense must be able to complete the "keep pass" play, the "counter bootleg" play, and the "waggle" play in order to experience success in the offense. If you are running "trap option," you must also be able to complete "trap- option pass." Those four action passes are the basic staples in this offense, and they are the keys to keeping the ball moving north and south. You must have a quarterback who can throw the ball accurately, and you must have backs and receivers who can catch it.

The first of the physical tools that we want our backs to concentrate on are their running skills. They should be north-and-south runners. It is inaccurate when coaches label the wing-T as a parallel offense! The only play in the offense that is ever parallel to the line of scrimmage is the sweep. However, the sweep becomes north and south once the back makes the cut. It is also amazing how those same coaches say the defense will run the sweep down with speed and catch it from behind. Most humorous of all is that those same teams do not catch it when they actually play against it. Remember, they have other threats to worry about and are frozen in place by the misdirection in the backfield.

Besides needing backs that are north-and-south runners, we need backs who will break tackles. We keep a statistic called "yards after contact," or YAC. This yardage is probably the most important statistic a running back has. We believe that if we gain between 100 and 150 YAC yards, then we will win the game, or at least have a big day offensively. Breaking tackles and being a north/south runner are two crucial qualities that running backs must have, regardless of their position.

Another physical skill we look for in our running backs is the ability to catch the football. We must have backs with soft hands who can catch the ball and turn upfield and gain additional yards after receiving the ball.

Blocking, though, is the most crucial attribute our backs can have. We require our backs to block. They will get plenty of opportunities to have the ball in their hands, but when the other backs have the ball, they must correctly execute their blocking.

We have been very successful in selling this philosophy. Our backs take great pride in their blocking. They are able to block big defenders and not be mismatched physically. We teach cut technique, and we always teach blocking at the hip. When blocking at the hip, a back might be outsized, but he can still get movement if he uses the proper technique.

Last, but not least, are faking skills. The wing-T is a misdirection offense. There are many times when we run a play and then run the companion play, which looks just like it, requiring the backs to fake. Those fakes help misdirection. They create deception, and they force the defense to be frozen in place, unable to read the ball and unable to pursue as quickly as they would like.

These are the skills we consider the most important that a running back can have. He has to run, he has to catch, he has to block, and he has to do a great job of faking. An unselfish back will do those four things. If our backs are all willing to be unselfish, then the end result will be that they all will end up with impressive statistics.

## SHOULDER SKILLS

The remainder of this chapter will deal with exactly what the wing-T running backs do on the field. We start with shoulder skills. We always start with the actual teaching of blocking. We put the backs, just like the linemen, down in a stance and teach them how to block. We do this first with bags, then with people. We teach blocking skills first.

The first fundamental we will start with is "shoulder skills" (Diagram 3.1). By senior year, the backs have done this drill for four or five years each. At the start of every practice, we use a big heavy bag to simulate the size and bulk that a defensive player will usually have. One of our players holds the bag, while another player blocks the bag. Shoulder skills include four drills in a four-part progression. The first drill is called "surface." Surface drill entails fitting into the bag in order to teach blockers how they should finish when they hit. The second drill is called "strike a blow," emphasizing striking a blow and rolling the hips. The third drill comes into play when we teach the footwork in conjunction with the block. We call this drill "step and hit." The fourth drill teaches backs to run full speed at the bag and execute a block and is called "run and hit."

### Surface

In this drill, we emphasize the fit, or the blocking surface, that we use. The wing-T requires that we teach the importance of shoulders in blocking. That is not old-fashioned or passé. We use shoulders as the primary striking point, but we also finish blocks with the hands. We are incorporating our hands into our blocks, but we are also using the hardness and the blocking surface of a shoulder. The surface of a block includes the side of the neck, the front of the shoulder, all the way down

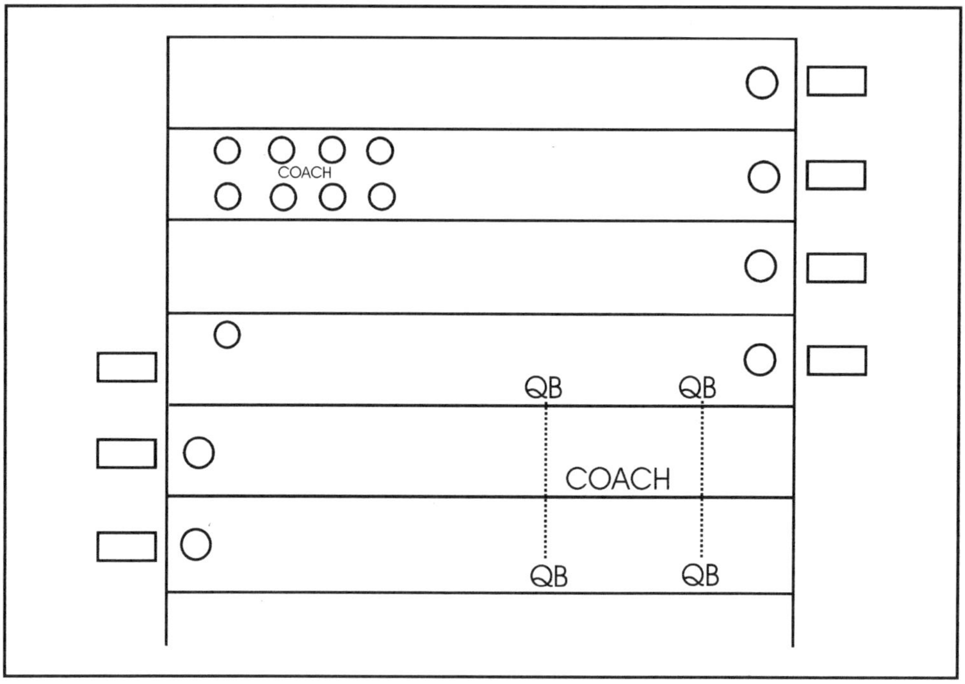


**Diagram 3.1**

to the elbow, the front of the arm, the fist, and even the pec. That is the surface which our backs will drive through on the bag when they make contact. In the old days, coaches would teach players to put their face in the numbers. But, as players made contact and put their face in the numbers, they were suffering neck injuries. In time, rules were legislated to prevent the teaching of face blocks. Blockers could no longer use the top of the head, or the facemask, as the initial striking point on a block. Many coaches still teach blocking by leading with the head. They just do not say it or print it anymore, because they do not want to be sued or have a liability problem. In the wing-T offense, coaches can sleep well at night because they know, morally, that they are doing the right thing by the players. We aim for the middle of the opponent when we strike him, but as we make contact, we slide the head so that we use the blocking surface described earlier. As our backs contact the defender, they drive their shoulder, drive their forearm, and drive their entire blocking surface through the bag. When they block, they block through the man, not at the man. When they make contact on the bags, they try to explode through the bag. The first thing we do is to have the backs get down in a six-point stance. We want them right up to the bag, so that their facemask is touching the bag. We want their knees under them and their thighs at a 90-degree angle to their lower legs. We want a nice, flat back. We want the bag to stay between the blocker's knees. If players block and tackle with the opponent between their legs, they seldom will miss.

In the "surface" drill, all the backs do is fit into the bag. As they fit into the bag, their head will slip to the side, and their hips will go down, but their eyes will stay up. We do all of the drills in practice on "sound cadence" (i.e., the first sound they hear). Sound cadence saves time and gives our players more reps. The command to the blocker is "surface, right shoulder, on sound." The coach will say, "Set," and all the blockers fit into the bag. Every two backs share a bag. If there are four blockers, then obviously, they need two bags. You need one bag for every two blockers you have. We want all the bags to be lined up on the sideline so that the bottom of the bag is intersected by the white sideline. All blockers will be facing into the bag, while the coach stands either behind or in front of his blockers so he can watch their eyes. Either coaching location is advantageous to the coach.

We have three drills going at the same time. All blockers will execute when the coach gives the command. By doing this, our coaches are mass teaching. All the backs are learning how to do this drill at the same time. The coach will try to see everything, and at times, he will not see everything, but that is okay. The players will be learning by doing rather than by watching, which is always better. Sooner or later, coaches will find any technique errors that might be occurring.

To review, the first drill is called "surface." Here, we will merely fit into the bag. We are not going to strike the bag yet, we are just going to fit in. We tell the back to go at the bag and slide his head to the side. The bag is still between the back's legs, he has a strong blocking surface, and when he simulates contact, he will place his forearm as if he were driving it through the bag along with his shoulder. The coaching points to emphasize while coaching this technique are that the eyes should be up. The blocker must be able to see how many clouds are in the sky. Check to see if his butt is down. The midsection of his body should be into the ground. If there is a blocker with his hips off the ground, he has not rolled his hips yet. Make sure each blocker is all the way down, hips into the ground. There should be a nice squeeze on the bag between the neck and the shoulder. Looking at the line of blockers, the coach can check all of them quickly, or he can check one guy at a time and then reset them.

When they are in a six-point stance, the blockers' toes should be flat. They do not want their toes curled under their feet because, when they strike, their knees will lift up off the ground. By flattening their toes, the blockers' knees will not come up, and their hips will roll.

The second half of the same drill is "surface" with the left shoulder. Make sure to emphasize both shoulders. The command will be "surface, left shoulder, on sound." All blockers will fit into the bag, while the coaches check for the key fundamentals. After using both shoulders, the blockers will switch. At this point, the man who just blocked will hold the bag, and the man who was holding the bag will work on surface. When the second blocker is ready to go, the coach should give the same two commands and have them repeat the drill.

### Strike a Blow

Phase 2 of the shoulder skills progression is "strike a blow." When players put bags down on the sideline, the white line is intersecting the bottom of the bags. When we strike the blow, we want the blocker to knock the bag off that white line. That is how our coaches know if the blocker is really striking a blow.

We use the normal six-point stance, with hands and knees on the ground and toes flat to the ground. Blockers are facing the bag, with the cage of their helmet on the bag. The coach will give the commands: "Strike a blow, right shoulder, on sound." This is a live hit. Our running back will cock back slightly to get momentum, then strike the bag and drive his blocking surface through the bag, knocking the bag off the line. The nose of the blocker will aim for the middle of the bag, then slide to the side as contact occurs, so that the shoulder and the forearm is the blocking surface which makes contact. That is a moral, legal block. It has hardness, and it is physical. As blockers finish, coaches should see the same fundamentals they see in the "surface" drill. Blockers have their eyes up, the bag between their legs, their hips down, and a tight neck squeeze between the blocking surface and the side of their neck.

Next, we do the drill with the left shoulder. We also switch the blockers. The man who just blocked will now hold the bag. The man who held the bag will now be the blocker. These two players work daily as partners and challenge each other. If one man feels that the hit was too soft, it is his job, as a good teammate, to tell his partner what he might be doing wrong. The coach, obviously, will do the same.

## STEP AND HIT

We are now ready for the third part of the progression, which is called "step and hit." In this phase of the drill, the coach should get the blockers up in a two-point stance with their forearms resting on their thighs. Measure the distance to the bag by reaching out and touching the bag. Blockers want to be about an arm's distance from the bag. The reason is that they will take a short, six-inch power step and then strike the bag on the second step. They have to be back far enough so that contact will occur on the second step. The blockers keep the bag between their legs as they line up.

We teach another fundamental that is extremely important to blocking. When a blocker blocks with his right shoulder, then he must step with his left foot. When people walk, and when they run, if they step with their right foot, then their left arm comes forward. Therefore, we use opposite arm and leg action when we practice this drill. If our backs strike with their right shoulder, then they take a short step with their left foot, and the result will be that the second step will be the contact step. Coaches teach this drill in phases. They first do the drill one step at a time, to check the first step. If the blocker is going to block with his right shoulder, he needs to step with his left foot. What should happen on the first step is that the blocker's toes should be replaced by his heels. That is all the distance the first step should cover. As he steps with his left foot, he cocks his right forearm. His right-shoulder blocking surface will drive through the bag. When doing this drill in steps, take the first step and hold it. Check for the chest on the thighs and the butt over the heels to prevent being overextended. Emphasize the chest on his thighs, so the blocker has the chance to block at the hip. He is not overextended; his chest is on his thighs, and he is low. He is ready for the second step. The coach will say, "finish," or "two," and the blocker will explode through the bag, with his third step following through naturally. As he finishes, he should have that same fundamental blocking surface, with his eyes up and a tight neck squeeze between the bag and the blocking surface.

Next, we do the same drill with the left shoulder. The coach is behind, watching all of his blockers at the same time. We are getting a lot of reps by mass teaching. Again, the blocker should take his first step and hold it. The coach should not allow the blocker to overstride with a big step. Rather, he should replace his toes with his heel. This is a six-inch power step, and on "two," he should explode through the bag. The third step follows naturally and is a result of the momentum carrying the back through the block. His eyes are up, his elbow is high, he should have a tight squeeze between his neck and the blocking surface, his chest is on his thighs, his butt is over his heels, and finally, he should have the bag between his legs. After the first blocker goes, the second blocker, who was holding the bag, comes over and takes his turn to block. The coach is standing back, watching all of his blockers, and can see if anybody is out of place. He makes his corrections and then is ready to move on to the next drill.

Once the players are to the point where they can take their first step, replacing their toes with their heel, they are ready to execute the drill without stopping on the first step. Do not make robots out of your players. Get past this part of the progression as quickly as they are ready.

**RUN AND HIT**

The final drill in the progression is called "run and hit," where backs will simulate blocking linebackers. The blocker will run at the bag and block it as if he were blocking a linebacker. When a halfback has to run at and block a defensive end, and he is in a diveback position, he will start from four yards away. If the fullback has to run through a hole to block a linebacker, or block a linebacker stepping up into the hole, he will be starting from four yards away. The "run and hit" drill puts the back in these types of situations. We also bring the bag right up on the blocker. The drill is now called "hit and run," which means backs hit first and drive the bag four yards. This is an alternative to "run and hit."

The same blocking fundamentals apply in "run and hit." If the backs block with their right shoulder, then they must step with their left foot first. It should work out so that contact will occur with the right shoulder contacting the bag on the fourth step, when he is four yards away. As the blocker drives the bag, he will drive the bag straight back with his right shoulder.

The final blocking fundamental is the finish. We teach our backs, as well as all of our players, to finish their blocks by swinging their tail. When coaches say swing the tail, that means the blockers will turn their butt into the hole in order to turn the defender. This is a case where blockers will use their hands to help finish the block. As they make contact, they drive the bag, using their off arm like a piston, and punch up through the bag. They bench press with that arm and turn the bag at the same time. The bag should remain between their legs. One of the cardinal sins occurs when the blocker approaches the bag, makes contact, and begins to swing his tail, with his feet outside the bag. He will cross over as he turns the bag. That is when he will lose the defender. Instead, the blocker should keep the bag between his legs and keep his feet apart. He should accelerate his feet on contact, but keep his feet apart through the whole block, finishing as he swings his tail.

The command we use is "run and hit, right shoulder, on sound." On "set," the blocker will take off, run four yards, drive the bag backwards for two steps, swing his tail with his feet wide apart, and drive the bag to the side for five yards. He can drive the bag farther, if he wants, further emphasizing the finish of his block.

Next, the drill is reversed so that it is "run and hit, left shoulder, on sound." The same fundamentals are used here as in the previous phase. As the back drives his forearm through the bag, his chest will be on his thighs, he will have a good, tight neck squeeze, his off arm will bench press, and his elbow will lock out. This is how he can turn a defender. He keeps the defender between his legs, drives his free hand into the bag, and bench presses. (This is one of the major reasons to do the bench press in the weight program.) As the back swings his tail, his butt should turn into the hole, and the man should stay between his legs. Next, his partner switches over and takes his turn. The man who held the bag is the blocker. The man who blocked holds the bag.

When our coaches do these drills, they are coaching a line of blockers. They can watch them all block, watch them all turn the bag, and check them when they finish. We blow the whistle to have them stop and hold their block, so we can check all of them. Have they finished in the correct blocking position? Do they have a tight neck squeeze between the side of their neck and the blocking surface? Is their chest on their thighs, butt over their heels? And is the man between their legs?

## TYPES OF BLOCKS

In addition to the shoulder skill progression, we teach the backs different types of blocks. There are two wingback blocks, which are called "gap" and "down," along with one diveback block, called "log." Regardless of what position the backs play, they all learn the wingback blocks, just as all linemen learn how to do waggle and sweep drill, and all running backs learn to execute all three types of motion. Coaches cross train all of the players so they learn all of the skills.

**Wingback Blocks**

All of the backs work on wingback blocks. The blocking bag simulates the defensive end whom the wing will block on the sweep. We put blockers in a wingback position about a yard back and a yard outside. The two wingback blocks are the "gap block" and the "down block." There are differences between the two blocks, and there are different times to use them. Anytime the defender is a player who likes to penetrate, the wingbacks use "gap" technique. They must cut penetration off . If he is not a penetrator, but is a reader who is playing on the line of scrimmage, the wingbacks use "down" technique. If there is any doubt in their minds, they begin with "gap" technique and react from there. Since the tight end has the assignment of "gap, read down" on sweep, he will block inside, leaving the wing on the defensive end. How the wing attacks him depends on his style of play. We use gap technique versus a penetrator and down technique versus a reader. If the end is a penetrator who runs upfield when the tight end blocks inside, then it is the coach's job to call the companion play and not try to run outside. If the end is not a penetrator and tries to jam the tight end and then seal into the hole, he has set himself up for down blocks. The wingbacks must be ready for either reaction. They must be ready for him to penetrate or to read and not penetrate. Coaches attempt to know by film analysis, stance, or alignment which technique the end uses, so our wingbacks can anticipate the type of block to use.

**Gap Block**

When we have called the sweep, the wingback has to live with it. He may have expected the end to seal, but instead he is a penetrator. The wing must block him anyway. He will use gap technique. His first step should be flat, for the inside foot of the tight end. It is like a pull step. The wingback's head will be across the front of the belt buckle of the penetrator. The key is to get the head across the front of the belt buckle in order to stop penetration. Even though we put the head across the front, the blocker must keep the defender between his legs. The bag (or the defensive man) is always kept between the wingback's legs when he makes this block. A common error is for the wingback to try so hard to get his head across the front of the defender that his feet wind up across the front as well. In that case, the defensive end can spin out of the block and beat the wing. We coach the wing to step flat enough so he can cut off penetration, but still be able to adjust the angle enough to keep the man between his legs when he makes the block.

We first drill the right wingback's block with the right shoulder. The command will be "gap left, on sound." Coaches should look for head up; good, tight neck squeeze between the blocking surface and the neck; chest on the thighs; back flat; butt over the heels; and the defender between the legs. We check the first step, the "gap step," the flat pull step for the inside foot of the tight end. The second step should occur on the contact phase. The "step and hit" techniques learned in shoulder skill period will finish the block. We then practice "gap block to the right," which is executed with the left shoulder. The first blocker will block once with each shoulder. Then the second blocker will block once with each shoulder. They then switch back and go to the next drill. The players get a lot of drills done in a short period of time, provided they are blocking correctly. On the first day of training camp, as well as the first day of spring practice, we allow 15 minutes for this period. This long shoulder skill period will enable us to teach thoroughly.

The reason we coach "chest on thighs" is that when the blockers make contact, they will make contact at the hip. The last time I checked, no one lifts weights with his hips. Players do not do presses with the hips. They are not doing squats with their hips, the way the do with their thighs. There is no strength in a man's hip. If backs block at the hip, they will push the defender all over the field. No matter how much he resists, they can still push him. They can do it with one hand. Take the biggest player on the team and have the smallest player push on his hip with just one hand. He will move him all around the field, as long as that hand is at the hip. One of the hardest things coaches will ever have to do is to get players to block at the hip. Once our blockers understand that principle, they will bury people. They will not just block them, they will bury them. The man who blocks at the shoulders has the toughest time. The defender has much of his strength in his shoulders, and all that resistance will defeat the block, or at least get it stalemated. This enables the defender's bench workout in the off season to help him defeat the block If our blockers strike at the hip, the defender has no strength there, and they will rarely be beaten. We paint a white line on the bag at about the hip area to emphasize the chest on the thighs and the importance of striking at the hip.

### Down Block

The second wingback block is called a "down block." On a down block, the defender is no longer a penetrator, so the blocker can put his head behind. Since the man is not a threat to penetrate, he will probably play parallel to the line of scrimmage and laterally up and down the line of scrimmage. Our wingback's job is to cut off this lateral/parallel movement. His head is placed on the upfield side of the defender, as opposed to in front. Backs only do this when they are absolutely sure that the end is not going to penetrate. Our wingback is one yard outside and one yard back from the tight end. He will then execute the block "down left." He will step with his right foot and block with his left shoulder. As the blocker's right foot steps, the toes of his left foot pivot as he moves his right foot. His second step will be with his left foot. The opposite arm and leg action still applies. We next drill the same block to the right. This will be "down right" for left wingbacks, and it is done with the right shoulder, with the head on the upfield side of the defender. He steps with his left foot, blocks with his right shoulder, and keeps his head behind.

### Log Block

After the backs have executed both wingback blocks, there is one more block which is executed from the diveback position. This block is called a "log block." The defender is aligned in a 9 technique on the outside shoulder of the tight end. The diveback is lined up behind the tackle's outside leg and is four yards deep in the backfield.

On this block, the first step should take off for a point one and a half yards outside the tightest man on the line of scrimmage. This could be a tackle, if the diveback is on the split end side, or it could be the tight end, if the diveback is on the tight end side. The first step only establishes the initial angle of takeoff. From there, the back must adjust on the basis of the defender's reaction. If the defender is sliding out, the halfback will let him go and wall off on the next inside defender. The guard will now kick out the defensive end, and the ball carrier will make his cut inside the guard. If the defender seals inside, then the halfback will adjust his path to pin the defender inside. The guard will then kick out the next man. The divebacks will execute this block with their inside shoulder. As they finish the block, they will finish by swinging the tail and taking the defender inside on a 45-degree angle, away from the line of scrimmage. The blocker must adjust to the defender on the basis of his reaction. The coach will put the blocker in a two-point stance and execute log block with the left shoulder. If he blocks with the left shoulder, he steps with the right foot. He will make contact with the head to the outside, swing the tail, and drive the bag in the opposite direction. His chest is on his thighs, and he has his butt over his heels and the man between his legs. We then will "log block" with the right shoulder. Do the two blocks and have the players switch. The man who was holding the bag gets to be the blocker, and the man who was doing the blocking gets to hold the bag.

That completes the blocking skill period, which covers skills we call "shoulder skills." In review, "surface," "strike a blow," "step-and-hit," and "run-and-hit" are the four main steps in our progression. Then there are wingback blocks and diveback blocks. Once the backs learn "gap," "down," and "log," they have learned the blocks they need to use.

## ROUTINE PERIOD

The next part of practice for backs is what is called the daily "routine" period (Diagram 3.2). This is the time when the coach will teach the proper stance and how the players should "take off." The players work on the first step for as long as it takes them to explode correctly. The four parts of this drill begin with the "stance." The second part of this drill is "bird-dog." The "bird-dog" drill is a one-step drill in which the players explode out of their stance as fast as they can for one step and then hold it to see if that first step is a good one. The next part of the period is "takeoff." When they practice "bird-dog," they can go straight ahead at a 45-degree angle, pull step to go lateral, or crossover step to go lateral. When they practice takeoff, they use those same first steps, but also take off and run. They can take off straight, take off at a 45-degree angle, take off with a pull step to go lateral, or take off with a crossover step to go lateral. The final drill during routine period is the timing of all of the motions, which can be mixed into the "takeoff" phase.

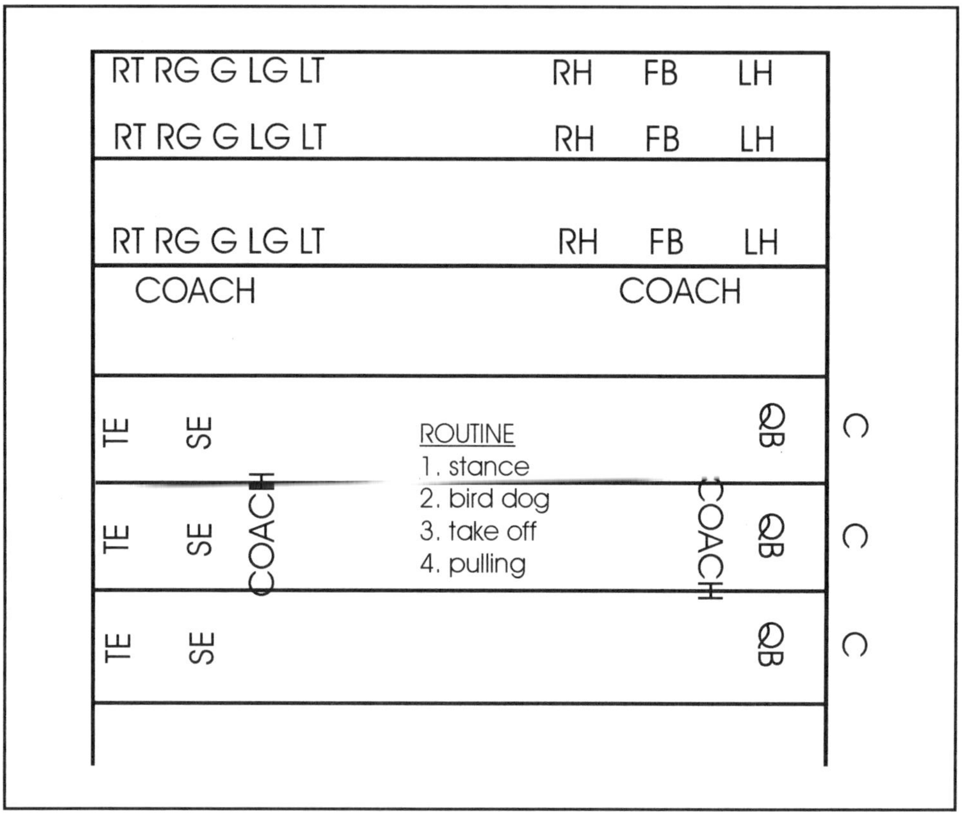


**Diagram 3.2**

## Stance

The first phase begins with the stance. Our backs learn the wingback stance, the diveback stance for the halfback, and the stance for the fullback, which are all the same. When coaches line this up on the field, they have all of their people in squares and on yard lines. Coaches want five yards between players and five yards from the players behind them. The first thing we teach in the stance is the feet. We use a stance where the feet are underneath the armpits. The feet should not be any wider so that the back can explode on the first step. The wider the feet, the tougher it is to explode because the first step will be shorter and less powerful. Backs need to be able to explode out of that stance. We coach a slight bend in the knees and a slight bend in the ankles. We tell the backs to get their heels up to the top of the grass.

The backs are in a two-point stance at all positions. The fullback is standing up; he does not get down in a three-point stance. The divebacks stand up and the wingbacks stand up. They keep their shoulders parallel to the line of scrimmage and their hands rest comfortably on their thighs. They do not want to push weight down into their thighs with their hands because that makes for a slower takeoff. The backs rest their hands comfortably on their thighs and even pat their thighs so that they are not grinding too much weight into their thighs. Some coaches instruct their players to put their hands down on their knees. We believe that that technique lowers the shoulders too much. We prefer to be more upright so we can see. Sometimes backs feel comfortable turning their toes out slightly so they can push off the ball of their foot. We have no problem with that. If the backs feel comfortable, they can use that stance. For the most part, however, the toes are pointing north and south, the feet are parallel and underneath the armpits, there is a slight bend in the knees, and the backs get their heels to the top of the grass.

Our running backs should be fairly upright, with their backs slightly arched and their eyes looking straight ahead so they don't give away their keys. The diveback and the fullback are in the exact same stance, feet parallel. The fullback is straddling the midline, so he is behind the center and the quarterback. The halfback is straddling the outside leg of the tackle. If the halfback is required to line up as a wingback, his alignment will change. The halfbacks will take their alignments from the tackle, because ends will always be changing. The ends could be tight, or split, or flexed to two yards; they could be unbalanced or not. There could be a slot, or there could be a closed-down split end. When our halfbacks align in a wingback position, they line up from the tackle in order to always start from the same spot. They align from the outside foot of the tackle. The wing's outside foot should be three to three and a half yards from the outside foot of the offensive tackle. The football is in front of the center, reached out as far as possible. The wingbacks align with their toes two yards from the back tip of the football.

Wingbacks line up according to the football and the offensive tackle. We want the wingbacks in the same position all the time, because they will be going in three-step motion. When they go in three-step motion, we want the back to be in the diveback position after the third step. On his third step, the wing in motion will be at the outside leg of the tackle. Timing of plays requires the wingbacks to line up from the tackle, who does not change his alignment, as opposed to the ends, who do change their alignment. Consistency requires the handoff to be in the same place all the time.

The wingback stance is the same as the diveback stance, with the exception of the inside foot. Wingbacks drop the inside foot back so that the toes are even with the heel of the outside foot. This facilitates the pull step and three-step motion. The wingback uses the pull step when he has to block a penetrating defensive end. This slight difference in the wing's stance enables him to keep his first step flat. This stance also allows the three-step motion to be quicker. This stance does not hinder the wing from going straight ahead, nor does it hinder him from releasing outside if he has to flare to block the fourth defender on the flank. The only change is that the inside foot is back, with the toes back as far as the heel of the outside foot. Everything else is the same. Shoulders are still north and south, square to the line of scrimmage. There is a slight bend in his knees, which happens when he gets his heels to the top of the grass, and he is upright, so he can see the defense to read it correctly.

Our backs are never down in a three-point stance. Sometimes we take the halfbacks and flank them out wide. They can use a wide receiver stance when flanked. We do not widen halfbacks very often. We want a four-back attack, with our backs in the core, so that we can execute the wing-T offense. The passing game is executed this way, and so is our running game. There should not be any tips for the defense.

**Bird-dog**

The next drill is called "bird-dog." In this drill, the backs explode out of their stances as fast and as hard as they can for one step. Coaches can check the first step by calling "bird-dog," plus a type of step with it. If the coach says to step straight ahead with the right foot, then the backs take their right foot and step straight ahead so that their toes are replaced by their heels. As they take that step with their right foot, their right arm should be thrown hard behind them. Their chest should also go down to their thighs. That is what coaches check for when they check the first step. The drill is called "bird-dog," because a bird-dog in the woods, pointing to a bird out in the field, would look just like this. He would have his nose pointing toward the target, his tail would be straight back, and he would be pointing with his whole body at the bird.

The first step we bird-dog on is a straight-ahead step. The command given to the players is "bird-dog, right foot straight ahead, on sound." To set up the drill, the coaches place all players five yards apart, with the backups five yards behind each other. The coach can stand out in front of the drill and see the entire drill. He can see who has not thrown the correct arm behind him, and he can see who does not have his chest on his thigh. The coach checks all the backs in the group, then tells them to relax and get ready for the next step. Everyone does the drill at the same time; that way, we are mass teaching. We are getting a lot of players reps at the same time. They are learning by doing rather than by watching, and they do a lot in a short period of time.

In the first practice of the year, "routine" takes 10 minutes. By the second or third practice, it takes five minutes, and by the end of the year, we can do this in two minutes.

The next step in bird-dog is a fire step. Their toes are still pointing north and south, but the step is on a 45-degree angle instead of straight ahead. The call is "bird-dog , fire right, on sound." Then they fire left, on sound. Next, the backs step with their left foot so that their left arm throws hard behind them. This step will simulate the first step in the log block, or any time we have to run for a point one and a half yards outside the tight man. It will be used on runs and on pass patterns. We coach the same take-off angle, so both plays look the same.

The next step will be a "pull" step to the right. Coaches will work the backs on the pull step, just as the linemen do. When backs take the pull step, the first step points the toes toward the sideline. That foot comes up and goes back down again. Since the backs are stepping with their right foot, they will take their left arm and throw it hard behind them. As with the quarterback in the 20 series, the most important part of this technique is to have the back foot pivot as the front foot steps. A common error is for the back to try to take a pull step without first pivoting his back foot. That will force the body momentum to go on a 45-degree angle, as opposed to straight down the line of scrimmage. It is very important to pivot the back foot on the pull step. Backs should step with their right foot, throw their right arm hard behind them, and pivot their back foot. This action will turn their shoulders and give them the necessary speed and momentum as they get into their block.

Coaches should continue to check the basic fundamentals: chest on the thighs, back foot pivoted, right arm thrown hard behind, and in proper bird-dog position. When the backs learn to master these fundamentals, the coaches know that they will be able to explode out of their stance at full speed.

On the sweep, we teach the halfbacks to cross over on their first step, because it is faster. When a baseball player steals second, he also crosses over from first base. To add momentum to the crossover, the backs take their backside arm and throw it across the front of their chest as they take off and run. We do not overcoach this, because it is not opposite arm-leg action like we normally emphasize. It is important to do this to enable the backs to get their shoulders turned as they cross over. When they take the crossover step, they throw that arm out in front of them, and then the opposite arm and leg action will take over naturally. We also practice the crossover step in bird-dog drill. Backs will cross over and hold it for one step. When crossing over, they rip their backside arm across the front of their chest so their shoulders will turn and enable them to get momentum into the crossover.

**Takeoff**

In routine period, the first phase is checking stance, the second phase is bird-dog , and the third phase is "takeoff." Players begin five yards apart and five yards behind one another. They all sprint off the line at the same time with the proper foot. They will explode out of their stance and sprint five yards at full speed. Coaches tell them which foot to take off with and which type of step to use. They explode out of their stance. They run five yards as fast as they can, and then it will take them about five more yards to slow themselves down. (You need 10 yards to do this drill.) Next, all the backs turn around and face the other direction. Now they explode with their other foot. If they exploded with their right foot the first time, then the second time, they explode with their left foot. After doing the drill once in each direction, they will end up in their original starting position.

If coaches want to work on pulling in the same drill , they have the backs face the sidelines. The coaches will then call, "take off, pull right, on sound." The backs will pull right, sprint five yards, slow down for five yards, then reset and pull left. The players explode out of their stance with a pull step. The first step is a pull step, and then they sprint down the line of scrimmage.

During routine period, our backfield coach will also work on three-step motion, one-step motion, and extended motion as part of his routine period. All backs learn all three types of motion.

**Handoff Drills**

The next part of the running back practice is called "handoff drill." Diagram 3.3 illustrates the handoff period.

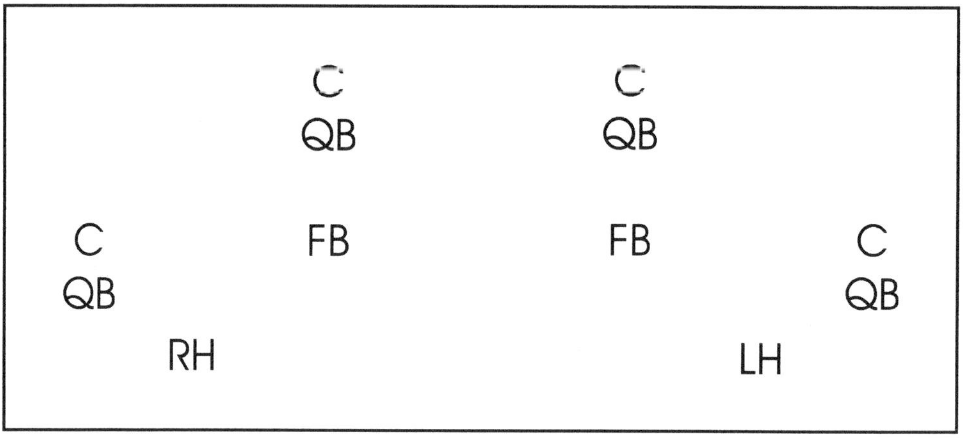


**Diagram 3.3**

All of the backs and all of the quarterbacks are involved in this drill. Our coaches teach extra players on the football team (e.g., the kickers or the players sitting out with an injury) to execute snap technique so there will always be a snapper in the drill for each quarterback.

There are four stations. In one, there is a center, a quarterback, a fullback, and his backup behind him. In another station, there is a center, a quarterback, and another fullback. One station will run fullback plays to the left; the other station will run fullback plays to the right. There will be two other stations about 15 yards down the field, and in each of those stations, there will be a center, a quarterback, and a halfback. The left halfbacks will be on one side, and the right halfbacks will be on the other side. The quarterbacks and the fullbacks could be working on the belly play. The fullbacks on the left work on belly to the left. The quarterback executes his footwork for the belly play, the fullback executes his footwork for the belly play, and then the quarterback finishes by doing a good job of faking. It is important for our quarterbacks to fake well. The fullback rotates from the left side over to the right side. Halfbacks continue working in their two stations on halfback plays.

If there are not enough players to fill two fullback stations, then it's okay to use only one. All stations are independent of each other. They use spacing boards during handoff drills. These are boards 16 feet long, one inch thick, and four inches wide, with paint on the spaces for the holes and the players. The backs work with these boards so they can line up according to where the linemen will be. This setup enables us to get lined up correctly on the practice field and not mistime the plays. The spacing boards consist of two separate boards so they can be picked up and moved if coaches want more space between the fullback stations.

The quarterback will rotate to each station as the period progresses. About one-fourth of the way through the period, the quarterbacks coach will be yelling, "Quarterbacks, rotate." They then rotate with the clock and go to the next station to work on a different technique. Every time they rotate, they work on a different technique.

The backs stay at the same station and work on the same play over and over again. Backs get many reps during this period. Coaches should allow five minutes for this period. They can reduce the period to two or three minutes, but if they use five minutes, it will guarantee a lot of reps on just a few plays.

The backfield coach and the quarterbacks coach will rotate around and make sure they can observe all the stations. They might miss something one time, but they will not miss it over the course of a few practices, and whatever needs to be corrected will get corrected.

**Pitch Drills**

The next drill the backs do is "pitch drill." In pitch drills, there are two different stations. There is a group with a center, a quarterback, a fullback, and a left halfback. This group will work options to the right. The quarterback is working on pitch technique during this drill. The halfbacks are working on catching the pitch. Diagram 3.4 illustrates "trap option."

There are no blocking halfbacks in this drill. There is a fullback who is faking, and there is the halfback who is receiving the pitch. There is also another fullback who holds a bag so that the fullback, after faking, can make a good block. There is an extra quarterback, who will be the pitch key. The quarterbacks will challenge each other during this drill. We want them to make it hard on each other.

The halfback establishes pitch relationship with the quarterback, which is five yards in front of him and three yards deep. As he catches the pitch, he bounces to the outside. He will bounce in order to stay away from the free safety in the middle of the formation. As the back catches the pitch, he will bounce from hash to alley to numbers to sideline. He keeps working his way outside. As he bounces, he starts up the field, sets up his block and then bounces to the outside. One station of backs is working on options to the right, while the other station of backs is working on options to the left. Both groups work independently on their own cadences and get as many reps as possible in the allotted time.

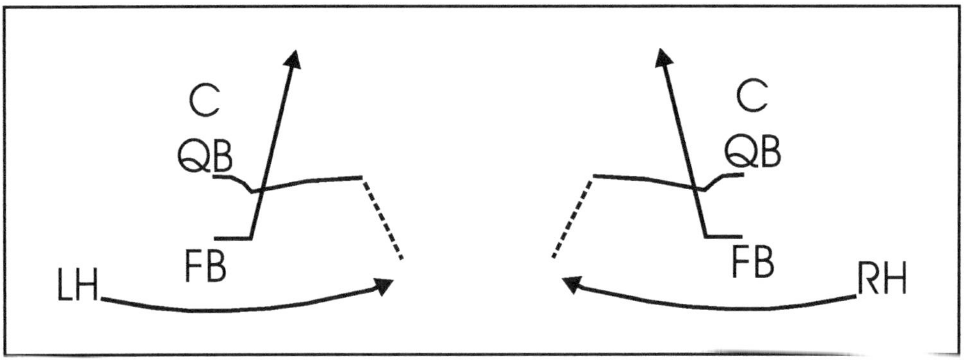


**Diagram 3.4**

## FULL BACKFIELD TECHNIQUE

The next drill is called "full backfield technique." Diagram 3.5 shows an entire backfield-center, quarterback, fullback, left halfback, right halfback-working on sweep to the right. They will work on any play which, during this period, the coaches feel they need to perfect. This is a great time to work on techniques that need to be corrected.

This is also a great time to work on most of the flank passing, keep pass, counter bootleg, waggle, and trap-option pass.

When working on sweep, for example, the quarterback takes the snap, hands the ball to the left halfback, and then fakes waggle. The left halfback runs the sweep; the fullback and the right half are assigned to block on this play. There will be an extra fullback holding a big bag, and an extra right halfback also holding a big bag. The players block the bags so that no one is just going through the motions. Everyone is executing the assignment and the technique for the sweep. While one group works in one place, the second group is in another. Both groups work on the same play at the same time. Each cadence is independent of the other, so as soon as they are ready, they can go on the next play.

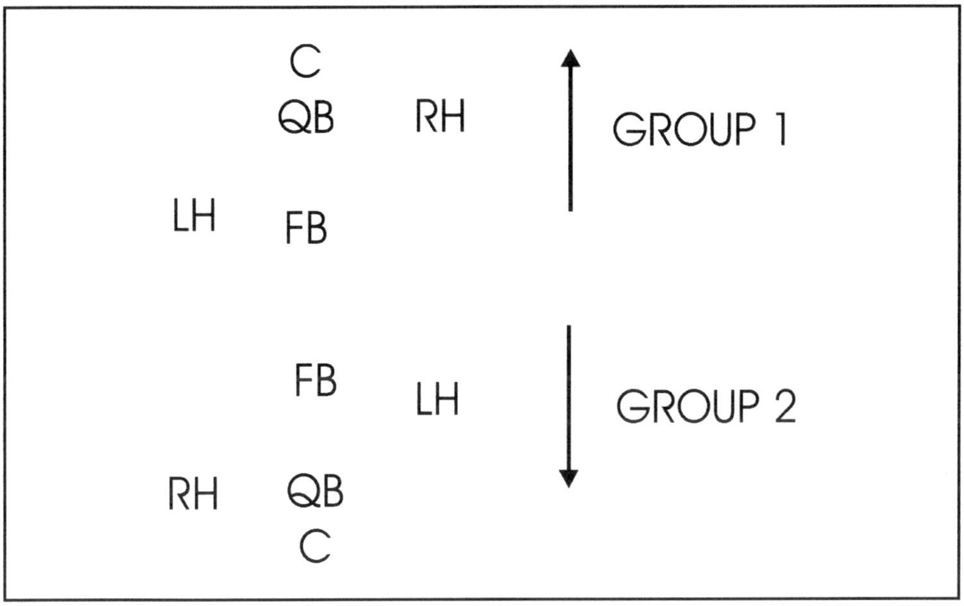


**Diagram 3.5**

## Passing with Ends

The final phase of our individual practice is a period called "passing with ends." Diagram 3.6 shows the backs working on the waggle play, where they fake the sweep to the right and the quarterback keeps the ball in the opposite direction. The spread end runs an out route. The fullback will block if the linebacker either threatens him or blitzes. If not, he is in the flat. The left halfback fakes the sweep and becomes a blocker. The tight end either runs a crossing route or splits a two-deep coverage. The backside halfback fakes a sweep block for one step and then runs a fly on the backside. In this drill, we are working on pass patterns, throwing the ball, and catching the ball.

Another way to do this drill is to have each quarterback and a line of receivers work on individual routes. The drill can be done with a full backfield and the ends, or with just the quarterback and the receiver throwing routes versus air.

Those are the drills the backs do in the practice plan: shoulder skills, routine period, handoff drills, pitch drills, full backfield technique, and "passing with ends."

## Technique and Footwork

As we discuss the exact techniques the backs use, along with their footwork for each play, our first play will be the sweep play. Many coaches think the sweep is the wing-T. Even though this play is one of the primary plays in the wing-T, the wing formation, and the sweep to the wing, it does not, by itself, represent the wing-T. The wing-T is much more. It is important to develop formation integrity and run-pass balance so that the defense will not overload to stop the sweep series.

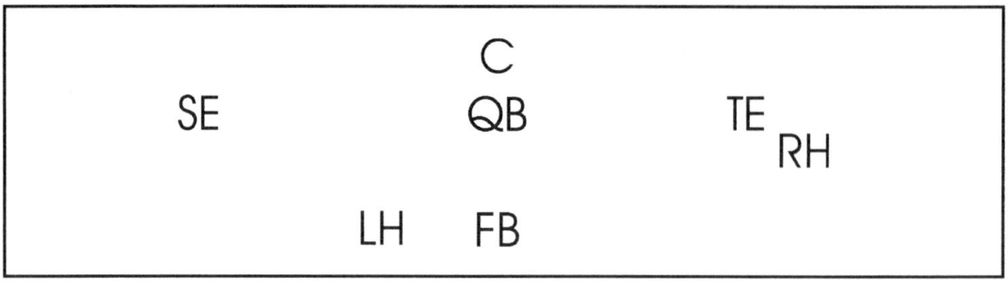


**Diagram 3.6**

## THE 20 SERIES

### 28-29 Sweep

The fullback lines up directly behind the quarterback, with his heels four yards from the back tip of the football. He should be straddling the midline with the quarterback and the center. The halfback will line up in a diveback position. His heels are also four yards from the back tip of the football. If he were to run the sweep from the wingback position, he would start in three-step motion and then execute the play from there.

When running sweep to the right side, the fullback will take a crossover step. His first step will go for the left foot of the center. As the quarterback reverse pivots on his first step, their shoulders are tight to each other. On the second step, the fullback passes the quarterback and makes what we call a "proximity fake." He will close down over an imaginary ball, grab his jersey, and sprint through the line of scrimmage to his blocking assignment. He will have his arms in, and the defense will think he has the ball. The quarterback does not fake to the fullback. As the quarterback reverse pivots, the proximity of his shoulders to the fullback and the action of the quarterback provide the picture of trap to the defense. As the fullback takes his second step and passes the quarterback, he will be faking into the line of scrimmage. The quarterback's back is to the line, and there is good deception to the play, with the fullback faking over an imaginary ball. The fullback blocks the area on the backside of the center. Sometimes the center will block that backside area and the fullback will adjust to his right and pick up a linebacker at the second level.

As the fullback crosses over for the backside foot of the center, the halfback will take his first crossover step, throwing his left arm hard across his chest to gain momentum. On the halfback's second step, the quarterback is ready to give him the ball. As he takes his third step, he will receive the ball.

The halfback's technique, after he has the ball secure, is to get his eyes on the down block by the wing. The halfback's eyes should be looking upfield as he runs across the backfield. Some coaches tell their halfbacks to catch the frontside guard before they cut. We coach our halfbacks to get outside the down block by the wingback on the defensive end, and then make a north/south cut. The halfback should turn up quickly.

The wider he runs, the more delayed he will be, and the more time he will give the pursuit to catch up. As the halfback crosses the backfield, he will stretch the sweep, get to the outside of the down block, and cut on a north/south path. As the halfback pops the line of scrimmage, running lanes will open up for him. He can break all the way back across the grain. Sometimes the whole pursuit will overrun the play and he can get the big touchdown run by cutting back. Sometimes the flank may be blocked very well, and the cut will be north/south or possibly to the outside. The major coaching point is to get the shoulders square and cut north and south.

There is a halfback drill for this play which really helps them to learn how to cut north and south. It is the "cone," or "four corner," drill. In this drill, the backs run and cut off of their right foot all the way around four cone as they make four cuts. They run across the cones to the right and plant their right foot as their eyes look to the inside. As the halfback plants his right foot, he steps upfield. In order to get his shoulders turned upfield, he will pivot his right foot. As his right foot pivots, his shoulders will turn north/south. He runs five yards and cuts, always keeping his eyes upfield. He repeats this technique until he makes four sweep cuts. He will go around all four cones and then go to the left. The backs get four sweep cuts in both directions. It is a pre-practice drill. They can work on planting their foot and pivoting so their shoulders turn north and south.

In review, the quarterback takes his first step on the midline. The fullback takes his first step for the left foot of the center. The halfback take his fist step by crossing over. On the second step, the fullback will fake over an imaginary ball, and the quarterback will continue with his second step on the midline. The halfback will take his second step to the handoff position. On the third step, the fullback continues through the hole. The quarterback will cross over on a 45-degree angle, and he will hand the ball off to the halfback.

The halfback will take the ball with his inside thumb down and the fingers of his outside hand spread straight from his belly button. As the quarterback lays the ball in, he will put the ball on his hip, and the halfback will let the quarterback bring the ball to him. The halfback should not reach for the ball. His bottom hand is the "table," and his top hand is the "stopper." The quarterback will put the ball on the table so that the nose of the football goes into the stopper hand and the ball carrier can tuck the ball away with either arm.

On the third step, the quarterback will make the handoff and continue to the flank, faking the bootleg. There will be great deception to this play because, as the quarterback reverse pivots away from the center, he pulls the ball into his belt buckle, keeps his elbows in tight, and as he reverse pivots, his back will be to the line of scrimmage so the defense will not be able to see the ball. With the proximity fake to the fullback, there will be effective deception in the play.

The mirror to this play, 28 sweep, is "29 sweep." The right halfback will now be the ball carrier when the play goes in the other direction. The wingback is executing a "gap block" or a "down block" on the defensive end.

**24-26 Fullback up the Middle**

The next play in the same package is 24 and 26 to the fullback. There are many different blocking schemes used for the fullback up the middle, including some schemes from the trap-option package. The blocking schemes include "on" blocking, "gut" blocking," and "guard trap" blocking. There are five or six different ways to block this play, and they will be discussed at a later time.

The fullback footwork adjusts slightly against odd or even defenses. The quarterback's footwork is also based on odd or even defenses. In an even defense, when the center is uncovered, the center will probably be blocking back to his left. Therefore, the fullback can take his first step for the left foot of the center. When running 24, the 4 hole is at the right guard. The fullback will run for the backside foot of the center, then break to the 4 hole. As the fullback makes the cut, his eyes are on the center's block. If the man the center is blocking fights across the front of the center's block, then the fullback will run the ball off the backside of the center's block. If the center gets movement, the fullback cuts playside.

If it is an odd defense, with the center covered, the fullback should run straight on the midline, through the quarterback and the center. The quarterback, as he reverse pivots, will pivot beyond the midline, allowing the fullback to run on the midline. The fullback will option run the defender on the center. Regardless of the blocking scheme, the fullback will find the hole once he sees how the center is blocking the noseguard.

On this play, the quarterback executes the same technique as he does on the sweep, except here he gives the ball to the fullback. He will fake to the halfback. The wingback will fake his sweep block and then block at the cutoff point. The quarterback makes a one-handed handoff to the fullback. The quarterback will "deal the cards." All handoffs will be made from forearm's length. The quarterback should never reach to make a handoff. If he has to reach the ball to the fullback, he will have poor deception on the play. The footwork of the quarterback will probably be poorly executed as well. The "26" is the opposite. On 26, the fullback starts for the right foot of the center and breaks to the 6 hole, which is our left guard's area.

If the play is 24 with "on" blocking, then everybody on the line of scrimmage blocks the man on him. The block on the noseguard versus a 50 defense will determine the cut by the fullback. He needs the midline. The quarterback will reverse pivot slightly beyond the midline, allowing the fullback to have the midline. The fullback will option run the center's block. The center will take his man in any direction he wants to go, and the fullback will cut off of his block.

**21-29 Waggle**

The next play in this series is "21 waggle." The backs will fake the sweep, and the quarterback will keep the ball to attack the flank. They all execute the same technique they use on sweep, at least for the first few steps. The quarterback will have the midline as he reverse pivots. The fullback will step for the left foot of the center, and the halfback will cross over. The next steps on waggle begin to change up. On the fullback's second step, as he closes over an imaginary ball, his path will widen to the outside foot of the guard and attack through the line of scrimmage, reading the linebacker. As he runs through, he reads the linebacker. If the linebacker blitzes the A gap or the B gap, the fullback will block him with his inside shoulder, and with his head outside. The point of attack is to the outside. The fullback's head is between the point of attack and the defender. If the linebacker does not blitz, the fullback is free to continue into the flat as a receiver.

The halfback, after he passes the quarterback on the fake, will gear down and block anyone who shows outside the right tackle's block. This is a very important coaching point on waggle. Many coaches will have the halfback who fakes the sweep run around the end. He can be a very valuable blocker on the backside of the quarterback. If the quarterback is forced to pull up, he has to get his shoulders upfield and is more of a stationary target. We need the halfback to be a backside blocker in case anyone is blitzing off the edge on the weak side of the play. The quarterback is attacking the flank and has the option to run or throw. The mirror play is "29 waggle," in which the quarterback bootlegs to the left. His read progression is deep, flat, or run. He will throw backside only when the free safety rotates with the quarterback's action. The wingback is a pass receiver. He will fake the sweep block and then run his route.

**22-28 Off Tackle**

The next play is called 22 and 28. This play is a great companion play to the sweep. If the wingback on sweep has to block a defensive end who is a penetrator running into the backfield, then he should not run outside, because that is such a tough block for the wingback. Against a defensive end who is not allowing the sweep, you should change the play to the off-tackle play, which is 22 and 28. This play hits off tackle, inside the defensive end who is penetrating, and takes advantage of his upfield charge. The coach calling the plays must know what the third defender, the defensive end, is doing. If he penetrates, run inside of him. If he seals, run outside of him.

The techniques for 22 are pretty much the same as the techniques for all the 20 plays, with one notable exception. The fullback uses 21 technique and will step with the right foot for the left foot of the center. On his second step, he will fake over an imaginary ball and then adjust his path for his blocking assignment.

This play can be blocked with "power blocking," where the backside guards pulls to kick out the end. It is then a double-team and kick-out. It can be blocked with "gut blocking," where both guards pull the way they do on the sweep, but the first guard guts and the backside guard kicks out the defensive end. It can be blocked with "tag blocking," when both the backside tackle and the guard pull. The guard kicks out the defensive end, and the tackle pulls through the hole and walls off inside. The fullback's blocking assignment is based on which blocking scheme we use. After the second step, the fullback will adjust his path according to the blocking scheme.

22 "tag" is one of our favorite schemes for this play, and it requires both the backside tackle and guard to pull like "counter trey." In that case, the fullback's first step is for the left foot of the center. On his second step, he fakes over an imaginary ball, and on the third step, he adjusts tight off the pulling tackle's tail and fills the area behind the left tackle.

The halfback's technique is to take the same crossover step he takes on the sweep, take one more step, and then bend for the 2 hole. He will bend for the inside foot of the tight end against an odd defense, or the inside foot of the tackle against an even defense. He receives the handoff on the inside from the quarterback. The quarterback will take his sweep footwork, but instead of handing the ball off outside, he hands it off inside. The quarterback does not have to reach to make the handoff because, if the handoff can be made at forearm's distance, the backs can run their course, and the play looks just like a sweep, except that it hits off tackle. Some coaches teach this play with an outside handoff, but that gives the halfback a tougher cut into the hole. If the play is executed correctly, the defense will not notice a difference in the play.

### Waggle Solid

The next play in the 20 series is "waggle solid," which requires the quarterback to keep the ball , but also to pull up instead of attacking the flank. The fullback takes his first step. On the second step, the fullback fakes over an imaginary ball and begins to attack his area. On the third step, the quarterback will step toward the flank to show the picture of waggle, but then drop back. The play turns into a drop-back pass. With waggle solid, both backs are blockers. This play will also keep one of the guards in so that there is as much protection as possible. It is a three-man route. As the fullback takes his footwork and fakes over an imaginary ball, he will break down in the hole and block that area. The halfback takes his footwork, gears down, and prepares to block the back side of the quarterback. This play gives coaches a drop-back game with waggle action and misdirection.

## THE 60 SERIES

It is important to be able call plays on the line of scrimmage and not have the players get confused. Many coaches call the "trap option" series with 20s, but we call them 60s to avoid confusion when calling them at the line of scrimmage.

**63-67 Guard Trap**

One of the first plays that sets up this series is a "guard trap" at the 3 and 7 holes. It could be "23 guard trap" or "63 guard trap," depending on the action we choose. The fullback will run a guard trap like "24 guard trap," but "63 guard trap" is one hole wider. With all the even defenses and 4-3 defenses that teams have employed lately, this play has become an increasingly major factor in game plans. If this play is called, and the defense is odd, the play goes back to being "24 guard trap."

Against an even defense, when running "23 guard trap," the backs will fake 20 action, and the quarterback will fake waggle. On "63 guard trap," the backs run that same 20 action, but the difference is that the quarterback turns and fakes trap option. This is the first play in the 60 series, because it sets up the series. On this play, the quarterback will take the snap and reverse pivot beyond the midline because the fullback steps for the front-side leg of the center, since he has a wider point of attack. The fullback will still step with his right foot, as he does in all 20 series plays to the right, but the difference is that he will step for the frontside foot of the center. On the 3-hole or 7-hole guard trap, the fullback must step for the right foot of the center because the point of attack is wider. The quarterback, regardless of his fake, must get beyond the midline. On the second step, the quarterback will make the exchange, and the fullback will make his cut. On the second step, the fullback will stay on course and begin to adjust as he receives the ball. After he has the ball, he cuts off the right tackle's block, which establishes the hole as he blocks down on the man over the guard. The guard will trap the first man outside the offensive tackle. The fullback will stay tight to the down block. A trap one hole wider affects the quarterback's technique, affects the fullback's technique, but does not affect the halfback's technique.

If the call is "23 guard trap," then after the exchange, the quarterback will cross over, make a great fake to the halfback, and sprint to the flat. To run the same play, but call it "63 guard trap," the quarterback will fake trap option, and the fullback's footwork will be exactly the same. The quarterback's footwork is the same for two steps. The only difference is that the quarterback will turn and fake trap option. As the halfback comes across the backfield, he will be the pitchback. The quarterback now must snap his hands back inside and snap his chin to his left shoulder. He will begin to pivot his right toe so that he can come downhill on his third step to fake trap-option action. The quarterback fakes to the playside instead of faking waggle.

**61-69 Trap Option**

When running "61 trap option," the point of attack is the flank to the right. The "61 trap option" is 20 technique for the backs. The fullback steps for the left foot of the center and will be a blocker. He will block either an area or a linebacker off the back side. If the center blocks back, the fullback will cut off his tail, get to the second level, and block the linebacker upfield. The halfback is the pitchback. He will sprint across the backfield the way he does on 20s, beginning with crossover footwork, and then he will establish pitch relationship with the quarterback. The quarterback takes two steps on the midline, turns downhill on the third step, and executes the option by reading the third defender.

The right halfback is assigned to his blocking assignment. He will flare and block the fifth defender, because the end will crack the fourth defender.

The quarterback will attack downhill, to the inside shoulder of the third defender. The backside guard will pull to log and will protect the quarterback from pinches or slants inside. The quarterback will get in the face of #3 and pitch the ball. If #3 comes right at the quarterback, then he will break down and step to the back he is pitching to. The pitch is taught two ways. The quarterback can use the basketball pitch, or he can snap his elbow and turn his thumb down. If the quarterback pitches and the ball is spinning too much, it makes the pitch hard to handle. If he cannot slow the spin with his thumb down, then the quarterback will use the basketball pitch. The ball will not spin as much with the basketball pitch. Normally, we teach the quarterback to turn the thumb down, snap the elbow, and the ball will rotate slowly. If the defense sends the third defender in his face, the quarterback will give with the hit the way a boxer gives with a punch. He wants a nice soft pitch. The halfback will be five yards in front and three yards deep as he catches the pitch. Against defensive players who slow play, or play cat-and-mouse, we want to attack them with the quarterback until they make a decision. If the defender is trying to slow the quarterback down on the way to his pitch, his momentum will be carrying him outside. The quarterback will give him a pitch fake, tuck the ball, and get to the option alley.

### 61 Trap-Option Pass

The companion play is "61 trap-option pass." If the fourth defender is coming hard up the field to beat the crack block, we throw a slant route by the wide receiver, in behind the strong safety (#4), to the void area he created by attacking the line of scrimmage. The backfield technique is exactly the same. The quarterback is on the midline for two steps. The fullback steps with his right foot for the left foot of the center. The halfback crosses over and establishes pitch relationship. The quarterback begins to attack downhill on his third step. On steps 4, 5, and 6, the ball should be thrown. Those should be choppy steps. The backside guard will pull to protect the quarterback as he throws the slant route behind the strong safety. If the corner chases the slant route, the quarterback can throw to the right halfback, who flared as if he were blocking the corner on the option play. If the strong safety stays back and the corner stays back, we could also pitch the ball to the trailing halfback.

### 61 Trap-Option Reverse at 9

There is a great play off the trap option series where the ball is pitched to the split end coming back through the backfield. The play is called "61 trap-option reverse at 9." The opposite would be "69 trap-option reverse at 1." The backfield technique on this play is the same as on the other 60s. The fullback will run to the backside flat, exactly as he does on waggle. He gets himself set up to block any defender who is chasing the play from inside out. The halfback uses the same action he does on "61 trap option," except he needs to get more depth as he crosses through the backfield, and especially as the quarterback gets ready to pitch the ball to the split end. The halfback will reach his hands as though he's catching a pitch. Between steps 4 and 5, the ball should be pitched to the split end. The quarterback should pitch the ball straight back, not in front, as if to pitch to the halfback. The spread end will appear as if he is intercepting the pitch. He then carries the ball around the opposite end.

**67 Counter**

There are other good plays in the 60 package. The "67 counter" is a play that will show the "trap-option" action. The quarterback will start downhill, as if he is running the trap option, and then hand the ball to the right halfback from the wingback position and run a counter play. On this play, the quarterback, the fullback, and the left halfback look exactly as they do on "61 trap-option crack," but only for the first two steps. The fullback then runs through the hole, bends, and blocks the frontside linebacker. The halfback continues to fake "61 trap-option crack." The wingback is not in motion. He leaves on the snap and takes the same footwork, as if he is going in three-step motion. After the third step, he runs for the outside leg of the left guard, where a double-team will occur. The quarterback will hand him the ball on the inside. The quarterback continues to fake the trap option, and the right halfback is the ball carrier.

**69 Counter Sweep**

A companion play is "69 counter sweep." This is an interesting play. Everyone executes "67 counter," but when the wingback receives the ball, he gets extra depth and runs a sweep around the left side. The fullback, the quarterback, and the left halfback will run "61 trap-option crack." On the fourth step, the quarterback will hand the ball to the right halfback. The quarterback then continues to fake trap option.

**67 Counter Bootleg**

There is a another companion play to "67 counter," which is called "67 counter bootleg." On this play, everybody uses the same action as on "67 counter," except that the quarterback will keep the ball at the flank and have a run-pass option. His first step is the same as it is on all 20s and 60s. The quarterback's second and third steps are the same as on "61 trap option." On the fourth step, the quarterback will fake the ball to the wingback-who is running the counter-with his hand and not with the ball. The quarterback keeps the ball in the crease of his pants and will attack the flank with the football. The receivers are the fullback, the tight end, and the backside spread end crossing. The left halfback passes the quarterback and will work downfield to block the first free man at the flank from the outside in. He uses "log block" technique with his left shoulder.

## THE 30 SERIES

### 31 Sweep

The last two packages of plays to review are the 30s and the 80s. The 30s are similar to the 20s, since they both feature a sweep play. The first play to review is "31 sweep." This is very similar to "21 sweep." The difference is that the line blocking is fire-on-backer. The halfback will cross over, receive the handoff, and make a good sweep cut when he gets outside the block at the flank. The line could make a six call, to pull the backside guard to wall off. Do not do this when playing against a penetrating eight-man front, because the defenders will be stunting and blitzing. Against those types of defenses, the line will block with fire-on-backer technique across the front.

Instead of the guards pulling to kick out the force, the fullback will kick out the force. The fullback on the 31 sweep will take a lead step, with his toes pointing north and south (like the belly cross block play), and then drive tight off the wingback's block to kick out the first defender outside that block. The difference on this sweep is that there is no buck or misdirection action. There is full-flow action with solid zone blocking up front. It is an effective alternative, because you can pick up the stunts with solid fire-on-backer blocking. If the defense is stunting, they are not keying the tailback or the guards, therefore there is no concern about the full-flow action in the backfield being too fast or bringing the defense to the play too quickly. The right halfback will use that same down technique on his block. The tight end will post the defensive end, thus setting up the right halfback's block.

The quarterback technique is exactly the same as it is on the 20s. He will hand the ball off to the halfback, as in "21 sweep," and fake the waggle. The big difference on this play is the fullback's action.

### 32 Off Tackle

If #3, the end, is a penetrator, the companion play in this package is "32," an off-tackle play. There will be a double-team on the man over the offensive tackle in an odd defense. If it is an even defense, the line will double-team the man over the offensive guard. The fullback will kick out the defensive end. The halfback will run directly for the off-tackle hole.

The quarterback opens directly to the halfback and hands him the ball. The halfback must have a chance to get quickly to the hole, so we make this handoff quickly, enabling the halfback to run directly off tackle. The wingback has a blocking assignment. The fullback will cross over with his left foot in order to get a good inside-out path on the defensive end. He will run to the tail of the double-team, as does the ball carrier. The ball carrier should run right over the tail of the double-team as tight as possible and as far as possible from the kick-out. It is an off-tackle power, and a good short-yardage call as well.

### 34 Blast

We can also run "34 blast" over the guards. On this play, the center and guard will double-team the noseguard, and the fullback will block the playside linebacker, with his head to the inside. The fullback will take off with his left foot, staying tight to the double-team, and isolate on the linebacker over the guard.

The halfback will use the same footwork and same technique he used on "32," except he must get turned up into the 4 hole quicker. The halfback gets his shoulders turned up fast and should be square in the hole, which invites the defense to overrun the play. The cutback to the back side often results in good yardage. The halfback must stay tight to the double-team and follow his fullback through the hole.

### 31 Roll Pass

The "31 roll pass" means that the quarterback will fake the sweep and then roll in the direction of the play action. On this play, the left halfback will block the defensive end. This play has the tight end running a corner route behind the corner. The fullback will run at the corner, as if to kick him out, and then slip into the flat. The left halfback will fake 31, come across the backfield, and log block the defensive end.

The first two steps are like 20s for the quarterback, like 31 for the fullback, and like 21 for the left halfback. On the third step, the quarterback will fake the sweep to the halfback and then roll in that same direction. The quarterback's pass progression is to look deep, then to the flat, then to run. He can throw the ball to the tight end deep, the fullback in the flat, or else he can run the ball if the flank is pinned down.

### 34-36 Counter

The rest of the 30 series are counters. They are blocked several different ways. In fact, "34 and 36 counter" to the halfbacks have been blocked with eight different blocking schemes over the years. The "tackle-trap" counter has been one of the best of the schemes. Another blocking scheme is "counter draw blocking," which has been exceptional, leading to many big plays and many touchdowns.

Another misdirection is the "counter crisscross" play. The "counter crisscross" is a play where the quarterback hands the ball off to one halfback, and the halfback hands it off to another. This play can be run either to a tight end or away from a tight end. It also can be run with two different kinds of blocking schemes. We teach the quarterback to open to the left halfback, as if it is a 32. He will take the ball and reach it to him. He wants the defense to see him give the ball so that they will begin to flow. The halfback will take a crossover step, as if he is going to run 31 sweep, and the quarterback will give the ball to him as soon as possible.

The fullback will block the way he did on 32. He will cross over to run a tight, kick-out path inside out. He will run for the outside foot of the tackle, and as soon as the tight end passes in front of him, he will kick out whoever is chasing off the back side of the tight end. When running counter crisscross, the blocking can pull the guard and the tight end, pull the guard and the tackle, or pull the tackle and the tight end. There are three different ways to block the play, depending on what kind of defensive spacing we see.

This play is one of the main reasons we teach the halfbacks to take the ball with their inside thumb down. When the quarterback hands the halfback the ball, the halfback can push it back to the other halfback without taking the ball and turning it over. The ball is placed on his "table" and, as he crosses the backfield, he will simply push the ball out. After the quarterback gives the ball to the halfback, he will fake waggle and bring defensive players with him. The wingback will not go in motion, but on the snap, he will use the same footwork he would use on three-step motion. He will get depth, as if he is coming back to his diveback position. On the third step, he should be back to where his diveback position is, receive the handoff, and run to the hole. As he clears the off-tackle hole, he will run north and south. The ball carrier does have one option left. The quarterback, who handed the ball off and then faked waggle, is running down the sideline. As the right halfback clears the line of scrimmage, he can pitch the ball to the quarterback. This is fun for the players to practice, but be careful allowing the halfbacks to pitch the ball in a game. We have seen it pitched right to a defensive corner, who ran it 60 yards the other way. Be sure that the defense has collapsed before trying execute this part of the play.

To complete the 30 package, we use "34 and 36 tackle trap counter" and the bootleg off the play. There is a lot of technique involved, and it is very important that this play is coached with detail. When running "34 counter," we will fake action to the left, and the left halfback will receive the ball, countering back to the right at the 4 hole. The 34 counter tells all the backs, except the ball carrier, that they are running in the direction opposite the football play. If they are running 34 counter, the play will hit over the right guard. All of the other backs will be running to the left. The wingback will go in three-step motion behind the fullback. As he clears the mesh between the quarterback and the left halfback, he will start downhill and log block the first free man on the flank from the outside in. The fullback will show belly and fake over an imaginary ball. Although the quarterback will not fake to him, the action will still indicate belly package to the defense. The fullback must run for the outside leg of the guard at full speed. As he takes off, he will cross over to get there faster. The fullback steps for the outside leg of the guard, fakes over an imaginary ball, and then blocks his area.

In the "tackle trap counter," the fullback must stay on course for his landmark. He should be in perfect position to block off the tackle's tail, as the tackle pulls to trap block. As the tackle pulls to execute the trap, the fullback fills tight off his tail and blocks the first defender who shows. If the defensive end is closing down, he blocks the defensive end. If the defensive end is up the field, he will not make the play, and the fullback will continue on to the next level. The fullback is a blocker on the play, but he will also fake to show the picture of the belly play.

The halfback carrying the football from a diveback position will rock his weight to the outside. He will throw his hips to the outside. He will not rock the weight and step with his outside foot, because that causes the halfback to run on a flat angle. As he rocks the weight, he will throw the weight to the outside. The first step will be with the inside foot. When he steps inside, he will use a "lead step"; his toes will be pointing north and south. The halfback will gain six inches of ground towards the line of scrimmage, keeping his toes north and south and his shoulders square. On the second step, the halfback's feet cross over. The third step squares his shoulders, his toes are still pointing north and south, and he will be square to the line of scrimmage, putting him in perfect position to accept the handoff.

The quarterback's technique is to reverse pivot, depending on whether he is facing an odd defense or an even defense. The ball carrier's path will bend, also depending on whether it is an odd or an even defense. If it is an odd defense, the ball carrier should run for the near foot of the center, which would be the left foot of the center when running 34 counter. The center and the right guard will double-team the noseguard. The center will step with his left foot and post with his right shoulder to elevate his pads. The right guard will use down technique to block the nose with his left shoulder at the hip and with his head behind. Both linemen will swing their tails driving the nose flat down the line of scrimmage. The ball carrier will stay tight to the tail of the double-team and explode through the line of scrimmage. We coach our backs to stay away from where the trapper is, because the ball carrier will trip over the trapper's feet. When that happens, the ball carrier is too wide.

If the noseguard is in a 0 technique, as in an odd defense, the aiming point for the halfback is the near foot of the center. If it is an even defense, the aiming point is a shorter hole, because the double-team will move over one man. The double-team will occur with the left guard as the post blocker and the center as the lead blocker. The double-team now will take place over the left guard. Therefore, the halfback bends his path for what we call a "short hole." A "short hole" means the back will run for the inside foot of the guard on his side of the line. In that case, the quarterback has to reverse pivot beyond the midline. If it is an odd defense, the quarterback will reverse pivot directly on the midline. If it is an even defense, he will reverse pivot six inches across the midline, because the halfback will run to a shorter hole.

One of the worst things that can happen on this play is when the quarterback reaches the ball out to the halfback. Instead, we want a close, tight handoff from forearm's length. When looking at this on film, there is a straight line of bodies: The fullback, the ball carrier, the quarterback, and the right halfback are all in a direct line, which gives deception to the play. It makes it hard for the defense to read. If coaches stop the film after the third step, and there is a line of bodies, then the players are executing the play correctly. The guard and the pulling tackle may also be in the line of bodies.

The quarterback will drag his right hand, keep his left hand in, and pump his arm as he attacks the flank. The ball carrier runs tight to the double-team. He can bend the play to any daylight. If the man being double-teamed fights across the face of the double-team, the ball carrier can break behind the double-team. Against an even defense, the double-team is moved a man over; therefore, it is a shorter hole for the halfback and more of a reverse pivot for the quarterback.

On "34 counter," the ball is usually given to the diveback, but it is possible to run the same football play and give the ball to the wingback, who will start in three-step motion. In that case, the right halfback would be in a diveback position. He can cross over and run to the flank in order to be a log blocker. We can also use a technique with the halfback called "right half dive." The halfback will dive to the outside to block the outside linebacker, as if he is running a load option. The fullback will go in one direction, the halfback will go in another direction, and the ball carrier will be in motion, which divides the defense. If the linebackers key the backs in the backfield, they have a tendency to divide and open up a hole for the ball carrier.

Another form of "34 counter" is run with both halfbacks in a wing position. The ball carrier will go in motion, but the other halfback will flare. He will flare as if he is blocking on trap option. The left halfback will go in three-step motion, and the quarterback will give him the ball. Be careful not to overcoach the wingback on this play. Allow him to go in three-step motion and aim for a point deeper than his normal diveback alignment. Tell him to square his shoulders to the line of scrimmage and let the wing and the quarterback work out the mesh. The quarterback makes the handoff from forearm's distance away and should not be reaching for the handoff. The quarterback takes the exact same footwork, reverse pivots, wraps his second step tight around the fullback, and then the wingback will adjust to the quarterback from there. The players work the mesh out between themselves.

**34 Counter Bootleg**

The last play in the 30 series is "34 counter bootleg." It is almost the same play as "34 counter," except the quarterback will have the ball, and the halfback will fake "34 counter." The quarterback will take the ball to the flank and execute a run-pass option. When we are pulling the tackle to run "34 counter bootleg," the fullback will widen his aiming point, because he is a blocker. He will cross over, but instead of aiming for the outside leg of the guard, he aims for the outside leg of the tackle. If there is any 5-technique penetration, he must block it with his head to the outside, with a right shoulder block. We are calling this play because, as we are pulling the tackle on the tackle-trap counter, the defensive 5 technique has been chasing the tackle inside. If the 5 technique does not chase, but we still need to call the counter bootleg, we call "counter bootleg solid," which tells the left tackle to block "on," instead of pulling.

If the fullback checks his area, and there is no 5-technique penetration, the fullback can release into the flat. If we call "counter bootleg solid," the fullback attacks the outside leg of the guard for his aiming point and now his block is on the linebacker. If the linebacker does not come, he will release to the flat and become a receiver. If the linebacker does come, he blocks him. The tackle and the fullback assignments are interchangeable, depending on how the tackle will block the play. The halfback will fake "34 counter" and always fake over a short hole. He will use the inside leg of the guard for his aiming point; this way, if the tackle pulls, they will not collide with each other. If the left halfback aims over the center when the tackle pulls, then they will collide. If he is on a short-hole course, then as the tackle pulls, he will come right off the tackle's tail behind him. The tackle's technique is to sprint to the opposite guard and then gear down. Even if the play is "counter bootleg solid," and the tackle is not pulling, the left halfback will use short-hole technique.

The quarterback will step across the midline to get to the flank quicker. The quarterback is beyond the midline and wraps tight around the fullback's tail. The fullback fakes over an imaginary ball. The quarterback will hand fake to the left halfback, dragging that hand as he goes by. The ball is tucked in the left side of his body, in the crease of his pants. As the quarterback attacks the flank, he has a deep receiver, a flat receiver, and a crossing receiver. He also has the option to run.

## THE 80 SERIES

### 83-87 Belly

The primary play in the 80 series is "83 and 87 belly." It involves a good deal of important detail for both the fullback and the quarterback. This play is one of the most productive plays in the offense. If executed properly, it can gain a thousand yards a season by itself.

The first variation is called "83 cross block" ("87 cross block" to the left). This play is 83, which means the fullback will carry the ball on a belly play. The right halfback will lead him through the hole. Our favorite blocking scheme when we run this play is cross block. The tackle's rule is "gap down-on" and the guard pulls to trap outside. The halfback is responsible for the inside linebacker. At the college level, we can cut the linebacker.

This play will show the same full-flow action as the 30 package. The halfback will take a short jab step out and up. (This is a very important coaching point.) From there, he must attack "through the hole," and his landmark is the outside leg of the guard, not the tackle. As he takes his second step, he will continue for the outside leg of the guard, reading the first defender from the nose of the guard out. This is his key for whether he will block inside or outside. This is also the key for the ball carrier to make his cut. If it is an even defense, and there is a man over the guard, then that defender will be the key, because he is the first man from the nose of the guard to the outside. If there is nobody on the guard, but there is a man over the tackle, then he is the read for the ball carrier and the blocker, because he is the first man on the line of scrimmage, from the nose of the guard outside. This defender's defensive reaction will tell the back whether to go inside or outside of him. The backs should run off their short jab step, out and up. As he takes his second step, he will continue for the outside leg of the guard and read the first defender from the nose of the guard out. If the tackle blocks down on the man over the guard, and the guard pulls to cross block the defensive end, the backs should run off the tackle's block. As they come through the hole, they will adjust their course. If the tackle blocks down and the defender fights outside the down block, the backs should run inside.

We use the same keys if the guard is uncovered, and the tackle is covered. The defensive man over the tackle is the key. If the blocker turns him out, the ball carrier and the lead halfback go to the inside. If the defender slants inside and the tackle blocks him down to the inside, the ball carrier and the lead halfback adjust and slide to the outside.

The left halfback will be in a wingback position. He will go in three-step motion. When he passes the quarterback-fullback mesh, he will attack downhill and block the first free man on the flank, from outside in. When working on this play in practice, we use an extra fullback to hold a big bag and move the bag so the backs will have to cut. There will also be an extra halfback holding another bag, so the log blocker can execute his blocking technique.

The fullback has specific footwork he should use. The worst thing he can do is get into the hole before the blocking has had a chance to develop. This play is like the sprint draw of the wing-T. The footwork is vital.. The first step by the fullback will be a lead step, with his toes pointing north and south. He will gain about six inches of ground toward the line of scrimmage, and he will keep his shoulders square. On his second step, he crosses over, keeping his shoulders square and his toes pointing north and south. On his third step, he also gains six inches of ground, with toes north and south and shoulders square. This step is the fullback's "square-up step," and this is when he will receive the ball. Since he has gained only six inches with each step, he will receive the ball deep enough in the backfield to read and make a cut. The halfback's body is about a yard to a yard and a half directly in front of the fullback. The quarterback reverse pivots beyond the midline to give the ball to the fullback and wraps tight around the fullback before faking keep pass. The cross block makes six bodies in a straight line as the handoff occurs, which adds deception to the play, even though it is a full-flow play. It will be tough for the defense to read what might happen here. Again, stop the film when it gets to the handoff point to see if the team executes the play with correct timing and deception.

The quarterback will reverse pivot to a 60-degree angle, beyond the midline. On his second step, he will reach the ball to the fullback's far hip. The quarterback hands the ball off on his third step, snaps his hands back in, and goes behind the fullback to fake "keep pass." On this third step, you will see the line of bodies starting to form, and the correct relationship forming between the halfback and the fullback. A common mistake on this play is when backs execute poor footwork and are running through the hole, side by side. If coaches see this happening, then one or more of the backs did not use the proper footwork, and the fullback will have no protection. It could be a fumble play. The fullback can be protected by keeping him a yard behind the lead halfback.

The belly is the same as an "iso" or "blast" from the traditional I formation. The lead blocker will be about one yard in front of the ball carrier as they go through the hole. The right halfback takes a jab step out and up on cross block, because he wants to give the cross block time to happen. The tackle will block gap down-on, and the guard will pull to trap. They need time to execute the cross block, so the halfback will jab step. The linemen can block the play with "blast blocking," double the nose, pull the backside guard around, and lead the halfback through. They can also block this play with "on blocking," where everybody blocks straight ahead.

As you can see, we have four or five different ways to block this play. The only time the halfback needs to take a jab step is if we call cross block. On any other blocking scheme, the halfback can run immediately for the outside leg of the guard with no jab step.

The belly is the top play in the offense. It will make many yards every year, but it has to be executed correctly. You do not want poor timing on this play, and it takes work to get the fullbacks to take correct footwork. The fullback must not be in too much of a hurry or be impatient. He can be "quick," but not in a "hurry." One of the biggest mistakes is when a fullback takes a lead step, crosses over, and, on his third step, runs immediately into the hole. When the fullback does that, the halfback will not be able to lead him through the hole and protect him from the linebacker, who is free to run through and cause a fumbled handoff.

**81-89 Keep Pass**

The companion play to the belly is "81 and 89 keep pass." Here, the quarterback will keep the ball in the direction of the flow. He will reverse pivot the way he did on the belly, and he will poke the ball into the fullback's pocket and snap it out quickly. He will fake to the fullback for an arm's-length ride, snap the ball back quickly, and get the ball up to a passing grip.

The halfback will be a legitimate receiver at the flank. From a diveback position, the outside halfback will run for a point one and a half yards outside the tight man. If the tackle is the tight man in the formation, the halfback will aim his first step for a point one and a half yards outside of him. Keep pass blocking will block down with the tackle and log with the guard. They may also block straight ahead. Regardless of the scheme, the halfback can help the block on the 5-technique defensive end. He will dive for a point one and a half yards outside the tight man, and on his way through to the flat, he will punch his left hand into the shoulder of the defensive end. He will then work his way up the field for two steps and bend to the flat. Halfbacks sometimes make the mistake of getting to the flat too quickly by running straight into the flat, thus forcing the quarterback into a longer throw than necessary. When this happens, the halfback catches the ball too close to the sideline, with no room to maneuver. The quarterback should be in a good relationship with the halfback and should be able to complete an easy pass to him, because he is the primary receiver. We like to run the play to a tight end or a spread end with a reduced split. The halfback can out-leverage the defense in the flat quickly.

A variation is to keep the spread end out wide and call "keep pass out" so we can throw an out cut to him. When trying to get the ball to the spread end, it's a good idea to keep the spread end wide. When trying to get the ball to the halfback, bring the spread end in and out-leverage the defense in the flat. Against a team running two deep and really jamming the spread end, his "out" route will convert to a fly, and there is a high/low read on the corner. The quarterback can throw the ball in the hole behind the corner. He can also throw the ball in front of the corner, to the halfback, depending on the corner's reaction.

The fullback, in keep pass, will use belly footwork. His steps will be lead, crossover, and square-up, and he will widen his aiming point to the outside leg of the tackle. The fullback will block the 5-technique area, which is the outside shoulder of the tackle. Against a 50 defense, the tackle could block all the way down to the nose. Then the pulling guard will have to log the defensive end, giving the fullback the defensive tackle. "Keep pass fire" will require the tackle to block on. The guard will pull to log the defensive end, and the fullback will then have the linebacker. We could also have the entire line block on, which will give the linebacker to the fullback and the defensive end to the motion halfback. The fullback will make a good belly fake and then block an area.

The left halfback will be sprinting in three-step motion. When he passes the mesh between the quarterback and the fullback, he will start downhill and execute a log-block technique on the first free man at the flank from the outside in.

The quarterback will give a quick arm's-length ride to the fullback, snap the ball back in, and get the ball ready to throw in a passing grip. He will get the ball quickly to the halfback in the flat. If he gets the ball to the halfback, the halfback can catch the ball and quickly get turned up the field . If the halfback breaks one tackle, he will run down the sideline for a big play. Sometimes our quarterbacks are a little gun-shy on pulling the trigger, and they wait too long, allowing the defense to react and catch up to the play. If the quarterback will throw the ball quickly off the mesh, the halfback will have the ball quickly, and will have a better opportunity to make big plays.

The halfback does not have to be in a diveback position. The coach can also put him in a wingback position. The blocking halfback could also be in a wing position or a diveback position. From the wingback position, the halfback can get to the flat quicker.

**83 Pass**

Another play in this series is the fake to the fullback and drop-back. Instead of the quarterback attacking the flank with a run-pass option, he can drop back. This is called "83 pass," with a suffix to attach the route. The right halfback will be in a wing position because he is one of the primary receivers on the play. The left halfback and the fullback are primarily blockers on this play. The quarterback takes the snap and reverse pivots, as in 83. The fullback takes the exact same footwork as before. As the quarterback meshes with the fullback, instead of attacking the flank, he drops back for three steps to throw. The left halfback will go in motion. If he is in a wingback spot, he goes in three-step motion, and if he is in a diveback spot, he goes in one-step motion. As he goes in motion, he will pass the fullback-quarterback mesh, then gear down to pass protect from inside out. This will result in the same blocking scheme that an I-formation team would use on the sprint-draw pass. The fullback will have the inside linebacker, and the motion halfback will have the outside linebacker in pass protection. If the fullback does not have to block, he will hook inside over the ball. If the halfback has nobody to block, he will flare. This play-action, drop-back type of play allows for five receivers in the route. As the quarterback reverse pivots, he fakes deep in the backfield. Not only does this move freeze the defense, but it also gains the quarterback depth away from the center. As he drops, the defenders are late in reacting, because they have been held by the depth of the fake to the fullback.

As the fullback fakes over the ball, he attacks the line of scrimmage under control. After the mesh, he will make a decision on whether he has to block the linebacker. If he does, he will break down, get into the proper football position, and be ready to pass block. If not, he can continue through the line and hook either outside or inside, depending on what kind of pass pattern he is running. As soon as the halfback passes the mesh, he gears down and works up into the line of scrimmage from inside out. If the outside linebacker or defensive end is blitzing, he must pass block him. If not, then he will flare with depth, get width, and become a fifth receiver for the quarterback to throw the ball to.

**83-87 Counter**

Another 80 series play is "83 and 87 counter." It calls for the same blocking schemes used on "37 counter crisscross." On "87 counter," the quarterback will hand the ball to the wingback. He will fake the belly with the fullback, while the backside halfback goes in motion to be a log blocker at the flank. The word "counter" means all of the other backs go away from the hole. The fullback will fake the belly as if he is running 83. He takes lead, crossover, square-up footwork. The quarterback will use the same footwork as on the belly, faking the ball to the fullback. He will hand the ball to the wing, who leaves on the snap and will not be going in motion. The wing's footwork is the same footwork he would use if he were using three-step motion. He takes three steps, and then he starts downhill to the hole, which is at the outside leg of the backside guard. The quarterback will reverse pivot, fake to the fullback, and hand the ball off on the inside. The backside halfback goes in on step motion. He runs across the backfield through the heels of the fullback, and as he passes the fullback, he will attack downhill and block the first free man at the flank from outside in. He will block with his inside shoulder and use log-block technique. The fullback's footwork is lead, crossover, and square-up and, as on all other counter plays, he has a blocking assignment. He will fill off the tail of the last man to pull. If we pull both the guard and the tackle, it will be off the tackle's tail. If we pull the guard and the tight end, it will be off the tight end's tail. He puts his head inside and blocks with his outside shoulder. The quarterback will hand the ball to the wing and attack the flank the same way as on keep pass.

**The Down Series**

Although the "82 and 88 down" is a belly play, it is a direct-hitting, quick, off-tackle play to the fullback. Since there is no deliberate footwork for the fullback, he will cross over and run as fast as he can. The quarterback, instead of reverse pivoting with depth into the backfield, will reverse pivot flat down the line of scrimmage. The quarterback gives the ball to the fullback with a quick ride into the line of scrimmage and then fakes option with the halfback. The playside halfback will be a blocker. He will block an inside linebacker or the strong safety at the cutoff. The backside halfback will go in motion to get in pitch relationship. If he is in a wingback position, he will go in three-step motion. If he is in the diveback position, he will go in one-step motion. He will be the pitchback on the option, so when the play is "82 down" to the fullback, he will fake the option with the quarterback. The fullback will cross over and run through the outside foot of the tackle. We tell the fullback to square his shoulders as soon as he feels the mesh, and get north and south. The quarterback will give the ball to the fullback off tackle.

The next play that comes off of this is "down option." When the fullback gets the ball (82 down), the play is blocked like a trap: down, down, pull the guard, and kick out. The "down option" play is blocked down, down, pull the guard, and log. The frontside halfback is a blocker either on the safety or on the inside backer or on the corner. The backs use the same techniques they used on "82 down." The quarterback will ride the fullback into the line, snap the ball back, and attack downhill to option the fourth defender. The guard will log block the third defender. The fullback has two options: (1) He can keep his shoulders square and run vertically through the line of scrimmage as he goes through the hole to block the free safety or (2) He can bounce to the outside to block the free safety. This option makes for less of a fake, but is probably more effective in getting the fullback downfield to be an extra blocker. Often, the free safety is very active and will support, so the fullback's block becomes critical. The quarterback can either keep the ball or pitch it to our halfback in motion. We will also use "keep pass" to a tight end-wingback, 83-87 pass, and 83-87 counter as companion plays to the down series.

**The Quick Belly Series**

The last part of the 80 package is the quick belly package, used to gain belly option when not running the 40 series. This package is an alternative to the triple option. The series features the quick belly option and the quick belly to the fullback. In our package, the quick belly is "84 and 86," which is a handoff to the fullback, followed by a fake option. The companion plays are "81 and 89 option," which call for a fake to the fullback and an attack down the line of scrimmage to run the option. We also have "84 scissors at six," which is a handoff to the wingback countering flow. The last play in the series is "81-89 waggle," which has been used with higher frequency in the last few years.

In the quick belly series, the fullback's footwork changes slightly. He will take a quick lead step, but his second step is a dive for the butt of the guard. It is a quick path. The quarterback will reverse pivot, give the ball, run the option, or give the ball on the scissors. The frontside halfback has a blocking assignment unless the play is scissors. The backside halfback will go in motion and be the pitchback.

**84-86**

The first play to start with is "84, to the right, or "86," to the left. This is a quick belly play and the fullback will take a lead step then drive for the butt of the guard. The quarterback technique is to jab step forward, reverse pivot flat, handoff to the fullback, and then fake option. The backside halfback will be coming in motion, three step motion from a wing alignment, or one step motion from the diveback position. The quarterback should be up on the balls of his feet so he can reverse pivot off his near foot. He reverse pivots flat down the line of scrimmage, reaches the ball to the fullback and rides him, snap his hands back in, and then fakes the option. The play can be blocked with different schemes up front, but works best with "fire-on-backer" rules, or zone blocking. The fullback can cut to either side.

**81-89 Option**

The next play in the series is "81 option." The technique for fullback is quick belly technique. The backs do the same thing, but the quarterback now pulls the ball and reads pitch or keep off the third defender. The backside halfback is the pitchback.

**84 Scissors at Six:**

On "84 scissors at six," the backside halfback will do the same thing he did on "81 option" and "84." He will go in motion across the backfield and become the pitchback. On "84 scissors at six," the quarterback is going to reverse pivot, fake the ball to the fullback, step back, and hand off to the right halfback. The fullback's technique is exactly the same as on "84." The ball carrier leaves on the snap, but he does not go in motion. His first step is back for depth, and his shoulders are square and facing the quarterback. From here, he should run right for the tail of the center and adjust to the quarterback. As he receives the handoff, his shoulders should be north and south as he goes through the hole. It is very important that he does not take a second step for depth. Rather, he should take his first step for depth, his second step for the tail of the center, and then he should be running downhill with his shoulders square.

This play is blocked a bit differently from the way "Sally" is blocked. It has the right tackle pulling and leading through the hole. The tackle is assigned to block the backside linebacker as he comes through the hole. He will read the center's block. If the center is blocking in the left direction, the tackle pulls through the hole behind the center. If the center is blocking in the right direction, the tackle pulls around the center's tail. If he pulls up through where the center is in pre-snap alignment, he should be in good shape. The ball carrier should make the same read as he attacks through the hole. If he goes right over the tail of the center, he will be able to run vertically and also be able to cut in either direction. The quarterback will ride the ball to the fullback, pull it back out, step back, give the ball to the halfback, and attack the flank. The opposite play is "86 scissors at four."

**81 Waggle**
The last play in this package is "81 waggle." This play has been popular of late, because many coaches have begun to instruct their inside linebackers to key the fullback. Rather than run "21 waggle" and have the fullback run to the play side of the center, thus bringing the linebackers to the play, the fullback will use "84" footwork until he passes the quarterback. He can bend back to the left, as on "21 waggle," and still become a receiver in the pass pattern. The pivotal problem occurs when the linebacker becomes a blitzer. As a preventive maneuver, we do not run this play if the defense has shown that tendency. It is very difficult for the fullback to start to the right of the center and then come back to block a linebacker lined up to the left of the center, if he is blitzing quickly. This play comes out of the game plan if the defense has shown a tendency to blitz inside backers.

The right halfback will be in a wingback spot and run the crossing route. His technique on this play is to start down through the middle of the two hash marks. As he does so, he reads the deep middle of the field. If a safety rotates to the middle, between the two hash marks, then at 10 yards, our halfback will break it off flat and stay between the hashes. He will not cross to the outside of the hash marks. He must now find an opening and sit down. As the right halfback runs down through the middle of the hash marks-and if he sees no one in the middle-he will split the middle of the field for a touchdown shot. If the two safeties stay outside the hash marks, the right halfback will divide the field down the middle. At the same time, the quarterback should be reading the safety correctly and then get the ball to the right halfback.

The fullback's footwork is the same as on "84"-a quick lead step to the right, diving right for the butt of the guard. As he clears the quarterback, the fullback will bend his path to the left and run in the flat. The left halfback will go in motion. As he passes the quarterback, he will gear down, work inside out, and be a blocker on the back side of the waggle. If nobody shows for him to block, he will flare. Rather than teach the quarterback to come all the way around and fake a belly play to the fullback, we simplify the action and have the quarterback reverse pivot on the midline, as on "21 waggle." He will execute the same footwork so that he does not have to learn another set of footwork. The play does not look any different to the defense than the belly play or a 30 sweep with all backs flowing. The fullback will fake over an imaginary ball, with the halfback faking sweep, just as he does on all waggle plays. The quarterback will attack the flank, with the outside receiver going deep, the backside inside receiver running the crossing route, and the backside outside receiver also going deep.

## SUMMARY

This chapter has presented a detailed description of everything the backs must execute in the wing-T offense. Included are many of the details that are important to the execution of the wing-T. Without those details, the wing-T is just a group of plays. Although they are nicely packaged plays, it is their details that make them successful. Anyone who wants to coach wing-T running backs needs to coach details very thoroughly. He will find that, when executed properly and with precision, these plays will gain a great deal of yardage.

# CHAPTER 4

# The Wing-T Receiver

In this chapter, I will discuss the wing-T receiver, or, as we commonly call them, our ends' techniques. We have in our program tight ends, and we also have spread ends, or wide receivers, or split ends-whatever you want to call them. All our receivers are all going to learn the same techniques. Again, we are going to cross-train our people. With very few exceptions, most of our ends will learn how to do every skill required of all the end positions.

## QUALITIES OF RECEIVERS

The single most important quality for the tight end, as well as for all the other positions, is that he be an unselfish football player. We must have a tight end who is just as willing to block as he is to run down the field and catch the waggle play. In terms of their physical attributes, the tight ends in our league average about 6'3" and 233 pounds. That does not mean that a tight end has to be that big, or that he cannot be smaller or bigger to play the position and perform well. But most successful teams have tight ends who are in the neighborhood of 245-255 pounds. That means that they are great big offensive blockers. These tight ends must be dominating players at the line of scrimmage. We also like an athletic tight end, because we like to throw to the tight end. He is the No. 1 receiver on many of our patterns, and we expect him to be able to get across the field or down the field and get open. Therefore, athleticism is imperative. When we are looking for a tight end, we want someone who is big enough and strong enough to block down on defensive tackles or defensive ends. It is extremely important that our tight end be able to gap block. He must be able to stop any penetration from a man playing 7 technique, inside him , or in the gap, or even all the way down on the tackle. He must be able to come down and execute a block on that defender. The flip side to that is that he also must be athletic enough to run down the field and get open against a defensive back. Usually, the tight end has to play against the safety, whether it be a strong safety or a free safety. Coaches recruit corners and put them at those positions, anyway, so the tight end needs to be athletic enough to get to the assigned spot on the field with the correct timing, and, hopefully, also get open. We work our tight ends in what we call "2-corner" drill, or one-on-one, versus defensive backs. They have to be able to win those matchups.

Our wide receivers, or what we call spread ends, are sometimes going to be off the line of scrimmage, and therefore flankers for us. Sometimes they will be on the line of scrimmage, and therefore split ends for us. You can call them wide receivers or whatever you want to call them; it makes no difference. Again, the first quality that we are looking for is unselfishness. We know that our spread end is going to be the No. 1 receiver on the majority of our routes, so, obviously, he has to have receiver skills. But we want a spread end who is also willing to block. That does not mean he has to be a great big, giant, physical specimen. He simply has to be willing to block, meaning that he has to be willing to go down in there and throw his body at a defender, if we call "option crack," or if we call a split sweep, where he has to come down on a defensive end. Whatever the case may be, we need a split end who is willing to come down inside and really strike someone. We try to teach all of our players to block with their head across the front and above the waist. There are times when we can cut. The majority of the time when our receivers block, they are going to have to block with their shoulders, and they are going to have to block hard. Whether they are asked to execute a crack block or whatever it is we would like them to do, their willingness to block is probably the most important thing they can have going for them. Will that split end run and hit somebody? Many wing-T coaches find that their best wide receivers, or split ends, are kids who played running back in high school in an offense similar to the wishbone-players who have some pretty good speed, but who also have been trained to block before. If you have a wide receiver coming from a high school program where they throw the ball 45-50 times a game, he is probably not the wide receiver you are going to get into your program. You are probably not going to throw the ball 50 times a game, unless you are just so good at waggling that you can do that. You can throw that often in this offense, but, normally, it is a ball-control type of offense that is based on running and play-action passing. Therefore, you will need to recruit a spread end who is unselfish.

Another key quality for receivers, of course, is that they have good hands. Receivers can get open all they want, and they can run great routes, but if they can't catch the ball, all that running talent is not doing much good. Can good hands be developed? I have seen it before. I have seen situations where a guy would come in as a freshman, and really not have a very good set of hands. The receivers coach would then work with him all through the season and the off-season and give the player a lot of drills and have the quarterbacks throw to him a lot. I have seen many players go from not having a good set of hands at all, to being top-quality receivers. Now, if receivers initially come to you with hands that are not so great, then obviously, you want a player who is either really fast, or who has great "shake-n-bake" moves, great quickness, or simply has a knack for getting open. Hopefully, then, you can help him to develop his hands as time goes on. Also, we all have experienced players who have come in as freshmen and graduated five years later, and their hands never got any better.

Finally, the ability for a receiver to run pass routes is essential. The receiver has to have either great speed or great quickness. Some guys can get open underneath and can run great routes and shake loose from the defender covering them, because they have really fine quickness and good moves. Some can burst off the line of scrimmage, give a head fake, give a jab step with a head fake, and find themselves wide open. Some receivers have the ability to really get a guy leaning. They can work one side of the defender or the other, and then break off in the opposite direction. Receivers like that, who have great moves, can make it in our league. They can be good receivers, especially in this offense, which contains so many intermediate routes. The flip side to that is to have a receiver who has tremendous speed. Obviously, at the college level, we can try to recruit those people. But they are hard to get, because every coach wants them. If you can get a guy with great speed, then a lot of things will open up for you in any offense, especially if that great speed player can also catch the football. Now you can get a guy down the field, you can throw him a fly route, or throw him a post route, or throw him a corner route. You can get him down the field and make some big plays with him and back the secondary off. This allows you to run the ball without the safeties and the corners, who are always sticking their nose up in the line of scrimmage, trying to be a factor in your running game.

It is most important to have players on your football team who are unselfish. You cannot have people who want statistics for themselves only. Athletes have to be happy with winning the football game and also with accumulating statistics as a team. When you have those kinds of guys, you are going to win. The worst thing that can mess those guys up is usually the attention give to them by the people in your town-patting them on the back, or else grumbling about the coach, or telling the kid that he should be a 1,000-yard rusher, or that he is not getting the ball enough. A kid buys into that. It causes problems. Your players have to buy into what you are teaching. They have to buy into a team philosophy. They have to be hungry and they have to be unselfish. Those are the principal qualities that we look for in our receivers.

As I go through the different things that our receivers do in every single practice, many of them are going to sound like some of the other descriptions in this book, because we teach everyone to block. We teach the same blocking fundamentals to all our receivers, all our backs, all our linemen. We teach the same fundamentals to our backs, our linemen, and our receivers when working on their first step and their stance during our routine periods. As I discuss this, some of our practice periods, such as shoulder skills and routine, will sound similar to what has been discussed regarding the other positions. But once we get through shoulder skills and routine in practice, then the descriptions of the duties of the spread ends and the tight ends become noticeably different from the descriptions for the other positions.

## SHOULDER SKILLS

The first thing our receivers start with, as we go to the individual part of the practice, is our "shoulder skill" period. Diagram 4.1 illustrates what this part of practice is like for our receivers.

You may have one coach, or you may have two coaches. If there is someone available to help your receivers coach, that's great. Then you can have two sets of eyes watching these drills.

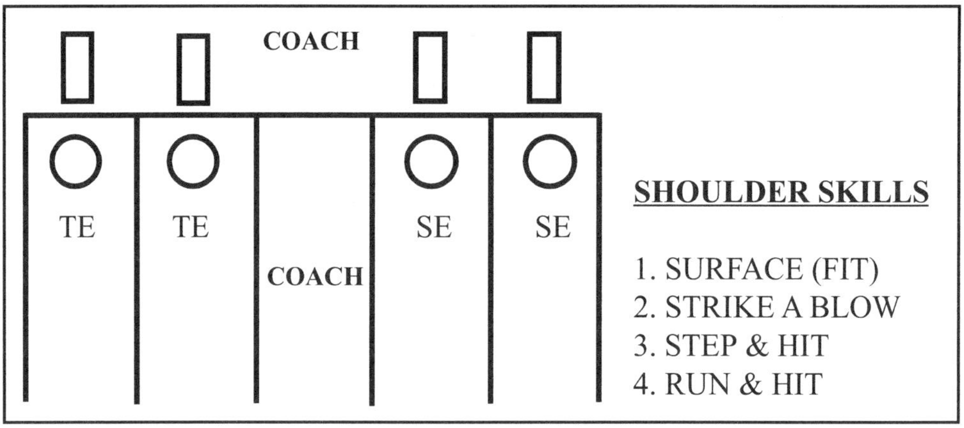


**Diagram 4.1**

Shoulder skill period includes, "surface," where we are going to fit into the bag and make sure we have the proper blocking surface. The second drill in the progression is "strike a blow." We position the players in a six-point stance for both drills. We will have the bag between the legs, and we will be working on a good blocking surface and then taking that blocking surface and actually driving it through the bag and rolling the hips. A receiver blocks just like a lineman or a back or anyone else in our program. The third part of this progression is "step and hit," where receivers work on taking the first step and then striking the bag. The final phase of the blocking progression is what we call "run and hit," which can be turned around to "hit and run." In "run and hit," receivers are going to block a defender off about four yards, or linebacker distance, away, and then finish the block after that. The opposite of the "hit and run" occurs when our receivers have to block a man who is directly on top of them, and then have to drive and run him, finishing the block that way.

We use the sideline for organizing "shoulder skills" drill. If we had four tight ends in our program, two tight ends would block two bags, which would be held by the other two tight ends. The wide receivers or spread ends would also be blocking the bags, with partners holding them. If we had four of each, that number would be optimal for the purposes of practice. If you do not have those kinds of numbers, then you should combine the groups and let one tight end and one split end work together and match them up that way.

The bags are intersected by the sideline. The bottom of the bags should be placed right on the sideline, and they should be placed between the five-yard stripes on your field. You can put them right on the corners of the five-yard stripes on the sideline. The coach stays on the inside of the action, so he can see the blockers from behind. Once in a while, our coaches move to the other side to look into the blockers' eyes.

## SURFACE

The first drill in the blocking progression is one we call "surface." When we do "surface," our players are going to be down in a six-point stance. The players know that when they get in those six-point stances, their hands and their knees should be spread enough so that the bag stays right between their knees. The six-point stance means that, basically, the cage of the facemask is right up on the bag. If you do this without requiring a helmet, you can tell your players to put their nose right on the bag. Their knees should be straight down from their hips. They should not have their butt cocked way back so that the blocker is sitting on his heels. We coach our players to position their feet so that their toes are not curled into the ground. We want their feet flat, and that way, when they do the drills, their knees will not lift up off the ground. This positioning will enable their hips to roll through the block.

The first part of this block is nothing more than a matter of fitting the blocker's surface into the bag. That's what we call surface. It is a fit drill. There is no hit. All we are doing is fitting into the bag. The blocking surface will include the thighs; the front of the shoulder, all the way down to the elbow; the forearm; and the fist, which is placed right next to the pec. At the contact point, the receiver is going to strike and drive that shoulder and forearm hard through the bag. The receiver is doing nothing more than fitting himself into the bag. There is not a lot to strike. There is not a lot of contact. (We will be doing that in the next drill.) The key coaching points are that the hips should be rolled down and through, the eyes should be up, and there should be a squeeze between the side of the neck and the entire blocking surface. If blockers squeeze the neck and the blocking surface, then they will squeeze the defender, which will give them a better chance to control him. Another point is that the receivers' toes should not be curled underneath their feet.

Your commands to your receivers are going to be "surface, right shoulder, on sound." Each fits in with his right shoulder. Next, you want to see them fit in with their left shoulder, as well, so the next command should be "surface, left shoulder, on sound."

## STRIKE A BLOW

One of the reasons why the bag is placed on the line, on the sideline on the field, is so the line can intersect the bottom of the bag. We want to see the player knock that bag off of that line. We want to really strike a blow. The name of the drill is "strike a blow." We want these guys to really strike the bag. We want to see if they can knock a 100-pound bag off the line scrimmage with one hit and not even use their feet. The strike has to be nasty. You want to see how hard your players will hit when they get a chance to block someone.

"Strike a blow" is done from a six-point stance. The blocker places his nose on the bag, both hands on the ground, knees straight down from the hips, and toes uncurled behind him. The player who is making this block is going to rock back just slightly and then explode through the bag, using that same blocking surface that I just mentioned and knocking the bag off the line. We will have him go with his right shoulder, then with his left shoulder, and then we will switch our guys around.

At the beginning of both training camp and spring ball, we ask players to hold their block so that the coach can check it. Now, if the coach is instructing six to eight different ends, they will all be on the line. Still, he's got to be able to coach them all, look at them all quickly, make the necessary corrections, and have them come on back. Everybody gets off on the "s" in "set."

## STEP AND HIT

The third step in the progression is called "step and hit." In this drill, we teach from a two-point stance. We want our receivers to be about an arm's length away from the bag. We tell the players to reach out and touch the bag. We want a good base. We are going to emphasize that we have the bag, or the defender, between our legs as a blocker. We are going to work on the proper footwork first of all, and then we're going to strike a good blow and block the bag off the line. This drill is first done in a two-step progression-step and hold-and then, after a while, we do the whole thing.

One of the key fundamentals in blocking is that, if a blocker is going to block with his right shoulder, his first step should be with his left foot. He should be vertically back off the ball as far as he is allowed to be. We want our players to take a short power step on the first step, and then make contact on the second step, where they will actually drive the defender. On the first step, the blocker replaces his toes with his heels, which constitutes the length of the step. The second step is an up step, which is done with his right foot. His right shoulder will make contact. On his third step, he will drive through naturally. Another important coaching point is for our blockers, when they step with that first step, to place their chest down on their thighs, because we block at the hip. The reason, as noted before, is that there is no strength in the hips. Players who work on the hip sled, doing squats and legs lifts, have all that strength get transferred down into the quad area and the glutes area-but not at the hips.

After you have worked step-and-hold for a few days, and you are satisfied that your players are keeping their chest on their thighs, their feet apart, and are stepping with a power up step so that their heels replace their toes and are not overextending, then the next thing you want them to do is the whole drill on one command-and watch the whole thing take place. Next, the players will do the same thing with their left shoulder, and they are also going to do the entire drill without stopping.

## RUN AND HIT

The final part of this progression is what we call "run and hit." We are going to have the receivers practice blocking linebackers who are lined up four yards away from us. We are going to have our receivers run at a linebacker as if they are going to be blocking a linebacker (or it could be a corner in the case of the wide receiver). Our receivers are going to run at the bag at full speed. When they get to the contact point, then the other fundamentals are going to fall into place. One of the things we tell our players to do is to drive the bag back a couple of yards, swing their tail, and take it down the line a couple of yards, just so they get a feel for what it is like to finish the block, as well as do all the other fundamentals.

One of the cardinal sins of blocking is when the blocker decides to start swinging his tail and finishing his block to the right, and then he throws both feet outside the bag. If the blocker's feet slide over and are all the way outside the bag, the defender will be able to penetrate at him. The blocker will not have the necessary control on the defender he needs to block. The defender can also spin out of this block. The steps and the footwork are short, choppy steps, and as he turns, the blocker takes his outside arm, throws it up into the numbers, and bench presses.

In one drill, we are going to have the blocker run for four yards, as if he's going to block a linebacker. When he does, he makes contact, drives the bag, and finishes the block.. The opposite of that is "hit and run." We also teach our receivers to block a man who is right on their nose-to drive him and then swing their tail and finish him. That action emphasizes leg drive. This drill is a good substitute for sled drill.

If our players execute the proper fundamentals, they will block at the hip, keep the man between their legs, and have good control of him they throw their shoulder and forearm through the block. We finish by having the receivers squeeze their neck and their shoulder and keep the defender controlled on that blocking surface.

## ROUTINE PERIOD

The next part of practice that our receivers go through is what we call routine period. Routine period is really a footwork period. This is where we have them concentrate on a proper stance and a correct first step. With the wide receivers, we teach two different stances. The tight ends can learn the wide receiver stance, which makes a total of three for them. The inside hand is always down for our receivers. That facilitates our release technique, and also our blocking and the way we teach our blocking.

Diagram 4.2 illustrates how we organize "routine period."

Routine period includes, first, work on the "stance," and second, our "bird-dog" drill, which is simply a step and hold (i.e., take the first step and hold it). And when we do this, we really throw the arms hard, and we have one arm that will point straight ahead, and one arm that will kind of point behind us. We will actually look like a bird-dog going out pheasant hunting when we do this. The third part of the progression is "takeoff," where we are going to work on exploding off the line of scrimmage for five yards with the correct foot. The last part is just for the tight ends, and only if you ask your tight end to pull on any of your blocking schemes. If you never ask your tight end to pull at all, I would not do this drill. It is a linemen's drill, but our tight ends have to pull through the hole and wall off on our counter plays; therefore, we teach the "tight end pulling" drills.

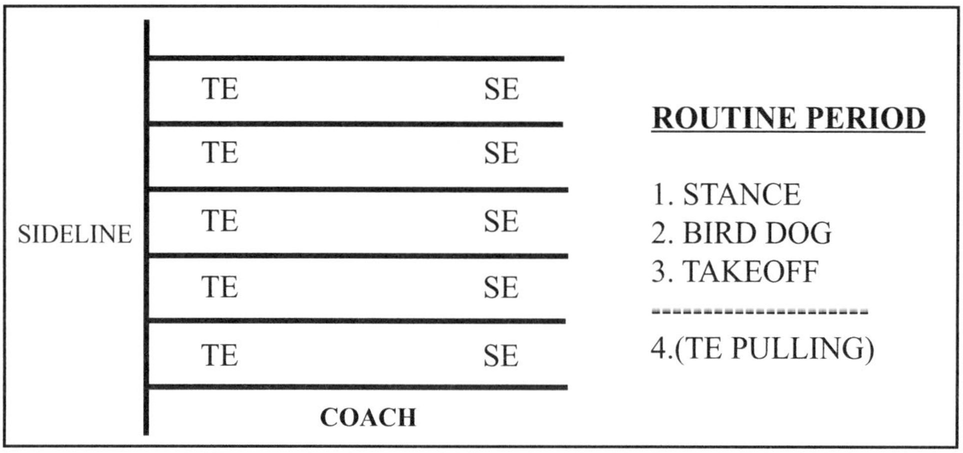


**Diagram 4.2**

During "routine," we want the receivers coach to be in a centralized location, as mentioned earlier. He needs to be in a centralized location, where he can see all of the receivers. What we do is we put all the receivers in a line, right behind each other, five yards apart and 5 yards in width. Now, the receiver coach can look out over his people and see all of them doing the drill at the same time, and he can make quick corrections. By following this procedure, we get in a lot of reps in a short period of time.

This drill for us starts out as a 10-minute drill on the first day of practice. By the time we finish our season, we're down to about two minutes. We go fast in this drill. Once you're convinced that your people are comfortable with the proper stance, then you do not necessarily have to work on the stance anymore. You can eliminate that from the progression. On "bird-dog," we step and hold at the beginning of the year, just to check the footwork, but we rapid-fire that "bird-dog" later in the year, meaning that we can go three steps very fast, and then on to the next footwork.

## STANCE

Since our receivers are always going to have their inside hand down, we must tell them which side the ball is on. The tight end stance is just like our offensive linemen's stance. First of all, they should use a narrow base. We do not want a big, wide, giant base because we want their first step to have power to it. We want their feet right underneath their armpits. That is as wide as they need to be. Their feet should be parallel. We do not want them to stagger either foot back. We want them to have a perfectly balanced stance so they can go in all four directions equally well. We want their toes to point in just slightly, because when they get down in their stance and bend their knees, their power-producing angles will still be going forward. If their toes are way out, and they get down in their stance, then their knees will point in the opposite direction. That is counterproductive to what you want them to do. (If you have a football player who is a slightly pigeon-toed, then by turning his toes in, it is actually going to help him, because it will lock in the power-producing angles.) We want our receivers' inside hand down and their off arm wrapped tight around their knee in order to lock in those power-producing angles in even further. We also want to emphasize the heels up to the top of the grass. If the receiver brings his heels to the top of the grass, he is automatically going to have bend at his ankles. As he gets into his stance, he should have bend at his knees, and he should have bend at his hips. We want him to have a nice, flat back in his stance. We want his hand to be extended as far in front as possible, yet not have any weight on it. We want him to be able to pick his hand up and down without having any weight on it. We want his hand as far out as possible, because we want the defense looking at that stance to think it is a run stance, even though it might be a pass play. Anther point is that, if he has too much weight forward or backward, the receiver won't have proper balance in his stance. By having proper balance, the receiver can go in all four directions equally well, with power. When I say four directions, I am talking about straight ahead, left, right, or even backward, if the receiver needs to be a pass protector. We want his inside hand down, because the No. 1 block the receiver has to execute is a gap block, where he blocks a defender in the gap between him and the tackle, or a defender on the tackle who might penetrate. We feel that, if he keeps his inside hand down, then it will be easier for him to take the pull step and get his head across the front.

The first stance we teach a spread receiver is a three-point stance. Eventually, we are going to have him stand up in a two-point stance. The fundamentals should be almost the same as they are when he takes a three-point stance. The advantage of being up, obviously, is that he can see a little bit better. He will have a better awareness of what is going on around him. Clearly, he can make moves on people who are right in his face. He can still get off the line of scrimmage quickly, as long as his feet are disciplined. Anytime we see our receivers start to false step, we put them back down in a three-point stance for a while and make sure that they understand what the fundamentals of stances are. Then we go back to standing them up again. The one thing that will make your receivers understand this message faster than anything is, if they have been in a two-point stance for a while, and, as a coach, you are seeing a bunch of false steps, you make them go back into a three. They do not like that three-point stance nearly as much as they like the two-point stance. It is of the utmost importance to eliminate false steps from our receivers.

When having them take a three-point stance, we teach our receivers to maintain a narrow stance. Their feet should be about as wide apart as a yard stripe on the practice field. We want the receivers' feet in a narrow stance, like a sprinter's. We want their back foot back. We are going to have them put their inside arm down and their inside foot back. We have them bend their knees and get their heels up to the top of the grass. We can look inside to the ball if we have to. There is no excuse for a wide receiver to be offside or jump the gun, because he can always turn his head to the inside, see the football, and move on the snap. He does not even have to hear the quarterback's cadence. He puts his back arm up a little bit, so he can throw his arm forward and really get his momentum generated to go straight ahead.

We tell our spread ends to go down into a three-point stance and keep their feet the same and stand up. That is the two-point stance that we like to use. We like their arms in a position where they can explode off the ball. What we would like is for our spread end to come off the ball just as he would in a three-point stance. We do not want him to false step. A false step occurs when the first step goes backwards. That means that the step has to come back to the line of scrimmage. What has happened to the receiver is that he has taken two steps and gone absolutely nowhere. When a man releases correctly off the line of scrimmage, he takes two steps and is a good two yards up the field. That is what we are trying to eliminate. That two yards can be the difference between scoring a big touchdown or being covered. We want to make sure the receiver does not false step, and that is what we are looking for in the stance by our receivers.

**Bird-dog**

The next part of routine period is what we call "bird-dog." Bird-dog is a step and hold. The receiver is going to work on one step at a time, and that is all he is going to do in this drill. At the beginning of training camp, we have our receivers take one step and hold it, and then we check to see if that step is where we want it. There are three different steps that we bird-dog with our receivers. The first one is straight ahead. The second one is what we call a fire step, where they step with their inside foot at about a 45-degree angle. The third step is a pull step. We have them pull step both ways, inside and outside.

We have the receivers work on firing out straight ahead. The tight end can work on firing out with his left foot and his right foot. For the spread end, normally, when he steps straight ahead, he is going to step with the foot that is back.

A "fire step" for us means that the receiver is going to step at a 45-degree angle with his feet, but his tail will still be pointed north and south, and his shoulders will still be square with the line of scrimmage. We do not want them to get overextended, because it is very easy for the receiver to be pulled out of his stance or fall down. He has got no power or balance when he does that; therefore, he is not going to be as effective either as a blocker or as a receiver releasing off the line of scrimmage.

On a pull step to the left, the receiver should take his left foot and step toward the sideline. It should not be a big, overextended, giant step. All he basically needs to do is pick his foot up and put it back down again. But the most important coaching point is this: If he picks up his left foot, then his right foot needs to pivot so that his toes are also pointing to that sideline. Another important point is that, if he steps with his left foot, then he should throw his left arm hard behind him. In this case, that will help him turn his shoulders.

## TAKEOFF

On takeoff, what we are going to do is have the receivers sprint five yards. We want them to get off the ball. It is not a long sprint. We are not interested in conditioning the receivers at this point. Instead, we want to see them explode out of their stance, but we are going to give them the foot that we want them to step with initially. On the practice field, what we are going to do is have the receivers sprint five, jog five, and then turn around. Then we can do the same thing, coming back with the other foot.

### Pulling Drill

We teach our tight ends what we call an 11-step pull drill, so that they can pull through the hole and wall off on certain counter plays. Therefore, they have to know pulling techniques. We are going to teach the pulling techniques at the end of our routine period, and we have only the tight ends do this. If you have only one receivers coach, send your tight ends to the offensive linemen for routine period. That way, they can work on pulling while you are working with the wide receivers on other things.

In the 11-step pull drill, if we are going to go to the right, the receiver will post up with his right foot first. His second and third steps both have him going down the line of scrimmage. On his fourth step, we want him to reach down with his left arm and grab grass, because this simulates where the contact is going to occur. If he were pulling to the right and going to log a defender, contact would occur on this step right here. If he is going to gut, or pull through the hole, then his fifth step is going to go straight up the field to finish the block. We want him to be nice and low. From there, six, seven, eight, nine, and 10 all go back to where he came from, and 11 is nothing more than getting back down in his stance. He should have completed a pull, and returned to where he started. When you teach this drill to your players, you want to walk them through it once or twice, but that's it. They have to learn to do it. I would do it where we walk them through it once, have them walk really fast, and then count the numbers for them the second time. After that, just say, "Set" and have them sprint all 11 steps. We do not want to make robots out of our players. We do not want kids out on the field doing things one step at a time. We want this drill to be smooth, fluid, and fast.

Our linemen grab grass on their fourth step. They dip their shoulders so they can rip through on the next step, because steps 4 and 5 are where they make contact on log blocks. Sometimes our tight end might have to do that, but most of the time-99 percent of the time-he is going to pull through the hole and wall off on a linebacker.

## BLOCKING TECHNIQUE PERIOD

The next phase of the receiver practice plan focuses on what the receivers have to do in terms of individual techniques. We begin with what we call "blocking technique period." The tight ends have quite a few blocks. They have individual blocks, but sometimes they are involved in combination blocks. They have to be able to execute the same blocks as the offensive linemen on a defensive down player. They also have to be able to execute the same blocks as our wide receivers on defensive backs.

## TIGHT END BLOCKS

### "On" Block

The first block we teach the tight end is the "on" block (Diagram 4.3). Just like everyone else, his head goes to the side of the hole, and he finishes the block by swinging his tail. We like to have the tight end take the man down the line of scrimmage parallel to the line of scrimmage. In "on right," he is going to block with his right shoulder; therefore, his first step is with his left foot. Contact occurs on the second step with the right shoulder. And he drives the defensive man to the right.

### Gap Block

Gap right means that there is a defensive man who has either lined up in a 7-technique inside shoulder, or in the inside gap, or possibly over the next player inside (Diagram 4.4). He is a threat to penetrate the neutral zone inside us. In this case, we put the bag inside and even with our tight end, so as to simulate someone who has just penetrated the neutral zone. On "gap block," when the receiver executes a gap technique, his head goes in front. We tell him to drive his head right across the front of the belt buckle and block with his left shoulder. Even though we are gapping in the direction to the right, the block is made with the left shoulder. This would be gap right. We have the blocker step with his right foot, and that first step is a pull step. The gap block technique consists of a pull step, and the blocker also puts his head across the front, blocks with his left shoulder, and finishes the man directly down the line of scrimmage. This is what we do versus any defender who is a penetrator or a threat to penetrate.

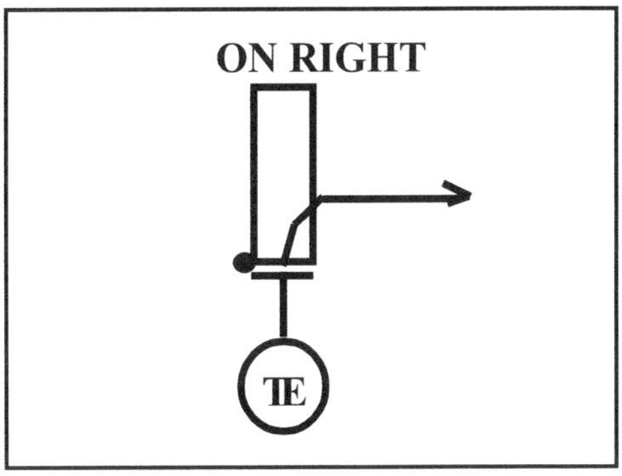


**Diagram 4.3**

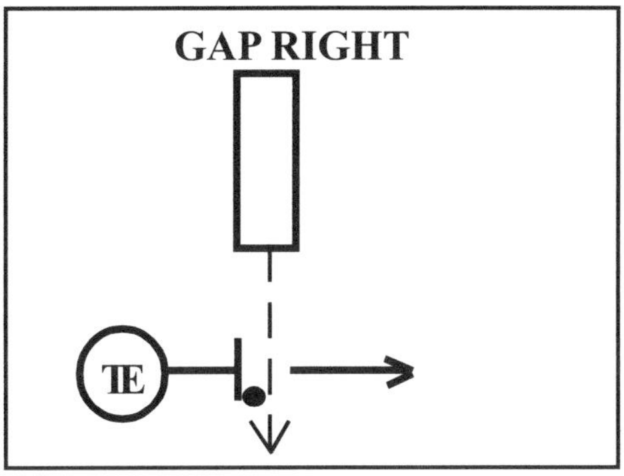


**Diagram 4.4**

**Down Block**

The next block is "down right" (Diagram 4.5). This same technique is our technique for lead or double-team whenever we double-team a player. On this block, you are simulating blocking a man who is over the tackle. We place the bag over top of where the tackle would line up, his ghost alignment. We are going to put our head behind on a down block, because we have determined now that this man is not a penetrator. He is a line-of-scrimmage, reading type of player. Therefore, we don't have to worry about putting our head across the front because he is not going to penetrate. "Down right" is executed with the right shoulder. Because the head is behind, we would step with the left foot. What happens in this block is that the right foot merely pivots, and the left foot steps, in order to get your shoulder square to your target. Contact occurs with the right shoulder. We finish the block down the line of scrimmage.

**Fire Block**

The next block is what we call the "fire block" (Diagram4.6). The fire block means that we are going to take the fire step that we worked on in bird-dog period, the 45-degree step, with our shoulders still square to the line of scrimmage. Our toes are still pointing north and south. We are simulating blocking a man who is lined up on the outside half of our body. We put the bag on the outside half of our body. When we say "fire right," we have to block the man who is to our right, but we also have to get our head to the outside. Therefore, even though we are saying "fire right," it is a left-shoulder block. The blocker will take a 45-degree step, toes north and south, shoulders square, and make contact with the left shoulder. The second step drives right through the crotch of the defensive man, and you are going to drive him, knock him off the ball. If you can knock him off the ball, that is great. If you feel you can do that, try to swing your tail and finish the man on a 45-degree angle back away from the direction that the play is going. We do not want our blockers to try to round off the block. What we want to do is block and drive the man back at a 45-degree angle and just knock him off the line of scrimmage. Once we have good control of him, then we will swing our tail and finish the block.

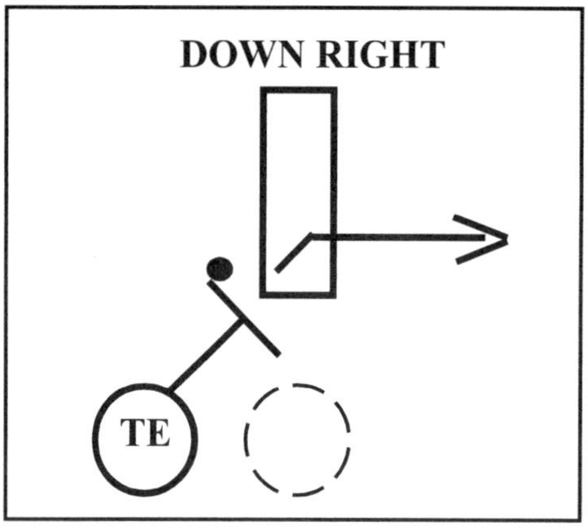


Diagram 4.5

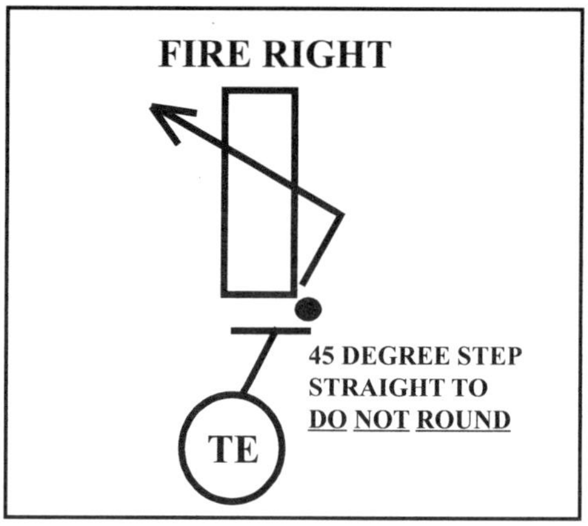


Diagram 4.6

**Reach Block**

The next block is what we call a reach block (Diagram 4.7). Reach and fire are very closely related. A reach block is used versus the defender who would be over the man adjacent to our tight end on the inside. When you take a reach step, you are either going to block this defensive lineman, if he slants to you, or you are going to climb up the field, right through his inside hip and try to cut off a linebacker. As a tight end, you are also often assigned to block a loose 9 technique and reach him. This would be a man lined up outside of you by a whole man. When we take the reach step, we are taking a flat 90-degree-angle step with the toes pointed north and south, shoulders square to the line of scrimmage. Then if that defensive man comes on an angle toward him, the blocker will go ahead and execute a fire technique after the reach step. The second step is right through the middle of the man. We will drive this defender straight off the line of scrimmage and later swing our tail and finish him off inside on a 45-degree angle.

**Bump Lead Block**

The next block we work on is what we call a bump lead (Diagram 4.8). Lead means you are going to double-team. It is our terminology for double-teaming. The blocking bag is placed on the offensive tackle. The tight end is going to come down as if he is going to double-team on the man lined up over the tackle. We get a good strike on this man and then climb vertically to the linebacker who is scraping. From there, the tackle takes over the block by himself, using wheel technique. (Wheel technique is explained in the offensive line section.)

**Post Block**

Our post block is done by the tight end when he knows that the wingback is going to come down and double-team with him from the outside (Diagram 4.9). If we are going to post lead and take the defender to the right, then the tight end is going to use his left shoulder. The tight end steps with his right foot, places his head to the inside, and posts with his left shoulder. What we do with our post block is try to raise, or elevate, the aiming point for the block. Normally, we block at the hips. But this is one time when you can block up in the numbers. We want to raise the defender up and elevate him so that the lead blocker can come down at an exposed hip. Once the post is made, the eyes should be to the inside. If there is a chance the linebacker might run through the C gap, the tight end must come off and gap block him. If not, then we can finish the double-team block, and the two of us, the post and the lead, will get our tail ends together, swing our tails, and take the defensive player flat down the line of scrimmage, parallel to the line.

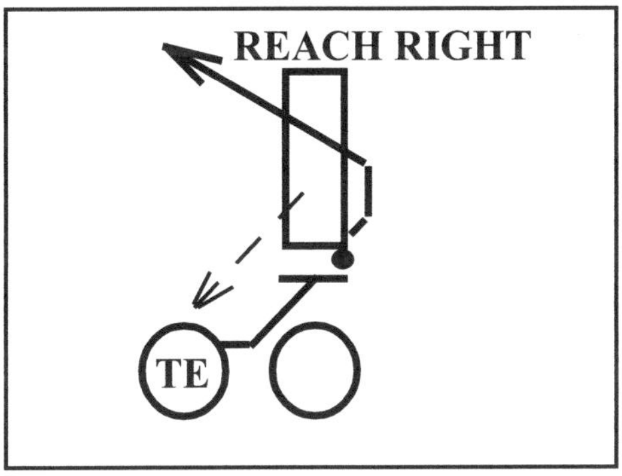


**Diagram 4.7**

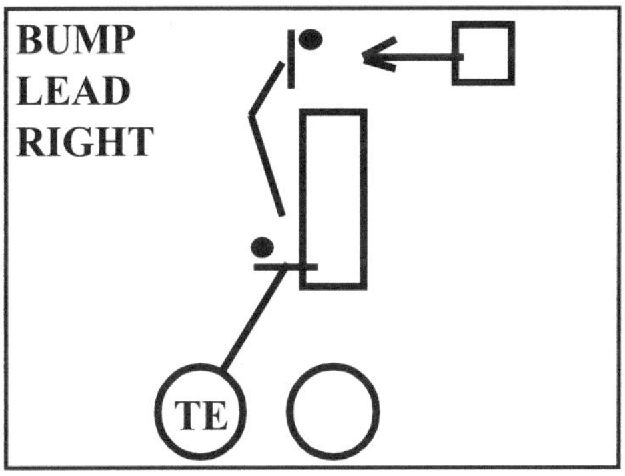


**Diagram 4.8**

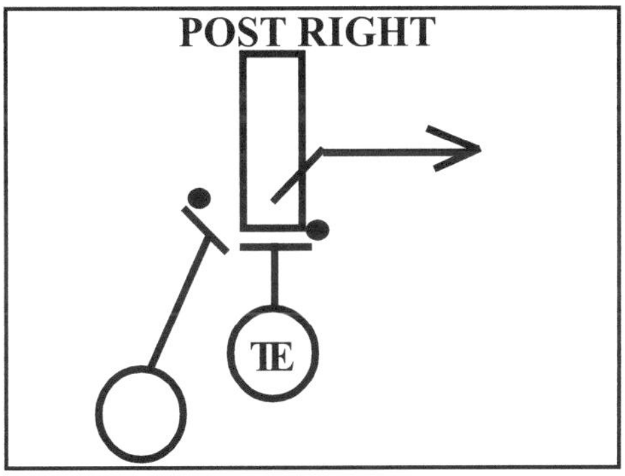


**Diagram 4.9**

### Cutoff Block

The last two tight end blocks are done with the tight ends and the spacing boards (Diagram 4.10). Those spacing boards are 16 feet long, an inch thick, and four inches wide. We need a set of spacing boards for our receivers to work on blocks. We want our tight end to be able to block at the cutoff. We will put a defender with a hand shield in a defensive back position above the play. We will then have him mix up the kinds of looks that he gives to the tight end. As the tight end comes across to the cutoff point, if that safety penetrates really hard, the tight end will gap block him by putting his head across the front. If the defensive player has backpedaled to the middle third, and then is coming, by the time we get to the cutoff point, we should be able to square up on him-and actually, at that point, use stalk block technique.

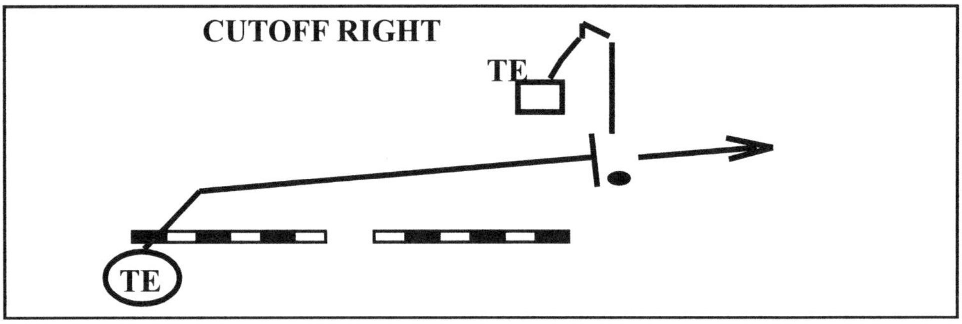


**Diagram 4.10**

You might also encounter a defender who is all the way over on the far side of the line of scrimmage, and thus simulate the tight end blocking all the way across at the cutoff. This will usually consist of the head across the front and gap blocking technique. That would simulate a sweep play to the opposite side from the tight end, common blocks that our tight ends have to make.

### Wall Block

The last one is our wall-off block, and it is the reason we taught the tight end how to do pulling technique (Diagram 4.11). The tight end will post up and pull down the line of scrimmage and turn up somewhere over the outside leg of the center or the outside leg of the guard on the far side. The tight end will wall off on a linebacker, who should be misdirected. Because most of these wall-off blocks are on our counter type of plays, where we start flow one way and bring a wingback through in the other direction, the tight end has to wall block through the hole and block the linebacker, who should, by that time, be scraping back to the hole. We tell the linebackers in the drill to take a shuffle step or two toward the middle and then come back on the tight end so that he has a fair chance to execute his blocking assignment.

## SPREAD END BLOCK

### Stalk

The first block is the one that the spread end has to use more commonly than anything else in our offense, and that is called the stalk block (Diagram 4.12). We have four or five parts to teaching this block that we think are very important. The first phase is similar to our shoulder skills in that we simply focus on the fit. We get our receivers

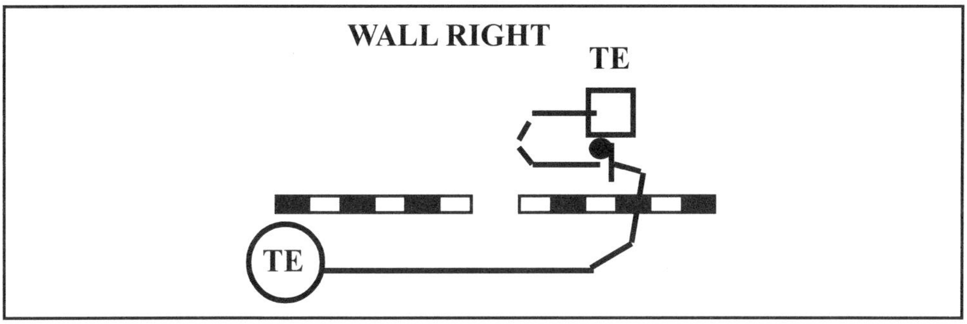


**Diagram 4.11**

and a defensive back, who could be another receiver simulating that position, locked up with each other. We start the spread end with his knees bent and his hands inside. Normally, we use a blocking shield to begin with during our early days of camp, but eventually, we throw the shield away and just have the spread end get his hands on the actual defensive player. We want him to bend his knees, put his hands on the inside of the man, and basically fit into the block and see what that feels like.

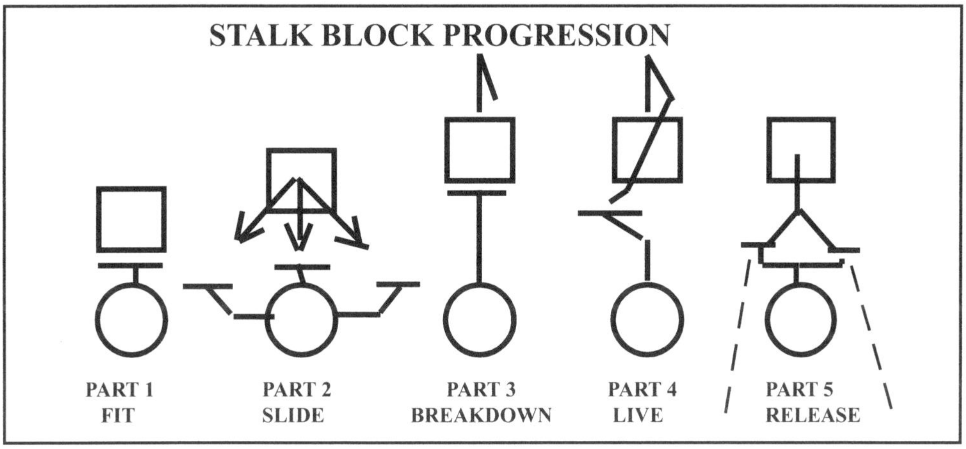


**Diagram 4.12**

In the second stage, we teach our spread end to slide his feet right and left. What we do in this part of the drill is take the defensive player and back him up to where he is about three yards away. We tell the spread end to get down as if he is ready to make contact. Now, the defensive guy has a three-way go. He can blitz fast to the inside, blitz straight ahead, or blitz to the outside. In this particular drill, we do not want him to head fake and try to go to one side or another. All we want from our spread ends is to get down in a good hitting position. If the defender goes inside, we slide left. We get squared up on him and we make the block. If the man goes outside, we slide to the right, get squared up on him, and make the block. If he goes straight ahead, we take him on as he comes. We are still fitting into the defensive man, but now we are doing it with him coming forward, so there is a little bit of contact involved as well.

In the third part of the stalk block progression, we have to learn when to break down. We just call this the breakdown phase. The defensive back takes the hand shield and he backpedals. When he breaks down and stops, or begins to drive forward, our spread end is going to break down at the same time. On the command, the spread end starts sprinting off the line of scrimmage. As soon as he sees the defensive man stop or break forward, he comes under control and gets into a good hitting position. There is no contact in this part of the drill. All we are really doing is teaching receivers when to break down. If the defender does not break down, we want the receiver to run him to the goal line every single time. If the defensive back is in man coverage and he has his back to the quarterback, turned inside-out facing the receiver, then we should run him to the goal line. He is not looking at anything else. Run him all the way to the goal line. That is two less bodies we have to step over when we pitch the ball.

The fourth phase of this progression, which is the live part, is the total combination of the other three. We call it "go live." Actually we are combining drills 1, 2, and 3. The defensive back will backpedal as the spread end comes off the line. When he starts to drive forward, our spread end breaks down. When he gets to a place where he can attack us, as he comes forward, we can let him go to his left, to his right, or up the middle. Our spread end, as he pushes off the ball, breaks down when the defensive back starts forward. If the man breaks inside, we slide inside and make the block. If the man goes straight ahead, we are in good position. If he slides to the outside, we slide to the outside to make the block.

The last thing we can do is have two spread ends facing each other. We have the spread end who is simulating the defensive player go ahead and use his release technique. We tell the spread end, who is simulating the blocker, to use his stalk block technique. Now, both of them can work techniques that they have to use all the time-and get better at doing them. One man is working on release techniques. He is going to drive forward and try to release inside or outside. The blocker is coming straight ahead. He is going to slide left, slide right, and then try to stop block the man who is trying to release around him. You should be able to turn this into a competition and have an especially successful drill.

**Crack Block**

There are four other blocks that we teach our spread ends (Diagram 4.13). These are all different from the tight end's blocks. The first one is called crack. We like this block. It is a change-up way to block the flank on option. Normally, our spread end is going to release and stalk #5 on the option. If we call option crack, then the receiver will post up inside, come flat down the line, and crack the fourth defender. The halfback, who usually blocks the fourth defender, will flare and stalk #5. It is just a switch in assignments between our spread end and our halfback.

When we crack block, we want to take a good pull step to the inside. We want to come flat down the line of scrimmage as far as we can go until we have to start turning up. It depends on how aggressive the strong safety is. If he sees option and he comes flying, we might have to go flat all the way down the line of scrimmage to crack him. If he backs off a little first, and then starts coming, or he read steps or freezes or pauses, by the time we get to a position to block him, we can usually start working up the field on that man. Our receiver should always start with a pull step down the line of scrimmage and then adjust to the strong safety from there. When we crack block, we want the head above the waist and the head in front so that it is legal.

**Cutoff Block**

Cutoff blocks can be simulated many ways (Diagram 4.14). A spread end who has to cut off a corner will simulate a play that goes away from the receiver in the opposite direction. Usually, in this case, there is no quarterback faking coming back to him. If the quarterback was faking waggle to our side, then we could fake a pass route and set up a waggle or a counter bootleg. But on a full-flood play away from the spread end, he must get inside out and cut off the corner on the backside.

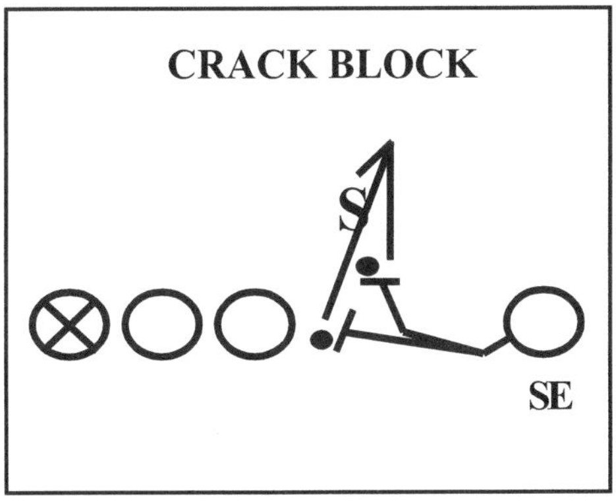


**Diagram 4.13**

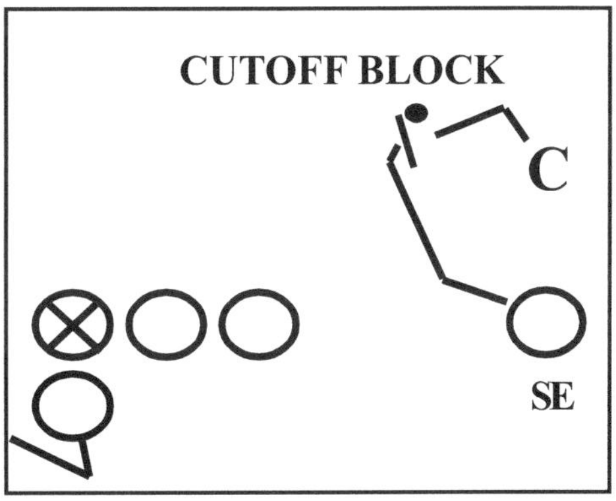


**Diagram 4.14**

**Down Block**

The last two blocks are related to each other (Diagram 4.15). A down block is done from what we call split alignment. Our spread end is four to six yards from the offensive tackle. He is going to come flat down the line of scrimmage and put his head across the front of the end man on the line of scrimmage. It is similar to a crack block, or a tight end's gap block. It is a down block, because we are coming from four to six yards outside, and we are blocking down on the defensive end. If the end manages to penetrate and beat us before we get there, we will climb to the next level. We usually do this in those instances where we know the end is a line-of-scrimmage player, and not a penetrator. We are going to come flat down the line of scrimmage, put our head across the front and block him. We would like to finish the block parallel to the line of scrimmage.

**Wall Rock Block**

The final block is what we call a wall rock block (Diagram 4.16). We are going to come down and fake the crack on the defensive end. We hope the end will penetrate or widen out to beat the spread end's block. When we use wall rock block, we are going inside to influence the end and make him either step outside or penetrate across the line of scrimmage. Then we go to the linebacker level and wall the linebacker off. In the meantime, we are going to run some kind of a play that comes up inside that defensive end. We are going to influence him to work out and then run the play inside of him.

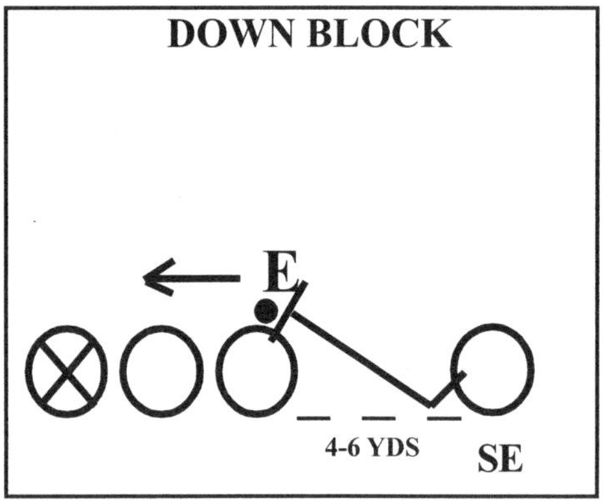


Diagram 4.15

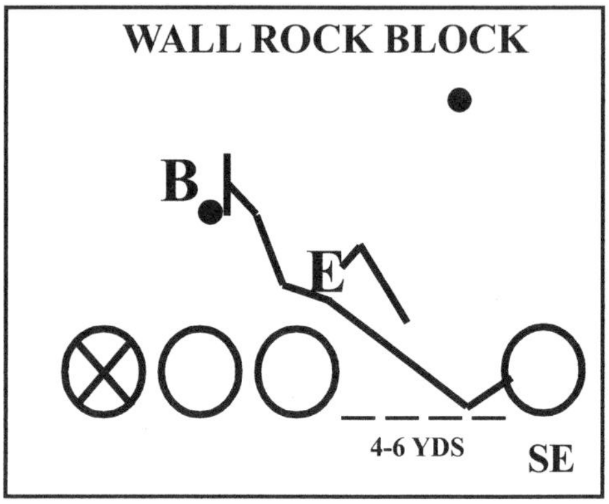


Diagram 4.16

## RELEASE PERIOD

The next part of the receiver practice plan is our release period, where we emphasize to our receivers the importance of getting off the line of scrimmage. We remind them that they cannot get jammed or held up at the line, and we back up our verbal instruction by working on their release techniques every day. We teach our receivers five release techniques, four of which are for both the spread end and the tight end and one of which is for the tight end only.

### Pull Release

The first release we work on is a pull release (Diagram 4.17). If our receiver needs to release to the outside, then he is going to take a pull step with his outside foot. On a pull release, he pull steps with his outside foot and then dips his inside shoulder, rip his inside arm through, and starts working vertically up the field as fast as he possibly can. This release can be used by a tight end on the line of scrimmage with the defensive end directly over the top of him, trying to jam him, or by a spread end with a corner in a press position, right up in his face. In either case, we need to be able to pull release around the defender. The spread end needs to pull release when he is running a fly route. We try to release outside on our fly routes to really stretch the secondary. Against a cover two-deep corner who is right his face and pressed, the receiver is going to release to his outside and run the fly. A tight end might have to do the same thing-take a pull outside release and then run his keep pass pattern, a seam route.

### Down Release

A down release is our second release (Diagram 4.18). It can be used by a tight end releasing off an outside backer or a spread end releasing off a corner-any situation where we want the inside release and also want to get vertical. If we are using a down release, we take a down step on a 45-degree angle to our inside. Our shoulder nearest to the defender must dip, and our arm nearest the defender must rip. We want the outside half of our body to dip and rip, and then get vertical up the field. One of the things that coaches should teach their players is how far up the field they should sprint at full speed. It is good to put a cone at least 10 yards up the field so that they do not just release off the line and gear down. That is not realistic to a game. They need to release off the line and then burst up the field.

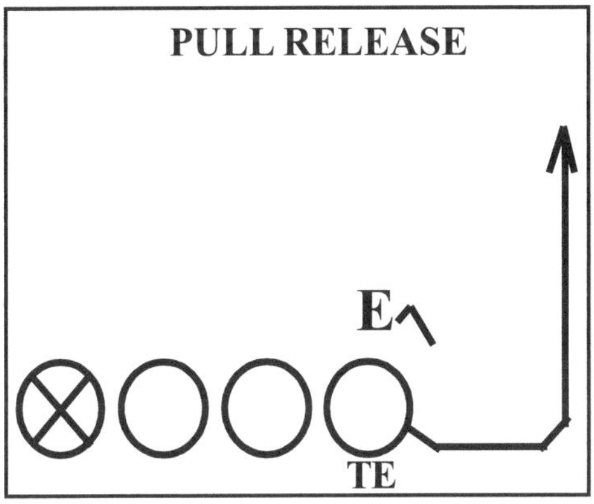


Diagram 4.17

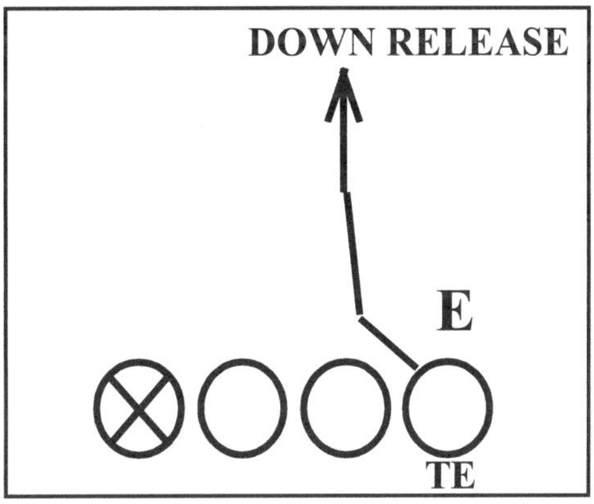


Diagram 4.18

**Fake Release**

On a fake release, we are going to fake to one side and release to the other (Diagram 4.19). We use several types of fakes, but a mere head fake can suffice. You can just throw your head to one side and then step with the opposite foot. You can step with left foot and then go to the right. Or you can combine both of those. You can head fake and step to the left, and then break to the right. Whatever works best for each receiver. There are a lot of players who like to do them in different ways. Most of the players I know choose to combine the head fake and the outside step and then try to release to the inside, or vice versa. They go head fake and step inside, and then release to the outside. There are times when our tight end has the release technique dictated to him (e.g., on a waggle route, a counter bootleg route, or a keep pass route). We do not let tight ends experiment with different types of releases on certain plays because of the way the base play is getting blocked. But there are also plenty of times that our tight end can fake release and run a drag route or crossing route to the other side. On pure drop-back, where we are protecting from inside out, our receivers can basically take the release they want.

**Swim Release**

On the swim release, obviously, we are going to try to swim right over the top of the defender, or right over top of the defender's hands and arms (Diagram 4.20). It is good to pin the arm in the direction you are releasing to. If the defensive man has his left arm sticking out at you as a receiver, and you are trying to release to your right (his left), then you want to take your hands and get his left arm off of you. You can pin his elbow, or you can swat his hands down. Whatever technique your coach is partial to, that will work. On the swim, we want to get the defender's hands off of us, and we want to punch right over the top of his arms with our near arm as we burst vertically up the field.

All of these releases-the pull release, the down release, and the swim release-can be combined. If you want to, you can head fake and swim or head fake and down release or head fake and pull release. You can combine the fake release with any of those.

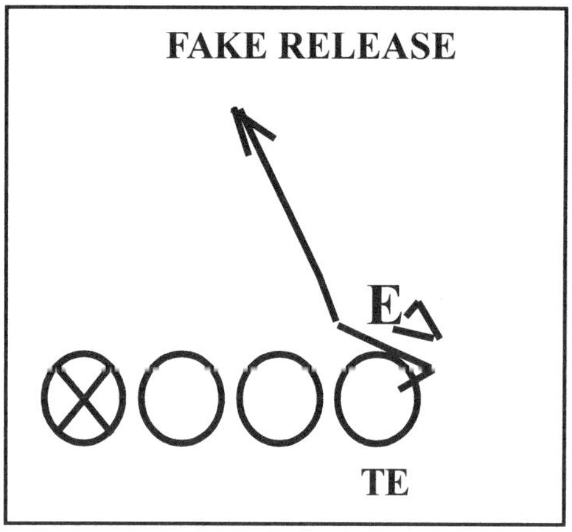


**Diagram 4.19**

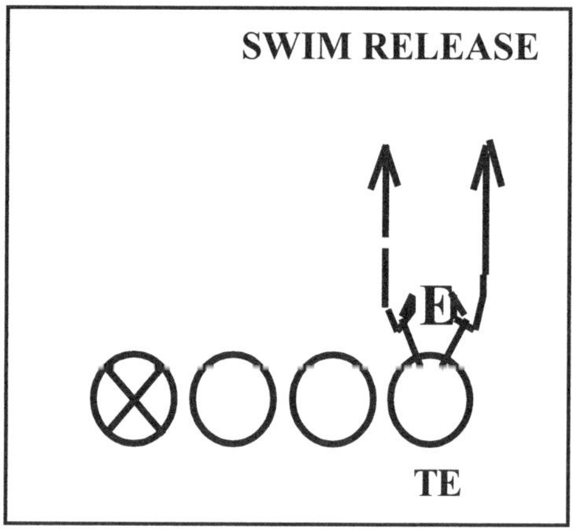


**Diagram 4.20**

**Block Release**

The last release that we want to talk about is strictly a tight end release (Diagram 4.21). This is a situation where the tight end has a 7 technique, or an inside shade, lined up on the inside half of him. This defender has shown a tendency to penetrate into the line of scrimmage and cause problems for our blocking scheme. The block release simply means that we are going to try to log this guy from outside in, but since he is penetrating, we cannot get it done without some help from the tight end. The tight end comes off on a block release. He is going to make contact with his head to the outside. If the ball is on the right, the tight end is going to make contact with the right shoulder; therefore, he steps with the left foot, hits the defender with the right shoulder, and in one continuous motion, bursts up the field. We do not want the tight end to hit, stop, hold, and then be late getting to his pass pattern. We want him to strike and take his second step in one continuous motion. It is done at full speed. There is no slowdown aspect. As he strikes, he runs his second step right to his route. There is no slowing down for the tight end, but if we make some decent contact, there is plenty of slowing down for that defensive player. Our guard, who has to log him, can pull, and since the defensive player has been slowed down, we can get that man log blocked.

### Pattern Drill

The next phase of the practice for our receivers is pattern drill. We have patterns that are specific to the tight end and those that are specific to the spread end, and we will work on those in this particular drill. We are trying to teach precise route running and are not necessarily working on releases. We are also not necessarily working on catching the ball. What we want to do is teach our receivers the proper depth, the proper footwork, the proper cut, and not have them mix and match other drills at the same time. You could work the release, the pattern, and catching the ball, all three at the same time. We often do that and call it passing with backs, or four-corner drill, or any type of team setting such as skeleton. The receivers get all that work in those periods, but in this drill, we are going to work on just the pass pattern and precise route running.

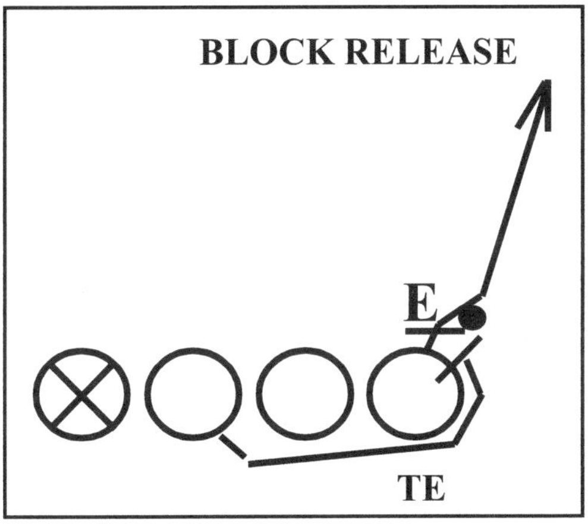


**Diagram 4.21**

## TIGHT END ROUTES

### Waggle Route

There are nine basic routes we teach the tight ends (Diagram 4.22). The first one is called our waggle route. On the waggle route, we want the tight end to take an inside or down release. We teach no faking in this release, because we do not want the defensive man leaning outside. We want the defensive player to seal down with us so we can log him. We want the tight end to take his down release inside and burst vertically, getting as deep as he can, running right down the numbers on the field. If the ball is snapped from the left hash, and our tight end was into the short side of the field, he will inside release, burst vertically to the numbers, and stretch the defense. It is amazing how many times over the course of a season a tight end will run that route, and the corner who is supposed to be in deep thirds, will come flying up and let the tight end go, leaving him wide open for a possible touchdown shot. We put a cone deep down the field and on the numbers. The tight end has to sprint to the cone. Normally, we put a cone at the depth that we want any kind of cut to be made.

**Step and Cup-Drag Route**

The second route is what we call step and cup-drag (Diagram 4.23). This is the backside route of our keep pass play for the tight end. If we need to worry about four rush players coming off the backside, blitzing the backside of the quarterback, we can run keep pass to the spread end side away from the tight end. Then we can use our tight end as a fourth blocker. The techniques on step and cup-drag call for the tight end to quickly check if either one of the two linebackers drops. He will step with his inside foot, cup back, and check the inside backer to the outside backer. If they both rush, he must stay in. If either one drops, he can go ahead and run his drag route over the center.

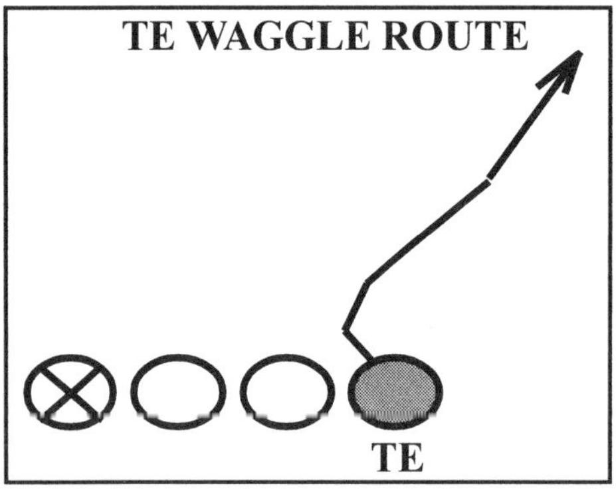


Diagram 4.22

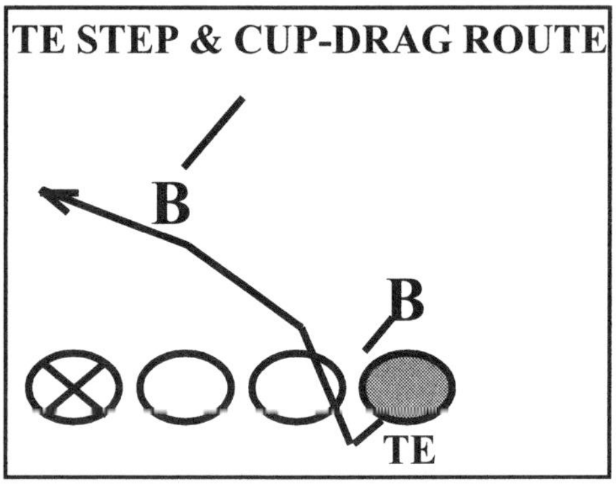


Diagram 4.23

**Seam Route**

The next route for the tight end is the seam route (Diagram 4.24). This is run when he has keep pass coming to his side. The tight end takes an outside release, usually a pull-step outside release, and he climbs to a point seven yards deep and three yards outside his alignment. As the tight end pull releases and gets up the field to that point, he is merely going to bend to the sideline and look over his outside shoulder for the football. The quarterback gets him the ball if the corner reacts to the flat route.

**Drag Route**

We run a lot of drags as crossing routes for our tight ends (Diagram 4.25). When we call tight end drag, or any route that has our tight end dragging, we usually show play action to the tight end side and have him drag back across to the other side. In that particular case, we want the tight end to drag on a shallow route and work for a point six yards deep all the way at the opposite sideline. If the defenders are reacting to play action, they usually overrun the tight end, and by the time they realize it, he is wide open in the opposite flat. We can use any kind of release, and we encourage our tight ends to use their fake releasing and so forth.

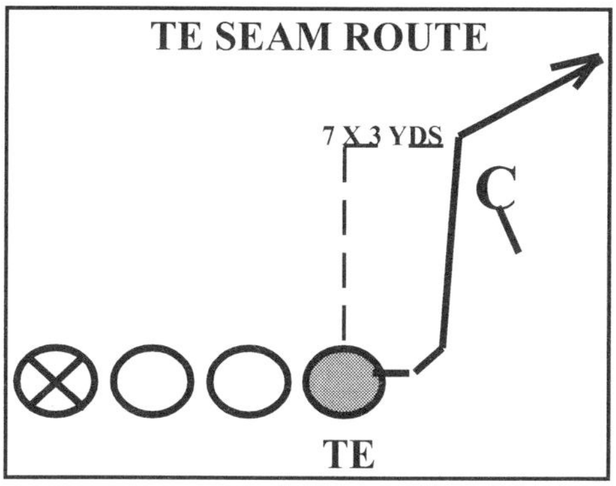


Diagram 4.24

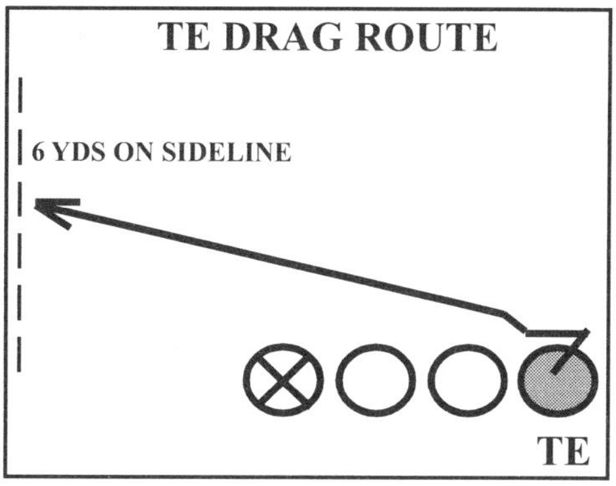


Diagram 4.25

**Hook Route**

Our hook route is similar to a spread end's curl route, which we also teach to the tight ends; therefore, we need to differentiate between the hook and the curl (Diagram 4.26). On the hook route, our tight end is on the backside of a play-action pass. We feel comfortable with releasing the tight end, and we do not need him to block. On a hook route, we are going to release outside. We will take a pull-step release and get vertical. We burst vertically to a point 14 yards down the field, and then we hook up. If the ball was snapped from the hash mark, and the tight end was into the short side of the field, we want him to get as wide as the numbers and then hook up and slide to an open area. If we show play action away from him, he is on the backside for the quarterback, and he is almost always open.

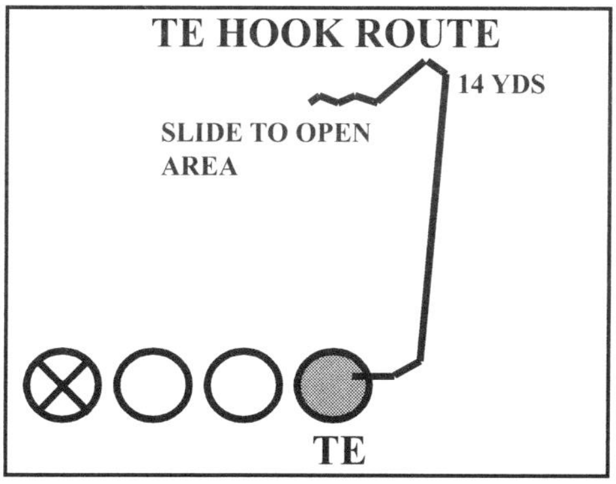


Diagram 4.26

**Crossing Route**

We use the crossing route for a tight end when he is on the backside of waggle, or for our counter bootleg play (Diagram 4.27). On this particular play, we want him to take an inside release, and we do not care how he sets it up because we are not trying to log the backside of the waggle. The tight end takes any kind of release he wants, but he has to release inside. He can combine pull release with fake, or down release with fake, or swim, or whatever. But he needs to release inside and get vertically down the field as fast as he can. We would like him to be between the two hash marks. He works to the area somewhere between 10 and 15 yards deep, where he is behind the linebackers. If there is a free safety in the middle of those two hash marks, or any safety, or any rotated defensive back in the middle, he breaks it off and stays in the middle of the two hash marks. We do not want him to cross the hash mark and work to the outside of the field. If there is no safety in the middle, we tell him to run right down through the middle of the field and be the deep threat. If we throw the ball back, this should be a touchdown shot.

**Hitch Route**

We teach the tight end a hitch route (Diagram 4.28). He has a lot of hitch routes in our offense, especially if we are running a smash combination. The tight end will basically burst off the line of scrimmage. When he gets to six yards of depth, he just turns and faces his numbers to the quarterback. There are other ways to coach the hitch, but this is very simple and direct.

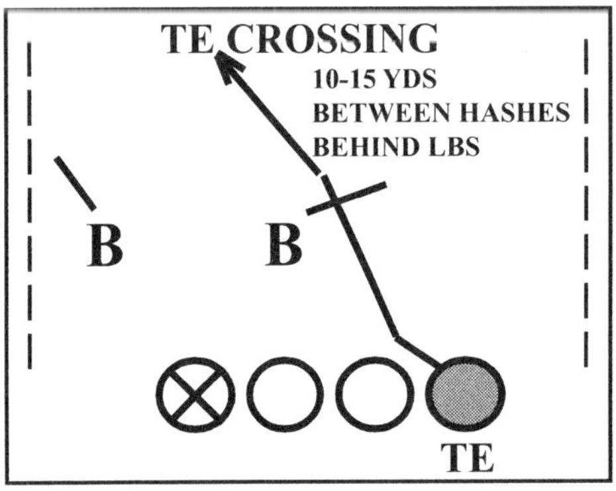


**Diagram 4.27**

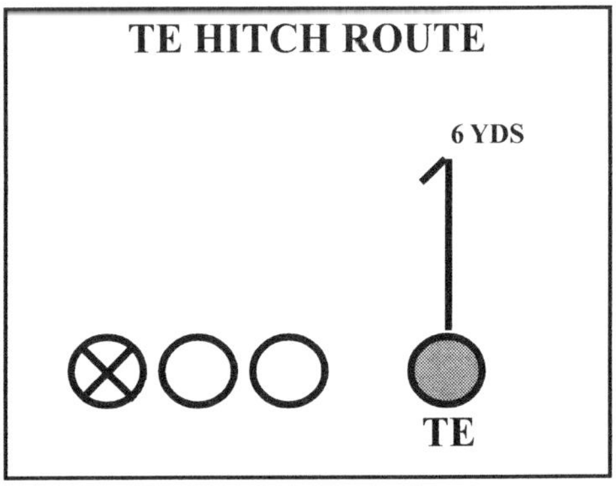


**Diagram 4.28**

**Out Route**

For the tight end, the out route can be run at 12 yards back to 10, if you have a quick tight end (Diagram 4.29). On a later-developing pass play, you can run it at 16 back to 14, or 14 back to 12, whatever times out best with your quarterback and receivers. Normally, when we do the out, we have our tight end in a flexed position. He is either flexed from the tackle or spread from the tackle, using spread end rules in a wide receiver stance. We are going to burst up the field, try to get the corner to turn his shoulders one way or another, and then break back to a point 12 yards deep. As we make this break, we want to lean forward into the cut, accelerate our arms as if we are going to go deep, and then plant and break. He also could run speed outs, where he does not come back to the ball, but simply rounds it off and tries to go full speed through the route. Right now, we are coming back, in the traditional sense, on a lot of our out routes.

### In Route

Last, but not least, we teach the tight end an in route (Diagram 4.30). Basically, it is a route that is anywhere from 14 to 18 yards deep, depending on how it times up with both the speed of your tight end and whatever passing action you're using. In this case, our receiver can go straight down the field and break to the inside. When he gets to his landmark, anywhere from 12 to 18 yards, he breaks flat across the line and is basically running away from any man coverage. As he breaks across, he settles in any hole in the zone he can find. Something similar to that is what we call a dig route. At 10 yards, we have our receiver fake to the post, and then at 18 yards, he breaks back across the field. We get the corner to back up, work to the middle, and then break away from him, creating separation to the inside.

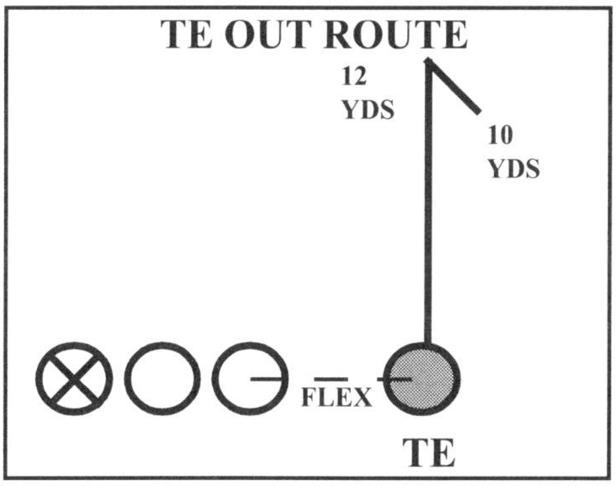


**Diagram 4.29**

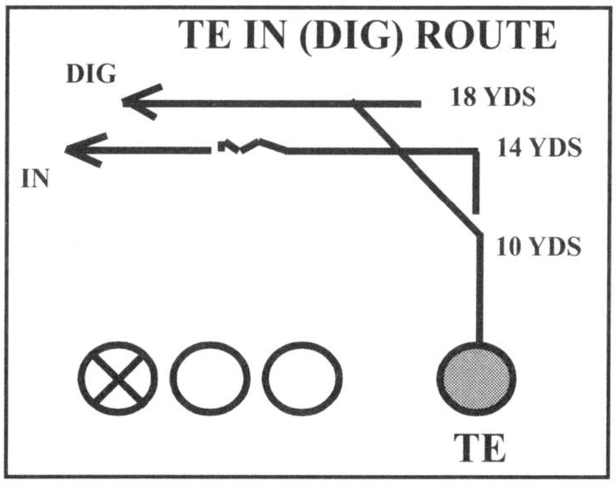


**Diagram 4.30**

## SPREAD END PATTERNS

### Post Route

We have nine basic patterns for the spread end as well (Diagram 4.31). They're obviously different and usually done from the wide receiver position. The first one is our post route. Our spread end will take his split, and as he pushes vertically about 12 yards, he breaks to the post. Most of our post routes are skinny. We want them to be a vertical cut, not really flat, where we come across to the middle of the field. In fact, what we would really like to do is split the area between the corner and the free safety as they backpedal into thirds. We want to stay away from the free safety. The spread end post route is going to split those two defenders. We want him to stay outside the hash mark when he runs a post.

### Out Route

The out route can be 12 back to 10, 14 back to 12 (Diagram 4.32), 16 back to 14, or

18 back to 16, whatever you want to teach, based on the timing of your play and the speed of your end. We want to capture one of the shoulders of the defensive back and get him to open his shoulders one way or another. We usually push vertically to a point about 14 yards, and then break back to 12. We have gotten a lot of mileage from out routes here in the last two years. Our quarterbacks are getting adept at throwing that particular pattern, our receivers are running the pattern very well, and we have a very high completion percentage with out routes. One of our favorite combinations is off waggles, keep passes, and counter bootlegs.

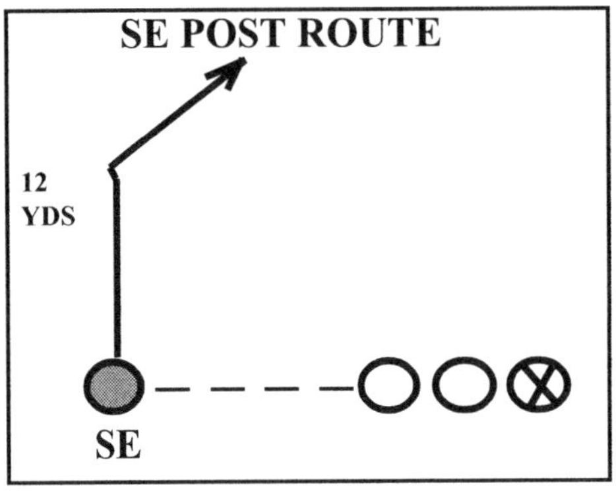


**Diagram 4.31**

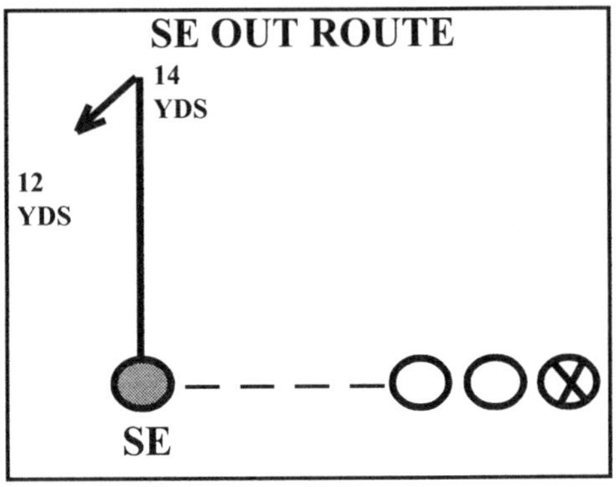


**Diagram 4.32**

**Fly Route**

One of the things we always insist on is, if we run a fly route, we want to release outside the corner at all times (Diagram 4.33). There is no excuse for releasing inside the corner. If the corner is pressed right up in your face, and you are assigned to run a fly, then you must take a pull-step outside release to get outside him. We want to get to a point six yards down the field, get the corner to lean one way or the other, and then burst outside of him. Obviously, if we can get him to lean to the inside, that is best. Somehow or another, we want to get his shoulders turned, or get him to squat his feet (fake hitch), and then release to the outside of him, bursting north and south up the field.

**Dig Route**

The dig route for the spread ends is the same as the tight ends, in terms of the route depth (Diagram 4.34). We want our receiver to sprint to 12 yards down the field, break to the post, and at 18 yards, once he has the corner really running with him, break flat across the line of scrimmage. If it is man coverage, he will run away from the man. If it is zone, he will sit in the open areas of the zones.

**In Route**

We also teach the spread end to run an in route (Diagram 4.35). The depth can be anything you want it to be-14, 16, or 18. We use a 16-yard in. We are going to push north and south and then break flat, parallel to the line of scrimmage, and burst away from man coverage. Or, if it is zone, as we break across the field, we will find the open zone and sit in it.

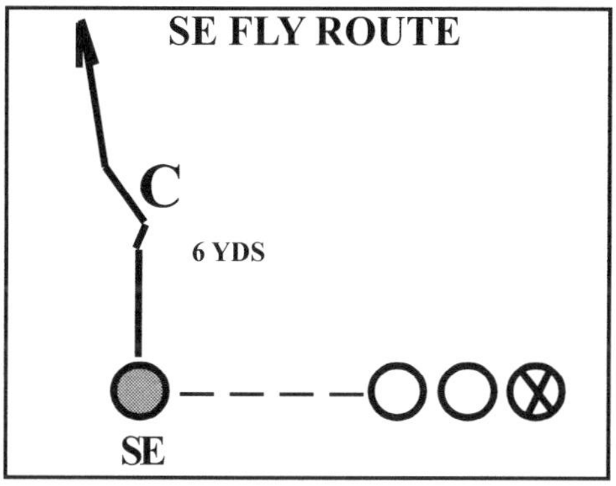


Diagram 4.33

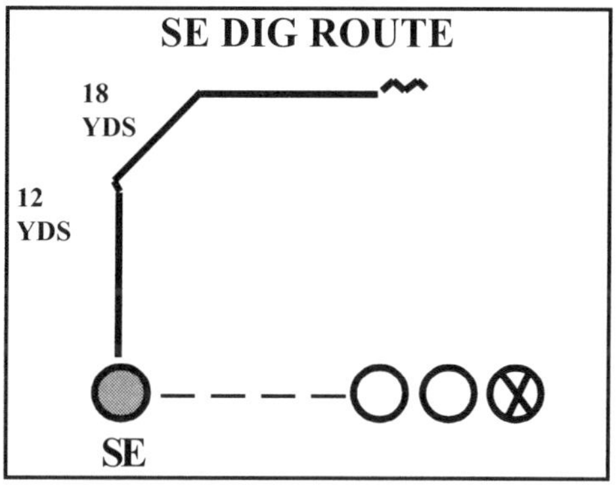


Diagram 4.34

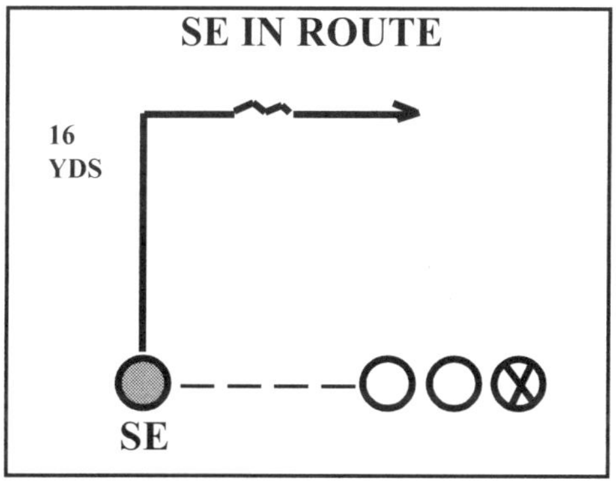


Diagram 4.35

## Angle Flag or Q Route

On the front side of our counter bootleg play, our spread end has been running what we call an angle flag route (Diagram 4.36). The angle flag is a push vertical, about four steps on a 60-degree angle, and then a burst deep to the numbers. Recently, we've started to work on a route we call Q route, which is similar to the angle flag. We want our spread end to burst vertically for about 12 yards. Somewhere around 12 yards, we want him to stick and step inside. He can head fake at the same time. But it is just one step to the inside, that is all we want. We want him to basically push off his left foot, stick step inside, plant his right foot, and then roll over and just bend the pattern to the area somewhere around 20 to 22 yards at the sideline. As he looks over his outside shoulder, that action bends his shoulders enough so that the quarterback can get the ball in there. Normally, in order to hold the corner, someone will be in the flat when we run the Q. I have seen people also run the post corner, where they come down, break to the post, and then break to the corner. Our Q route pretty much does that for us, but faster, much faster, using the slightly different technique of a stick step inside, roll over back outside, and burst.

### Slant Route

Our slant route can be run off a three-step drop, and also off our trap-option pass action (Diagram 4.37). We are going to come off the line of scrimmage and attack the outside shoulder of the corner, trying to create width. When we get to six yards, we are going to make a skinny break. We want to break on an angle that is about halfway between 45 degrees and 90 degrees. So you can call it a 22-degree angle if you want, but it is halfway between a 45 and a flat break. We will gear down in the open seam and run away from man coverage.

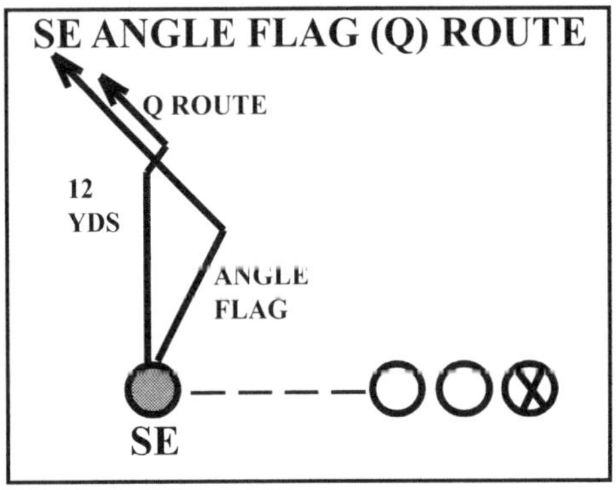


**Diagram 4.36**

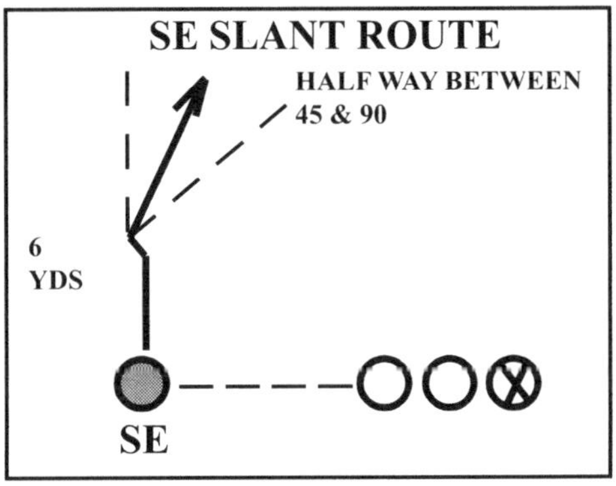


**Diagram 4.37**

### Curl Route

Our curl route is very specific (Diagram 4.38). We are going to split about 12 yards between the spread end and the tackle. We do not want to be over-split on the curl route, because we are going to threaten the flat with another one of our receivers. On the curl route, for the first two to three steps, we stem slightly inside. Then we break vertically up the field. We want to really burst, and we want to run like we are going to run a fly route. At 12 yards, we are going to plant our outside foot and come right back down the stem of our route. Once we start down the stem, we can slide to an open area, if we need to do that, in order to be in a good passing lane back to the quarterback. Normally, we simply come right down the stem of the route. If the corner is going to really sit on this, then in combination with the curl, we can run a route called stutter, where at 12 yards you stutter your feet, or basically gear down, and then burst on the fly. The stutter and the curl route work hand in hand.

### At 5 Route

The last route is what we call an "at 5 route" (Diagram 4.39). If you are going to put your spread end in a split alignment four to six to eight yards from your tackle, this becomes a valuable alternative on the backside of waggle. The spread end will step down as if he is going to sweep block for just one step. Next, he climbs vertically to a point about five yards up the field, and then he becomes the crossing receiver, just as the tight end was on the backside of waggle. He will start down the middle of the field, and we want to keep him right between the middle of the two hash marks. If there is no safety between the hash marks, he is going to split the hashes and go right down the middle and deep. If there is a safety between the hashes, somewhere between 10 and 15 yards he breaks it off and stays between the hash marks, not crossing the hash marks to the outside of the field.

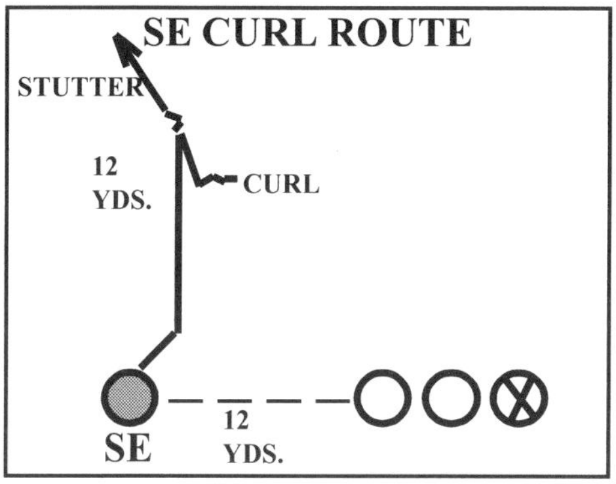


Diagram 4.38

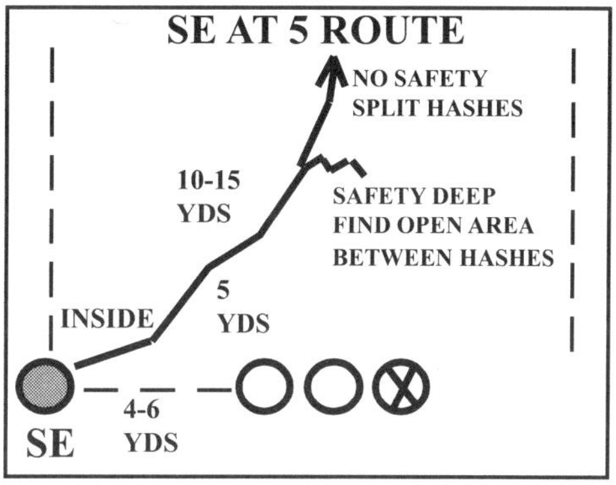


Diagram 4.39

## BALL DRILLS

As you notice when you go through this practice plan, the receivers work on releasing off the line of scrimmage in a separate drill. They work on patterns in another drill. And then they work on ball drills, which is another type of drill. That is really what comprises the three parts to running a route: your release, your pattern, and your actual catching of the football.

Next, I am going to discuss the ball drills that we do. There is nothing revolutionary here. All of you who have been coaching for quite a while probably have lots of different ball drills that you do, and they are probably the same as these. Or maybe you have some different ones that are better. But, in any case, these are the ones we believe cover the fundamentals that we need.

### Tuck and Cover Drill

The coach pairs his receivers up, with one football for every two guys he is working with (Diagram 4.40). We tell the receivers to throw the ball at all different strike points. We want them to throw the ball right at their face, over their right shoulder, over their left shoulder, and at their numbers. They should throw it low, throw it low to the right, throw it low to the left. We work on catching the football in all those different ways. They just play catch. It is that simple. But we want them to concentrate on the fundamentals of catching the football. We tell our guys that the only catch made with your thumbs together is the ball that comes at your upper body, straight down the middle. We tell them to put their pinkies together for all the other catches, and turn their thumbs out, so that they are not fighting the ball or pressuring the ball away from them. We also emphasize the fact that as soon as they catch the ball, they have to tuck it away. Then, if contact is going to occur, they can cover it up. Those are the three most important points that we try to accomplish in this drill: catch, tuck and cover, and catch the ball at different strike points. We do not want our receivers to always catch the ball in one place in this drill, because that makes it really too easy on them. We want them to practice making those catches that are away from their body, that are down low. There are going to be a lot of times in games when the ball comes and it is not going to hit you right in the exact strike point that you expect.

**Bad-Ball Drill**

The next drill that we do with our receivers is what we call a bad-ball drill (Diagram 4.41). There are lots of ways to set this up, but what we do is have a line of receivers standing one behind the other. The coach will be back five, 10, or 15 yards away, whatever he deems necessary in terms of the length of the throw. Each receiver takes off across the field. The coach is going to throw them a bad ball. We want the ball to be thrown low. We want the ball to be thrown high. We want the ball to knuckle by taking the ball and holding it at the back tip and throwing it with a locked elbow. The receivers really have to concentrate on catching it. The first guy runs across the field and catches a ball from the coach. Next, he runs over to the other side of the drill. Then the next receiver will go. You can get a lot of reps on a lot of bad balls in a short period of time by doing this drill. We try to provide a five-minute period for ball drills every day, and we feel that you can get at least two ball drills per five minutes.

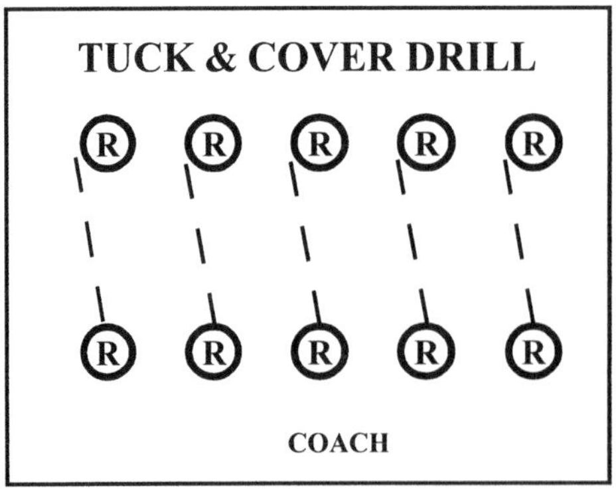


Diagram 4.40

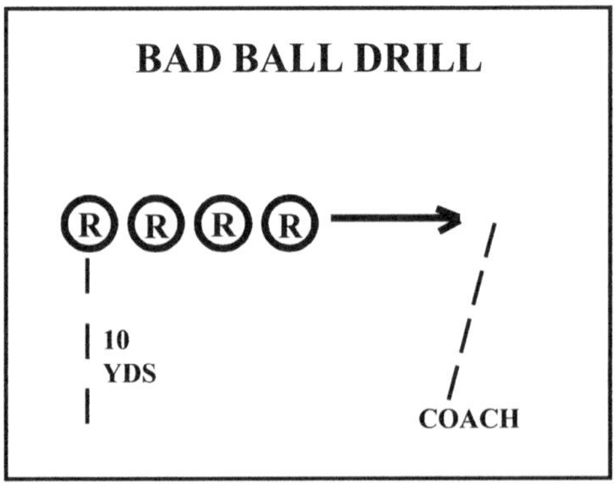


Diagram 4.41

**Break-Point Drill**

I want to mention two things about this drill: First, we do not work on the release, and second, we do not work on the pattern. All we are doing is putting receivers in the place where they would have finished their pattern and then having them accelerate to the football from what we call the break point. We are going to throw them the ball and work on the fundamentals of catching the football. If the ball is in the upper body, right down the middle, we will catch the ball with the thumbs together. If the ball is away from the body, up high, we try to catch that ball with the pinkies together and the thumbs spread out. What happens is, if the ball is away from your body, and you put your thumbs together, when the ball hits your hands, it tends to bounce off your hands and away from your body. Whereas, if you turn the thumbs out, then the ball hits your palms, and it tends to bounce back toward your body.

**One-Handed Catch Drill**

Our next drill focuses on the players concentrating so intensely that they can catch any football with just one hand (Diagram 4.42). We will throw the football over their shoulder, about where we want the fade ball to go. You can throw the ball up and over, and try to hit the outside shoulder. You can also throw a ball on more of a straight trajectory and have the receiver work on bringing that ball in with one hand. But the important thing here is, as many times as you do it with your right hand, you probably should do it twice that many times with your left hand, if you are a right-handed receiver-and vice versa, if you are left-handed. Our line of receivers will go straight down the field, and the coach will throw the ball in that direction, and they can work on catching the ball with just one hand. Then the next guy goes, and the next guy goes, until we are finished. As the receivers wait, the coach will run down quickly and throw the ball from that end down their way. Now the receivers are working with their left hand. The coach moves around, but the receivers do not have to move around. You save time in your drills, and you are not wasting time. This goes back to our racehorse practice philosophy.

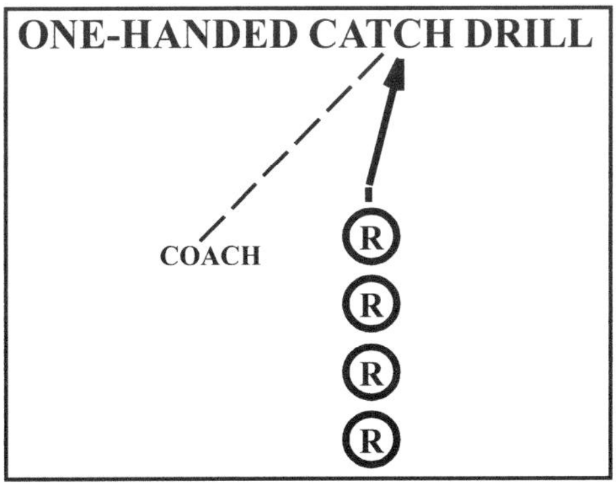


**Diagram 4.42**

## Turnaround Drill

In the turnaround drill, we simulate a man running a route (Diagram 4.43). He turns around quickly, and the ball is already on him. He has to focus, catch the ball, and get it tucked away, all within a relatively short period of time. You hear many coaches talk about throwing on the break. If the quarterback goes back and sees the receiver break, and he lets go of the ball, if he has some strength to his arm, that ball is going to be traveling before the receiver can get his eyes focused back to the quarterback. In that situation, the receiver has to have fast focus, good concentration, and the ability to get the ball tucked away when it is right on top of him. Sometimes the quarterback will see that a receiver is going to be open. He will be getting pressured in the pocket, and he will need to get the ball off a little bit early. Because of this, you must have your players trained to get their head snapped back around, to get their eyes trained on the football, to focus, to concentrate, and to get the ball locked away. The receivers are facing away from the coach. The receivers have their backs to the coach. We will tell them whether we want them to turn over their right shoulder or turn over their left shoulder. We want our receiver to snap his head around and get his shoulders around as quickly as possible in whichever direction we are working on. We work equally on both directions. The coach is going to give the command as he lets go of the ball. The ball is in the air by the time the receiver gets his head and shoulders snapped around. We usually do this drill from about 10 yards apart.

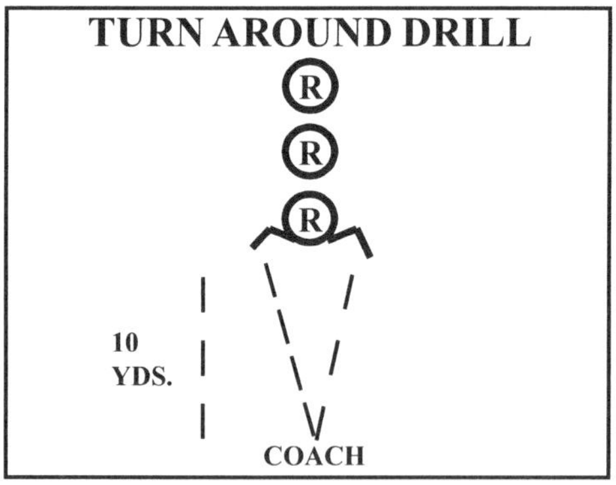


**Diagram 4.43**

## Comeback Drill

In this drill, the receiver is going to come back to the coach, or the quarterback, and catch the ball on the way back to him (Diagram 4.44). We take the release and the route out of this drill. All we work on is the actual coming back to the quarterback. You have heard a lot about receivers running a route with coverage on them and having to turn around, come back to the quarterback so that their numbers face the quarterback (so that the defender is behind them), and their body seals the defender from the throw. You can be open with guys close to you, as long as there isn't a man in the throwing lane between you and the quarterback-assuming the quarterback has pretty good zip on the ball and can get the ball there with confidence. When the receiver gets his shoulders snapped around, what you want him to do is be able to come back to the quarterback. If he just turns around and stands there, the defensive back can then react through him to the football and swat the ball down. If you have pushed the coverage enough to make a good cut, and you make the break, and, as you see the quarterback, you come back to him, you then have a chance to keep the separation between you and the defender, or at least keep your body between the ball and the defender. The receivers are about 10 yards away from the coach. The receiver who is going to catch the ball takes a step forward to simulate the last step in his pass pattern and then plants his foot and comes driving back to the coach. We want him to come right back down his stem toward the coach and we are going to throw him the football. You can have him plant his left foot and turn back over his right shoulder, or plant his right foot and turn back over his left shoulder. Once the ball is tucked away, we want to burst up the field. We do not want to get into the habit of catching the football and stopping. That is a bad habit that you want to teach your players to avoid. It is really important that as each kid catches the ball, he tucks it away, covers it up, and turns and bursts up the field. We put a line of cones about 10 yards up the field, so he has to break all the way past the cones. This helps the receiver to get used to catching the ball and turning upfield and running. You do not want your players catching the ball and falling to the ground, or catching the ball and slowing down. Once they have the ball in their hands, that is when the action should begin.

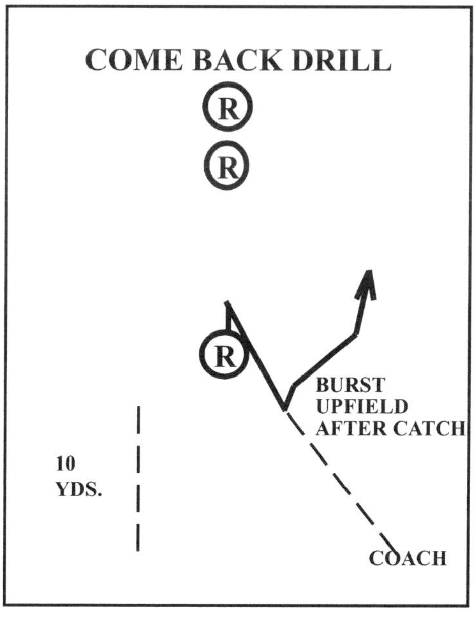


**Diagram 4.44**

## Sideline Drill

In high school and college, you only have to have one foot in bounds when you catch the football (Diagram 4.45). We teach our receivers the same drill that the pro coaches teach theirs. We learn to do our little tap dance on the sideline. For a number of reasons, we are going to teach them to keep both feet in. If they are concentrating on it, one foot for sure will probably stay in, maybe even two. We have had a lot of receivers make catches, right at the sideline, with both feet in bounds. Another reason is, if the receivers ever do make it to the pros, then they will have already been trained in those techniques. We know that sometimes a receiver is going to catch the ball on the dead run, get one foot down, and step out of bounds. But if this is coached into them thoroughly enough, they will tap dance on the sideline and try to keep both feet in. Sometimes that is not possible. It is not always possible at the pro level, either. But we are going to work on it right from the very beginning of their freshman year, all the way on through their career. We set a receiver who is going to catch the ball about five yards away from the sideline, and we have the extra receivers lined up right behind him. We take the final step of our route, one step forward, and then break back toward the line of scrimmage toward the sideline. The coach is going to throw the ball, simulating a quarterback throwing the ball on a comeback or an out. Our receiver will catch the football and try to tap dance right on the sideline, keeping both feet in, and catching the ball. Sometimes they even drag their feet and fall down as they are catching the ball and trying to keep both feet in bounds. We like to get each receiver four or five throws on two different drills every time we do a ball drill period.

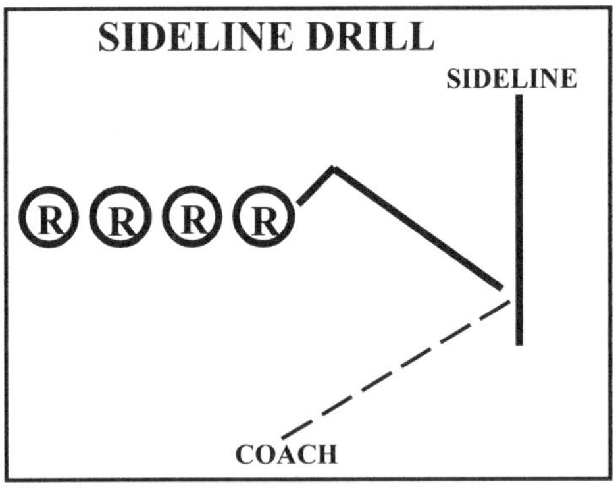


**Diagram 4.45**

## Distraction Drill

We like this drill because it forces our receivers to concentrate, which is a big help, especially if they are going to be try to catch the ball in a crowd (Diagram 4.46). Our distraction drill can be set up lots of different ways. One of the easiest ways we know of is to have two receivers serve as the distractors. Our line of receivers is going to run straight across the field. The coach, from about 10 yards away, throws the football right between the two distractors. The distractors, only two to three yards apart, wave their arms, jump up and down, and put their hands between the ball and the receiver's eyes to disrupt his concentration. As the receiver runs across the field, he has to focus on the football, keep his concentration on the football, and not allow those players to be any kind of a distraction to him at all. As he catches the football, he goes across to the other side. Once the receivers are done running in one direction, then they start from the other side and run in that direction, and we throw the football. Now, they are looking over their left shoulder instead of their right shoulder, as they run horizontally across the field. One variation that helps out is to have two lines of receivers on the opposite sides of the field, and have both run across in opposite directions. You throw the ball to the back receiver, and the front receiver acts as a distractor. We try to simulate those game-day situations as much as we can.

**Gauntlet Drill**

The final ball drill that we do is a drill we call gauntlet (Diagram 4.47). Here, we really try to make the receivers concentrate on catching the football. We do that by trying to strip the ball, trying to knock those receivers down, anything that may cause problems for the receiver. In this phase of the drills, we are working on making sure that each receiver has caught the ball and tucked it away. As he turns up through the gauntlet, we try to do everything we can to get that ball out of his hands. We have two lines of receivers forming a gauntlet, or a tunnel, with the receiver turning up into that gauntlet. The players in the gauntlet are going to strip him, they are going to bang him with hand shields, they are going to bump him. They are going to do anything they can to try to make him lose the football. We put our receivers really close to the gauntlet. As they start to run, the coach, from about 10 yards away, will throw the ball at the first line of gauntlet defenders. As the receivers come across, they catch the ball and have to turn up immediately into the gauntlet. This drill gives them good practice at turning up the field and getting the ball tucked away quickly so that it does not get stripped.

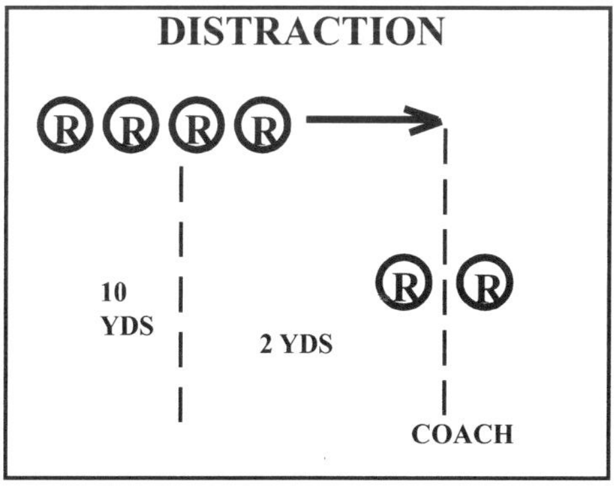


**Diagram 4.46**

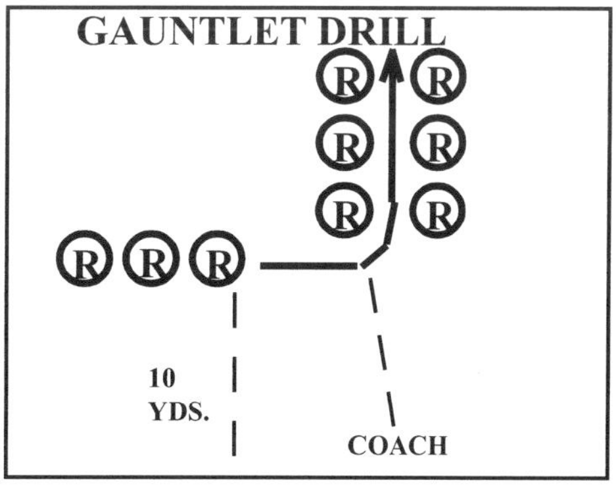


**Diagram 4.47**

Those are the basic ball drills that we do. They are not revolutionary, and I am sure that you as a coach have come up with even better ball drills than this. But these are the things that we want our receivers to concentrate on when they catch the football: catch, tuck and cover, getting upfield, learning how to come back to the quarterback, learning how to keep their feet in bounds, learning how to concentrate on the football when they are getting distracted, learning how to keep the ball tucked away when they are getting swatted and stripped and bumped and everything else. We do the drill five minutes almost every day of the whole year. When we first start doing it in training camp, and then again the first day of spring practice, we allow 10 minutes for the period so our coaches will have plenty of time to introduce all these ball drills to the players and get reps on it. Shortly thereafter, it becomes a five-minute drill.

## PASSING WITH BACKS

The last part of the individual portion of our receiver practice plan is what we call "passing with backs" (Diagram 4.48). Passing with the backs concerns the receivers and the running backs getting together with the quarterbacks and running pass routes. This can be an individual drill, or it can be a group drill. We do it at least once a week each way. You can have more than one drill going on at the same time. Sometimes we have had as many as four different drills going on at the same time, where our quarterbacks are just dropping back and throwing a certain route to a certain type of receiver. If we want to get a lot of work on throwing the out route to our wide receivers, we will have one quarterback do that. Possibly another quarterback will be working on throwing the corner route to his tight end, or the angle flag, or the crossing route. We just give them one route at a time in that particular setting.

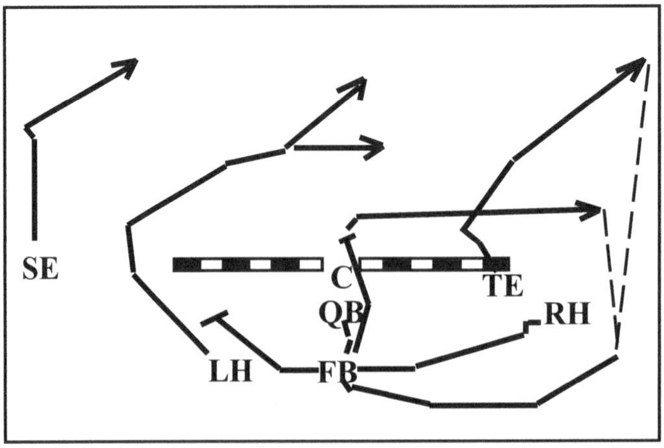


**Diagram 4.48**

We also try to do a lot of group work as well, where the entire backfield and the ends run through what they would do on a certain passing play. Take, for instance, the 129 waggle, which is where we fake the sweep to the left and the quarterback keeps the ball and bootlegs out to the right. In this case, our tight end is going to take a down release and go vertically and get deep on the numbers. Our split end is going to run a skinny post and stay outside the hash mark on his side. Our left halfback is going to run the crossing route, where he can split two deep or break across the middle. Our right halfback is going to go in motion and fake the sweep and then block the backside of the quarterback. Our fullback is going to block the linebacker if he is a blitzer, and if not, he is going to slip out into the flat. The quarterbacks come up, and they call the cadence. All the backs and all the tight ends run the pattern. One thing that you can do to spice up the drill a little bit is to put a free safety in for the quarterback to read, or else put some corners in and have them just back up or come forward. As a coach, you can direct what you want the defensive backs to do, so that you can also control what the quarterback is going to see in terms of a read, and who he should be throwing to. We tell our quarterbacks when they do this drill that if we repeat the same pattern, they should not throw the ball to the same guy twice. We want our quarterbacks to keep mixing up their throws so that they get practice at throwing all parts of a particular play.

# CHAPTER 5

## The Wing-T Offensive Linemen

This chapter will deal with every technique that an offensive lineman has to use in our offense. We will begin with the qualities that we look for in our linemen, position by position, beginning with the offensive center. I start with the offensive center because, in our offense, we put the best people we have down the middle. We need a strong, athletic center, just like our quarterback and fullback. We feel our football team is similar to a baseball team. In a baseball situation, you want to build strength up the middle-your pitchers, your catchers, your middle infielders, your center fielders. Those people are vital to the operation of your baseball team. It is exactly the same with the wing-T. We want to have a strong center, a very good quarterback, and an outstanding fullback in this offense to make it work as effectively as possible.

As we look for the desired qualities in our offensive linemen, we go through several testing procedures. We test our players on anything we can think of that will give us useful information. We use the same combine workout that the NFL scouts use. We will test all our players in their height and their weight, their bench press, their 40-yard-dash speed, their vertical jump, their broad jump, their 20-yard shuttle times, and the list goes on and on. We test them in about as many areas as we can come up with, areas we think will give us useful information on the athletic abilities of our players.

Once we have that figured out, we take all the "big men" and we look at their test scores. We find out which ones are the best overall athletes. Those are the players who are candidates to play center for us. Often, we have two or three different players who can play center. Our second opening for a big man is at tackle. Next come the offensive guards, who don't have to be big, but do have to be among your best athletes. As a clarification, when I say the best big man plays center, I mean that he should be one of our finest athletes, in terms of his test results, who is also a big man. He is the guy we are going to put at center. The guards should be very good athletes, without respect to size, although, clearly, the bigger they are, the better it will be for our offensive line.

### CENTERS AND THE SNAP TECHNIQUE

We must first teach our center the proper hand-up technique. We feel that we can take anybody and teach him the snap technique that we use in the wing-T offense, so our center doesn't have to be someone who has played the position before. Regardless of his experience, in time, he will learn to execute the snap technique properly. The best way I can illustrate this point is through the following example: If I were at a clinic lecture someplace, in front of a large audience, I might pick out somebody who has played football, yet has never snapped the ball before in his life. In front of all those people, I could teach that person how to snap the ball in a little over five minutes. In short, the techniques we teach our players are both easily learned and easily taught at every level.

We want our quarterbacks and our centers to work every single day on the hand-up technique, which is what most people refer to as the quarterback-center exchange, or just simply, the snap. The snap technique is the most important skill in football; after all, nothing else will happen if you do not snap the ball correctly. We teach our quarterbacks to put their hands straight up in the air, with their fingers pointing vertically north and south. They then turn their hand a quarter turn to the right, if they are a right-handed quarterback, or a quarter turn to the left, if they are a left-handed quarterback. The V between the thumb and the forefinger should point straight up to the sky. We want to take the hand and bring it down so that the hand is parallel to the ground when we stick our hand under the center. If we do that, we should be able to take the snap with one hand, and not use the left hand, if I'm a right-handed quarterback. The quarterback is going to be only wrist deep under the center.

When we teach snap progression, we teach a three-part progression to the center snap. The first thing we do is get the quarterbacks to hold the ball exactly the way they want it to come from the center. When the ball comes up the quarterback, we would like him to receive the laces in his hand, in order to get the ball into a passing grip as quickly as possible. We want the fat of the ball between the V of the thumb and the forefinger, and we want the quarterback to have his hand on the back half of the football. This is exactly how it should come up from the center.

There is no turn to the center snap. The center does not snap the ball and turn it as he snaps it. He brings the ball straight up. We describe this motion with the center's hand as the same motion he would use if he were down in the basement and had to turn on a lightbulb with one of those cords hanging down that turns the lightbulb on. The center is going to grab the cord and pull it. That is the movement that the center's arm and hand should take as he delivers the ball. As he brings the ball from the ground, he brings it straight up. The first few times that centers do this, their forearm will snag right across their thigh, and their thigh will bruise a little bit. But the bruising subsides quickly, and they learn how to handle it.

The three-part progression works like this: We have our center down in a good offensive lineman stance. The first part of the progression we call the fit. We want our quarterback in a fairly narrow stance. We want him to be only wrist deep under the center. We do not want him any further than wrist deep under the center. We want him as upright as we can get him. There will be a slight knee bend. The quarterback will take the ball and get in his good stance. He will hand it to the center, who then takes the ball from the quarterback and brings it down to the ground in the opposite motion that he would use to snap. He gets the feel of the ball, of where it should be as he hands it to the quarterback. He reverses the trajectory of his arm motion back down to the ground. After he has done that, he passes the ball back around to the side. The quarterback will take the ball again, put it in the good grip in which he wants to receive it, and pass it back to the center, who will again take the ball and bring it back down to the ground. The important point here is that our center must get a feel for where that ball has to come when he brings it up to the quarterback. We will repeat this hand-up as many times as we have to, until we feel that the center has that motion down.

The next part of the progression is called the six-inch snap. In this part of the progression, the center will take the ball and snap it to the quarterback. He is going to snap the ball from somewhere around his knees, at least six inches off the ground. All that happens right now is that the quarterback directs the center in terms of where that ball came back. The quarterback will tell him the ball did not come back far enough, or that it came back too far. It is too far to the left, too far to the right, turn to the left, turn to the right, whatever that direction might be. The quarterbacks really need to know how they want the ball, and your best center coach, a lot of times, after a few years in the program, will be your quarterbacks.

The third part of this progression is the full snap. At this stage, the center will use all his fundamentals. We would like the ball stretched out as far in front of that center's face as possible, because that gives our offensive line room where the defense has had to back off. Our center knows how the ball needs to come in, because we did fit. He knows how the ball should snap when he snaps the ball and how it should feel as he brings it up to the quarterback. We should be able to execute this snap in a short period of time, as long as we have coachable people. When fumbles occur, the quarterback and the center need to communicate. If that ever happens in a game, we give both players minuses, regardless of whose fault it was, because those two need to communicate with each other.

## OFFENSIVE GUARDS

Your offensive guards will actually have a lot of fun playing in this offense, because they get to pull, trap, block down, kick out, and lead the backs on the sweep. The wing-T is not the kind of offense where your linemen either go straight ahead or straight back all day long. In this offense, your linemen have a lot of fun because they get to do everything. They really get to showcase their talents and their abilities.

The offensive guards must have good coordination. They must be able to pull, and also to maintain their body control and balance as they pull. There are a lot of athletic movements involved in the offense, and so the offensive guards must have good body control and must be fine athletes. They have to be big enough to block down on a defensive lineman. Sometimes people think you can put the 5-9, 160-pound kid at offensive guard. Maybe that will work in high school, but it certainly will not work in college. There are many times when guards have to block on or block down against some big football players in college football. Consequently, guards have to be at least big enough to block down on a large-size defensive lineman.

The guards also have to be fast enough to pull out on the flank and lead a swift running back on the sweep or on an option play, or the quarterback on the waggle. The guards must have good athleticism to be able to pull and lead those backs on the sweep. The average center in our league weighs about 250-260 pounds. He is usually at least 6-2. The offensive guards in our league are actually big people. They are usually in the 6-3 range and about 270 pounds. In high school, I know that you are not going to have those kinds of kids. You cannot recruit who you have to play with. Therefore, you are going to have a mixture of different body types that are going to be on your offensive line. I would suggest to you, though, that you put your best big man at center, your quickest big man at left tackle, and then your best line athletes at offensive guard.

## OFFENSIVE TACKLES

These are the big linemen in your offense. They are the players who are going to be asked to block down on defensive tackles or block straight ahead with "on" technique on defensive tackles. They must have considerable size to play that position. We say to put your best line athletes at guard, and then take your big men and find out who is going to be your center. The rest are tackles. I would say your quickest tackle needs to be on the left side, assuming you have a right-handed quarterback; on the right side, if you have a left-handed quarterback. You want to be able to protect the quarterback's blind side. If he is your best athlete, you do not want him to be taking a lot of blind-side shots. We want that guy to play 11 games. The tackles are our largest people. They do the least amount of pulling, yet they do some pulling. We do cross-train all of our players to play all of our positions. Therefore, they must be athletic enough, and they must have quick feet to be able to execute those pulling assignments. Also, more important, they must be able to execute a gap or a down block, where they have to step down inside and cut off penetration, or block down on a defensive tackle who is lined up inside of them. Our offensive tackles are great angle blockers. They must be able to block down on angles. We are always going to try to scheme to get our tackles to be able to block on angles as often as we possibly can in our offense.

## OFFENSIVE LINE PRACTICE PLAN

The next topic I am going to discuss is that which covers all the techniques that we teach during the offensive line practice plan. Many of these skills will be repeated by other position groups, because we teach blocking skills and shoulder skills to all of our position players.

**Shoulder Skills**

The first thing we do during practice with our offensive linemen is shoulder skills period (Diagram 5.1). If you want to use sleds, or if you want to come out from chutes and boards and do those kinds of skills instead of shoulder skills, that is fine. If you want to combine them, that is fine, too. We do use the sled at times, and we will use chutes and boards next year, at times. But the first thing we do on the first day of every practice and training camp, spring ball, whatever, is we teach shoulder skills.

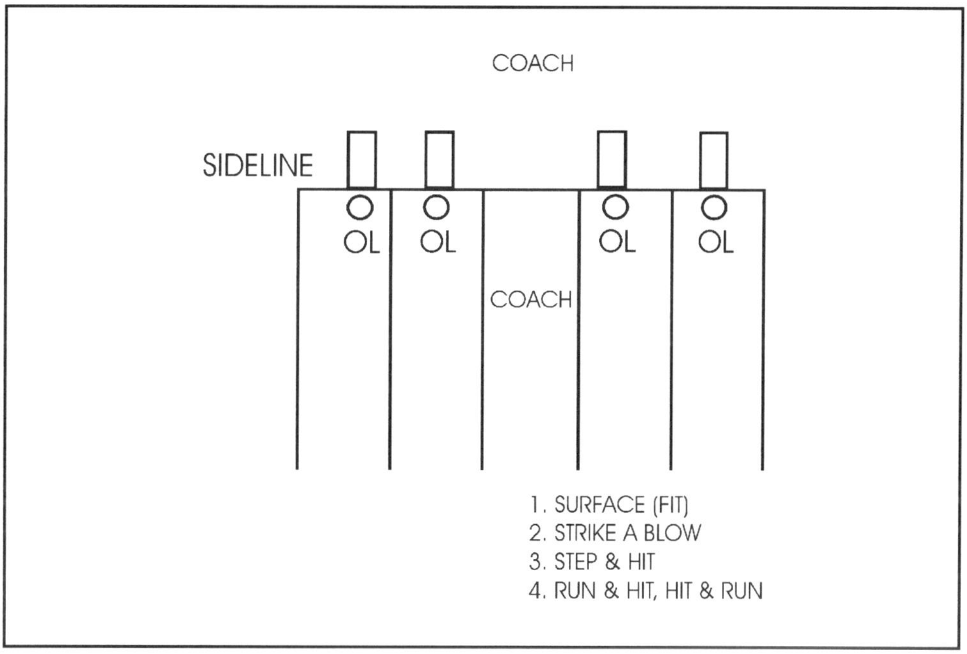


**Diagram 5.1**

There are four parts to this blocking progression: The first one is called surface, which is nothing more than a fit drill. We do the surface drill from a six-point stance. There are some fundamentals in blocking that we emphasize all the time, namely, keeping the defender between your legs, having your chest on your thighs, keeping your butt over your heels so you do not overextend, and finishing your block by swinging the tail. Our six-point stance means that our hands, our knees, and our feet are touching the ground. An important coaching point is that the toes should be flat and not curled underneath the feet. We do not want to curl the toes underneath the feet because, if we do that, as the blocker strikes, his knees will lift up off the ground and we will not be emphasizing rolling the hips.

Surface merely means that we are going to fit these men into the bag. There is no contact, no strike in this drill. We are going to have them form a good blocking surface and fit themselves into the bag. When we block, we drive our forearm and our shoulder through a bag. We do not want to block "at" the man, we want to block "through" the man. As we make contact, the blocking surface includes the side of the neck;, the front of the shoulder, all the way down to the elbow; the front of the forearm; the fist right next to the pec; and the pec. As we make contact on a block, we explode, and we drive that surface through the bag. During surface, we are going to fit these young men into the bag and make sure that their surface is correct. We cross-train all of our players on all the techniques and we mass teach, meaning that we structure as many drills as possible so that all the players are working at the same time. Therefore, lots of players get a chance to do lots of reps. We feel the players learn more by doing than they do by watching. We are going to try to get as many of them in a drill as we can at the same time.

Using all of our offensive linemen, we have one bag for every two players. We line all the bags up on the sideline, going right down the line, and our blockers are lined up on the inside of the field. The bottom of the bag should be intersected by the white yard line. All the blockers are facing into the bag. The coach can stand back and look at his linemen from behind. From behind them, he can see what kind of strikc angle they have. He can make a lot of corrections from this angle. The coach can then come around to the front, and he can watch their eyes to make sure their eyes are looking where they are supposed to be looking. We do all of our drills on the first sound. We do not waste time with a whole bunch of cadence during practice; we get more reps without doing it that way. We do the drill with one shoulder, then we repeat the same drill with the other shoulder. After that, the blocker gets up and holds the bag, and the person who just held the bag will come down and take his turn to execute the blocking assignment. We emphasize some key fundamentals in this drill. We want to make sure the blockers' eyes are up. We want to see them looking up to the sky. The coach can stand in front, and he can see that the eyes are up, or he can stand from behind and see the other fundamentals. When we are behind, we are looking to see that the blockers have a good surface and that the bag, or the defender, is squeezed between the side of the neck and that blocking surface. We want to get a tight neck squeeze. If we are going to control this defender, the best way to control him is for us to have him between our legs and to squeeze him with the blocking surface and our neck. We want to see the off arm posted into the ground. It is also very important that we see the hips down and make sure that the toes are flat and not curled.

We need to check just a couple of things at the outset of this drill: We want to see that our players are in their six-point stance, and we also ask our linemen to put their facemask right on the bag. If you are doing this in preseason, and you are not using helmets, you can tell them to put their nose right on the bag, if you want. We want a direct angle up and down in their knees. We do not want them cocked way back or hunched back on their heels. We would like them to be upright. We would like their knees right under their hips. We do not want their toes curled into the ground.

The second part of the progression is also done from the six-point stance. The second phase is called strike a blow. In strike a blow, we want to do exactly that. We want to really strike the bag and roll the hips through; we want to make contact hard enough so that the bag is knocked off the white yard line. We want to have hardness here. This is explosion. This is full speed live, in terms of the hit. All we are going to do now is to see if the hips roll through the block. We will do the same drill again, only with the left shoulder. The command to the players would be "Strike a blow, left shoulder, on sound." .

Part three of this progression is what we call step and hit. This is a very important phase of the entire drill because we are true to a fundamental principle in all of our blocks: Our linemen get down in their stance. The center has the ball, and he reaches the ball out in front of him as far as he can. The guards will put their hand down on the center's toes. That puts the guard's back off the ball as far as he is legally allowed to be. Our helmets must break the plane of the center's belt as he gets down in his stance. That is a legal position for an offensive linemen to be in. Because of that distance, contact really is going to occur on our second step.

The one thing you want to avoid is an over-elongated first step. You want the first step to be a good six-inch power step, with the second step driving through the defender, or the bag, in this case. What we want, and what I mentioned as a fundamental that is a very important principle in our blocking, is that anytime we are going to block with the right shoulder, we are going to take a short, six-inch power step with that left foot. When using the right shoulder, the left foot will step first. When using the left shoulder, the right foot will step first. This holds true in all blocks. We begin to teach that principle in this part of the blocking skills or shoulder skills progression. That is why this drill is called "step" and hit.

What we do in this drill is we take the first step and then drive through the bag. At the beginning of training camp, or the beginning of spring ball, when we take the first step, we ask the players to step and hold it so we can check that their first step is exactly the way we want it. If we are going to block with the right shoulder, we want the blocker to take a short step with the left foot, with his heels replacing his toes. That is all the farther the step is. We do not want the blocker to be over-elongated. If the first step is too big, the blocker does not have the proper balance that he needs to block. If he gets any contact from the side, he is going to lose his balance. We are going to do the step and hit, and the first few times we do it, we are going to say "set," and they are going to take the first step and hold it. Then we will say finish, or count to two, and on the second command, the players will block through the bag on their second step. Their third step will actually follow naturally right with them. Another important fundamental in this phase should also be emphasized: We would like our blockers to be as close as they possibly can, every time they make contact, so that their chest is on their thighs. When we take the first step, we are not only going to look at the step, but we are also going to make sure that the chest is down on the thighs. The reason we want the chest on the thighs is that we want to block at the defender's hip. Defensive player have all their strength in their upper body, but right at the hip, a man has no strength. He cannot lift weights with his hip. So if we block him at the hip, we can push him all over the field. An old guy like me can do it with one hand, so imagine what a big, strong 300-pound guy can do if he really delivers a strong blow at the hip. He can devastate defenders. You do not have to be bigger than everybody you play against in order to devastate them. You can be a great blocker if you use great technique. This drill really starts to teach that technique.

As the season progresses, after we have mastered the first step, then we will just say, "Set," and we do the whole block without holding on the first step. When our players get lined up, we want the bag between their legs and about arm's length away. We ask the players to reach out and touch the bag, and that is about as far away as we want them. That will put us in just about the right spot to take that first step, the power step, and then on the second step, explode through the bag. The third step will then follow right behind.

When two players have executed this phase of the progression, we switch, and the other two players come over and take their chance. If you have 20 linemen to coach, then you are going to need 10 bags, and you will put 10 guys right on the line.

The final piece of the progression we call either "hit and run," or "run and hit." These are two different drills. In one drill, we are in close to the bag. We can be at arm's distance away from the bag, the same as in step and hit. When the coach says, "Run and hit, right shoulder on sound," the players then step with their left foot, throw their right arm hard behind them, and drive the bag straight off the ball. To finish the block, they drive the bag for four yards, and then drive it four more yards to the right. This drill is hit and run.

The opposite of that drill is run and hit. In run and hit, we want the blockers to be about four yards from the linebackers, or from the bags. We are going to simulate blocking linebackers in this drill. All the same fundamentals will still apply. If we call "run and hit right shoulder," the blockers are going to take off with their left foot. On the fourth step, they will make contact. When we make contact, we are going to drive the bag back, and then we are going to swing our tail and drive the bag to one side or the other. That incorporates the final fundamental that we are looking for. When we say swing the tail, we want to hit the bag so that our tail turns toward the hole. We want to finish the block by moving the defender down the line of scrimmage, which is going to create horizontal openings when we run the offense. We want to drive the bags, or the defenders, in a lateral direction. We do not want to create linebackers when we block. If the defender is up close, and our offensive lineman is blocking that defensive lineman right on his nose, then when he makes a great hit, knocks the guy four yards straight off the ball, and the defender falls off the block and makes the tackle, then all we did was to create another linebacker to stop the play. It is far better to make the block and then swing our tail and finish the block down the line of scrimmage. Now, we have created a horizontal opening, a lateral opening, so the hole is much bigger. We are not only going to work run and hit as though we are blocking linebackers, but we are also going to work on finish, so we can now swing our tail and drive the bag in a lateral direction down the line of scrimmage, parallel with the line of scrimmage.

One major problem to avoid is this: As the blocker swings his tail, if his feet, as he begins to swing his tail around, come outside the bag, then he is going to lose the defender. The defender will spin out of the block, or step out of the block, and we will have lost it. As we swing our tail, we must keep our feet apart, accelerate our feet on contact, and keep that defender between our legs. This is an extremely important coaching point.

One of the things that you will find right in the middle of our playbook is a big section that says right there in black and white, that we do not teach the head as the initial point of contact. We feel that that is immoral; it is also illegal, and it causes neck injuries to players. We feel that we can rest very comfortably at night, knowing that we are teaching a sound, moral, ethical, legal block. We still finish with the hands. We can be up-to-date in terms of hand usage, but when we actually make contact with a defender, we would like to use the shoulder and really strike the man. The blow is much harder when you strike with your shoulder than when you lead with your hands. The other point we believe is that people who teach "lead with the hands" are really trying to cover up the fact that they are really "leading with the face." We feel that leads to the same problems that the NCAA has tried to outlaw. Therefore, we believe in the shoulder block, we like it, but we do use hands to finish. This drill is a great time to demonstrate that.

That is a long explanation for a drill that really only takes about 5 minutes once all the players learn how to execute. The first day of practice, first day of spring ball, we plan 15 minutes so we can walk through it, talk through it, make sure all the new players learn. But after our linemen have done this for a while, the drill is cut back to a 10-minute period, and then it goes down to a five-minute period. Once you really understand the drill, you can eliminate the surface phase and start with "strike a blow," "step and hit," and "run and hit," and you can get all that done in three minutes. Everybody on our team is going to do this all at the same time.

**DAILY ROUTINE**

The second part of the offensive line practice plan is what we call our daily routine

(Diagram 5.2). In routine period, we teach the stance, and we are also going to teach what we call bird-dog, which really is the first step you take when you strike or when you fire off the ball. We will teach takeoff in a couple of different ways, and we will also teach pulling.

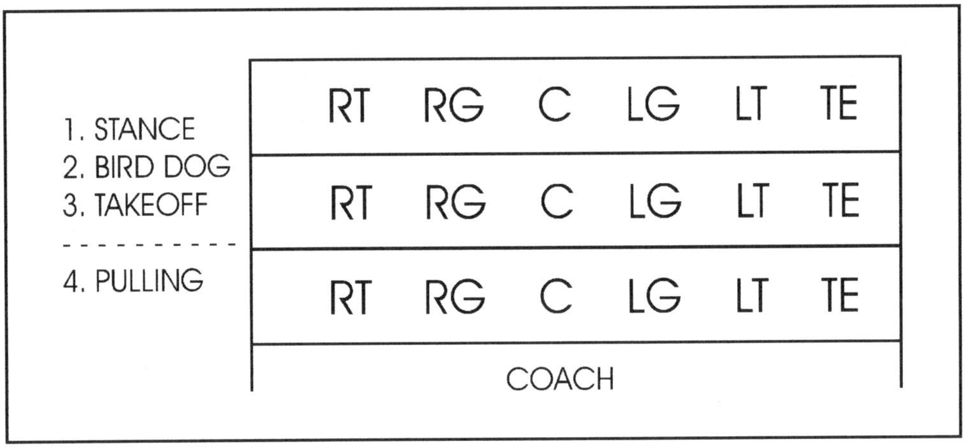


**Diagram 5.2**

If we had three offensive lines, we would take the offensive center and put him directly in front of the coach, facing the coach. We would take the right guard and put him five yards to the right of the center. The left guard would be five yards to the left of the center. The right tackle and left tackle would also align in their positions. Their backups would line up five yards directly behind them. Behind our offensive center, the second-team center aligns five yards away. If we have third- and fourth-team centers, they are each five yards farther away. The same thing holds true for the left guard, the backup, then the extra guys, all five yards spaced. As a coach, I can stand out in the front of this drill where my center is, and I can see all of my players, all at the same time. If you are doing this, then you are mass teaching. You are teaching everybody on your offense the same footwork, all at the same time. This enables you to get through a lot of fundamentals in a really short period of time.

### Stance

The first thing that we are going to do in our progression is teach the stance. This is very important. We want to teach a parallel stance. I know some wing-T teams will put their dominant hand down and their dominant foot back. We do not believe in that. We would like to have a perfectly balanced stance. We will instruct our offensive linemen to put their feet about armpit's width apart. The wider your stance, the less power you can generate on the first step. One of the things that you will have to do as the season wears on is to keep reining in your big offensive linemen. You should bring that stance back in, because they have a tendency to get really wide, and you want that stance fairly narrow. The next thing we tell the offensive linemen is to turn their toes in slightly. The reason is, as the linemen get down in their three-point stance, the power angles that are created in their legs will be locked in. As they get down in their stance, and as they bend their knees, those power angles are locked in. On the other hand, if their toes are pointing out to the sideline, and they get down in their stance, the power angles are not going straight ahead. If they turn their toes in slightly as they bend they knees, their feet will often straighten out and point north and south. We want those knees pointing straight ahead. We want to lock those power-producing angles in. We want to create some knee bend, and as we get down, we are going to bend our knees and bring our heels to the top of the grass so that we have a bend in the ankle, a bend in the knee, and a bend in the waist. We are going to allow our players to put their dominant hand down. It does not matter to me if their right hand is down or their left hand is down. The offensive linemen can have either hand down-whichever one is dominant.

For our tight end , we definitely dictate which hand is going to be down-always the inside arm. When the tight end is on the left side, he has a right-handed stance, with his right hand down; when he is on the right side, he has a left-handed stance, with his left hand down. We feel this is important because the tight end blocks down and gap blocks so much. We want that inside hand down to facilitate his gap step or his pull step in order to block down inside more efficiently.

We have the linemen take their down hand and reach out as far in front as they can, without putting any weight on their fingertips. When the offensive linemen are down in their stance, the defense should never be able to identify who is pulling or pass blocking. The defense should never be able to read our stance. Linemen should look the same every time. When we get down in our stance, we want to make sure that the defensive linemen cannot read us. In some programs, when the linemen are leaning way back, it is definitely pass or draw. When they are leaning way forward, it is definitely run. We would like to look the same all the time: Feet narrow. Toes pointed in. Arm reached out in front as far as possible.

The nondominant hand is going to lock in. We are going to wrap the wrist around the knee and lock in a power-producing angle. We do not want the off hand up on the thigh pad. We also do not want the off hand down on the knee, because that starts to raise the body up. We want the off hand wrapped around the knee, and we want to lock a power-producing north and south angle into the knees. This type of stance allows us to make blocks with the chest on the thighs. From this perfectly balanced stance, our linemen can go in any direction.

We introduce this stance on the first day of training camp or on the first day of spring ball. We give quite a bit of time for teaching during this period. The offensive linemen will have the coach talking them through the stance drill for quite a while, until they fully understand what a good stance looks like and feels like.

**Bird-dog**

In the first phase of what we call "daily routine," we just coach the stance, making sure our players are assuming their proper stance. We do not want to give up on any of these fundamentals throughout the entire season. The second phase is a drill we call "bird-dog" drill. In this drill, we work on exploding into the first step. All it is, is one step. We coach a bunch of different first steps for our players to take. As they take these steps, they will step and hold just to see if they are taking the proper first step.

**Straight-Ahead Step**

The first step we look at is called "right foot straight ahead." When we step straight ahead, that is the step that we use for an "on block." When we take the first step, our heels will replace our toes. With the foot that steps, that same arm will throw hard behind us. As we step, we are going to step and hold it, so that the coach can check all of his players. When they hold, each lineman should have a good base, butt over the heels, not overextended, and the chest should be down on their thighs. If we step with the right foot, we throw the right arm hard behind us. We throw the left arm hard in front of us, and we look like a bird-dog, out in the field, pointing to our prey.

Once our linemen know what the first step should look and feel like, we will rapid-fire this drill. Instead of stepping and holding, we are going to go three times faster, and we can hold it on the third repetition, if we want to. We simply practice the first straight step on command, then reset, step again, reset, and continue on command until we freeze the last repetition.

**Fire Step**

The next step we practice is called a fire step. A fire step means that as our feet move, we have our toes pointing north and south, and on the first step, the toes will continue to point north and south, but the foot will step at a 45-degree angle. This step relates to what we call a fire block. We practice taking a fire step and hold it, bird-dog it. It does not take long for the coach to correct all of his guys once they actually know what they are doing. Players who have been in the program for four or five years really know what they are doing, so, at that point, the coach doesn't have to correct anybody.

**Reach Step**

The next step that we work on is called a reach step. On the fire step, we went on a 45-degree angle, and the toes stayed north and south. On the reach step, we step at a flat 90-degree angle, with the toes still pointing north and south, which keeps our shoulders also pointing north and south. During this drill, as each player steps to the right on a flat, lateral 90-degree angle, his toes are still north and south, and he still has his bird-dog position, with his chest on his thighs. Then we will go reach step left on sound, step, and hold it. Obviously, a reach step ties into our reach block. When we get to teaching the reach block to our players, we will use the first step, which is called a reach step.

**Pull Step**

The next step is the pull step. The pull step relates to many of our blocks. We can be pulling on the trap, or we can be pulling to lead on the sweep. We can be pulling to gap block a defender who is lined up inside of us. As we take a right pull step, the lineman steps with his right foot. He basically picks his right foot up and puts it back down again, but his toes will point directly to the sideline. The most important coaching point is that the backside foot must pivot at the same time. As you step with your right foot, the right arm throws hard behind you, in order to help the backside foot pivot, and help generate momentum for the pull step. As the puller throws that arm hard behind him, he gets his shoulders turned, he gets his backside foot pivoted, and he gets his shoulders facing in the direction that he needs to go.

When practicing the pull step, we are going to take the first step and hold it. One good way for a coach to check this footwork is to stand to the side. However, rather than run all the way over to the side to change positions, the coach can tell his players to face the sideline. What the players will have done, then, is to turn around in their stance; we will have saved a lot of time, and the coach will not have to run all the way around the field over and over. The coach can check to see if the players' back foot pivots or not. He can check to see that each player has his right arm hard behind him and that he is in the bird-dog position. The players' left foot should be pivoted all the way around. Both feet should be pointing to the sideline. When we take that step, instead of being right on the same yard line, the right foot can actually step back a little bit so that when the lineman pivots his right foot, he has a little distance between his feet, and he has a little bit better base between his feet and under his body.

Those are the four steps we work on most often during bird-dog period. Straight ahead, fire, reach and pull. If we can master those four steps, most of our blocks will come off those four steps for the first step of the block. During daily routine period, stance was the first phase, and bird-dog footwork was the second. The third phase is what we call "takeoff."

**Takeoff**

When we do takeoff, we can do it in any direction. We can go straight ahead, or pull right, or pull left, or we can fire right or left. When we do takeoff, our linemen, as we say the command, will sprint five yards as fast as they can. They will slow themselves down for the next five yards. They are going to run 10 total yards, but they are going to explode out of their stance for the initial five yards. As we do this, we always tell them to take off with either their right foot or their left foot. We want to see them explode out of their stance with the correct foot. If you do this enough, it becomes second nature. At first, you might have to think about it a little bit, but as you do it, repeat it, and it will become second nature to your players. I can tell you that it takes a long time to explain these drills, but on the field, it is 10 minutes during the first practice, five minutes during the second practice, and it stays five minutes all the way through training camp. By the time the season rolls around, this is a tree-minute period. Your coaches can go fast. Check the stance, bird-dog the four types of footwork, take off whichever way you need to take off, and do the pulling drill.

We do takeoff drill two different ways. We can explode out of the stance and sprint, or we can have the linemen do a thing we call duck walk, which simulates keeping your feet apart as you drive a man off the ball. The first thing we always do is just take off straight ahead on sound. All the linemen are in a good stance. All are going to take off with their right foot on sound straight ahead. After all the players have gone in one direction and they have gone 10 yards, sprinting for five and decelerating for five, they are going to turn around and face the other direction. You as the coach have to move down to the other end of the field, and now they are going to take off with the left foot on sound. Then you should be back in the original position you started in. Next, we repeat the drill, emphasizing the duck walk. Our players have been taught to keep their feet apart as they make contact and drive the defender. All of them will be practically duck walking as they come out of their stance with their feet apart. We feel that is necessary in order to keep the defender between the legs.

In the next portion of the same drill, you can work on another step. As you repeat the drill again, your first step now is going to be a pull right step. Again, sprint five yards and decelerate for five. Then return using a pull left step. We can also work on taking off and using any kind of footwork we want-straight ahead, fire, reach, pull, whatever we need to see as a coach. We do it rapid-fire and do it fast, because as a coach, all you have to do is be able to see the footwork that you want to see each day.

**11-Step Pulling Drill**

The last thing we do in daily routine is called an 11-step pulling drill (Diagram 5.3). When the players do this drill , they take 11 steps. Actually, they take 10 steps, and on their 11th step, they are getting back down in their original position. We walk our linemen through a pull technique where the linemen pull flat, work up the field as if they are going to wall off, or log block, and then come back to the same spot that they lined up in. We walk our linemen through it about one time, so they can see what we want. Then we sprint through the complete sequence. We do not want to have our linemen walking through this, counting steps, the whole year, because you can make robots out of them. We do not want to do that in the 11-step pull drill.

If we are going to pull to the right, simulate a log block, and come back to the original position, with the 11th step nothing more than getting back down in your stance, it is a 10-step drill. The first step is a pull step to the right. Take the step and hold it. On the second step, we are going to attack the man we are logging. The third step continues along the same path. On the fourth step, we reach down and grab grass, and we want to dip the shoulder. The fourth step is where contact occurs. It occurs with the inside foot and the inside shoulder making contact. Step five comes straight up the field. We simulate swinging our tail and starting to finish the block as the off arm comes into play. On step six, we bench press and start to turn the defender. Step six also starts each lineman back to his original position, followed by seven, eight, nine, and 10. Then we simply turn around and get back down in our stance, which is the 11th step. We do the 11-step pull drill to the right, then do the 11-step pull drill to the left. We are only going to count this for the player once; after that, we are going to run through all 11 steps at full speed. The first step will be the pull step on sound, two, three, four, grab grass, five turns vertically up the field, six starts you back from where you came from, seven, eight, nine, 10, and 11 is merely getting back down to your stance.

In summary, our daily routine period includes checking the stance, making sure the stance is good; bird-dog, firing out for the first step and holding it; takeoff with any step you need, sprint for five, decelerate for five, and turn around to go in the other direction. The final phase is always the 11-step pulling drill.

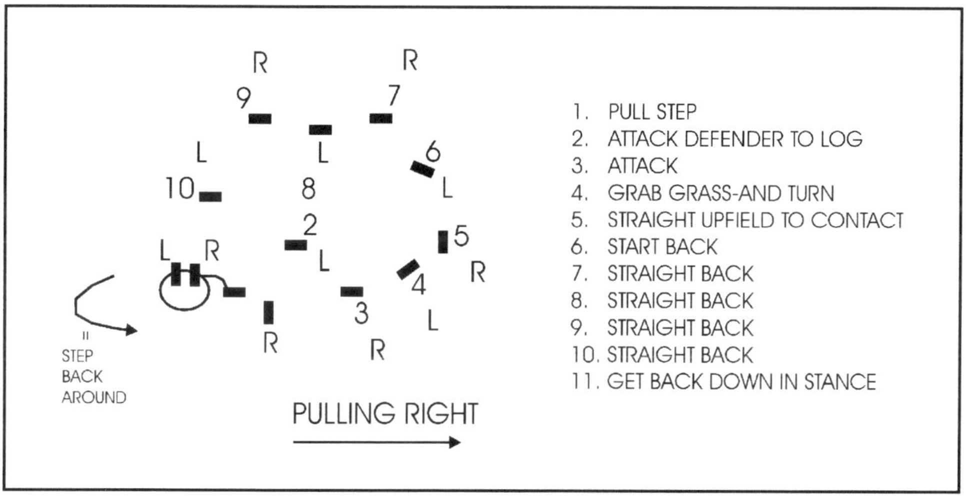


**Diagram 5.3**

## BLOCKING TECHNIQUE PERIOD

The next part of the practice for our linemen is what we call blocking technique period. We have two different types of blocks. The first type is called a single, or individual, block, and we have five of them. These blocks are one-on-one blocks performed by a single player. The second type of blocks are combination blocks performed by more than one player. Each of these different types of blocks begins with one of the first steps we have already taught and relates specifically to one or more particular plays in the wing-T offense.

## INDIVIDUAL BLOCKS

### On Block

The first block is called an "on" block (Diagram 5.4). This block simulates a defender lined up directly over the top of an offensive blocker. We are going to simulate the defender with one of the big bags at first, and then it will be a body after that. The first three days of camp, we use one of the big bags directly in front of one of our offensive blockers, and on the line of scrimmage. When we says, "On right," we are blocking with the right shoulder. We are going to finish the block, the defender, or the bag flat down the line of scrimmage, parallel to the line of scrimmage to the right. Of course, the opposite of this is "on left." The technique we emphasize is that, if the blocker is going to strike with the right shoulder, then he must step with the left foot. As you strike the man, you begin to swing the tail, keeping the man between your legs, and then take him in a flat direction to the right, down the line of scrimmage. "On left" means to strike with the left shoulder, drive the man in a left direction, and take your first step with your right foot.

At first, we use the big bags. We will get two blockers, along with two linemen holding the bags. Our blockers are all on one side, and our bag holders are all over on the other side. As a coach, I can be on either side. I want to be able to look at the blockers from behind, and I also want to be able to look at them from behind the defender. We can watch how the players come off, and we can see their eyes, and see if their eyes are correct. The blockers will be down in a three-point stance. They are about an arm's distance from the bag. We begin by blocking "on right," meaning we take our first step with the left foot, strike with the right shoulder, swing the tail to keep the man between our legs, and then drive them to the right. We ask both players to bring the bags back. The blocker and the bag holder pick the bag up and bring it back together. The man holding the bag now gets a chance to come over and be the blocker. Once the blocker has finished "on right" and "on left," he then goes over and holds the bag for the other man to block. When our blockers finish, they hold the position of their block so we can tell, as a coach, if they have the good blocking fundamentals that we taught during shoulder skill period. Once your players understand what is expected of them, they should be able to execute "on block" right and left. Once their partner executes it, they can go on to the next block. You can get a lot of blocks done in a relatively short period of time. Once training camp really gets going, or once the season gets going, and we do not have to wear shorts and T-shirts anymore, then we won't block the bags anymore. We will bring our defensive people down, and we will actually block bodies that move. This is actually a much more realistic drill to do than blocking bags all the time. But the bags are a great place to start because they allow us to emphasize the technique, and if a blocker uses that same technique when he blocks a live body, then he is going to be a great blocker.

### Gap Block

The second block we teach is what we call "gap" (Diagram 5.5). It is a very important block for us, and it is used to cut off penetration. In this drill, it is very important that the man holding the bag lines up in the neutral zone. You want him even with the blocker, as if a defender just penetrated the line of scrimmage. You want him in the position he would be in if he were directly in the gap between the blocker and the next adjacent offensive lineman. It is important to have the bag in the neutral zone so that the blocker has to pull step flat down the line, get his head across the front of the bag, and finish the block down the line of scrimmage. When we draw blocks, we draw the shoulder surface and we draw where the head is, so that our blockers know which shoulder to block with. We actually make contact with the right shoulder when we gap block to the left. It is just the opposite when we block "gap right." In that maneuver, we pull step with the right foot, block flat down the line of scrimmage, and finish the block in the direction to the right. We teach our players to get their right ear across the front of the defender's belt buckle. Even though we are going to pull step and gap block, we still want the defender to stay between our legs. Our gap block means we are going to be blocking with our head across the front of a defender, and we will be pulling inside, toward the line of scrimmage or toward the football. As a wing-T coach, you are going to see a lot of opponents try to penetrate the line of scrimmage against you, and so this block is very important.

**Diagram 5.4**

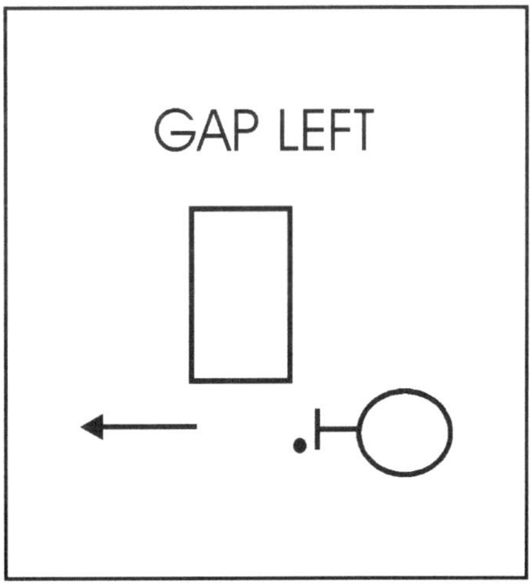


**Diagram 5.5**

### Down Block

The next individual block is called the "down" block (Diagram 5.6). This is used when blocking a man lined up inside of you. The defender is lined up over the adjacent blocker inside of you. This could be a tight end blocking down on the man over the tackle, or it could be a tackle blocking down on a man over the guard. It could also be the center blocking back on a backside defensive lineman, or it could be the guard blocking down on a noseguard. We use "down" technique only when we know that the defender will not be a penetrator. If there is any question as to whether or not the defender might penetrate, we use our pull step and a gap technique.

When we are blocking down, our head goes behind. When we block down left, we are going to make contact with the left shoulder, and our head will go behind. As we make contact, we swing our tail, and we finish the block right down the line of scrimmage, creating a lateral opening in the defense. On down right, the blocker would be on the left side of the bag, and he would block in the right direction and finish the bag to the right, parallel to the line of scrimmage. One thing about the down technique. If we are going to block with our left shoulder, in order to keep all of our fundamentals in place, we want to be able to step with the right foot and block with the left shoulder. Therefore, when we down block, as we step with the right foot, we will get up on the ball of the left foot, and the left foot will actually pivot a little bit so that we can take off and make contact with the left shoulder. Contact will occur on the second step. Notice that the fundamentals we learned in shoulder skill period are right in place and carry forward to technique period.

### Fire Block

If you recall, the fire step is a 45-degree step with the toes pointed north and south. The fire step relates to the "fire" block (Diagram 5.7). This block is executed when you want to block a man who is lined up on your outside shoulder. On fire right, the defender is on the outside shoulder of the man blocking to the right. Our first step is a 45-degree step, with toes still pointing north and south. On the second step, we are going to drive the inside knee and the left blocking surface-the forearm and the shoulder-through the inside of the man, right down the middle of the man. We are initially going to knock the defender back on a 45-degree angle, and then we are going to swing our tail and take the man back to the inside if we can. Most important, we would like to see a good, hard strike on this fire block. It is going to be a left shoulder block when we block fire right. The other thing that is important to emphasize is that when we fire block, we are going to lower our strike point. Instead of the hip, we are now going to block on the thigh pad. We are going to bring the strike point down just a little. A lot of times, we will be firing out on a linebacker four yards away, and that strike point will lead us to an opportunity to possibly cut the linebacker. We are allowed to do that in college football. As a high school coach, even if you block at the thigh pad, you should be okay. If not, use the hip as an aiming point.

When blocking fire right, we will have the bag on the right shoulder of the blocker. The first step is a fire step. The second step is the contact step. On the second step, we want to drive the inside knee and blocking surface right through the middle of the man. We want to drive the knee right through the crotch area and drive the left shoulder right through the defender's outside thigh. Finish the block. Bring your third step, and begin to swing the tail and take the bag in the opposite direction.

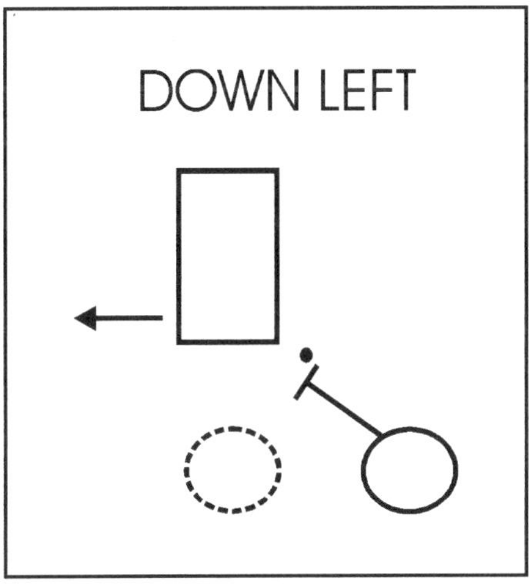


Diagram 5.6

Diagram 5.7

**Reach Block**

The final individual block that we coach is what we call the "reach" block (Diagram 5.8). We have already taught our reach step during bird-dog drill. The reach block relates to the reach step. On a reach block right, we will reach step with the right foot. A reach step means you step at a 90-degree flat angle with your toes pointed north and south. After the first step, it becomes a fire block. Your first step is a reach step, and after that, you are executing fire technique. The bag needs to be placed at least in the gap between the blocker and the next adjacent blocker. It really should be placed over the next adjacent man to the outside. If the blocker is a right guard, the bag should be placed over the right tackle. If the blocker is the right tackle, the bag should be placed over the tight end. If the blocker is a center, the bag should be placed over the right guard, when we reach right. If the blocker is good enough, he can take a reach step, execute fire technique, swing the tail, and take the defender back inside. But if we can execute the reach block by getting squared up on the defender, getting the man between our legs and driving him by maintaining contact, then we have done a heck of a job as an offensive lineman.

These are our five individual blocks. They are the one-on-one blocks. They are the first blocks that we teach. They are essential to everything we do. There are some other blocks, trap and log, that we could teach as individual blocks, but we get those blocking techniques in our combination blocks.

**Diagram 5.8**

## COMBINATION BLOCKS

### Cross Block

The first combination block that we teach in the wing-T offense is what we call "cross" block (Diagram 5.9). You will notice that when I refer to combination blocks, I am talking about two-on-two. We have a blocker, another blocker, a bag directly in front of the first blocker, and another bag directly in front of the second blocker. "Cross block right" means that the man on the right is going to use down left blocking technique. He will block with his left shoulder, his head goes behind the defender, he swings his tail, and he takes the bag in the left direction. His first step is with his right foot. The blocker on the left, who is the inside blocker, is going to execute trap right. He is going to take a pull step to trap, or he can take a slight drop step, depending on how much width he needs in order to get this cross block executed. Then he will work up into the line of scrimmage, inside out, with his head behind the defender. As we make contact, we swing our tail and take the block directly down the line of scrimmage. It is essential that the blocker blocking down left finishes his block parallel to the line of scrimmage, while the blocker blocking trap right also finishes his block parallel to the line of scrimmage. We are trying to create a lateral opening in the defense so that we can run through a gaping hole with our offense. To execute this in practice, we are going to use four reps. We will cross block right. A blocker blocks down left, and the other blocker blocks trap right. Then you come back, and the blockers switch sides. Now, the man who before was on the inside comes over, and he blocks down left. The man who blocked down left moves to the inside, and he now blocks trap right. Both guys get to execute both techniques-the down and the trap. After the two blockers have had their turn to execute it, then the two players holding the bags come over, and they take two shots each at blocking the cross block.

The opposite of this block is "cross block to the left." That takes four more reps for us to get through. You are looking at a total of eight reps to get all the players to do each skill from both sides. If we cross block to the left, the man on the outside, or the man on the left, would block down right. The man on the inside would block trap left. In a cross block situation, if our linemen are split with a two- or three-foot split, the bags, or defenders, are directly in front of each of the blockers. The trap blocker has the responsibility, as the trapper, to adjust to the down blocker. If there is a collision between these two , we feel it is the trapper's fault. The trapper must come as tight off the down blocker's tail as he can, without bumping into him.

**Diagram 5.9**

**Gut Block**

"Gut" block is a combination block with two blockers (Diagram 5.10). It could be a center and a guard, a guard and a tackle, or a tackle and a tight end . When we execute the gut right technique, the man on the outside, the blocker on the right, blocks down left. He is going to hit with his left shoulder; therefore, he steps with his right foot. As he makes contact, he swings his tail and drives the defender flat down the line of scrimmage, perfectly parallel to the line of scrimmage. This block is used when blocking down on a defensive lineman and pulling around for a linebacker. The man on the left blocks gut right. He is going to put his head behind, and he is also going to block with his left shoulder. He will finish his block parallel to the line of scrimmage. Both blockers will do both skills and then switch, with the bag holders coming over and both blocking gut right. After that, we work on gut left. Here, the blocking techniques switch. The man on the left blocks down to the right, finishing the block in the right direction, parallel to the line of scrimmage. The man on the right blocks gut left with his right shoulder and finishes his man in the right direction. When we execute this block, we would like the two blockers to line up as they do in a normal situation in a game where they have a two- or three-foot split between them. We want the first bag directly in the gap or over an adjacent blocker. The first bag will be on the line of scrimmage in the gap. The second defender, or bag, will be stacked behind the first defender, directly behind him. As they step through this block, we want no space between the blockers' tails.

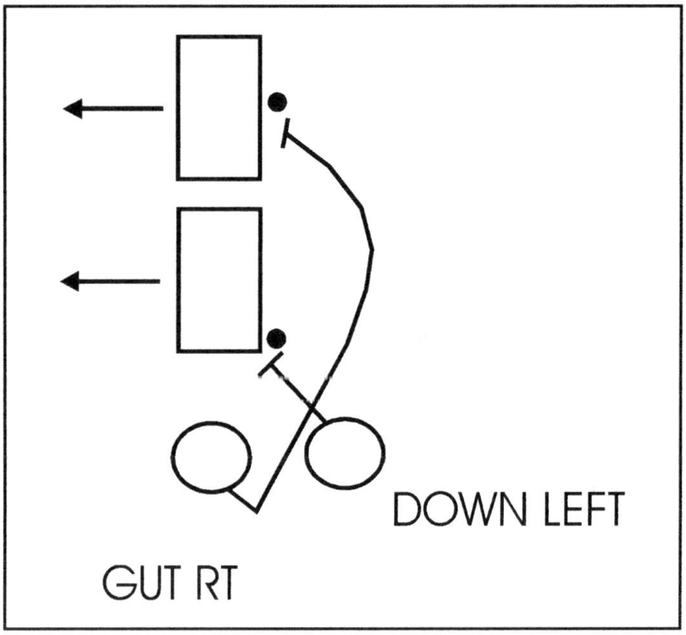


**Diagram 5.10**

### Scoop Block

The next combination block is what we call "scoop" (Diagram 5.11). We can scoop to the right or to the left. In this block, we have two offensive blockers versus two defensive players. If we are using bags, the defender on the line of scrimmage will have one of the big bags. The defender who is off the line of scrimmage will have a smaller shield. What happens on a scoop block is that one of the two blockers is going to block the defensive lineman on the line of scrimmage, and the other blocker is going to come upfield and block what we simulate as a linebacker. When we do scoop, the two blockers are actually going to read and get a feel for the defensive lineman. The outside blocker takes a fire step, a 45-degree step, and his block is called fire right. The inside man is going to block reach right, so he takes a reach step. As they take their footwork, the rule is that the covered man takes a fire step, and the uncovered man takes a reach step. These players could be a center and a guard against an even defense, or they could be a guard and a tackle against an odd defense. They could even be a tackle and a tight end against the 4-3 defense. On the scoop, the outside man takes a fire step. As he does so, the inside man takes a reach step. If the defensive player steps to the inside, then the guard reads his inside foot. If the defender steps to the inside on an angle, a slant, or a pinch, the guard knows that he will now take that block over. If the defender works straight ahead, or works to the outside, as the guard takes the reach step, the guard will now climb on a 45-degree angle, right through the inside hip of the defensive player, and cut off the linebacker scraping through the playside. If the defensive lineman slants inside, our inside blocker takes the reach step and then becomes a fire blocker on the defensive lineman as he slants inside. Next, the lineman who took the fire step will climb and go block the linebacker scraping over the top. The fire blocker, as he fires on the way to the linebacker, is going to take his inside arm and punch the slanting defender into the offensive guard to help generate some momentum for the guard's reach technique. Scoop left is the opposite. Here, we have the man on the left block fire left, while the man on the right, on the inside, blocks reach left.

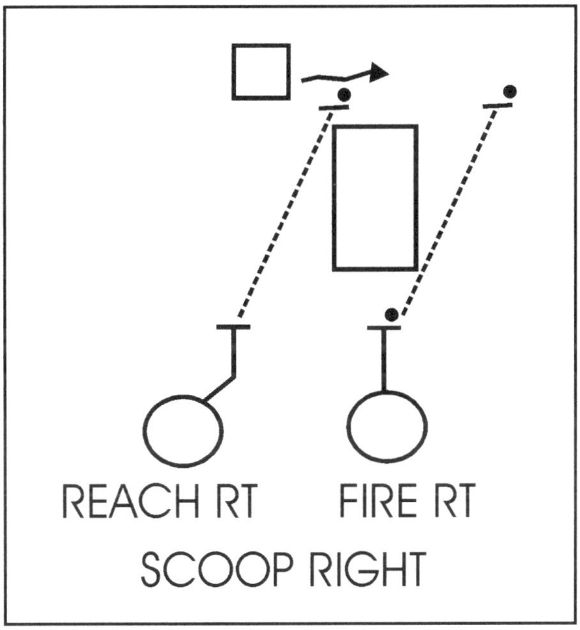


**Diagram 5.11**

**Over Block**

An "over" block is exactly the same as the scoop, except it is more predetermined (Diagram 5.12). This block is used on the backside of an option that is going away, wide to the flank. An example of this has the left guard and the center using over block technique on the noseguard and the backside linebacker, with an option going to the right. The center, or the man on the right, is going to take a fire step with his right foot, just as he does on a fire block, except that he is going to take his inside arm and rip through the outside arm of the defender and just climb. If there is contact, we want him to rip through the defender so that the defender turns his shoulders. The left guard, or man on the left, executes reach right. He will take the defender over with a little bit of contact help from the outside man, or the man on the right. It is just like a scoop, but it is predetermined that the blocker on the right, or to the outside, is going to go ahead and go to the backer every time. Obviously, the opposite of that would be over left, which is used backside when the play goes in the other direction. A great coaching point on this block is to make sure that the man on the right gets good contact as he rips through the defender on the way to the linebacker. We do not want to avoid contact; rather, we want to make good contact. We want to rip through the defender and really turn his shoulders, or open his shoulder for the reach blocker to come through.

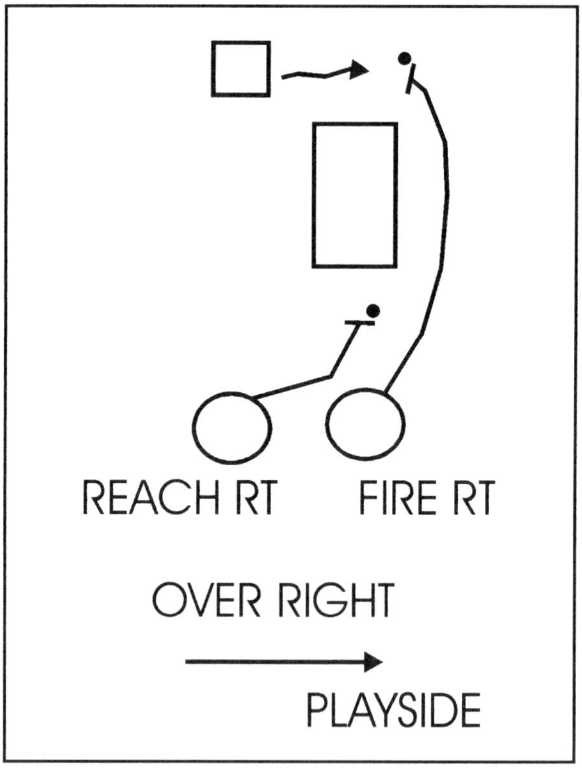


**Diagram 5.12**

**Lead Post Inside-Out Block**

The last combination block we practice in the wing-T offense is called "lead post inside-out" (Diagram 5.13). This block is a three-on-three block. What we are simulating is a double-team down and trap out. The blocker in the middle will be the post blocker. If we are going to lead post inside-out to the right, that means that we are going to be trapping to the right. The man furthest to the left is going to pull and trap to his right. He is going to use his right shoulder, his head will be inside as he makes contact, and he will finish his man down the line of scrimmage to the right. This creates the lateral opening in the defense that the wing-T is trying to achieve. The middle man will be post left. He is going to post with his right shoulder, swing his tail, and then take his man in the left direction. The man on the right is going to block down left. The key coaching point here is that the post blocker must not be so strong that he knocks the defensive man off the line of scrimmage. We do not want to do that. We want to create the lateral opening. The post should not be so strong that he knocks the defender back. The other thing is, the post is going to step with his left foot; he is going to strike with his right shoulder. As he feels contact from the man to his outside, who is blocking down left, the two blockers, with their tails together, should swing their tails and take the defender down the line of scrimmage. If they get tight to each other, they should keep their tails together, and they should not get split. When the defensive man splits the double-team, it is because the blockers do not have their tails together. The trapper will pull inside out and trap his man with his right shoulder and take him in the right direction. One additional point on the lead post: The post blocker and the lead blocker have to be able to pick up their two men on any kind of a stunt. Once in a while, we see a linebacker who steps up in the A gap. If that happens, the center will come off his post, or the inside man will come off his post. He will execute what we call gap technique on the penetrating linebacker. In that case, the offensive guard, or whoever the outside blocker to the right is, comes down on the nose and thus becomes the primary blocker on the nose. This is known as a "conditional" post. That is, you are going to post block the man all the way. You will come off that post only on one condition, and that is if the linebacker blitzes inside of you in the A gap. If the linebacker scrapes to the playside and the noseguard loops or angles away from the down blocker, the post should take his block over by himself. He has stepped with his left foot and blocked with his right shoulder. He should have his head inside of the nose. If the nose tries to go in that same direction, he will swing his tail and take the defender parallel to the line of scrimmage and down the line. When that happens, the down blocker can come down, get a good punch on the nose, and then climb for the backside linebacker who is scraping over the top. Often, the climbing angle will have to be vertically up the field, depending on the speed of the backside linebacker.

The man in the middle is going to block post with his right shoulder, so he is going to step with his left foot and block with his right shoulder. He is going to block a little bit higher because we want to elevate the defender. This is one time that we will block up in the numbers. We want to elevate the defender so that his hip is exposed. The man furthest to the right is going to block down to the left, and he should be right at the hip. The two of them should swing their tails and take the man straight down the line. The man furthest to the left will block trap to the right. He takes a pull step, adjusts tight off of their tails and then traps, with his right shoulder inside out to the right.

As we practice this block against the many different looks we see from the defense, we rotate each lineman through each of the blocking positions. The man on the left moves around to the right and will now block lead. When each player has gone through the block three times, then the three players on defense get a chance to come back over on the offense, and they get to do it three times. You want to make sure you repeat this drill three times with each group so they all get to be trap blocker, post blocker, and lead blocker. When you finish, the next thing you want to do is switch the defense (e.g., a defensive lineman covering the man on the left, a defensive lineman on the man on the middle, and a linebacker on the man furthest to the right).

During our blocking technique period, we can practice any of six combination blocks and five individual blocks. There is simply not enough time to work on every one of our blocks during every practice. The offensive line coach needs to pick out the blocks that his players need the most work on, and those are the ones that he should repeat each week.

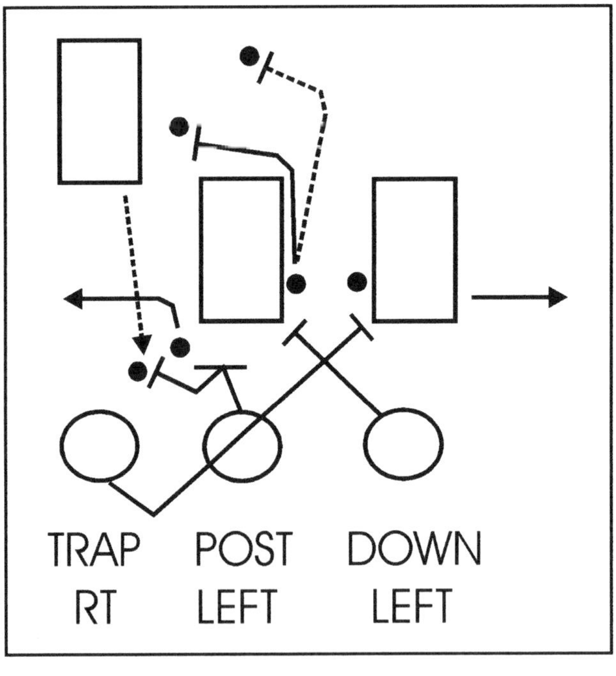


**Diagram 5.13**

## PULLING DRILLS

The offensive line practice plan starts each day with shoulder skills. The next thing we do is our routine period. Then the linemen have a blocking technique period. Finally, we finish with our pulling drills, which consist of a sweep drill, a waggle drill, a gut drill, and a trap drill. We teach all of our linemen to pull within these drills, and we will cross-train our linemen to play all the positions. A center learns the guard techniques, a tackle learns the guard techniques, and our guard learns how to do all the blocks. Everybody learns everything. We cross-train everybody. By mass teaching, we have a chance to do that because we can get so many reps quickly. We teach all the linemen all the techniques for one big reason. We want to be able to play our best five, all the time, regardless of what position they may have started out in. We may go through part of the season with our five best linemen playing, and then, all of a sudden, our right guard gets hurt. If our backup right tackle is the sixth best offensive lineman, then he has learned every technique that a guard has ever had to learn from day one. As a result, our next best lineman can step right in there, and all we have to do is brush him up on assignments, because he has learned all the techniques.

**Waggle Drill**

In this particular drill, every lineman is a guard (Diagram 5.14). We use what we call a spacing board. This board is 16 feet long, one inch thick, and four inches wide. It marks the spaces in the offensive line. It has three dark spots that represent the offensive linemen: the first dark spot is the guard, the second dark spot is the tackle, and the final dark spot is the tight end. The board also has light spots that represent the amount of split between each position. All the linemen will line up on the first dark spot on the spacing board. We lay those spacing boards on the ground as wide as where the center's feet would be. We have all the linemen in two lines, waiting to play the two guard positions. On each side, there will be two players holding a bag or a shield, or just going live with pads. We want to have the first defender in a position where the first guard will pull and log on the waggle. We want to have the second defender in a position where he simulates a corner who has just blitzed off the edge and has started to penetrate the backfield. We can put the two defenders side by side either on the line of scrimmage or off the line of scrimmage, or else we can put them in tandem behind each other, or we can move them around, depending on what we are going to see by the defense and what defensive problems we are experiencing. Versus a 50 defense, we will have a defensive end on our tight end and a corner or a strong safety who has blitzed into the backfield.

We are going to do waggle drill to the right and to the left, and we are going to do the drill rapid-fire, as fast as we can, in order to get as many reps as we can. In five minutes, the linemen get a ton of reps. The first way we do the drill is "29 waggle," which means we fake the sweep to the left, while the quarterback waggles to the right. We can do this drill with or without the quarterbacks. The first guard, the right guard, is going to take a pull step on his first step. He will then attack the first defensive player. We coach him that the kick-out angle and the log angle should be exactly the same. The kick-out is going to be with the head inside, and it will be with the right shoulder. The log will be with the head outside, and it will be with the left shoulder, when going to the right. However, the angle of approach, as we approach the defender, must look exactly the same so that a log block appears to be a wrong-shoulder kick-out. As the guard takes a pull step, he adjusts. He is coming on a kick-out angle, but he wants to execute log block technique on the defensive end. He will swing his tail and try to take the defensive end back into the line of scrimmage. The first guard is the log blocker. The backside guard is either going to kick out or lead the quarterback up the field. The backside guard, who is the left guard on "29 waggle," also has a first step that is a pull step. On his second step, he crosses over for depth. If he is pulling to the right, his pull step will be with his right foot; he will cross over with his left foot to gain about a yard of ground into the backfield, and then he will flatten out and attack the flank. When he does that, he allows the fullback to go in front of him. The crossover step will allow the fullback to go in front of him and block the linebacker or become a receiver in the flat. As he crosses over, that step gives him about two yards of depth into the backfield, because he has already lined up off the ball in his stance. He should be about two yards from the back tip of the ball as he comes across the backfield. From there, he is reading the flank. If we have a corner who has blitzed into the backfield, the backside guard will trap him out, putting his head inside, and finishing him on a 45-degree angle back into the backfield. This is done because we do not want to try to outrun penetration. If the defense has had penetration, even if it is by the defensive end, the first guard will gut, let the penetration go, and the backside guard will kick the penetration out. The quarterback will take his two steps on the midline and begin to attack the flank. If the backside guard has kicked out, the quarterback will step underneath the kick-out, and he can either run or throw from there. If we get the flank logged, the quarterback can continue on his path, get around the end, and have a good end run. If there is no penetration, the backside guard will listen for a "go" call, lead the quarterback up the field, and block the next threat that shows. That threat will either be a corner or a defensive back. If those defenders have dropped off, the guard can look to his inside for a linebacker scraping on second contain.

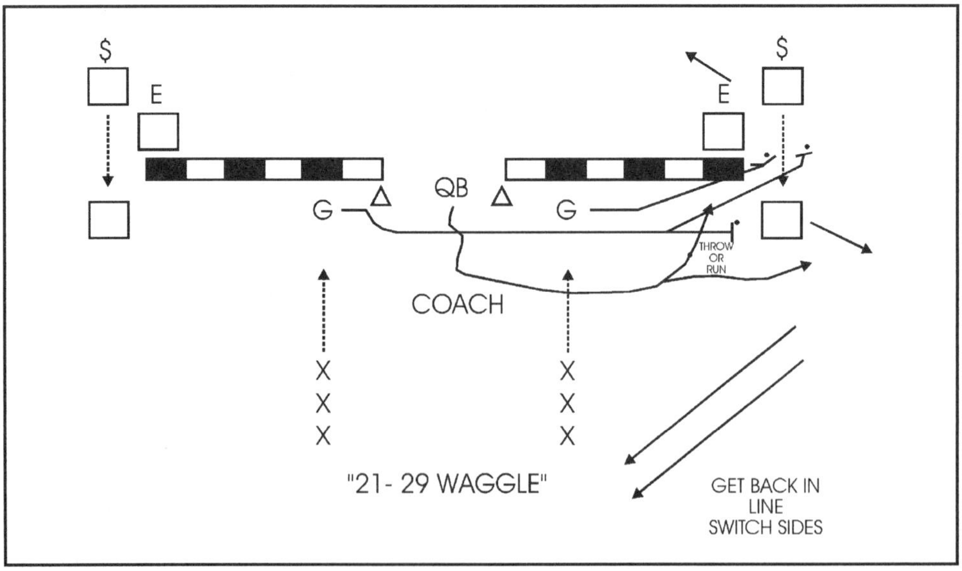


**Diagram 5.14**

You can do the waggle drill with or without the quarterback. The guards pull, while our other offensive linemen are holding the shields. As they pull to the right, the second two guards go sprinting up to the line of scrimmage and get ready to go waggle in the other direction. The coach quickly makes the corrections that he sees. The guards who were just blockers on the play now grab the shields. They hold the shields, and the two linemen who were holding the shields come to the back and get in line to play the guards next. After that exchange takes place, the next two guards have already sprinted up to the line. The coach now calls waggle to the left, or "21 waggle." The next two run "21 waggle," so they go to the left. The first guard pulls and logs, and the backside guard pulls, crosses over, and kicks out. We can rapid-fire the drill. It is 29 waggle, 21 waggle, 29 waggle, 21 waggle, 29 waggle, boom, boom, boom, boom, a lot of reps. If you do the drill this way, you can get tons of reps in five minutes. Every time your guards go, the next time they come to the back of the line, they switch sides so they can be the other guard. All of our pulling techniques are taught like this.

**Sweep Drill**

The sweep drill has the same type of set up as the waggle (Diagram 5.15). Every lineman is going to play guard. We are going to cross-train again. We have two guards up in position, in the guard spots, on the spacing boards. The cones are now placed two yards deep in the backfield and right on the inside leg of the tackle, which is marked by the second dark spot on the spacing boards. The coach is in a central location. The guards are down in their three-point stance, and the coach says "21 sweep," or sweep right, or whatever direction he chooses.

The first guard is going to pull step on a 45-degree angle away from the line of scrimmage. On that step, his eyes go right to his target. We have two players holding shields in the positions where we are going to have to execute the sweep blocks. If we are playing against a penetrating strong safety or corner, we put the shield two yards deep in the backfield. The first guard is the kick-out guard. His first and second steps are at a 45-degree angle away from the line of scrimmage. His third step flattens out, and his fourth step starts downhill tight off the wingback's block. The wingback is blocking down on the defensive end. The guard is going to work inside out and wants his head inside, whether the defender has penetrated the backfield, or whether he has to go up the field to kick him out. This is a right-shoulder block when you are going to the right, a left-shoulder block when you are going to the left. This footwork will allow us to come downhill and get an inside-out path on the kick-out block. If we ever run sweep to a diveback side, it also allows the diveback to get out of the guard's way so that there is no collision. If you pull the guard flat down the line of scrimmage and then try to run the sweep to the diveback side, the guard and back run into each other.

The backside guard takes a pull step with his right foot, and he sprints flat down the line of scrimmage until he gets to the other guard's position. When the backside guard gets to the right guard's position, he is going to gain a little bit of depth so he can step around any trash. The backside guard must not get knocked off by penetration. As he pulls, his eyes go immediately to the playside inside linebacker, and he needs to be ready for the linebacker to be scraping to the outside. The guard is going to come around the wingback's block, or through the first opening he can find in the line of scrimmage that will enable him to cut off the linebacker scraping. The guard is going to wall the scraping backer off, so his head will be upfield, and he will use a left-shoulder block. We want him to finish his block back toward the line of scrimmage.

On the coach's command, the first guards execute sweep right. As soon as they make contact, the coach makes any corrections he needs to make. The two guys who played defense will hand the shields to the two guys who just played offense, and the two guys on defense will now run to the back of the line and get lined up for their turn to play guard. While that is happening, the next two guards have already sprinted up to the line of scrimmage, and they are in position and ready to go. The coach says sweep left, "29 sweep," and the first guard goes and kicks out; the second guard goes and walls off. While those two are doing that, the next guards run up to the line and get ready to go to the right on the next repetition. Every repetition is rapid-fire in order to get as many reps in as you can. We have taught all the linemen how to play guards on waggle and also on the sweep.

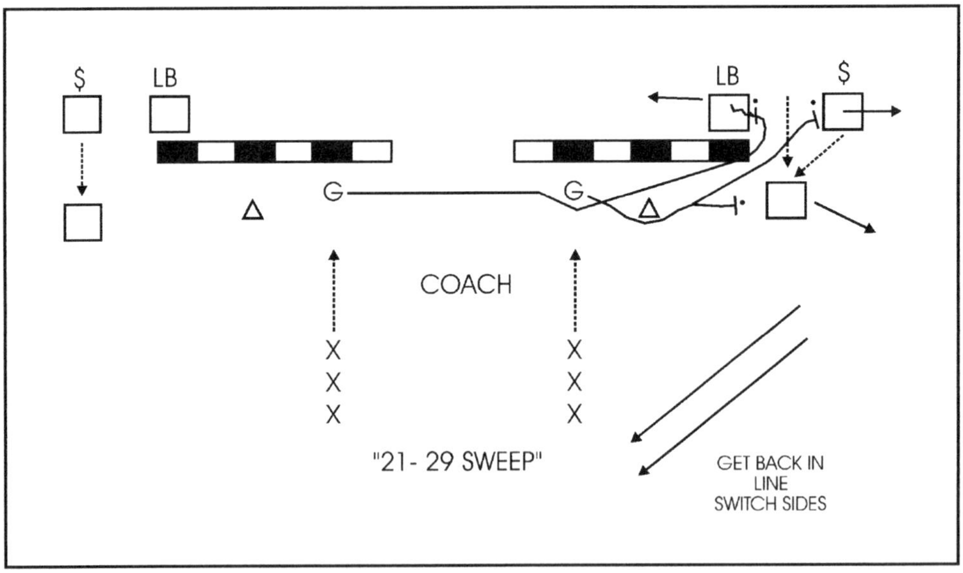


**Diagram 5.15**

We can do the same thing with any trap play, any gut play, or any kind of play where we are pulling guards (Diagram 5.16). We do the exact same drill and just set the defense up the way we want it. If we were going to run "22 gut," the first guard is going to pull step. He is going to gut around the tight end 's block, and he will be looking for the linebacker who will be scraping into the off-tackle area. As the guard comes around, he blocks the linebacker with a wall-off technique, with his head upfield and blocking with his left shoulder. The defensive end is the penetrator; that is why we are calling this play. The backside guard pulls flat down the line as fast as he can, and he kicks the end out with his right shoulder. While the blockers are making the bag exchange, the next guards sprint up. The bag holders come to the back of the line and get ready to be guards. The next two guards run "28 gut" to the left. We are alternating right, left, right, left, right, left. Every time the guards get a chance to come back and get lined up, they switch sides so they can get a chance to do all the techniques.

Gut right, gut left, trap right, trap left-whatever kind of pulling technique you want to work on for that particular day can be done in this fashion with this drill set up this way. We generally work on sweep and waggle drill all year long, and add trap and gut drills as we need them.

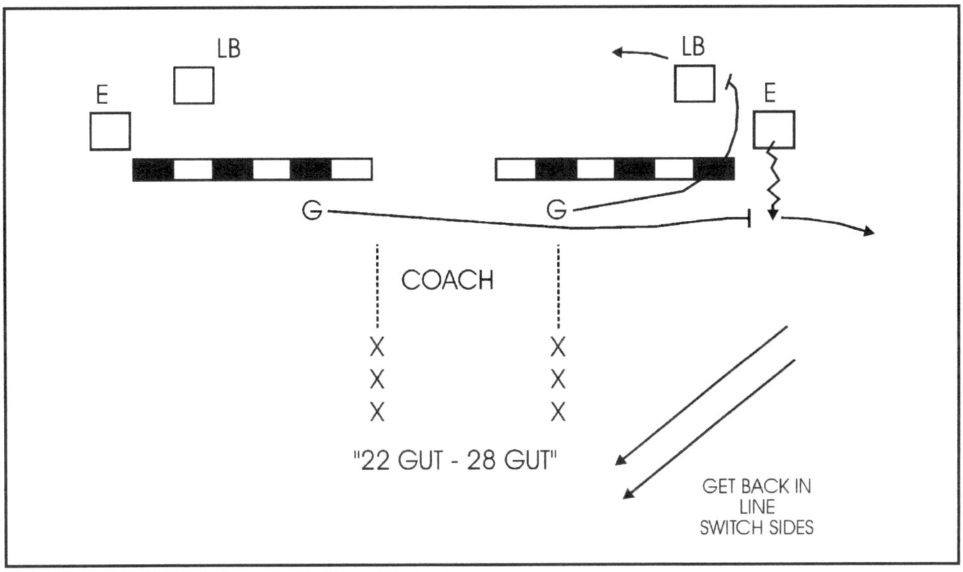


**Diagram 5.16**

## PASS-PROTECTION DRILLS

### Mirror Drill

The next drills that we are going to work on with our linemen are our pass-protection drills (Diagram 5.17). The first drill that we do is called mirror drill, and we do this with partners. The partners should be two or three yards apart. When we first do the drill, we have the linemen put their hands behind their back. We do not want the linemen using their hands in this drill yet, because we want them to learn to move their feet. We will start this drill with one blocker in a good pass-blocking position. We want good knee bend, head up, back arched, neck pulled, and the shoulders back. The other player, who is simulating the defense, is going to go back and forth, right and left, and make his partner move his feet and mirror him.

On the coach's command, one partner starts moving right and left, and our blocker will try to keep that man between his legs, just as he always does on any block, and slide with him, keeping his feet apart all the time. As they mirror, they slide their back foot first. This allows them to always have space between their feet. What you do not want is for the blocker to open up and move his front foot first. This would allow the defender escape avenues behind the blocker. We do the mirror drill with all the offensive linemen facing a partner. We do it with all our linemen at the same time. Then we switch and the other man comes over, and he gets a chance to do the drill. This drill constitutes the first phase of our pass-blocking progression.

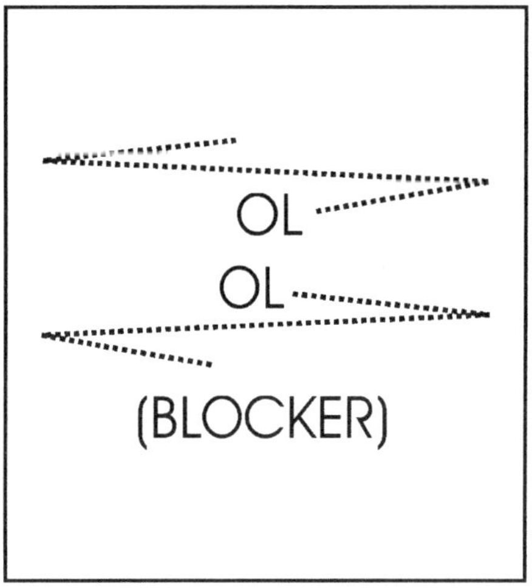


**Diagram 5.17**

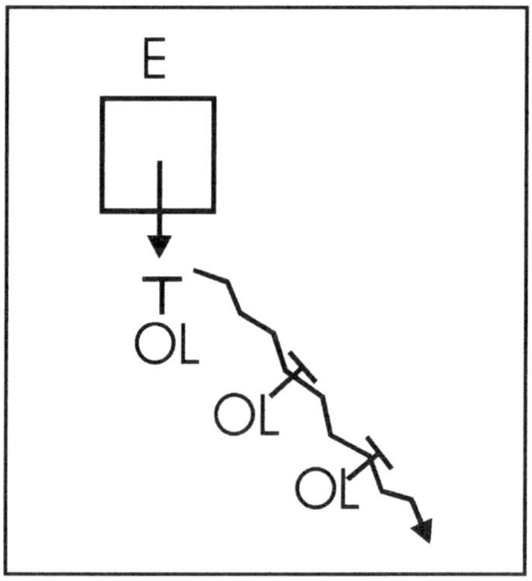


**Diagram 5.18**

**Jam Drill**

The second part of the pass-protection progression is jam drill (Diagram 5.18). In this drill, our offensive pass blocker is going to assume a good pass-blocking position, with knees bent, shoulders back, neck pulled, and target with his hands. He is going to block through the picture window created by his hands at his target. The defensive partner will come forward. The blocker will jam one good shot, then recoil and separate. The defensive man will keep coming. Then the pass blocker will jam again, lock him out, and ride the defender upfield past the quarterback. We emphasize keeping a good body position, pass rusher between the legs, good knee bend, neck pulled back, all the proper fundamentals we have taught in our other drills.

### Mirror and Jam

The next thing we want to do is incorporate both the mirror and the jam by combining the first two drills (Diagram 5.19). Our offensive blocker is going to get into good position. The defensive man is going to go sideways and then attack the blocker, forcing the blocker to jam him. The defensive man can go back and forth, left and right. Whenever he wants to, he can attack forward. Whatever simulates a pass rusher rushing an offensive lineman is what you want this defensive man to do. We will have our defensive man head fake to one side and then go to the other side, and we want our offensive blocker to execute a good jam on him.

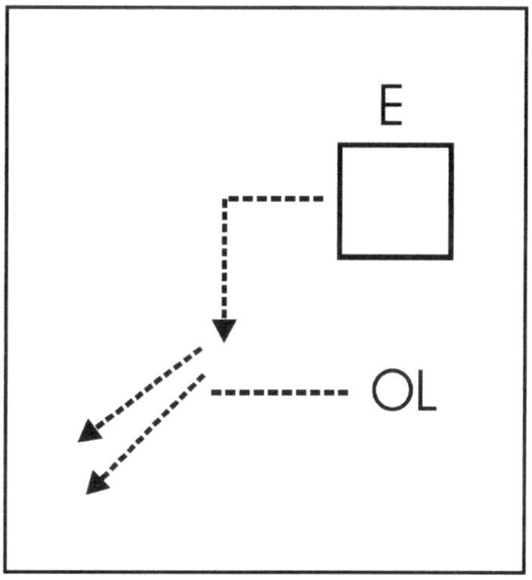


**Diagram 5.19**

### Kick Step

The next part of this progression is what we call kick step (Diagram 5.20). On kick step, we are simulating blocking a wide rusher coming off the edge. The defender is going to come off the edge as if he is trying to get to the quarterback deep in the backfield. The offensive pass blocker already has the rusher quite a bit outside of him. The key is to intersect the pass rusher without the blocker opening himself up to getting beat inside. The one thing we do not want to do is turn the shoulders. If we turn the shoulders, we open up a clear path for the pass rusher to come inside of us. What we coach is to keep the shoulders square and cut the rusher off by taking an intersecting angle and keeping inside-out position on him, so that if the rusher does come back inside, we are in position to block him. We will do that with a technique we call the kick step. The kick step means that we are going to step back and out with the outside foot, while trying to keep the shoulders square the whole time. We might have to kick step once, we might have to kick step again. The rhythm is kick step and slide, kick step and slide. The outside foot will kick step. The inside foot is what we call our post foot, and that post foot slides. We can kick and slide as many times as we have to in order to get the amount of width that we need to intersect the wide pass rusher. What we must not do is run way outside the rusher and open up the inside path to the quarterback. We want to keep inside-out leverage as we kick step backwards.

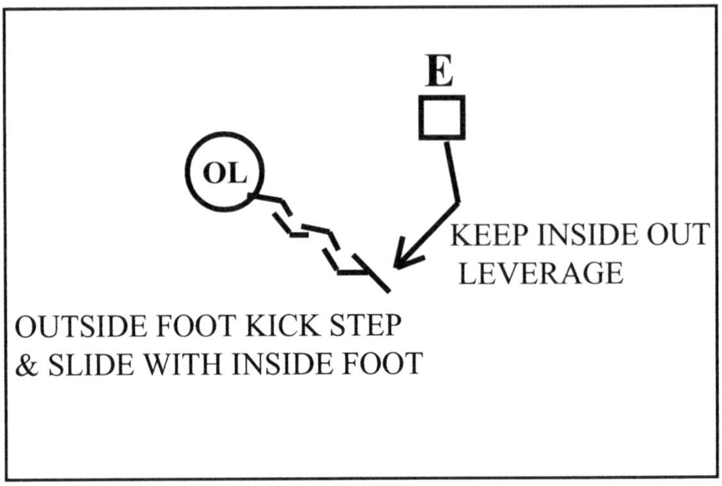


**Diagram 5.20**

**Stunt Pickup**

The last part of our pass-blocking progression is what we call stunt pickup (Diagram 5.21). We use four players to do this drill. We usually teach our offensive linemen to do this against offensive linemen, and then we will do this against the defense live. The two pass rushers can do anything they want. One rusher can go inside, but we have to be able to block him. The other rusher can go outside, but we also have to be ready to block that rush. The two pass rushers can execute stunts or twists. The rusher on the outside, a defensive end, for example, may come crashing down inside; as he crashes, the inside man takes a step forward and then loops to the outside.

We coach two ways to pick up these kinds of stunts. The first way is to man the stunt, which implies that the blockers are going to block their man, regardless of where he goes. In order to do that, the pass blockers have to be able to get on two different levels. The tackle has to step back a little bit on the snap and get a little bit more depth than the guard, or vice versa. We also have to be able to switch with our man and not run into each other. One way or another, we have to make sure that our two pass blockers do not knock each other down. If you are a man-to-man team, and you are going to block man-to-man all the way, then it is really important to get the pass blockers on different levels as they cross each other so they do not pick each other.

The other way to pass block stunts is with zone protection. When you zone it, that means you are going to pass the stunt off. In order for two linemen to zone off a stunt, two things have to happen: First of all, the blocker who sees his man loop must yell the direction of the loop. As soon as he sees the looper go, he has got to yell, "Outside, outside, outside!" Next, both of our pass blockers are going to block their man until they hear the outside or inside call and until they feel the other blocker knock them off of their man. What happens is, as the penetrator comes down inside, our outside man keeps pass blocking him. As the inside man sees the loop, he yells, "Outside, outside!" and he steps right through the hip of his adjacent blocker. He will knock him off, and he will take the block over, forcing the outside blocker to pick up the loop. Two things are important: One man must recognize and call the loop, and then he must turn and knock the other blocker off the penetrator so that blocker will know that he is to pick up the looper. One thing you must be careful of is that you must stop the penetrator first, because you have plenty of time to come off on the loop. The defense does not have to run a stunt. They can pass-rush straight up the field. The pass blockers must always be prepared to block the man on them. They have to block the man on them and be honest about that block until they hear the call and feel the bump. The blockers must not anticipate and leave early.

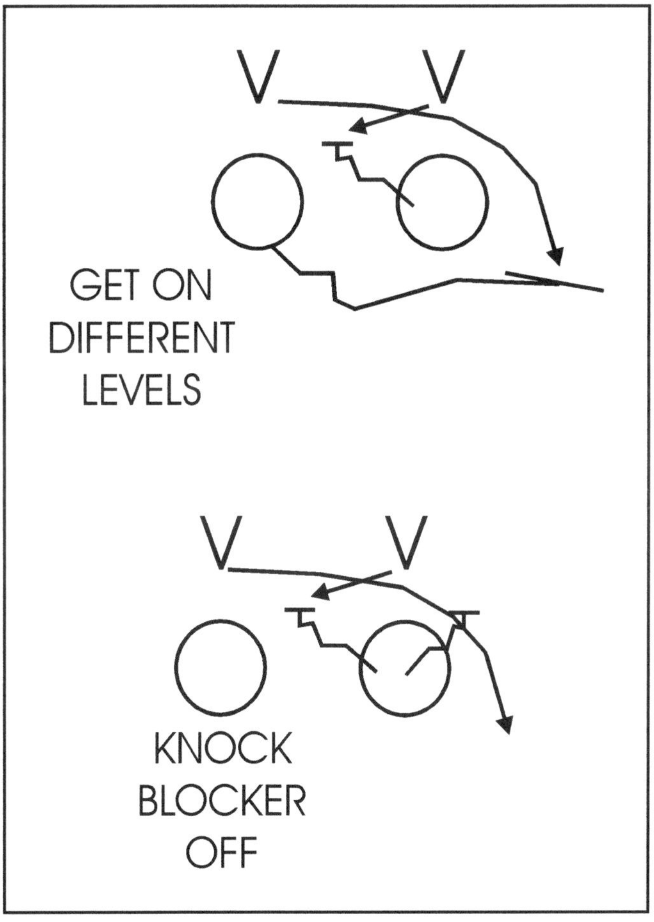


**Diagram 5.21**

## MIXED GROUP WORK

The final parts of our practice plan for our offensive linemen involve group work and team periods. We have a period that we call mixed group work which is essential to the offensive line. There are two parts to mixed group work. One is called internal and the other is perimeter drill. Both go on at the same time.

### Internal Drill

This is the part of practice where the offensive line-both guards, the center, both tackles, and sometimes the tight end-work on inside running plays (Diagram 5.22). They also have a set of backs in the drill. The defense has the front 7, or front 8, whatever the front is, with no defensive backs in the drill. What we work on are our internal run plays. We want to go off tackle and up the middle, for the most part. We might throw a pass once in a while to keep the linebackers honest. We might, once in a while, run an outside play or an option to keep the defense from pitching down inside.

We are going to take the same number of plays and run them over and over again until we get the inside game blocked the way we want. No matter what play we run, we are going to get the internal blocking scheme down so that we can block each front we will see. If we can move the ball inside in this kind of a drill, where the defense knows it is an inside run, then it will be much easier to run the ball once we start mixing it up with our flank game and passing game, and put 11 people out on the field, when the defense does not know what is coming.

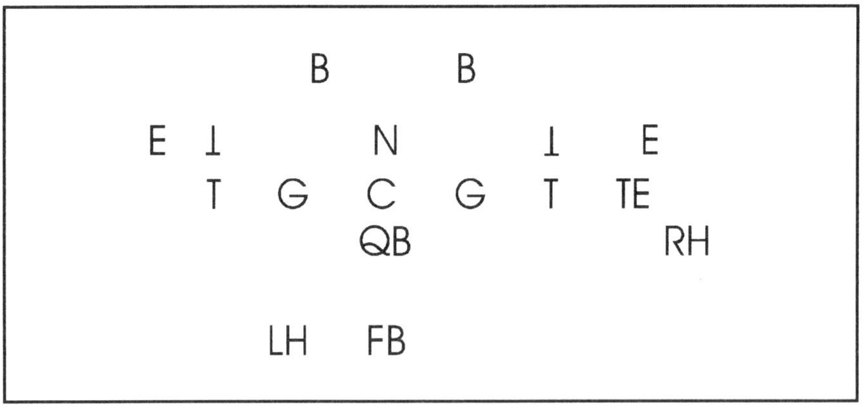


**Diagram 5.22**

### Perimeter Drill

While internal drill is going on, we have another drill going on at the same time which is called perimeter drill (Diagram 5.23). Perimeter drill is the opposite of internal drill. It contains all our outside running plays, flank passing, and plays where we want to protect the flank and the quarterback. We run bootlegs, waggles, sprint passes, and our perimeter running game. The defense in this drill has all their linebackers and all their defensive backs. If defensive ends drop into coverage or also force the run, then we have them in the drill. There are no defensive linemen in this drill, nor are there any offensive tackles. Just as in internal drill, where there are no wide receivers and no defensive backs, this drill has no tackles and no defensive linemen. The center can be one of your good centers or not. We can put the noseguard in this drill and then have one of our good centers execute his blocking technique. Most of the time, we use one of our substitutes to snap the ball.

This drill is going on at exactly the same time that internal drill is going on. Players can rotate every other day, or they can rotate halfway through the drill. If the drill is 10 minutes long, you can have the guards and the backs and the tight end switch after five minutes, and then do the same thing with the linebackers and the defensive ends.

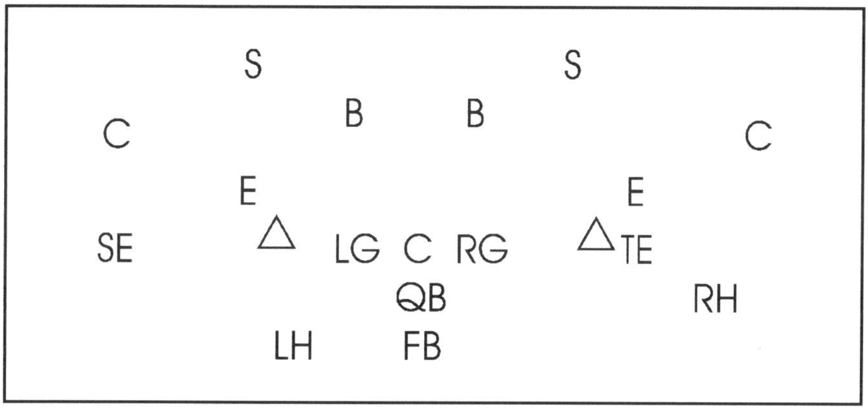


**Diagram 5.23**

## Passing Game
During the second part of mixed group work, we work on the passing game. In the first part, we focused on our running game. We have an internal drill and a perimeter drill, mostly runs, both going on at the same time. When we have mixed group work and work on the passing game, we again have two different drills going on at the same time.

## Pass Skeleton
At one end of the field, we will have a quarterback, a right half, a tight end, a fullback, a left half, and a split end (Diagram 5.24). They will be throwing pass routes against the defensive coverage people, including the defensive ends, if they are drop people, the linebackers, and the defensive backs, running whatever coverage we need to see. This is called pass skeleton, or "skelly." We are running routes against the coverages and executing our reads.

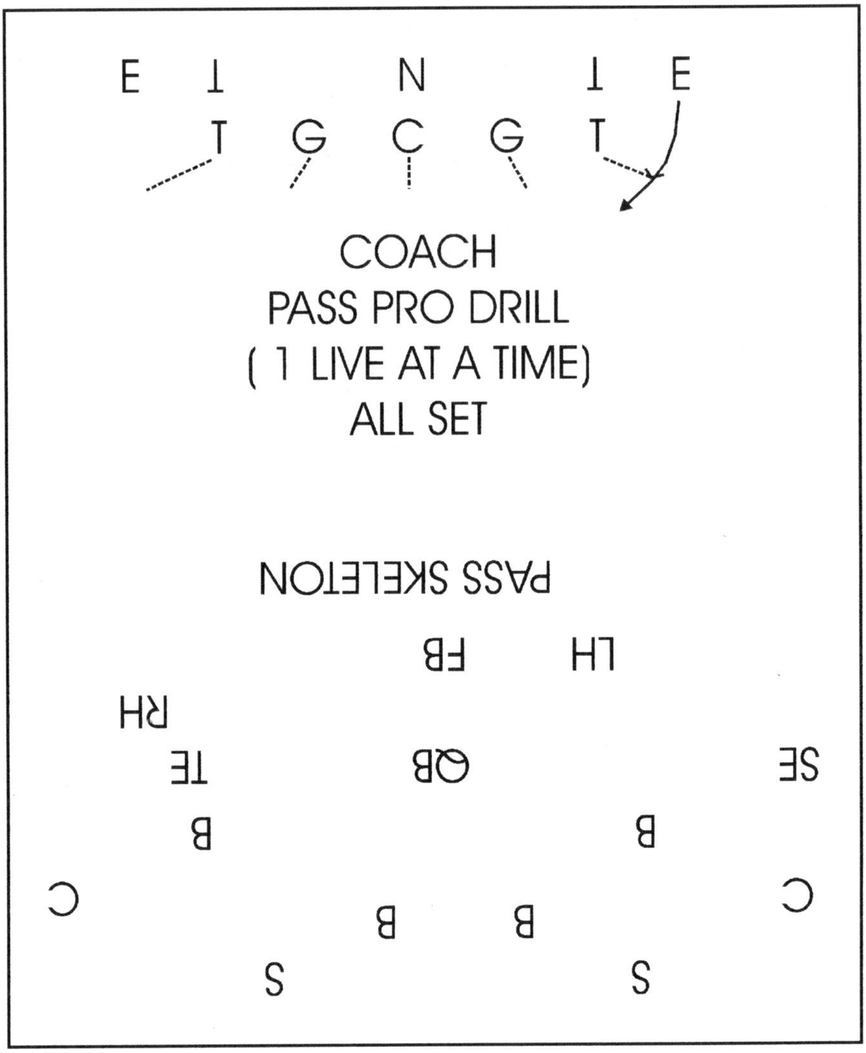


**Diagram 5.24**

**Pass Pro**

While this is going on, down at the offensive line end of the field we have a drill in progress called pass pro. We have five interior offensive linemen, all down in their stance and ready to go. We put the defensive players across from them. We might use a noseguard, a defensive tackle, or a defensive end. The coach will stand back and indicate to one of the pass rushers that he is live on the play. There is only one rusher going at a time. However, the offense does not know which pass rusher is live, so they all have to take a good set. All the offensive linemen are working on exploding out of their stance and getting out of their stance quickly and working on a good pass set. But only one of them will actually end up blocking a live rusher. It is up to the offensive coach to decide which defender is live. We also incorporate the stunt pickup against the defense by having two-on-two, three-on-three, three-on-two, or any combination we need to see from the defense.

## SUMMARY

What I have detailed in this chapter is everything we do with our offensive line and every technique we teach our linemen throughout our practices. We cannot teach them every techniques, nor can we use every drill in every practice. What we do is to pick out a couple of single blocks, a couple of combination blocks, and then work those blocks until we feel as though our players have those down pat and can execute them well. Then the next day we will go to others that we did not cover the first day, and pick those up. It is the same thing with our waggle drills or any of our pulling drills-one day using waggle drill or sweep drill, the next day possibly gut drill. Our teaching strategy is based on the week's game plan and whether or not we plan to run a lot of sweeps or a lot of waggles. In our pass pro drill, we try to get as much of that work in as we can each day. We are going to do skeleton almost every single day. Mixed group work is something we are certainly going to do all through training camp and spring football. As the season progresses, we do less and less of mixed group work and more and more of team work. Each practice, though, contains the basic elements we have discussed, all of which clearly reinforce the fundamentals and techniques we use in the wing-T offense.

# CHAPTER 6

# Wing-T Game Planning

In this final chapter of the book, I will address how we game plan for the wing-T offense. It is my opinion that coaches put too much pressure on themselves trying to come up with some magical game plan every week, when they really do not have to do that. The plays in our offense have rules. If you block the rules, the plays will take care of themselves. We feel, as an offensive staff, that the most important duty on game day is to make sure that we have coaches who are disciplined and assigned to watch defenders. If you are going to run a play to the right, then you count defenders. This is the foundation for all the blocking rules I have described in the previous chapters. You count defenders, and then you attack #3. If the #3 defender is penetrating up into the backfield, that tells us we should be running inside him, off tackle, or possibly farther inside—internal—depending on how #2 reacts. If the third defender is sealing down inside, then we should either be running at the fourth defender or throwing play action in behind the fourth defender, depending on his reaction. The wing-T offense is a sequence-oriented offense. It is an offense that allows you to say, "If they do this, we will do that." In order to be able to make those decisions, you must be disciplined as a coach and watch the defenders. We have coaches on our staff who are responsible for watching #3, #4, and #2 all the time. If we have extra guys, we would like them to watch the free safety and the trail player from the backside. Our whole basis for making game plan decisions is to watch the defensive players. From that point on, you don't have to be a magician. All you have to do is be able to call the companion plays according to the defender's reactions. And you can really torture a defense.

In this offense, you have three or four base series of plays. If you stick with those base series, watch the defenders, and call companion plays, you will not need anything else. We have our sweep series, our trap option series, our power series, and our belly series. We do not really need anything else. We just make it work. There are some companion plays that can help you break some keys now and then, but for the most part, you ought to be able to make your offense work just by your coaches watching the defenders and their reactions.

### OFF-SEASON FILM STUDY

The coaches on our staff do not talk about game plans at all, until we have completed an exhaustive, off-season film study. This task involves at least three coaches, and it probably takes a good five to six hours just to cover the offense for one game film. Clearly, with that kind of effort and time put into it, it is not something that you will necessarily do during each week of preparation for each game. The other thing that you will run into as a coach running the wing-T is that you may be the only team in your league that runs the wing-T, which hinders you in trying to learn how your opponents will defense you. When I was the head coach at Edinborough, we were the only team in that league that ran the wing-T. I always try to be as unique as possible with what we do both offensively and defensively. If there are a lot of other teams running wing-T in your league, then maybe the defensive people in your league are getting used to seeing the wing-T offense and also getting better at stopping it. However, your best film and your best scouting report are going to come from analyzing your own film from previous years. When you exchange films with your opponent, you get possibly three games. Maybe the first two are against I-formation teams, and the third one is against a one-back passing team. What did your offense gain from that? You might not have gained anything. But by studying your own film in the off-season and how the defenses react to you, you can get a good feel for how a particular team is going to try to defend the wing-T.

**Play Charts**

Our off-season film study begins by reviewing and diagramming each play that was run the previous year (Diagram 6.1). We are going to use one piece of paper for every play that we ran against our opponent in the previous game. Possibly the first play called was 121, where the quarterback is going to reverse pivot, hand the ball off to the halfback on the sweep, and then come on out and fake the waggle. What we do when we break the film down in the off-season is draw in our formation, which is 100. And then we draw in the defense we are facing, by jersey number. There are no E's and T's and D's in the diagram, just jersey numbers. When we put the defense down by jersey number, this teaches us a lot of things. By putting down No. 80 on the diagram—representing possibly one of their outside linebackers or a defensive end—we can find out if he is flip-flopping to the wide side of the field, or if he is going to our tight end all the time. We can determine whether he goes to the strength of our formation all the time, or into the short side of the field. There are a lot of different things that you can learn before you ever have the ball snapped, just by putting the defenders into jersey numbers. You obviously can learn who the starters are, and who the backups are. Then, with your game program, you can pretty much figure out if there are seniors at certain positions, and since they are graduating, who will be taking their place the following year. You also need to be able to study the individual defensive personnel and how good they are. You need to ask yourself the following: What can they do well? What can't they do well?

The next thing that we do differently from some staffs is not only assigning jersey numbers to all the defenders written down, but also noting every bit of their reaction to the play. We want to get as many reactions for these people drawn in as possible. We want to see who forces the sweep. We want to see if the free safety stays in the middle or not. We want to see how the linebackers key and how they react. We want to know what kinds of techniques the people play up front. This information is readily available to us; all we have to do is go through a game film. We may have to run the play back 22 times to do this. You should not have to, though, because you know who your own people were supposed to block. Consequently, you should be able to at least begin to draw their blocks in, and then start drawing the reaction from the defense. We draw the defensive player all the way to the play.

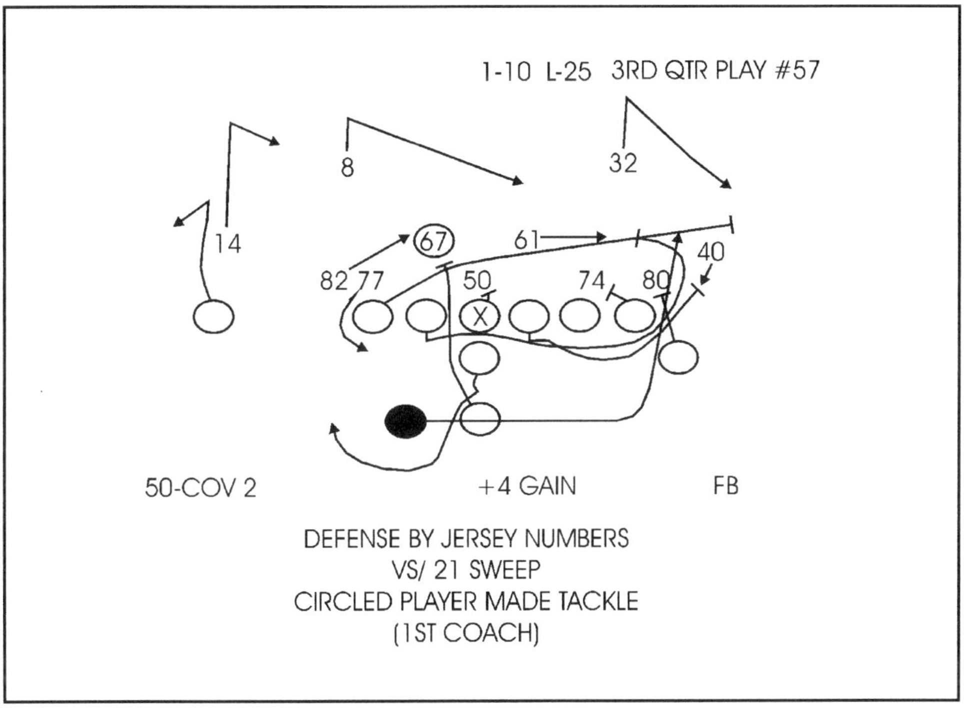


**Diagram 6.1**

Let's just say, for instance, we ran 121 sweep to the right, and No. 67, the backside linebacker, was the guy who made the tackle because our fullback was not able to get to him coming up through the line. Or maybe our faking and our ballhandling was not good enough to keep him from flowing. If No. 67 flew out of there and made the tackle, we put a circle around his number. That way, at the end of this exercise, we can keep track of how many tackles each of these people is making against us, and who is the biggest nuisance. We can determine who we have to misdirect, who we have to make sure we get blocked. We learn a lot by taking time in the off-season to do this.

On each play chart, there is a lot of information around the edges. For instance, we want to write down on the diagram the down and distance. Let's say that for this play it was first down and 10 yards to go; then we would write "1-10." If we were on the left offensive hash mark and the wide side of the field was to our right, then we would put an "L" or "LH" for the left hash mark. The next information we want to record is the yard line. If we were on our own end of the field, we would record that as minus (-25); if we were on the opponent's end and going into score, that would be plus(+25) to us.

In the corner of our sheet we put the quarter and the play number. What this does for you is enable you to find plays by the number of the play. Clearly, if it is the third quarter and you have run only 26 plays, you might be in some trouble on the scoreboard. Conversely, if it is halftime and you have charted 38 plays, then you probably have been doing a great job at controlling the football and helping your defense out. At the bottom of the page we are going to write in what the defense is. If we are seeing a 50 defense with a two-deep secondary, we write down "50 cover 2." We also write down the result of the play. If this play gained four yards before we got tackled, and if we did get the play stopped for less than an "efficient play," we write down what stopped the play. If the play was "efficient," then we only record the result. If we make four yards or more on first or second down, then that is what we call an "efficient" play. If it is third down and one, and we make two yards, that's an efficient play, because you made the first down. If it is third down and eight, and you only made six yards and had to punt, that is not an efficient play. An efficient play is a play that makes the first down, or the required yardage. For first and second down, our required yardage is four yards per play. If we gain four yards per play, that puts us in third and short. If you break a tackle, you gain more yards, and then you're down the field quickly.

That is the information we gather for just one play! It takes quite a while to do during the off-season. It usually takes us about six to eight minutes per play, sometimes as long as 10 minutes, depending on how well we see the jersey numbers on the film. But we will do that for every play of the game—every single play. One coach's job, while we are watching the film and running it back and forth, is to write this information on pre-made sheets that we use to record the plays. You can save yourself a lot of time if you can make sheets with the blocks already on them. Down and distance, hash mark, yard line, quarter, play, defense, any comments you want to make, are written on this sheet. We make a block for all those different information items. And then we have the center and the two guards and the two tackles drawn in pre-snap. We can immediately begin on each play and try to save ourselves as much time as possible. It takes time to do this, and you have to be dedicated and committed to it. But it is the very best thing you can do to garner information on your opponents. As I mentioned earlier, before we ever start a game plan meeting, the first thing we have to have done is this off-season film study so that we can gain as much information on our opponents as possible. That is the first phase of our game planning, and it takes a while. We have one of our three offensive coaches do this, and while he is busy, we have a second coach and a third coach doing other jobs.

## Down & Distance, Field Position Tendency Chart

The second coach's job during off-season film study is to create what we call a "Down & Distance, Field Position Tendency Chart" (Diagram 6.2). Across the top of the chart we make a column for all the possible downs and distances that we can have. We will have a column for 1st-and-10, second down and 11-plus, and then all the second-down yardage situations. We do the same thing for third down. We have a column for third down and 11-plus, and all the third-down yardage situations. We also will have a column for fourth downs. If there is ever any question about how many yards to go for a first down, for example, on 2nd-and-11-plus, we might put in parentheses that it was for 15 yards. What we have now is all the downs and distances across the top. We write all the field positions down the sides. We start from the plus-five-yard line to the goal line, going in for a touchdown, which is what we call "goal line." Let's say we get the ball 1st-and-5, and the defense is a 6-5. Then we will write 6-5 in the box formed by the column for first down and the row for plus-five to goal line. When we review this later, this entry reminds us that the opponent is in a goal line defense at the 5-yard line. We just mark down in each corresponding box whatever we see the opponent run. Obviously, you have no 2nd-and-11s from inside the 5-yard line, so that will be crossed out because it is not possible to do from the 5-yard line.

| DOWN & DISTANCE/ FIELD POSITION TENDENCY | | | | | | | | | | | |
|---|---|---|---|---|---|---|---|---|---|---|---|
| | 1-10 | 2-11+ | 2-10 | 2-9 | 2-8 | 2-7 | 2-6 | 2-5 | 2-4 | 2-3 | 2-2 |
| 5 TO GOAL | 65-1 | | | | | | | 65-1 | | | GAP 8-1 |
| 20 TO 5 RED ZONE | 44-1 | | BLITZ BLITZ | 44-1 | | | BLITZ | | | | |
| 50 TO 20 4 DOWN | 44-3 | | | | 44-3 | | 44-3 44-3 | | 44-3 | | 44-1 |
| -20 TO 50 3 DOWN | 50-1 50-2 50-3 | 50-3 | | 50-3 BLITZ | | 44-3 | | 50-3 | 44-3 | | |
| -5 TO -20 | 44-3 | BLITZ | 50-3 | 44-3 | | 50-3 | | | | 50-3 | 50-3 |
| GOAL TO 5 COMING OUT | 44-3 | | | | 50-3 | | | | | | |

**Diagram 6.2**

As we progress down the chart, we have a row for the plus-20-yard line to the plus-5, and that is what we call the "red zone." We will chart opponents' red zone defenses and whatever they run in that red zone area. We write them in the corresponding blocks. The next area we call "four-down territory," from the 50-yard line to the plus-20-yard line. It might be four-down territory for you, or it might not be. It depends on what your field goal kicker's range is. Some years we make this area the plus-40-yard line to the plus-20-yard line, depending on our field goal kicker's range and what we want to consider "four down" territory that year. The next area, working down the side of the page, is our "three-down territory," from our own 20 out to midfield, or wherever four-down territory starts.

Continuing down the chart, we have the minus-5-yard line to the minus-20-yard line. That is when you are really "backed up" and you really need a first down. At the bottom of the page, from the goal line to the minus-5-yard line, is called "coming out." In this area of the field, you are talking about plays that are run from your own goal line to the minus-5-yard line. This is when you really need to get off your own goal line, not get sacked in the end zone for safeties, and not have your ball carrier stopped in the end zone for a safety. We try to run safe plays down here, so that we do not turn it over and give the opponent an easy touchdown drive. Those things do happen once in a while, but I think if you plan against it, you can minimize it.

What we want to know from this chart is which defenses our opponents were in with regard to all these different field positions and down-and-distance situations, represented by each of the blocks on the chart. When we game plan, we do not necessarily need to plan for all these downs and distances. For example, on second or third down, we may say that anytime it is second down and 9-plus, anything higher than 9-plus, we know that they are going to be in some kind of man-to-man coverage and possibly some kind of a blitz. Maybe their percentage is really high, possibly 90 percent blitz or 90 percent man coverage, when it is second down and 9-plus yards to go. We will take out our game plan sheet, and we will list second down and 9-plus as an area, or a down and distance grouping, and now we can condense and combine the different defenses that we see in there. The same thing holds true for 2nd-and-short and third-down situations.

Every week, you may have a different set of guidelines for what constitutes short yardage and long yardage, based on how your opponent reacts. That is the beauty of doing it this way. You can get better tendencies. If you preprogram defensive tendencies into your own mind, sometimes you will be calling plays against different defenses that might not be the best plays to call in those situations. We try to make these charts preseason. We make 11 of them, one for each of our 11 opponents. We have these charts prepared in advance, and all we do is fill in the blocks as we are watching the films in the off-season.

As we are breaking down the film in the off-season, one coach is doing the play diagrams, and one coach is doing the down & distance, field position tendency chart, filling in all the blocks. Here we are finding out what the tendencies of the defense are. Maybe this week they play short yardage on third down and one, and as soon as it's third down and two, they don't play short yardage anymore. But next week, you face an opponent that plays short yardage all the way up to third down and three. Every week it might just be a little bit different, and this chart helps us tell exactly what the opponent's defensive tendencies are, not only by down and distance, but also by field position.

**Personnel, Scheme, Attack, Comment Sheet**

Let's say you have a quarterbacks coach who also coaches the running backs, and you have a line coach and a receivers coach—that's the minimum that you need in order to coach the wing-T and do it well (Diagram 6.3). If so, you have three coaches working with your offense, and so you have three things to do when you are conducting your off-season film breakdown. The third item we prepare during the off-season is a sheet for comments with regard to scheme of attack, personnel, or any points of emphasis we want to note for the following season. There are three columns on this sheet. The first column is for comments about the opponent's personnel. When we talk about their personnel, we are talking about their starters and their backups—the comments we make about their personnel as we watch the film. For example, if we have observed that No. 17 backs up the free safety, who is No. 14, we can make a list of all the backups so that you know who is going to take over for any seniors who might have been playing on defense the previous year. If we notice that No. 60 was injured against a certain team, we can write that down. We may note that this player, if he has a serious injury, may not be as good next year, or perhaps might be a defender we don't have to worry about attacking as much. Anything that refers to the opponent's personnel we put in this first column.

| PERSONNEL, SCHEME, ATTACK, COMMENT SHEET | | |
|---|---|---|
| THEIR PERSONNEL | THEIR SCHEME | OUR ATTACK |
| #17 BACKUP FOR #14 FS<br>#60 INJURED VS SDSU<br><br>#58 BACKUP LB<br><br>#7 SLOW TO CONTAIN | DE #75 PLAY TRAIL FOR REVERSE<br><br>DE #77 DOES NOT TRAIL BLITZ IN RED ZONE 17 YD<br><br>SLANT TO TE 1ST DOWN | BEGIN OFF TACKLE<br><br>ATTACK LEFT DE WITH OFF TACKLE PLAY<br><br>FS #10 NOT GOOD DEEP COVER, THROW PLAY ACTION POST |

**Diagram 6.3**

The second column is reserved for comments on the opponent's defensive scheme. For instance, if their backside defensive end does stay home, and he trails the play, and he does look for reverses, that is valuable information we need to write down. If we see that No. 75 on the backside does stay home and look for reverses, but also that No. 77 on the other side does not stay home, then we know that we want to run our reverse to No. 77. Here is another example: Maybe our opponent blitzes only in the red zone. Maybe the only time we really have to worry about calling plays to beat the blitz is when they get to their red zone. Obviously, that is another of their tendencies that we need to write down, and there are many more. Anything that relates to their scheme and how they do things goes in this column. These notes provide wonderful references for the following year, when we once again make our game plans.

The last column is reserved for comments on our attack—in other words, what we want to do when we are attacking this team. Maybe we are seeing an eight-man front and we decide to begin off tackle. We decide that the left defensive end is the guy we should attack with our off-tackle power play because he is the guy who comes running up the field all the time and does not really squeeze or seal the off-tackle hole. Those are the kinds of things that we want to know—where, who, and how we should be attacking. Possibly, we observe that their free safety is not a good deep cover guy, and so we can throw the post in behind him. Maybe we notice that he is a really strong run defender, so we make note of the fact that we need to be throwing play action, and that we will need to throw it early and often. Anything we say about the opponent's defensive scheme or our attack or their personnel goes on this piece of paper. The third coach involved with the off-season film study is busy making notes in all these areas as we break down last year's film.

Along with the off-season film study, we want to compile as many statistics as we possibly can. We want to get as much information as possible about our opponent. We would like to make a preliminary game plan, even in the off-season, in terms of how (based on last year's defensive scheme) we are going to attack them in the upcoming season. We take all of this material and store it in a notebook and file it away. We save it, and we keep film studies on our opponents from as long as five years back. When our opponent changes head coaches or a new scheme comes in, we simply empty out the notebook and start over again. That has happened quite a bit in our league, so we have had to start a number of new notebooks. At least four different teams in our league have changed coaches while I have been here. Each time, that means we prepare a different notebook, plus information on any new opponents that we might have to play. We save those notebooks, because we never know when we are going to have to play those guys again down the road. Maybe in a playoff game, maybe in two years when our schedule changes. Who knows? We keep all that stuff filed. We get all the previous year's film study done in the off-season, and we keep it until the next year when we have to play them. Then we can get the notebook out, watch the film again quickly, and refresh our memory from the notes we have previously made. We can see notes that indicate that this is exactly how we said we thought we should attack them, based on what we saw on film the year before. Obviously, we must now watch the film and see what they are doing differently this year. Have they changed their scheme? Maybe they are now a

4-4 team instead of a 50 team. If this happens, it does not mean we wasted our off-season film study, because we can still learn a lot from it. We really believe in it. We do not even consider talking about any game plans during the season unless we have first done this in the off-season. We think it is an extremely important exercise.

## IN-SEASON FILM STUDY

Our in-season film study is based upon the information that we receive from our film exchanges with our opponents for that particular year. The most important thing that we are looking for is the statistical data we can get in terms of what defenses they play in certain downs and distances and key field positions. We use the same type of chart in which we can see the downs and distances across the top and the field positions down the side. We do another fully separate chart. If this were the 1996 season, and we obtained three films on each of our opponents this season, then the information from the three 1996 films that we received get plugged into a separate chart. The one we do for ourselves in the off-season is kept separate. Thus, we have two different charts. What we are trying to accomplish is to determine what types of statistics we are going to find from putting all the defenses that they are currently using into the blocks, into the down-and-distance field position situations. Is it the same as what we saw against ourselves in the previous off-season film study? That is the first thing we are looking for from this year's game statistics. We want to get a true feel for this opponent. We want to know when they are going to blitz. We want to know what their short yardage defense is. We want to know when they use those short-yardage defenses. We want to know what they do on first down. We want to know what they do on second down and long. These are the kinds of things that we have to find out. What is their red zone defense? What is their coming-out defense? We are trying to find out what types of tendencies they might have for each of these situations and whether they are the same as or different from the previous year's tendencies? We find that most of the really good teams we play against have a defensive package—a basic defense they believe in—and most of the time that is what we see from year to year. But there are always going to be change-ups. The opponents are going to change or add coverage. They might move their line on you, add a stunt or a new blitz once in a while. Thanks to our off-season and in-season film study, we should be able to nail them down. If they are not studying themselves, then we are going to have a tremendous advantage over them. If they are studying themselves and changing things up on us, again, it still goes back to how disciplined we are as a coaching staff to find out how their defenders react on game day, and how adept we are at calling companion plays to account for those reactions.

Besides establishing what is the same about our opponents from year to year, we also look for is what is different this particular year. Therefore, we go back to our off-season film study, review it, watch the film quickly, read the comment pages, and look at the statistics that we have previously seen. We want to know what is different now. Have they made a new scheme? Are they using a new scheme? Are they blitzing more in the red zone, blitzing less in the red zone, blitzing more on first down, playing more man-to-man coverage? What are the things that are different this year from last year? It has been our experience over the years that when an opponent changes from one year to the next, then you are probably going to see what you found in those films leading up to your game. You are going to see the new defense. Lots of teams go to new schemes and change up their defense year by year. If they change it up, that is basically what you are going to see. In that case, your off-season film study was done in vain, except for personnel notes—and then again, sometimes not. We have one particular opponent in our league who played a 4-3 defense. But one year we went up to play them, and lo and behold, we faced a 6-1 defense the whole game. They beat us. We were caught a little flat-footed by their 6-1 defense, because they had never shown even one single snap of 6-1 defense. They beat us with it that particular day. We did not adjust quickly enough. We thought we could do some things by formation that we were prepared for. It just did not work out. The next year, we had a great game plan, thanks to our off-season film study for that 6-1 defense. When we got the film of this team the following year, and we started watching all their games, again, they were 4-3 on every snap. We did not see any 6-1 defense. We made our game plan in response to their 4-3 defense, but, just in case, we prepared a small package of plays that we thought would hurt the 6-1 defense. We had that package of plays ready to go, if, in fact, they did the same thing to us that they did a year before, which was to show 4-3 defense leading up to our game, and then play 6-1 defense against us. We were ready for that the second time, and of course, the second time we beat them, because that is exactly what happened. We got 6-1 defense the whole game. We ended up using the smaller package of plays, but the key is that we had that stuff practiced, we had it thought out, we had it well conceived in advance. When we saw the 6-1 defense, we simply went to it, stayed with it, and actually had a fairly big day. Those are the kinds of things that you can gain from your in-season and off-season film study. Again, gather up all the statistics. Find out what is different. Finally, if there is a new scheme, are you going to be ready for it ?

## SETTING UP OUR PLAN OF ATTACK

Once we have all of the information gathered from both our in-season and off-season film study, we are going to figure out how to set up our plan of attack. There is a basic rule of thumb that we use in establishing a game plan. Our basic premise is, if the defense is a seven-man front, we want to begin by finding the flank. If it is an eight-man front, we begin off tackle. Let me discuss how we come to that conclusion. What we do is take our basic wing-T 100 formation and draw in a seven-man front (Diagram 6.40. We take an imaginary line and draw it through the outside foot of our tackles. Now, we want to count how many people are in the box—how many are between those tackles' outside feet, and how many are in the front, and what is the offense's relationship to the defense. We need to know our ratio of defenders to offensive players. In most seven-man fronts, we have five offensive linemen inside the tackle box; with our ends removed, they have five defensive players. We call that equal strength. That does not mean that any play between those tackles is not going to work. That is not true. But what it does mean is that we will begin the attack at the flank by attacking playside #3.

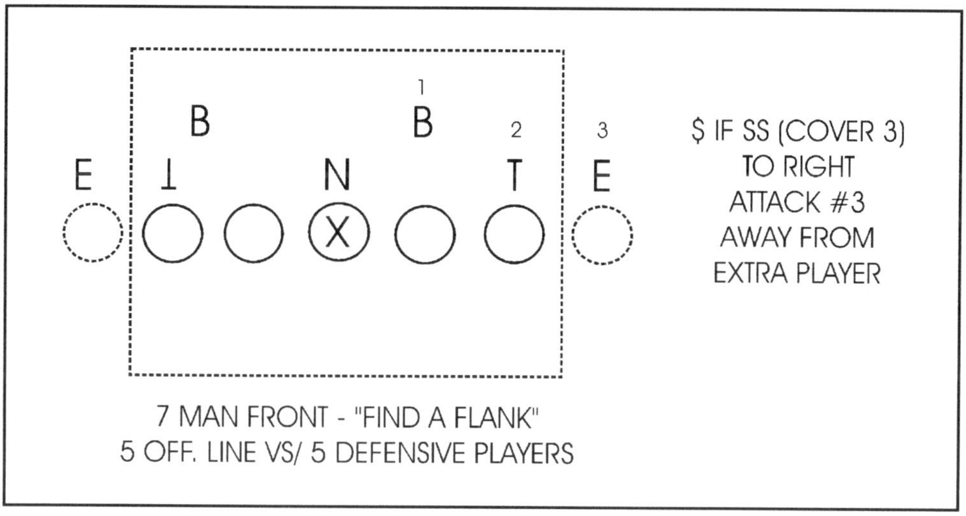


**Diagram 6.4**

If it is a seven-man front, that gives the defense four defensive backs. They can either give you a two-deep shell and balance up their secondary, or a three-deep shell and overload their secondary to one side or another. Consequently, we begin our attack at the flank. In other words, find the flank and attack the third defender on the weakest side of their defense. For example, let's say they put the strong safety over to the defensive right, which is our offensive left. They are going to put that strong safety to the left because maybe that is the wide side, or maybe that is the strong side. You have to figure that out by film analysis and also by game-day observation. Now, what they have done is to put an extra run defender with the front seven to make it like an eight-man front, except they have kept the three-deep secondary in the back row. Probably our best flank is to attack away from that rotated safety, especially if he is up close to the line of scrimmage, because he is an extra defender to that side. Therefore, we will begin our flank attack on the right, away from the strong safety. From that point, we begin to read the reactions of the defenders and adjust accordingly.

If it was a two-deep type of secondary and they were pretty well balanced, you do not necessarily have a strong safety you can attack to or away from, but what you do have now is that two-deep look. Versus the two-deep look, what we would like to do is attack where we have the flanking angles. If we had our wingback on the right in a position where he outflanked the third defender, we would probably begin our flank attack by attacking that third defender, whom we have outflanked with the wingback's blocking angles at the line of scrimmage.

That is our seven-man-front philosophy. In either case, two deep or three deep, we begin by attacking a flank. If you draw that imaginary line through the attack-side A gap and count defenders, you can easily determine which defender is #3. We begin our attack by attacking him, and then we want to see how he is reacting. If he is a penetrator up the field, we try to go off tackle inside him and find out what #2 is doing. If this third defender is sealing down, and he is stopping the off-tackle play, then we want to come outside of him. Next, we want to know what the fourth defender does. If he is really aggressive on the run, obviously, the play-action passing behind him should be good. If the #4 defender is soft on the run or slow to react, then we just keep running right at him until we can force him to come up more aggressively. It is a continual cat-and-mouse game all the way through the game. It may look different in the first quarter than it does in the fourth. The third man may be a penetrator up the field. If so, we are going to run off tackle. But if #2 is penetrating as well, then we know that we need to go inside of #2 also, with a play from our internal game. If #2 is not a penetrator, and he is going to seal down, then we will just stay right there, off tackle, until something changes. In order to do that and not run the same play all the time, we need to have a couple of different plays that hit each area from different series. As an example, 22, our buck off-tackle play, which can be blocked tag, gut, and power, conflicts with the sweep. Our 82 down or 82 gut, in the 80 series, also hits right, off tackle, and provides another look, another way to attack that same 2 hole, inside the #3 defender. Here, we are not merely running the same play all the time. Instead, we throw in different formations and run those two or three or four plays—whatever we have—out of different formations. Next, we start using some motion and some shifting, and before we know it, everything looks different to the defense, even though all we are doing is attacking their weakness inside #3 penetrating upfield every time. It is important to have play packages, to have more than one way to attack defenders in a defense. I talked about that early in the philosophy section. Begin the attack at the flank and then read the defenders and find out what their reactions are.

For an eight-man front, we draw the imaginary line through the outside foot of the tackles, and we count the number of people inside the box (Diagram 6.5). In our eight-man-front game plan, we will split our tight ends a little extra, taking them out to five feet, sometimes six feet, and see how far the defensive ends will come out with us. If the defensive ends are a 7 technique, where they are assigned to play on the inside shoulder of the tight end, we can stretch them a little bit as the tight end comes out. Now, the defensive end is no longer in the off-tackle box area, so, against an eight-man front, we begin our attack off tackle, because we have five blockers, and they have four defenders in that box. This five-on-four gives us a numerical edge, and so we begin in the off-tackle area and go from there. Again, if #3 begins to come back down and seal , even though he might be lined up wide, if he is going to seal hard, we can now take the attack back to the flank and focus on what the fourth defender does. If #3 stays wide, but #2 starts working out or upfield, then we can go to our internal attack inside #2. It all works together. That is our basic premise for beginning our game plans for those two defensive fronts.

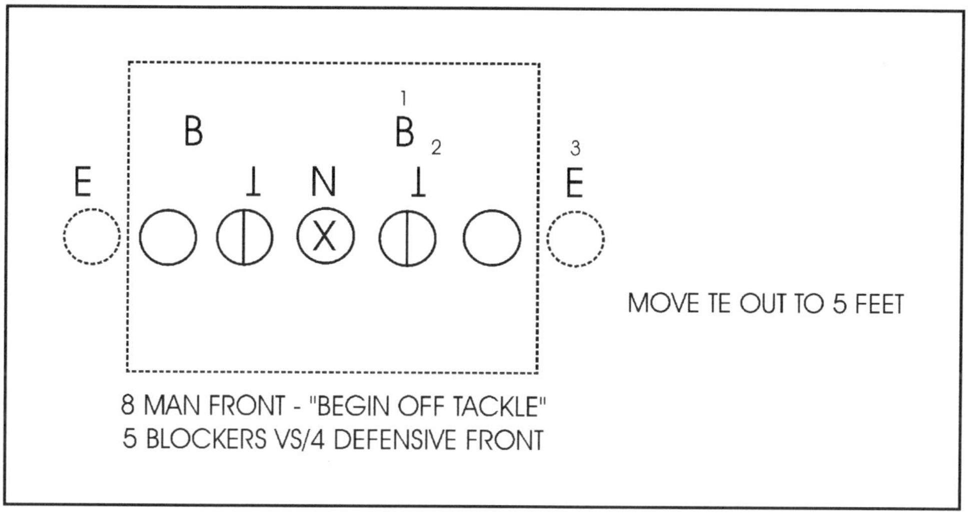


**Diagram 6.5**

If we say that we begin our attack at the flank, or begin our attack off tackle, that means exactly that—we start there. But the cat-and-mouse game, or the chess game, between the coaches continues throughout the game. As we get into our game, maybe #3 seals at the beginning of the game, but by the second quarter, he is penetrating upfield because of how we have been attacking him. Now, that is the time to change our focus as a play caller and take advantage of his reaction and run the ball off tackle. If the guys on defense are watching them, and our staff is disciplined, we will know exactly what plays to call. We just call the companion play and attack the other area, the void area, or the vulnerable area, however we describe it. You do not have to be a genius to make these play calls. You do not have to come up with some magical game plan every week. You can run your same offense from the first week of training camp, all the way through to the championship game, and not have to change anything. You just have to be ready to react to how those defensive people are reacting to you. Again, in order to do this, you need to have play packages, companion plays. If you block the tight end down, you ought to be able to hit outside of him, or inside of him. If you block the tackle down, you ought to be able to hit outside of him, or inside of him. Those are play packages, and they can be run with a number of different backfield actions, depending on how the linebackers are keying. You might want to use a certain action one week, rather than another. But that is basically how we call our plays: we just watch the defenders' reactions.

## COACHES' GAME-DAY RESPONSIBILITIES

I would like to discuss briefly the coaches' responsibilities on game day (Diagram 6.6). As you know, we number the defensive people in the defensive fronts. Let's consider a 50 defense, for example. Let's say we are going to run a play to our right.

We draw an imaginary line through the attack-side, right A gap. (It would be the left A gap, if we were going to the left.) Whoever the defenders are outside that imaginary line from the inside out are the defenders for whom we are going to set up our attack. We number them from inside out. The first guy is #1 (usually the linebacker over the guard in a 50 defense). The second guy from inside out is #2, usually a defensive tackle over our tackle. The third player from inside out, probably the defensive end or outside linebacker, is #3. The man closest to the flank who is in a support position and who will cover the pitch on the option and take the flat or the curl zone in passing—the closest man to the line of scrimmage—is #4. The furthest man in the secondary, or the guy who is going to cover deep in their secondary, is #5.

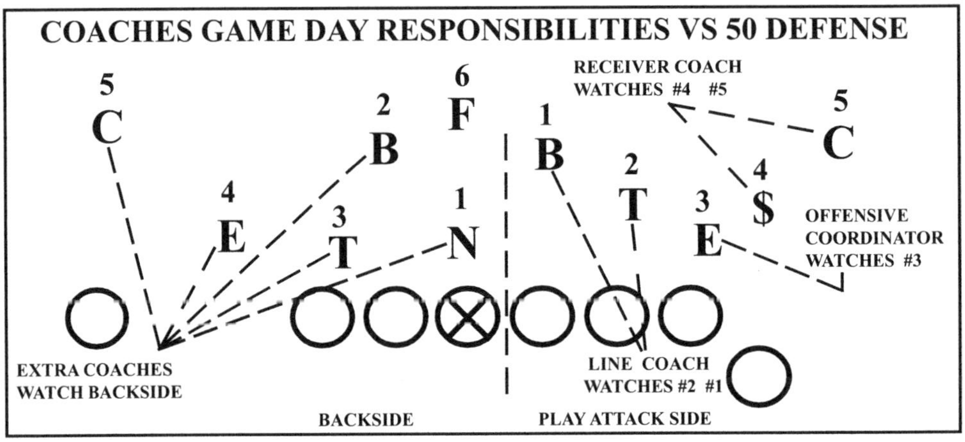


**Diagram 6.6**

Who watches these people? We assign #3 to the offensive coordinator. Our offensive coordinator should call the play, because he knows which direction the play is going; he sees the defense and finds out where #3 is aligned. He will watch #3 on this play rather than our own guys, because he wants to know what #3's reaction is. We will know what our own guys do by way of what happens out there on the field. We'll hear all the noise and ruckus. As a head coach, I am in control of the game also, and I am watching our players. But our coaches cannot be. They must be watching their assigned defenders. Let's say this #3 is a seal guy who is going to seal down and take off tackle away from us. We can bring our attack out here to #4. Our receiver coach watches #4. We want him to know how hard this guy is attacking the flank. If we run to the flank, how hard is he coming at us? Is he soft, is he hard, is he quick to react, is he slow to react, what is his reaction? We want to know exactly what he is doing. We would also like our receiver coach to watch the fifth guy as well. If he can see both of these guys, we get a little more information out of it, and we get a feel for the types of coverages and support systems that the defense is giving us. It is important for the receivers coach to see #4, and if he can see #5, that's great. If he can't see both, he must know what #4's doing. If you have extra coaches, then you can assign another extra one to #5 playside. The line coach is responsible for watching #2, so he has to know the second defender's reaction. All this information is being stored, and between series, we feed all this information into the guy who is watching #3, our coordinator, who then analyzes the information. If the line coach tells him that #2 is sealing and he also sees that #3 is penetrating up into the backfield, then that is all he needs to know. He knows we are going to take our attack and go right inside of #3 and run off tackle. If #2 is sealing, then #3 is sealing, and we then know that we have to take our attack outside and either go right at #4 with the run or behind him with the play-action pass. As for the offensive line coach, he must see #2. If he can also see #1, that's great, because that will tell us if they are doing any blitzing or cross firing or stunting.

The backside of the defense is counted as follows: The first guy is #1, not a zero. If they have a head-up nose, we do not count him or call him a zero; he is the first defender on the backside of the play. As we work toward the backside of the defense, the next defenders outside of the nose are #s 2, 3, 4, and 5.

As we look at the 4-3 defense, it is still a seven-man front (Diagram 6.7). Depending on whether or not you have a tight end in the game, the defense might show some eight-man-front looks as well. However, again, let's say we are going to run to the right. Then the attack-side A gap is the right A gap, between the center and the guard on the right. Counting from inside out, the defensive tackle is #1, the defensive end is #2, the outside linebacker is #3 (or those two could possibly be reversed). If we have a tight end and a diveback in the backfield, the backer might stack in over the tackle, and he will thus become #2, and the end will become 3. We try to attack this defense a lot to the spread end side, and we usually get the outside linebacker in a hip look to the spread end side. The man closest to the line of scrimmage in the secondary is usually the #4 player and the flat cover guy. The man who is deepest is usually the deep player or the halves or thirds cover player. Off the backside again, the first guy is #1, and then 2, 3, and 4, as we work our way out. Again, we begin our attack by attacking #3. If we can put a tight end in the formation, then the defensive end will probably move out, and the backer will come inside over the tackle. Now that the end is #3, we can watch his reactions so we will know whether to go inside or outside. Against a 4-3, we like to attack #1, the split end side. This makes the outside linebacker #3, while the tackle and the end are #1 and #2, respectively, and the corner and safety are #4 and #5, respectively. Again, we begin our attack by attacking #3 and finding out what his reaction is going to be and then continuing from there.

In the 4-4 defense or eight-man front, let's say that the play is being called to the right (Diagram 6.8). Once we have drawn the imaginary line through the playside A gap on the right, we count from the inside out. Again, the backer and the defensive tackle can be reversed, but those two guys, depending on their positioning, are #1

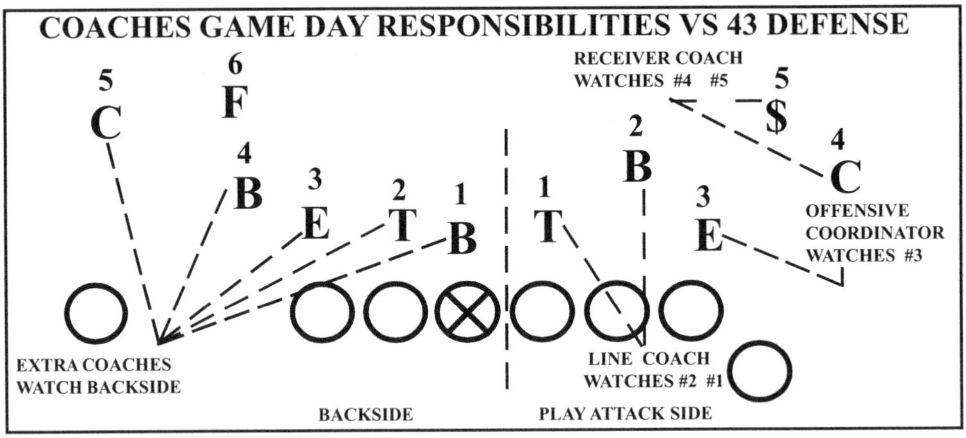


**Diagram 6.7**

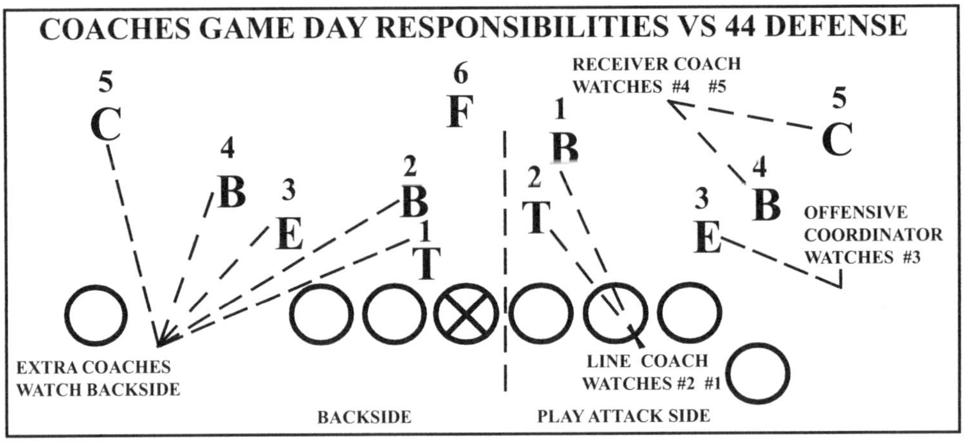


**Diagram 6.8**

and #2, however they sort themselves. The defensive end is the third guy. As for the outside linebacker or the strong safety, it does not matter which of those two is #4. Remember that E's, T's, and B's are irrelevant. This player is #4. When we refer to the defenders, we say that is #4. We do not say that is a safety or a backer or a corner. Outside, the thirds player is #5. Versus a 4-4, eight-man front, we begin our attack off tackle. If we put a tight end wide and stretch his split, we will usually widen the defensive end a little bit. Now, we can begin our attack off tackle. If the defensive end is not going to spread with our tight end's flex, then we get our flank game back because the tight end and wing have outflanked the defense.

Let's review these three defenses and talk about who each coach watches. First, the 50 defense: Coordinator watch #3. Call the play and watch #3 and know how he is reacting. Line coach, when you hear the play, make sure you know what #2 is doing and attempt to find out what #1 is doing. Receivers coach, make sure you know what #4 is doing and try to find out about #5 as well. When we have a couple of graduate assistant coaches on our staff, then they are assigned to watch the backside guys, to see who trails, to see if any reverses can go, and we also want them to watch the free safety in the middle and see if he is coming out of the middle in an attempt to be a ninth run defender. If he is, we know that we can call post routes in behind him if we can beat the corners.

Looking at the 4-3 defense and again talking about who is assigned to watch defenders, we start with #3. No. 3 could be the backer to a split end side, or he could be the end to a tight end side. Regardless of which one it is, he is the guy who the quarterback coach or the coordinator or the play caller will watch . Our line coach watches #2. Again, we want our line coach to try to figure out what #1 does as well. Our receivers coach is watching #4. If the corner is closest to the line, he is #4. Also, we want him to know what #5 does. If we see extra guys (e.g., free safety, trail player), let's find out how those guys are reacting and whether or not we can go for the post or the reverse or whatever we might be looking for.

The final defense will be the eight-man front. Who watches whom? Again, this is pretty simple. The line coach watches #2; if he can see #1, that's great. The coordinator calls the play and watches #3. The receivers coach watches #4 and #5, but especially #4.

## PRACTICING GAME DAY

As coaches, one of the things we ask our players to do is to practice every day of the week for game day. How many times a week does your coaching staff practice what the coaches should do on game day? This is something that we insist that our offensive staff work on every week. At the beginning of the week, we are busy breaking down the film, making the scouting report, compiling all the statistics, and making the game plan. We have a lot of things to do at the beginning of each week. But, as the week winds down, and as the game day approaches, in those last two days before the game, most of the work in terms of what the coaches have to do, in terms of clerical things, and written things, is virtually finished. And so, at that point, they have got a little extra time left. What we want them to do is to practice game day. How do we do that? We take those guys in a room and we put last year's game on, or we put on the game from the past Saturday that our opponent played. We would rather see the defense to the wing-T. Even though we are not seeing the previous week's game against the wing-T, it is still good to watch the defenders and how they react. We will know that the next play is going to the right. The coordinator will watch #3 on the right side of our offense, the line coach will watch #2 and possibly #1, and the receivers coach will watch #4 and possibly #5. Maybe our two graduate assistants will watch the free safety and the trail player. Next, we turn on the film and run one play through, completely. We go around the room, after the play has run, and we ask, What did #3 do? Line coach, what did #2 do? Receivers coach, what did #4 do? Then we turn the film back on, run the play back, and watch those three guys again. We are going to check ourselves. Did that defender really do what we said he did? By going through the plays one at a time, and stopping the action on film, there is no running it back and forth while the coaches are trying to find out what happened. Did #3 seal or did he penetrate? If you did not watch closely enough, or I missed it, you need more practice. If you as the head coach are the play caller, that means you need to be watching #3. You need to practice this on game day as well. And if you assign that responsibility to somebody else, then he has to practice it in your place. You need to know those informational items, and you need to know them on game day in a hurry.

When the play is over, it sounds something like this: "Line coach, 2's penetrating. Receivers coach, 4 is real soft. We can run at him; he's backing up." Now, as an offensive play caller, I see that #3 is sealing. If I know that #3 is sealing, and I know that #4's soft, then I also know that my next play call should be at the flank. Or, let's say I just watched #3 penetrate, and I know that #2 is also penetrating because the line coach just told me that. In that case, I can run internal. But that is not going to happen on game day, and you are not going to get good at that if you practice it. You've got to practice game day as coaches, just as your players have to practice game day as players. That is something that we do all the time after we have the game plans done, and after all the scouting reports are done. It is exactly what we do on game day, and it is important for us to understand how those defenses work and how those defenses are numbered and what we call. In order for all of us to be on the same page and call everything together, we practice our assignments on game day.

## WRITING THE GAME PLAN

The next thing we need to talk about is exactly how we write the plan. When we do a game plan, what exactly is written on pieces of paper that we make up during that particular week? What exactly do we have with us on the field or in the press box on game day?

### Summary Page

The first thing we do is put a summary page on the game plan (Diagram 6.9). On the summary page, we summarize the opponent's defense. This does not require a long explanation. We keep in mind always that our players will be more inclined to read something that is less cumbersome, less burdensome, less detailed, and less complicated. Keep in mind, then, that if you try to make it as simple as possible for your guys, they will read it and they will study it, which is the ultimate goal. Our offensive scouting report could include hundreds of different details about our opponent's defense, but we don't want all that information in there. We want to know the base front spacing. We want to know the front change-ups. We want to

U.S.D. VS/ U.N.D.
OCT 22, 1996

1. UND IS A 7 MAN FRONT. THEIR #1 SPACING IS A 50 DEFENSE AND THEIR TOP CHANGE UPS ARE EAGLE STRONG AND WEAK. THEIR BASE COVERAGE IS COVER 3 AND THEIR TOP CHANGE UP COVERAGE IS COVER 2.
2. BEGIN YOUR ATTACK AT THE FLANK. USE SHIFTING TO GET MISMATCHES. YOUR PRIMARY FLANK PLAYS ARE:

| | |
|---|---|
| 121-929 | 988 DOWN OPTION |
| R21-BL29 | LF 988-RT182 DOWN OPTION |

3. IF #3 SEALS YOUR PLAY ACTION GAME ATTACK #4 WITH:

| | |
|---|---|
| 929-121 WAGGLE SOLID | 989-181 KEEP PASS |
| BL29-R21 WAGGLE SOLID | LF989-RT181 KEEP PASS |

4. IF #3 PENETRATES YOUR OFF TACKLE GAME WILL INCLUDE:

| | |
|---|---|
| 182-988 DOWN | 122-928 TAG |
| RT182-LF988 DOWN | RT122-LF928 TAG |

5. IF BOTH #2 AND #3 BOTH PENETRATE YOUR INTERNAL GAME WILL INCLUDE:

| | |
|---|---|
| 187-983 CT | 124-926 G.T. |
| RT187-LF183 CT | RT124-LF926 G.T. |

**Diagram 6.9**

know the base coverage. We want to know the primary change-up coverages. We want to know the goal line and short-yardage defenses. We want to know the long-yardage defenses and whatever else we deem really important for that scouting report. We do not put a lot of information in the scouting report, and we also try not to put in too much information on the game plans either.

Here is a brief example of what a summary page on the game plan might contain. Let's just say we are getting ready to play the University of North Dakota. Our first paragraph on this game plan, page 1 of the game plan sheet, would probably look like this:

"UND is a 7-man front. Their number front is a 50 defense. Their front change-ups are eagle strong and weak. Their base coverage is cover 3, and their top change-up coverage is cover 2. They use a 6-5 goal line and eagle strong on short yardage. In long yardage situations, they play 2 man under coverage."

Notice that that is a basic, brief description of what the opponent's defense is for that week. This is all the players need to know. We know that they play a seven-man front and that they are basically a 50 package. We know what their change-ups are, and we know they use cover 3. We know what their goal line, short-yardage, and long-down defensive packages are, and we know the basic change-ups they use. That is plenty of information for our players in terms of what we need to summarize about our opponent's defense. Remember, this plan gets handed out to the quarterbacks and the coaches two days before game day. By then, they have already received the scouting report, and they have already practiced for two or three days against this defense. These are things that they already know, and not something that we need to hammer into them.

The second paragraph on page 1, the summary page, is where we begin stating our plan of attack. In this case, we are going to begin our attack at the flank because the defense is showing a seven-man front. We are going to use shifting to get mismatches or whatever else we might use shifting for. We are going to change formations on them. We might use shifting, or we might use motion, or we might not do any of that. But we begin our game plan at the flank. Our two base plays, the plays we think are going to best attack the flank, are listed in red. Now, red simply means that something is hot. If it is in red, it is hot, and we are expecting to use it a lot in our next game. A play listed in blue is something that is not so hot, something that we have in the game plan and that we practiced, but not something we're planning on running as our focus for this particular game. It could become red listed as the game goes on, just as these red listed plays could become blue listed as the game goes on, depending on the reaction of the defense. Here, we describe our attack at the flank, and we list our primary plays. You might have a sweep, an option play, or whatever else you might want. We try to list all of those same plays from different formations. For example, if we decided on using 121 and 929, our sweep play, we might also choose to run it from red 21 or blue 29 or any different formation from which we could plan on running that play for that particular week. We will also have an option listed. We try to list an option, a flank run, and a flank pass every week that we think we can make go. We are going to run them a number of times. For example, we might choose 988 and 182 down option, left 988, right 182 down option, which are the same play from a different formation. You might have two or three or four different formations you want to run that same play from.

The next part of the discussion will be the flank passing game. We have attacked #3 with our flank attack, and now we are anticipating that #3 is sealing, trying to stop the off-tackle hole. We know we are going to keep attacking the flank. But now, if #3 seals, and we know that #4 is also aggressive, then we focus on our play-action passing game. We're going to say that if #3 seals, our play-action passing game attacks #4 with the following plays: For example, we might run waggle solid, and we would list that out of two different formations. We might select our keep pass, 989, 181, left 989, and right 181 keep pass. These might be the plays for the week that we selected to throw the ball in behind the fourth defender when he reacts hard to the run action. Those are the plays that we would red list. In other words, those are hot, they are primary. We plan on running those a lot. And we plan on repeating those. Of course, they could become blue listed, depending on how the defensive reactions change during the game.

Next, if #3 penetrates, and #2 is sealing, then we would need to package our off-tackle attack. We simply write what that includes, and again, we put a play down out of a couple of different formations. For example, we might use 88 down and 22 and 28 tag. Between the down play and the tag play, we have something that will hit inside of #3 if he is penetrating, and outside of #2 if he is sealing. We list the hot-listed plays for each particular situation.

In the last paragraph here, we deal with it if #2 and #3 are both penetrating. Our internal game might now include our halfback counter game and our fullback trap game up the middle. These are just hypothetical examples, as I pointed out earlier. We will want to fill these red plays in with anything we choose for that particular week. That tells us and our players how we are going to begin our attack, and how we are going to evolve the attack in terms of the primary things that we want to run and repeat frequently.

There are a lot of things that we can call, and there are a lot of things that are going to be companion plays to our plan of attack that may not be red listed. But you are still going to practice them, anyway, because the reactions during the game may change, and what was red listed before, may become blue listed now, and vice versa.

This finishes page one of the game plan and how we write it up. There are five quick paragraphs. If we had a sixth one, it would include our drop-back passing attack. In terms of the wing-T, the four areas that we want to attack in every game plan are internal, off tackle, flank run, and flank pass if #4 is aggressive.

**Hit Charts**

Pages 2 and 3 include diagrams of the formations, as well as a list of the plays that we are going to run from each formation (Diagram 6.10). Page 3 is identical to page 2, except that it contains the mirrors of the formations. We will have wing formation in every game plan—tight end and wing to one side, and spread end and diveback to the other. Right after that we will have what we call slots, or what look like slots. You have a spread end and a wingback on the same side, and a tight end and the diveback on the other side. To help us stay organized, we put the spread

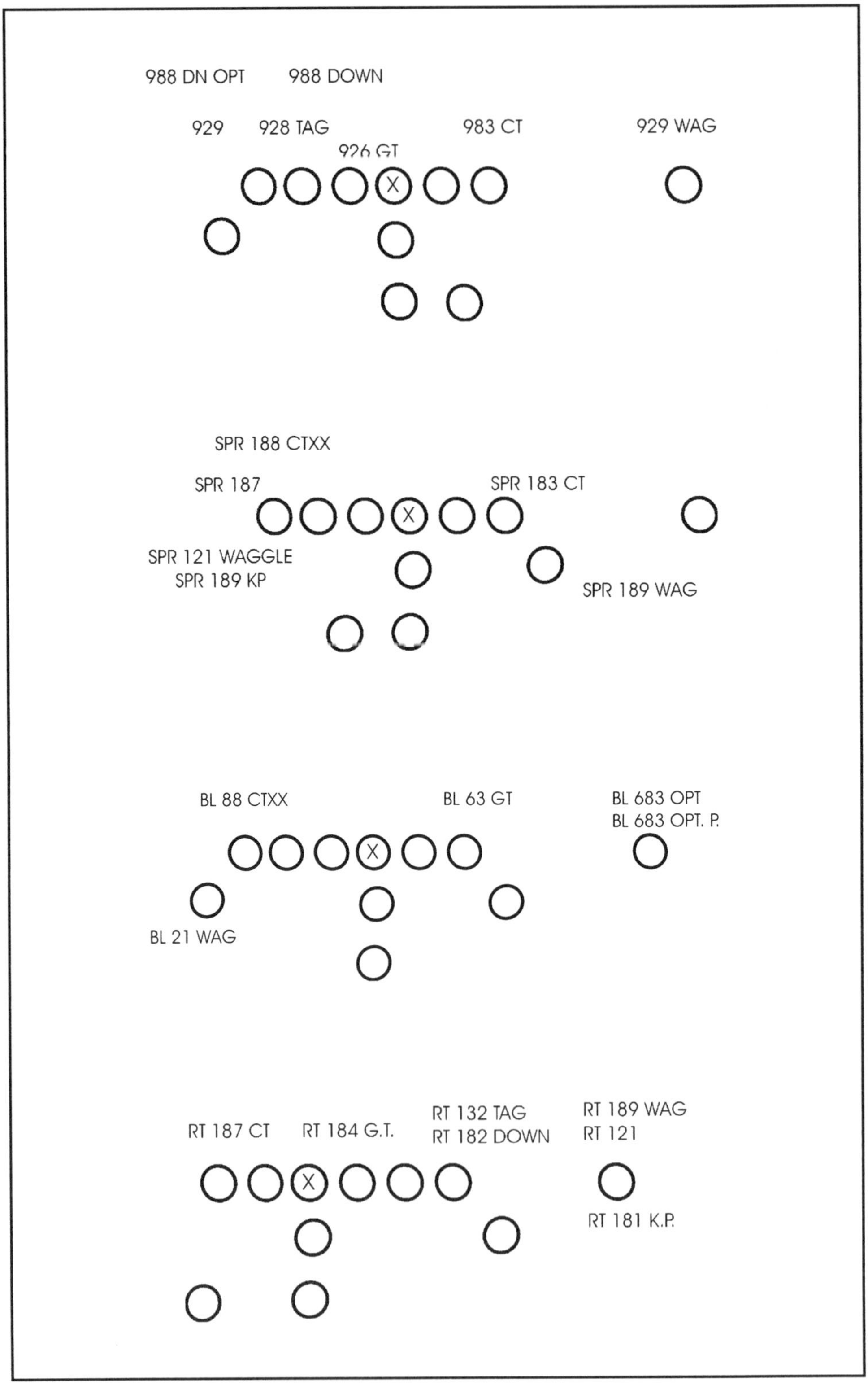
988 DN OPT
988 DOWN
929
928 TAG
926 GT
983 CT
929 WAG
SPR 188 CTXX
SPR 187
SPR 183 CT
SPR 121 WAGGLE
SPR 189 KP
SPR 189 WAG
BL 88 CTXX
BL 63 GT
BL 683 OPT
BL 683 OPT. P.
BL 21 WAG
RT 187 CT
RT 184 G.T.
RT 132 TAG
RT 182 DOWN
RT 189 WAG
RT 121
RT 181 K.P.

**Diagram 6.10**

end to the right on one page and in all the formations, and to the left on the next page. Then we have double wing. In this, we have used wing, slot, and double wing. We write in the plays where they are going to hit out of each formation. Finally, we will have unbalanced. Wing, slot, double wing, and unbalanced will be addressed in every game plan, and the plays are written in where we are going to run them. This is how we write the plan on pages 2 and 3: We put the formations down, we write the plays that we are going to run out of each formation, and we write them in the areas where the plays will actually hit. We put run plays on the opposite side of the line of scrimmage. We put pass plays on our own side of the line of scrimmage in the backfield. Wherever the ball is going to be, that's where we write the play in. If we have some plays that we really like, ones that we think we are going to repeat a lot, then they are listed in red. The ones that we think are not going to get repeated a lot, but are ready, are listed in blue.

There are a lot of college coaches out there who fill in from flank to flank and have as many as 16, 18, 20 plays from each formation. What you will notice is that if you are doing this right, in the wing-T, you will run many of the same plays from each different formation—wing, slot, double wing, and unbalanced. You not just running different formations, but you are running the same plays out of those formations, and your kids are getting better at executing, and the defense has trouble recognizing. Throw in motions and shifts and you have a double-edged sword. You get the best of all worlds in terms of the defense not being able to recognize what you are trying to do.

Both pages 2 and 3 are what we call hit charts. They are in cellophane, and our coordinator has them with him at all times. He will especially refer to those pages between series during the game. He can talk about the plays that he has already run, he can look over those play sheets, and he can pick out all the plays he might need in any situation. If we got stopped on one particular series of downs, we do not want to waste too many possessions, so we have to address why we got stopped. If the defense is doing something different with their scheme—say we planned on #3 being a seal guy, and now he is penetrating, and we planned on #2 being a penetrator and now he is sealing—we know we must adjust and go off tackle. We go back to those play charts and now start circling the plays that are going to hit the defense off tackle, just to remind ourselves, and then start using those plays and keep the chess match going. Finding out how the defense is going to play over the course of four quarters is the key, as well as adjusting with the defense as they adjust to you. They may change it up on you once, but then go back to their base on the next play. That is why you have to be disciplined as coaches to watch those players all the way through the game. If we get all the way through the second quarter, and they have not once done anything differently, then we figure we do not have to watch those defenders anymore. We can watch our own guys and see how they are holding up against the players they are matched with. If the defense changes, then we are right back watching defenders so that we can adjust our offense.

The coordinator does not look at any of that stuff while the offense is out on the field, running the offense. Those first three pages are basically pages that he should be looking at between series, while he's talking to the other coaches, and while they are gathering as much information as can possibly be accumulated by those three guys, or four or five, or whatever number you have.

**Critical Call Sheet**

The next page, page 4 of our game plan, consists of what we call "critical" calls (Diagram 6.11). A critical call for us is any play where, if we do not make the required yardage, we will lose possession of the ball or lose a direct opportunity to score some points or give the opponent a direct opportunity to score points. In general, third and fourth downs are critical calls: goal line and red zone offense, two-point plays, specials, and coming-out calls. For example, third-and-1 is critical in most field zones, but if we are in four-down territory, then we have two downs in which to make the required yardage. We can then call the play on third down according to that. We try to make it on third down every time, so that we keep ourselves out of those critical fourth-down situations. Sometimes we can get third-and-long situations, and if we just get half of it back, and are in four-down territory, then we can go for the other half on fourth down. In that case, third-and-long may not be considered critical. Maybe we are a little too far out for the field goal kicker, yet a little too close to be punting. That is a great time to go on fourth down. I think we see a lot more teams going for fourth down now than in the past.

**Third Downs**

The first "critical" category is third down and one or less. We always have at least two choices in this situation, sometimes a third one. The next critical call is third down and two or less. These calls may be the same as on third-and-1 or less, but they also may be different. To me, making two yards on third down is a lot different from making six inches. Therefore, we obviously put different kinds of choices in this category.

The next critical call is third down and three to four. If you are a good, solid run team, and you are running the ball and making yardage, you probably will have a lot of third down and three to four calls throughout the course of the game. You want your best plays in your game plan for this situation. When we get to this down and distance, we run our best football plays right here. What are your best football plays? Whatever is red-listed for you, basically, those are your best football plays. They are the plays you felt you were going to use in this game plan a number of times and get a lot of repetitions on them. A lot of times in this situation, we like our waggle, bootleg, and keep pass plays, plays that are flank-pass oriented in nature, because that gives the quarterback more options.

The next critical call is third down and five to eight. As a wing-T football team, and as a run-oriented football team, we want to try to stay out of these kinds of situations as often as possible. These are still third downs that are makeable with

U.N.D. CRITICAL CALLS
OCT 22, 1996

3-1 OR LESS (DEF)
1.
2.
3-2 OR LESS (DEF)
1.
2.
3.
3-3 TO 4 (DEF)
1.
2.
3.
4.
5.
6.
3-5 TO 8 (DEF)
1.
2.
3.
4.
5.
6.
3-9 PLUS (DEF)
1.
2.
3.
4.
5.

GOAL LINE DEFENSE (DEF)
1.
2.
3.
4.
5.
6.
COMING OUT OFFENSE (DEF)
1.
2.
3.
SPECIALS
1.
2.
RED ZONE OFFENSE
1.
2.
3.
4.
TWO POINT PLAYS
1.
2.
3.

**Diagram 6.11**

parts of our package, if we have prepared for them. Sometimes we will have a three-step-drop passing game, or maybe a five-step drop, or maybe our good play-action drop-back , and we can throw those short to intermediate routes that are easy to complete and can get us the required yardage. Or, possibly, we are just stubborn, and we think we can make eight yards anytime we want with our sweep play, or our waggle play, or whatever. We fit it in here, depending on what we think we have to do or can do to gain five to eight yards and keep possession. One of the things that we always do is write down in parentheses what the expected defense is for that particular down and distance. What is the predominant defense we are probably going to see in that down and distance? For five to eight yards, we usually have about six choices, just as we do for three to four yards. It could be more, it could be less, depending on what we feel we need for that particular week.

The final category is third down and nine-plus. We usually have five or six choices in this instance, but we also know that if we are in third down and nine or more all game, we are probably not going to win. In that case, we would be in trouble no matter what we're doing, but let's have the best possible plays we can have for nine or more yards in this category. Obviously, we are either going to have to throw the ball down the field further, or maybe hit a trap in a long-yardage situation, or use some kind of an option. For the most part, third down and nine-plus is a pass, draw, screen kind of a down. We do not necessarily like play action in third and long because the defense does not honor it. But sometimes that might the best blocking scheme we have, so we have to go ahead and use it.

All of those situations discussed here require critical calls—third down and one or less, two or less, three to four, five to eight, and nine-plus. The plays we use are all third-down yardage plays that we have used over the years. As we look at the down and distance, field position chart from our off-season and in-season film study, we may find that one week it might be third down and three to four, and the next week it might be third down and three to five. It is also possible that what is considered intermediate for some teams changes for others. One week it might be that seven-plus is all blitz; therefore, that will be our long-yardage category for the week, instead of nine-plus. Distances may change slightly, week by week, but as a standard rule of thumb, these are the downs and distances that we will use most of the time. Again, they are all critical calls. If it is fourth down and one, and we are going for it, then that is the same—it is a "critical" call.

We have our coordinator refer to this list while the series is going on, in case we get to one of these situations. We may find that, all of a sudden, we are into a coming-out offense, or we are really backed up. We are only on our own 1-yard line. What did we have planned for that? The beauty of page 4 in our game plan is that all of these situations are thought out well in advance. They are planned for when we are in the staff room, and it is nice and cool. There is no pressure, no fans yelling at us. We can take our time and be deliberate and think about it. We can look at the defense, try to find the weaknesses in it, and mark down some calls that are going to work in those particular situations. We do all this when we are nice and calm—not in the heat of battle, when the crowd is screaming and everybody is telling us we don't know our butt from a hole in the ground and can't make a decent call. All those kinds of things can add up during the game and distract us. That is why we want to have these critical calls formulated well in advance; so all we do now, when that situation arises, is to look at our chart, which tells us what we need to do. Example: It's third down and one, we are expecting a double-eagle defense, and here is where we are going to attack because that is the weakness of it. We know what we have planned for this team coming into the game in this situation.

We just look at the chart and call it. We are always going to keep track of ourselves. How well do we do on third down and one or less? We keep a running count, starting with game one; when game two comes, we add that to game one; when game three comes, we add that, so that we have a running chart on ourselves. How are we doing on these critical calls? We are evaluating ourselves all the time. What is working? What is not working? What defenses are we seeing? What defenses are we not seeing? We are constantly updating and revising and renovating this list on the basis of how these defenses are trying to play us.

**Goal Line Offense**

On the right-hand side of page 4 are other kinds of critical situations. The first one we write down is our goal line offense. We would like that goal line offense to be somewhere between four and eight plays. We would like to start spring ball with the plays that we like to run down on the goal line, go all the way through training camp, and games one, two, and three and try to keep this as similar as possible from week to week, so we get good at executing this. We do not want to be changing up what we are doing down here in the most critical area on the whole field, by doing something we have never had a chance to execute. Coaches ask themselves how it is that their offense can drive all the way down the field and then, when it gets to the goal line, it can't score. Was it bad planning? Was it that we didn't analyze thoroughly enough the defense that we were going to see? Was it that we did not get better at executing our package the way we should have? With our goal line offense, we try to keep it very much the same all the way through the year and just get better at it.

**Coming Out**

The next situation is called "coming out." What is the defense going to do when we are backed up inside our own 5-yard line? We are going to write the defense on the chart. Of course, it is there as a reminder to our play caller so he knows that if he is not seeing that defense, then maybe he will have to change his calls. Coming out means we are backed up inside our own 5-yard line. This is a case where we do not want to be handing the ball off deep in the backfield. We do not want to be throwing late over the middle. We do not want deep drops where we could be sacked in the end zone. We want to be able to hand the ball off on direct teaming action if we can, and make some yardage and get the ball at least up to the 4-yard line, where we can punt with our normal amount of room. We have to be able to get off our own goal line. We make this plan way early in the week, and we practice it in our practices. We tell the kids that we are going down to the other end and we are going to practice coming out. Again, the key is well-thought-out calls prior to having to make those same calls under game pressure.

**Specials**

The next area on the sheet is for our "specials." By specials, we mean plays that we do not normally run much of, but that we have in the game plan for that week for a particular reason. Maybe we have a reverse play in our plan. Maybe we've seen on film that their trail player is undisciplined and does not look for the reverse. So we put a reverse play in, practice it, and have it listed with our specials. A great time to call those kinds of things is whenever we get a turnover in our opponent's end of the field. We can use these kinds of things as momentum breakers. Other specials we use are the halfback pass, any kind of new screen, a play requiring special personnel, anything that is special for the week—something that we do not normally do a lot of, yet think that, at the right time, against this particular team, it is going to break on them.

**Red Zone Offense**

Next is the red zone offense. The red zone offense refers to when we are at the plus-20-yard line, going in to score a touchdown, all the way until the 5. When we get around the 5-yard line, the goal line attack starts to take over. What are we doing in the red zone? Are there special plays or patterns that we want to use in the red zone? Maybe yes, maybe no. The other thing that we can put in for a red zone attack is what we do not want to do. More than likely, we will continue doing whatever has worked best for us to get us down the field in this category. We then list the things that we do not want to do. As an example, maybe in their red zone, our opponent is a blitz team. That being the case, we will not want to run certain plays, so we simply mark down that we do not want to do this or that. This past year, I believe we scored in the red zone every time, except a couple. There were only two times in the red zone that we did not score. I thought the coaches did a good job last winter. We studied it. We called up other schools and asked them the kinds of thing they tried to do in the red zone. Our offensive coordinator, Blair Hrovat, did a tremendous job on his study and found out a lot of interesting things. The most important thing we learned is to continue doing what has been successful for us in the past. That way, we won't screw ourselves up. The point is not to try to get too fancy down there. Do your bread-and-butter stuff and make it work. Keep in mind that the defense might change personality down there and, as a result, you might want to do some different things.

**Two-Point Plays**

Last, but not least, down in the bottom right-hand corner, are our two-point plays. This is so important. If you study hard enough, you will find your opponent's defense defending the two-point play somewhere in your film library. Basically, we are going to write down what defense they run here. We are going to try and figure out what plays are going to beat that type of defense. We want this planned way in advance, because it is a lot of pressure when the game comes down to a two-point play, especially if it is right at the very end of the game. What we found over the years is that it is not always the one at the end of the game that is the deciding factor (e.g., those occasions when you went for two points two to three times earlier in the game, and then the game ends up with a score that indicates you would've won if you had made any one of those previous two-point plays). We had a situation this year when we got to the goal line on the last drive of the game and we were nine points down. We had gone for two once before that and did not make it. If you figure that you get those two points back, and you are only down seven points, look at the potential difference that makes in the outcome of the game. Now, if you can score that last touchdown, you can go for the two-point conversion and win the game. Or if you made the two and you are only seven down, you can kick the single point and go overtime. You never know when that two-point call that you write down on that piece of paper is going to make or break the difference in the game.

I believe that every one of these categories on page 4 of our game plan sheet is critical. And by critical, I mean exactly that. You are either going to give up possession of the ball, or you are going to lose a direct opportunity to score points right there in that particular down and distance or area of the field. You do not want to be predictable. You do not want to necessarily do the same thing every time you get down there. But you also want to be good enough to be able to execute your offense when you get down there and maybe do it from a different formation or with a different shift, or with different motions or whatever. Try to give the defense a different look, but also try to keep as much continuity in your attack as you possibly can.

## ATTACKING DEFENSES

I am now going to go over some simple game planning that we do, and I will take all three defenses that we have been talking about all through this book and illustrate how we might attack each with our base series and with our base play packages.

### Attacking the 50 Defense

As we start with our 20 package, I will show how the companion plays work and then discuss how the companion plays work, depending on the defensive reactions (Diagram 6.12). If we are going to run to the right and attack the third defender, then the first play we are going to run is 121, our buck sweep to the right. We're attacking the flank because a 50 defense is a seven-man front, and because we think by film study that the third defender is going to seal when we block our tight end down and try to keep the off-tackle hole from opening up. As he seals, #4 is soft on the film that we see, so now we know we can run the sweep right at #4. What is the companion play to that? If 3 is still sealing and 4 is coming hard against the run, we want to run 121 waggle solid. On that particular play, the quarterback fakes the sweep, starts his waggle footwork, gets #4 to react up to force the sweep, but then as he drops back , we throw the ball right in behind that fourth defender. That is 121 waggle solid complementing 121 with regard to #4's reactions. If the third defender is not sealing anymore, and he begins to penetrate up the field to try and stop the 121 sweep play that we have been running, we want to run our off-tackle play, which is 122 tag. Again, we can show buck action,

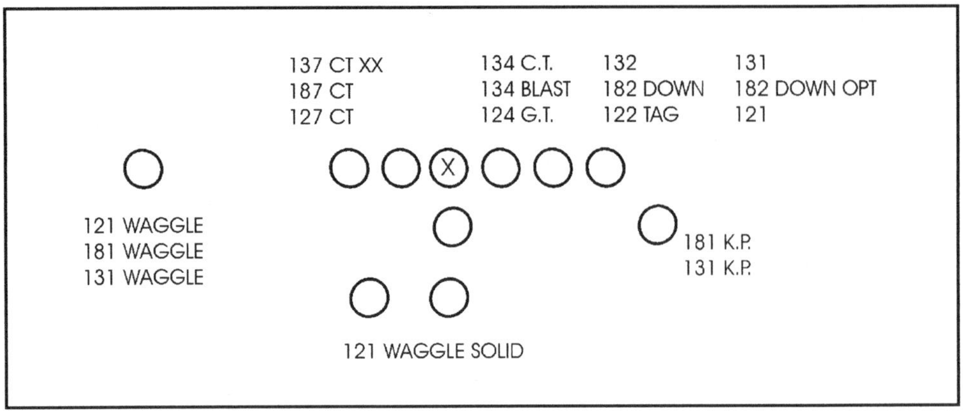


**Diagram 6.12**

hit the play off tackle and use a variety of blocking schemes, of which we like tag the best, which means tackle and guard both pull. This is nothing more than the old counter trey or counter gap blocking that all the pros run. Everybody at every level runs this same thing; #3 is penetrating, and #2, who has been sealing to stop internal runs, now wants to get up the field in order to stop this 122 tag by penetrating. We know our answer is to run 124 guard trap. We are going to come right back under the #2 defender and take advantage of his upfield penetration to stop 122 tag. If 2 seals, obviously we will stay off tackle. If 3 seals, we will go outside the flank. If 4 is soft, we will continue attacking the flank. And if 4 comes hard, we will throw in behind him. Those four plays—121, 121 waggle solid, 122 tag, and 124 guard trap—comprise a play package that takes care of all the reactions you are going to see from the people you have decided to attack on the playside. There are additional things you might want to consider to complement the four plays you already have selected.. One of them is some kind of a counter coming backside, where the inside people are over-pursuing. The 127 counter would be a great complement to any of the four calls as an inside play. That would be an inside play to take advantage of quick inside linebacker flow. Then the outside play we would use would be 121 waggle. Now we complement the sweep with the fake and come all the way backside with the quarterback and attack the flank with a run-pass option. There is our 20 series, flank to flank. As you look at this game plan sheet, we have an answer for any reaction that the defense can do to us from flank to flank, and each looks the same for the first two steps. Every single thing we do looks exactly the same for the first two steps. We could now expand these six plays to other formations or motion for different looks, yet still attack with the exact same thought processes.

We want to continue to do these same things, but we want to do them with a different backfield action. Let's explore our belly package now. We start with 182 down option. We are going to run option, faking the 82 down play , off tackle, and the quarterback keeps the ball and he comes on out and options the fourth defender. We either block down on the third defender or log him. We can do other things, if he is a penetrator, but we start with the down option. We are running the down option because we can log and get the inside sealed, and we can get outside and attack #4. If #4 is fairly soft, we feel we have a good play here. As soon as 4 becomes aggressive, then we want to go to 181 keep pass and throw the ball in behind him. Each play complements the other. If #3 decides he is going to penetrate rather than seal, we adjust with 182 down, we trap that #3 right out, and we run the ball right off tackle. We have taken advantage of that third defender's reaction, and again, we are figuring that #2 is still sealing. If #2 is coming up the field, there are a number of things that we can do. We can go with a counter trap. We can do anything that hits inside of #2 quickly. We can run 184, which is our quick belly. Certainly, we could run some kind of a 34 counter or 36 counter to our halfback on our 30 action. We could run 34 blast, which looks like the 80 package in some respects. But we are going to have something that hits internal, and hits inside of #2 if he gives us that upfield penetrating reaction. Again, we want to build in some kind of counter in case they flow too hard. We have 187 counter, where the quarterback fakes the belly and hands the ball off to our wing coming back. We can use counter crisscross blocking, or we can use counter tag blocking, where the tackle and the guard pull, or we can pull the tight end and the tackle. It just depends on what your defensive problems are. Also off that 80 series, we would like to have something that comes backside wide. We have an 80 waggle, so we say 181 waggle. We have basically been getting the same kinds of things done that we did with our 20 package, but with a different backfield action. It does not have to be 100 formation. We can go right 100, we can go red, we can go spread 900. We can mix these formations up many different ways. All these packages just get the same things done. If you add the shifting in formations, and you have a couple different play packages from several formations, then you do not really need much else.

How about our 30 package? What can we do out of our 30s? We have our 131, which is our power sweep. If #4 is soft, we have our 131 keep pass. If #4 is aggressive, we have 132, which is our power off-tackle play. We again have 134 blast. We also have 134 counter or 136 counter to take advantage of #2 being a penetrator. We have 137 counter or counter crisscross, where the halfbacks hand the ball to each other. We have our 131 waggle to the backside. That completes another package of plays that you can use, where you have flank-to-flank offense, and you have play packages built in such a way that no matter what the defense does to react to you, you can go ahead and take advantage of that reaction with a companion play.

I would not run this offense unless I had at least two packages, and unless I could run every companion play in the package—and run them from all the formations and to both sides of each formation. Then, and only then, do you have a true wing-T offense. You have answers for what the defense gives you. You do not need zillions of plays. You can run the same plays, run them from different formations, use different motions, different shifts, and it looks like a zillion different things to a defense. You are simply running the same four or six plays that you have been running from the first day of training camp using the same attack concepts in every package. Your kids are getting better and better, and the defense is still trying to figure out what you are going to do to them next. That is the beauty of this wing-T offense. This is why we believe in it so much. When I was a football player in college, we had the split-back veer as our offense, and the coaches used to brag about how they loved it so much because it was an offense where, if the defense did this, then we did that. We took advantage of their reaction. The wing-T does the same thing for you.

**Attacking the 4-3 Defense**

Against the 4-3 defense, I would encourage you to run your base offense (Diagram 6.13). You know that the 4-3 defense is a seven-man front, but because of the even spacing, it retains some of the properties of an eight-man front. One of the things we do is split the tight end five to six feet. You might get a defense where the defensive end is on the tight end in a 9 technique, the defensive tackle is in a 3 technique over the guard, and what you have done is really spread and opened up the off-tackle hole, putting a great deal of pressure on the Sam backer, the man playing on the outside shoulder of the tackle. You have created a lot of space for him to step up and plug. As soon as the 9-technique defensive end starts to move down inside, of course you can recognize it right away, and then your flank game's going to be good. We would probably start this attack off tackle. If you go back to our 20 series, we would probably start this package with 122 and block it with either tag or power or whatever blocking scheme we wanted to use. As soon as we could get 3 to close down some or move his alignment, then we'd go to the 121 sweep, but would probably begin off tackle. Then we have 124 guard trap for when #2 becomes a penetrator. Again, we have 121 waggle solid in case the fourth defender comes really hard and we want to throw the ball in behind him. We have 121 waggle, which hits backside, away from the flow at the flank, and 127 or 167 counter backside on the inside. So now we have inside, internal, off tackle, and flank. We have flank passing, so we have a way to get in behind 4. We have counter and we have something that counters flow back to the flank. We have flank-to-flank offense, with the first two steps looking exactly the same, and the ball can be in any one of six different points. But the play looks the same to the defense. Blocking schemes look the same; so does the backfield action. We would begin with 182 down if we were going to go to our 80 package. Then, when 3 became conscious of off tackle, we would go 182 down option and get the down option play and use those two as complements. If is soft, and we continue to run option, and if he's not, if he's aggressive, 181 keep pass in behind him should be good. We have 184 inside and could use our quick belly package, or we could use counter flow. We have 187 counter, which counters the flow back to the weak side. Obviously, we have our 181 waggle, which counters flow back to the outside. As you see, these are the same plays that we just attacked the 50 defense with, only with a different starting point, and with adjustments in our blockings. Your rules and attack concepts will hold up versus all the defenses.

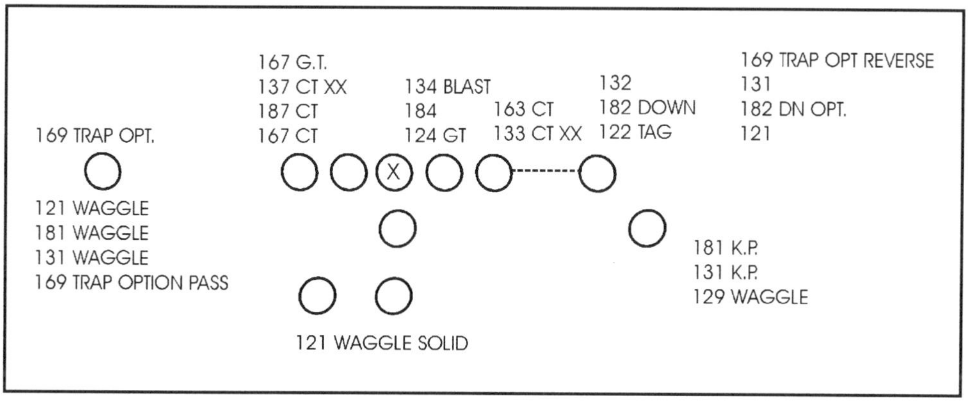


**Diagram 6.13**

If you want to go with the same type of setup, and you want to run your 30 package, then 132 is our off-tackle play out of the 30 series, and that is what we would start with and then judge how #3 is reacting. Then we might go to 131 as a companion play. Next, we could go to 131 keep pass if #4 is really aggressive, where the quarterback fakes the sweep, keeps the ball in the same direction, and has a run or pass option to throw in behind the corner or the #4 defender. Our 134 blast is the internal play that goes with that. Our 137 counter crisscross would be the inside counter, and then we have 131 waggle for a play-action pass that counters the flow to the outside. At the outset, when the defense overcommits, we can go inside of them or outside of them, depending on how that backside trail player runs, and how fast the whole defense pursues to the football.

Also, against the 4-3 defense, we want to attack to the spread end side. We would like to run 100 formation, but we can choose spread 900 and run to the left as well, or red formation, or unbalanced. But we want to attack the spread end against this defense. We are going to go with guard trap a little bit wider and trap the #2 defender, the contain defensive end. We would use 167 guard trap and judge the defender's (defensive end's) reaction. If the end is going to seal on the trap, then we want to be able to log him and go outside with trap option, which would be 169 trap option, crack, or however we want to block it. We run trap option, especially if 4 is soft and 3 is aggressive, or we can go trap-option pass if 4 is really aggressive. Then the complementary play would be 169 trap-option pass. Now we have inside, outside, and outside pass. We could run some gut plays and some internal guard traps to give us an internal game. Our 67 guard trap would almost be considered off tackle, depending on how #2 is reacting. Of course, we can run our counter crisscross, our trap-option reverse, and our waggle plays back away from the spread end. We could run our 133 counter crisscross, which would give us an inside counter, or we could run 163 counter, depending on whether or not we want to have the halfbacks hand the ball to each other. We have 169 trap option reverse, where we can bring the spread end back across and pitch him the ball off the trap-option series. Of course, 129 waggle is a good complement to all of this. You can see by looking back, even with the right halfback in three-step motion and flow beginning to the spread end side, that we have flank-to-flank offense. That offensive look is going to look exactly the same to the defense as the first two steps, regardless of where the ball attacks. The first two steps are going to look exactly the same, no matter where the ball ends up attacking. That is the beauty of this offense: It's flank to flank, with motion, without motion, and we can have direct hitting plays, counter plays, whatever we need.

**Attacking the 4-4 Defense**

Against the 4-4 defense, I would again strongly encourage you to start with your base football plays (Diagram 6.14). Begin there, and adjust your blocking schemes to fit the 4-4 defense. All the rules are in the book for you, so you can just take them and start to create. Since the 4-4 defense shows an even front and the tackle is uncovered, we would take the tight end and split him five to six feet to see how far the defensive end will widen out with us. If we can create a big bubble between the defensive end and the defensive tackle, that will give us a vulnerable off-tackle area , and that is where we would begin our attack. Starting with the 20s, we would start with 122, since we are starting off tackle to attack an eight-man front. We will select tag as our basic blocking scheme. Once the third defender becomes conscious of stopping the off-tackle area, 121, our sweep play, would serve as our companion play. Once #4 becomes really aggressive in his attempt to stop the sweep play, then 121 waggle solid enables us to show the same look, with the quarterback faking the sweep to the left half and starting his waggle and then dropping straight back and throwing the ball in behind 4. We show the sweep look and throw the ball right in behind him. If 2 is a big penetrator, then we can go 124 guard trap or gut or guard-trap gut, or whatever it is that we favor as an internal blocking scheme. Again, you can see we have four plays that attack the playside of the defense, and we can go inside, off tackle, outside, or we can throw a play-action pass in behind the fourth defender. We also have the same look for two steps with our counter game, where we could run 127 or 167 counter, hand the ball off to the right halfback, who is the wingback coming back, countering the flow. Then we add 121 waggle, which counters the flow to the outside, with the quarterback having the run-pass option.

A different backfield action, with the same kind of conflicts for the defense, would be the 80s, or our belly action. We would start with 182 down, because it gives us a direct shot at an off-tackle play, and as soon as 3 becomes a seal-conscious guy, we would adjust with 181 down option as the companion play. One other thing that we like to do against the 4-4 defense is to use the 83 cross-block influence, which is kind of a companion play to 82 down. We can go 83 cross block and influence the right halfback. He steps at #3, as if he is going to come down on him, and then turns out, and the tight end goes across on the linebacker, and we cross block. We use the 83 footwork, as opposed to 82 for our fullback, and now we have a little bit

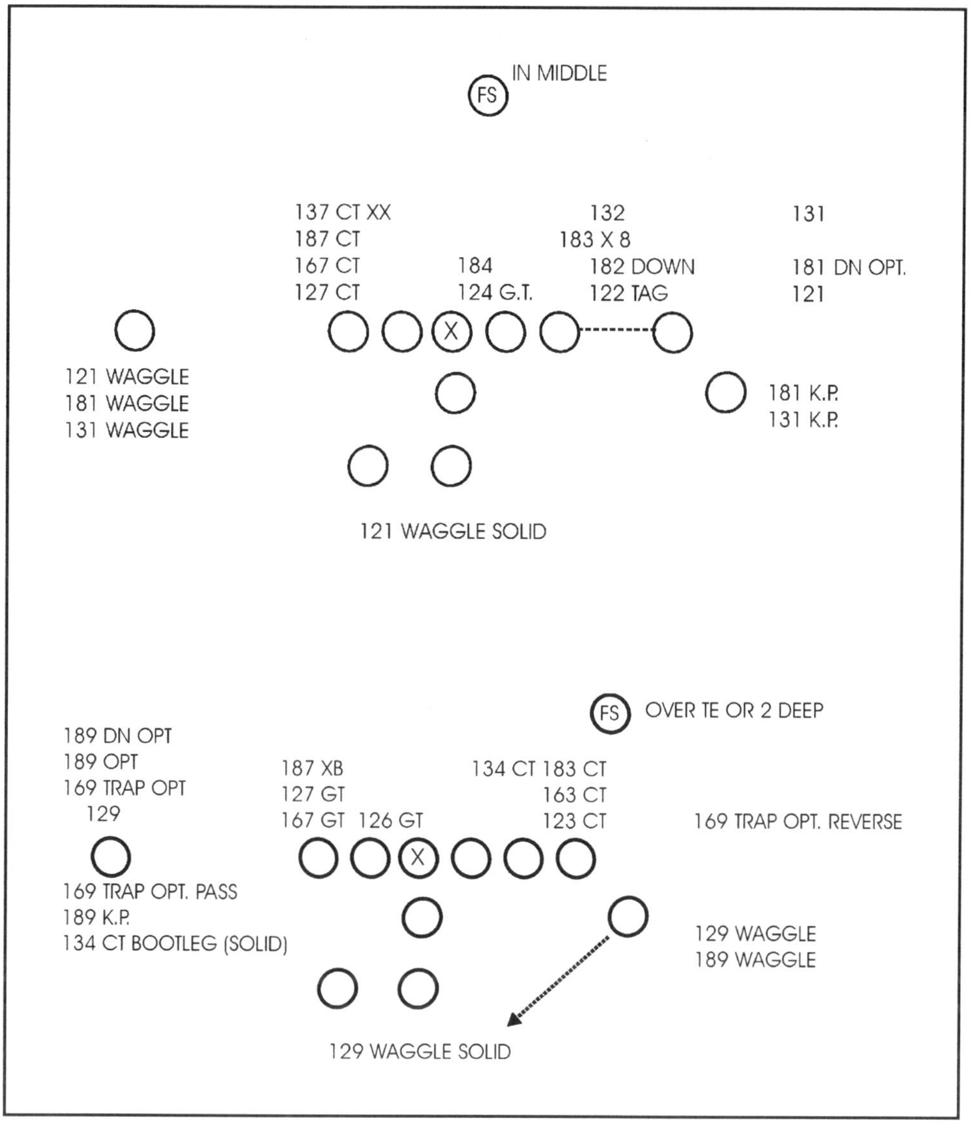


**Diagram 6.14**

more of a deliberate path that allows him more of a cutback opportunity than a direct path, as 82 down would. That would be something that we might use in conjunction with 82 down. You have an internal play. We can go quick belly, 184. We can use some kind of a counter tackle trap play that will get us inside of #2, such as 187 counter, to counter the flow back inside. We have 181 waggle, which again counters the flow back to the outside.

We are not big on the 30 series against eight-man fronts unless our opponent is one of those teams that uses all four guys inside and is always doing A- or B-gap stunts. One guy stunts A, the other guy goes B, and they keep mixing that stuff up on you. Our 30s will offer a better sweep, because we can fire block everybody; instead of pulling guards, we can let the fullback be the lead blocker and kick out. Now we can pick up all the internal blitzing and still get the sweep run correctly. We would start with 132, the off-tackle play—double-team down, kick-out, good old-fashioned power football. Our 131 is the sweep we use when #3 becomes seal-conscious. We use the 131 keep pass to the flank when #3 is soft. The 181 keep pass would be the same thing within the 80 series to attack to #3's side if #4 is really aggressive. If we get the fourth defender coming hard for down option, 181 keep pass should hurt him. They cannot stop everything. For counter plays, we have 137 counter or counter crisscross, and the halfbacks can hand the ball to each other; in that case, 121 waggle or 131 waggle would be fine as well.

Against the 4-4 defense, if the free safety likes to stay in the middle and be a middle third defender, this is how we like to run the package. Once that free safety becomes strong-conscious, or he comes over in a two-deep alignment, or he is going to come over and line up and play man-to-man on our tight end, then we would like to run the entire package of plays by putting the back in motion across the backfield and running that same packages of plays back to the weak side. Then, back to the weak side, let's start with our internal play. Our internal play would be 126 guard trap, or gut, or guard trap gut. We can also use 167 or 127 guard trap, which is a little bit wider. We can go outside with the 129 sweep, which would be our sweep outside to the left. Then off of that, we would have 129 waggle solid, if #4 is really aggressive, so we can throw the ball in behind him. That gives us all our plays to the playside. We can also attack back to the weak side. We can run 123 counter or 163 counter and hand the ball off to the halfback coming back through. We have 129 waggle, which is part of this package. We can then add the other dimension of the trap option. We can use 169 trap option with crack, for example, or 169 trap option pass. Now we have a flank-to-flank offense with the 20 series, but we are also including the trap option as well. Because, again, for the first few steps, it all looks the same to the defense, and they do not know where the ball is going to hit. We can even add 169 trap option reverse back to the left side. We are attacking the defense at all points, and the look is exactly the same to the defense for the first two steps.

If we wanted to get into our 80 package, we could run 187 cross block. We could run 189 option or 188 down option, some kind of option play to the wide side, and attack #4. We can go 189 keep pass if #4's really aggressive. That gives us a chance to throw the ball in behind him. We have our 134 tackle trap counter, which looks just like the cross block series and provides us with a counter. We could add 134 counter bootleg, or solid, with the tackle staying home, either way, and fake the tackle trap counter and keep coming outside to the flank. All those things are good. We also have 189 waggle, which allows us to attack outside to the weak side against flow. We could also have 183 counter, which gives us a counter inside from the 80 series. As you can see, we can build a heck of an attack. Look at all this football we have got here to attack the 4-4 defense with only one formation. All we are doing is running the same plays, either strongside or weakside. To me, that is enough right there for 10 game plans. We can simply add our series in on the basis of how the defense is playing, or we can use the series that are best for our kids.

# ABOUT THE AUTHOR

Dennis Creehan is the defensive coordinator and the outside linebackers coach at Rutgers University. His 28 years of coaching experience include successful stints at the high school, collegiate, and professional levels.

He began his coaching career (1971-74) at Keystone Oaks H.S. in Pittsburgh, Pennsylvania, after a stellar playing career as a strong safety at Edinboro University. A three-year starter for the Scots, Creehan served as team captain in his senior season, earned first-team all-ECAC accolades, and helped lead Edinboro to Lambert Bowl honors. At Keystone Oaks, he served as offensive and defensive coordinator and also coached wrestling and baseball.

In 1974, Creehan was the tight ends coach and recruiting coordinator for Johnny Majors at Pittsburgh. He then served as the offensive coordinator at Carnegie–Mellon for a single season, before returning to Edinboro for four years as defensive coordinator prior to the 1976 season.

In 1980, Creehan was appointed head football coach at Edinboro. During his five years at the helm of the Scots' gridiron program, four of his teams were nationally ranked. For his efforts, he received three conference coach-of-the-year honors.

From 1985 to 1987 and 1991 to 1992, he was the defensive line coach and special teams coordinator for the Edmonton Eskimos of the Canadian Football League. During his tenure with the Eskimos, Edmonton was 35-16, won two conference titles (1986, 1991), and appeared in the Grey Cup (1986).

From 1987 to 1989, Creehan was the outside linebackers coach at the University of California–Berkeley, while current Rutgers head coach Terry Shea served as the Bears' offensive coordinator. Next, he moved to San Francisco State, when he was appointed the head football coach and assistant athletic director for the Gators.

In 1992, he returned to the head coaching ranks when he was named head football coach at South Dakota. During his five years at the helm of the Coyotes, Creehan resuscitated a struggling program and led his teams to 28 wins, including 26 in his last few years at South Dakota. In 1997, Creehan moved to Arkansas State, where he served as defensive coordinator for a season, before assuming his present position on the Scarlet Knights' staff.

Creehan is widely respected as one of the most outstanding defensive coaches in the game. In addition to authoring a two-volume set of books on the wing-T offense, he has developed a best-selling, 11-volume series of videos on the wing-T. Creehan is a popular, well-respected speaker at coaching clinics.